A TRIUMPH OF CO-OPERATION OVER ADVERSITY

*The History of
Donaghmore Co-operative Creamery Ltd.
(Founded in 1927)*

Published in Ireland by
Arderin Publishing Company,
4 Parkview, Portlaoise, Co. Laois (Tel: 0502 / 20356)
in conjunction with
Glanbia plc.

© Glanbia plc.
Published in 2003.

ISBN 0 86335 046 1 (paperback)
0 86335 047 X (hardback)

Cover design by Penhouse Design Group, Powelstown House,
Stradbally, Co. Laois.

DESIGNED AND PRINTED BY LEINSTER LEADER LTD., NAAS, CO. KILDARE.

A TRIUMPH OF CO-OPERATION OVER ADVERSITY

The History of Donaghmore Co-operative Creamery Ltd. (Founded in 1927)

Written and edited by
TEDDY FENNELLY

Contents

Preface

The co-operative ideal is based on the pooling of small resources to create new enterprises which are democratically owned by the shareholders. It is an ideal that has empowered and enhanced the lives of millions of people around the world who, as individuals, have either underachieved in the free market or have been exploited by powerful business interests or oppressive regimes.

The co-operative revolution was well established and thriving in Britain, in mainland Europe and in America before it took root in Ireland in the closing decades of the nineteenth century. Unlike British co-operative activity which centred on urban retailing, the Irish co-operative movement was based on agricultural processing and marketing. Dairying, which has a history in Ireland dating back thousands of years, has played a central role in the movement as it developed in this country.

The founding father of co-operation in Ireland was Horace Plunkett. Though a Protestant, unionist and member of the ascendancy class, he empathised with the hardships endured by the mostly Catholic and nationalist peasant farmers. His deeply held conviction was that the way forward for a socially, politically and religiously divided country was through co-operation. The movement's tentacles spread out into the communities and into the homes and hovels of rural Ireland. The co-operative society, which often became synonymous with the local creamery, enabled farmers to take control, to some extent at least, of their own affairs. Producers got a fair price for their milk and a market for their butter.

The creameries developed into important daily social occasions for rural folk, where local news and gossip was traded and where every puck or kick of a ball in a hurling or football match was replayed and analysed. Romances and many a marriage emerged from the new social opportunities presented by the co-ops' activities.

Political independence came in 1922 but the early years of the Irish Free State was a difficult time for the economy and for farmers, in particular. With a stagnant economy at home and a weak demand abroad for Irish exports, farming prices hit the floor. Many farmers were forced out of dairying and reverted to home buttermaking for an income. A bitter all-out milk war ensued as the creameries battled for a diminishing supply of milk. It was a recipe for disaster. Dr. Henry Kennedy, the chief executive of the Irish Agricultural Organisation Society (IAOS), the umbrella body for the creameries, (later to change its name to the Irish Co-operative Organisation Society – ICOS) introduced reforms which included a plan for rationalisation in the traditional dairying regions and setting up new creameries in areas not already served by co-ops.

Coincidentally there was a renewed interest being shown at the time by farmers in the Donaghmore area to start a creamery and Dr. Kennedy's timing on his initiative to open up new regions to co-op creameries was just perfect for those already pushing the project in the corner of Laois near the borders of Tipperary and Kilkenny. Fr. Thomas Henebry, a curate in Killesmeestia, was conscious of the

economic benefits that a local creamery might bring to the area and set about winning support for the idea wherever he could. The old Union buildings at
Donaghmore, which had been built and used as a workhouse in the immediate
post-Famine period but had lain idle for many years, were eyed out by the organising committee as a suitable location in which to base their operations.

Sixty-nine members attended the first annual general meeting of Donaghmore
Creamery Society on 5 May 1927, which was chaired by Fr. Henebry. Included on
the committee of twelve elected were men of differing political and religious persuasions and farmers of big acreage and small. By deciding to leave their differences aside and to work together in the interest of the common good, they set a
shining example for committees of management in future years to follow. When
one remembers that this was a mere five years after independence and the bitter
Civil War that followed, the example set by the pioneers of the Donaghmore Co-op
for others in the infant Irish Free State, in which politics and religion were such sen-
sitive and divisive issues, should not be underestimated.

The doubters, and there were many, believed that the short term prospects for
Donaghmore were poor and the long term forecast was absolutely bleak. The
creamery was based in a non-dairying area and the organisers lacked business
experience and capital, they said. There were question marks over the level of
farmer participation in a venture new to the district and in the creamery's ability to
procure an adequate milk supply. How could such a shaky venture succeed at a
time when other similar undertakings, long established in traditional dairying areas,
were falling by the wayside? Nor could the initiators have picked a worse time. The
country's economy, depressed in the 1920s, went into almost terminal decline in
the 1930s with the onset of the economic war with Britain. To many it seemed, at
best, a risky venture that became riskier by the year.

Yet Donaghmore managed not only to survive but eventually to prosper. Despite
their early reservations, the IAOS supported the project, providing it with an invaluable advisory service, obtaining legal advice and acting in an advocacy role and as
an intermediary between Donaghmore and other agencies, such as government
departments.

The committee faced up early to the reality that there were not sufficient milk
supplies from the immediate area around Donaghmore. Because milk is such a
perishable commodity, and farmers of the day depended mostly on their horses
and donkeys for transport, it was imperative that the suppliers' journey with milk to
the separation station was as short as possible. Committee members knew that, if
the Creamery was to have access to an adequate milk supply, auxiliaries would
have to be built convenient to the areas where most of the milk was available.

They also knew that it was a priority to have the auxiliaries up and running as
soon as was possible and so prevent other new creameries being created or exist-
ing creameries spreading their wings into the Donaghmore catchment area. The
first area targeted was Coolrain. An auxiliary was opened there in early 1928.
Raheen was opened later in that same year and Spink followed in 1935. Although
Coolrain was forced to close, through lack of milk supply in 1939, the branches at
Raheen and Spink went on to become vital organs of the Donaghmore operation.
Mountmellick was later to join the Donaghmore family, thus spreading its wings in
Laois countywide. The Society continued to expand, adapt and thrive until it
became part of the Avonmore group in 1973. Clonaslee Co-op, in which
Donaghmore had a shareholding from its beginnings in 1962, merged with

Avonmore some years later. Monasterevin, after amalgamation in 1973, was linked up with Donaghmore to form a major region within Avonmore, which itself later merged with Waterford Co-op in 1997 to become Glanbia, one of the biggest dairy food producers on the planet.

The forecasters of doom had said that it was the wrong business, in the wrong place, at the wrong time. But they overlooked one important detail. It had the right people; talented, progressive, strong-willed individuals. The giant oak that is Glanbia, owes much to the acorn sown by Fr. Henebry and nurtured by dedicated committees, management, workers and suppliers of Donaghmore spanning 75 years.

At the helm through thick and thin, was the Society's indefatigable secretary, J.P. Kelly, a man of vision and substance, if there ever was one. Time and again he guided the good ship through turbulent waters and against all the odds. A man of great foresight and ingenuity, he introduced diversification and innovation to the Donaghmore operation with spectacular effect.

Nor was he a shrinking violet. When the going got tough J.P. was seen at his best. He was fearless in the face of powerful adversaries and shot from the hip with deadly effect. He possessed a clear logical and analytical brain and didn't beat about the bush when he had something to say. From time to time, and for various reasons, in the interest of Donaghmore, he faced down criticism from government departments, the IAOS and even key people within his own organisation, including its first chairman.

His clash with Fr. Henebry came at a time when ordinary mortals had reason to fear the collar and the power of the Catholic Church. The Society was only two years in existence and its viability was still very much in question. The chairman was enraged when voted down by the committee on a choice of bankers' issue. He refused to sign the minutes at the following meeting, saying that they were incomplete. Fr. Henebry had crossed the line as far as J.P. was concerned. "Minute books are not kept to give vent to the speeches of the chairman or any individual ...," J.P. retorted. He went on to tell his reverence that he should be ashamed of the disgraceful scene he had created. Fr. Henebry had said that he was "ignominiously insulted" by the committee who had voted down his motion, but J.P. was of a different opinion. "It is you, and you alone, who ... cast the insult. You have insulted the intelligence of the other members of the committee." J.P. continued to condemn every single aspect of Fr. Henebry's offensive behaviour and dissected his every argument before delivering the *coup de grace*. "I cannot understand your attitude ... though I have tried, and tried hard ... certainly you have stooped to practices unworthy of your calling in order to achieve your ends ... Does this contain the true spirit of co-operation? Is it for the material welfare of the Society? I am exceedingly sorry that I find it necessary to address you in this tone but I, at least, have the interests of our little Society at heart and I will uphold them whatever the cost."

J.P. continued to uphold the interests of the Society "whatever the cost" for the following thirty-five years. Fr. Henebry was left with no option but to resign. Meanwhile the Society walked the tightrope and the new chairman, Edward Sheeran, was forced to seek a wage cut of 10% for all staff in his first year in the position due to the depressed butter sales. Two years later, in another cost-cutting exercise, the salaries of the managers, secretary and dairymaid were again cut by 10%. Donaghmore struggled on from year to year in the early decades due to this willingness by management and staff to make sacrifices when necessary and their ability to work together in the interest of the good health of the Society.

Its survival was heavily reliant on the marvellous ingenuity of its secretary. Donaghmore had its own electrical supply in 1931, thanks to J.P.'s intervention, one of the first businesses in rural Ireland to be given a connection and with widespread rural electrification still a long way into the future. J.P. not only encouraged the grinding of corn for local grain growers but he put a mill, which he owned, at the Society's disposal at a knockdown price. As a further service to local farmers, with the committee's approval, he set up a store at Donaghmore, and later at Raheen and Spink, selling seeds, fertilisers and other goods for the household and farm. He became an agent for Ranks, the millers, buying grain from farmers over a wide area and while he earned commission on purchases, he ensured that there was a significant spin-off for the Society. The AGM in 1934 heard that the purchase of grain had turned what was a trading loss for the Society into a profit. Three years later, the annual report recorded that "without the milling, store and grain trade it would be utterly impossible for us to carry on the creamery side of the business".

It was this ability to adapt and diversify that enabled Donaghmore Creamery to survive through the most difficult years and to capitalise on the opportunities provided in the better times. During the war years, a time of severe fuel shortage, the Society harvested turf for its own use and also to earn valuable income. A hatchery was established in the mid-forties and operated successfully for some years. The store business grew and prospered. An advisory service was provided for milk suppliers and shareholders.

Donaghmore did not get its head safely above water until the 1950s, when milk supplies rapidly increased and the country's economic situation gradually improved. The dramatic improvement in Donaghmore's fortunes is reflected in the milk intake figures. In 1951 it was over one million gallons for the first time. By 1968 it had risen to more than seven million gallons. The supply had risen so sharply, indeed, by the early 1970s that the committee realised that the Society would have to invest a huge capital sum in upgrading the facility at Donaghmore. This was considered a risky proposition in the fast changing circumstances in the farming industry that prevailed at the time, as Ireland prepared for entry into the EEC. It proved a crucial factor in members opting to amalgamate with the Avonmore group, which had a huge new facility at Ballyragget.

Kelly had the title of secretary but he was effectively the chief executive of the Society from its inception until he stepped down, due to ill health, in 1964. He called the shots even if his remuneration did not reflect his input or level of responsibility. Through all his years at Donaghmore, Kelly worked alongside the Grogans, William and Donal, father and son, who boasted a proud collective service of over forty years as managers at Donaghmore. Other key personnel included Billy Wallis, manager from 1969 until 1973 and joint manager for the previous eight years, Joe Butler, who managed the Raheen Branch very capably for a long number of years and Ben Moran, who gave many years of dedicated service as manager of the Spink Branch.

The executive staff were supported and guided by a very progressive management committee over the years. These men were elected by the shareholders (farmers/suppliers of milk) and represented their interests at management level. The exceptional calibre of these men is amazing. Farmers all, they displayed a high level of business acumen, foresight and adaptability. To the fore among these great men was George Galbraith, a firm admirer and mentor of Kelly. His was a strong voice on the management committee for almost half a century. In later years he was first chairman of the Avonmore Federation of Creameries, the forerunner to complete amalgamation in 1973. His son, John C. Galbraith, was company accountant before replacing J.P. Kelly as secretary in 1964.

Another influential committee figure was Bobby Bennett whose father, R.F. Bennett, was a member of the first management committee and with whom he was present at Donaghmore on the day the Creamery opened for business in 1927. Bobby was chairman from 1967-73 and led the Society into the amalgamation with the Avonmore group in 1973. He later became vice-chairman of the Avonmore Board of Directors. The names of Edward Sheeran, chairman 1930-40 and Patrick J. Kavanagh, chairman 1947-66, must also be mentioned specially in the roll of honour for the first 75 years of Donaghmore Creamery.

Donaghmore was crucial to the successful formation of Avonmore Creameries. Amalgamation was a big decision to take for such a proud and independent association and not all members agreed with the move at the time. Along with South Tipperary and Barrowvale, it was one of the big three societies in the amalgamation. Had its members decided not to join, it is likely that South Tipperary would have looked to its future in another direction. This would have left Avonmore a much smaller and weaker group. But Donaghmore did join and helped make Avonmore one of the major players in the Irish dairy industry.

In its 75 years Donaghmore has impacted upon a lot of people. Donaghmore Creamery Butter was on the shelves of grocery stores and on the tables in households throughout Laois and its hinterland for generations. It played such a regular part in the daily lives of people that it was almost taken for granted. Farmers throughout Laois and further afield have benefited from regular milk cheques and through the provision of supplies, stores and services needed in their business.

The Society's operations provide good employment, throughout County Laois and beyond, in places where it is most needed. Donaghmore has infused new life into the rural areas and towns where it has Branches. Apart from the obvious spin-offs to the local economies, the Donaghmore presence has also helped the social, sporting and cultural life of these areas. It has survived because of the capacity of people from diverse backgrounds to work together through thick and thin for the common good and because of its constant preparedness and ability to face new challenges. The Society, it could be said, is the embodiment of the principles of co-operation.

Though now a relatively minor part of a huge conglomerate, Donaghmore Co-op has managed to keep its unique identity, carved out by its proud history of enterprise and durability. This book tells the story of 75 years of achievement at Donaghmore and the men and women who made it all happen.

The main sources for the history are the minute books dating from the Co-op's beginnings until the mid-1960s and the correspondence deposited in the files of the IAOS (now ICOS), which complement and expand on the records held at Donaghmore and often assess people and events from a different viewpoint. Similarly, the people interviewed come from different backgrounds and approach the story from varied perspectives. Their personal reminiscences provide an invaluable insight into the personalities, the events and the work practices of a bygone era, as well as the changing times and fortunes at the Co-op over its first 75 years. These combined sources reveal an incredible amount of detail of the day-to-day operations at Donaghmore and much of that detail has been retained in the book for the purposes of record and to tell the full story of Donaghmore Co-op – the story of the triumph of co-operation over adversity.

The Research and Editorial Team

Seán Hearn (Chairman): A native of Co. Wexford, Sean joined Avonmore in 1981. He worked as Manager of the Raheen Branch, then the Donaghmore Branch and then as Regional Manager of the Donaghmore/Monasterevin Region. In 1990 he took over the Feed Division of Avonmore. He also serves at committee level in the Irish Grain and Feed Association, of which he was President in 1995. He was appointed Commercial Manager of the combined Avonmore/Waterford feed business at the time of the merger in 1997. This business, Gain Feeds, is now the No. 1 animal feed brand in Ireland. Seán, who is a member of Portlaoise Rotary Club, now lives with his wife, Eileen, and three children in Portlaoise.

Michael Igoe (Research and Project Co-ordinator): Joined Avonmore in October 1976 as Regional Office Manager in the Donaghmore/Monasterevin Region. He served nine years in Donaghmore, eight years in Portlaoise and four years in Ballyragget. Since his retirement in 1997, he has spent two years in Avonmore/Glanbia House and one year in Portlaoise working on special projects. He is married to Elsie (formerly Keating from Mountrath) and has three children, Anthony, Selena and Katherine.

Ger Lawler (Research): Began working at Raheen Branch in August 1948. He was not yet 14 years old. He was in his 51st year of service with Donaghmore Co-op when he decided to call it a day on 3 October 1998. He worked in many capacities but for the most part in a clerical capacity at Raheen. Married to Maura (nee Bergin), there are three children in their family, Poilin, Geraldine and John and five grandchildren.

Teddy Fennelly (Writer and Publisher): Editor of the Leinster Express for 20 years. He was founding President of the Portlaoise (now Laois) Chamber of Commerce. Among his previous books are *Fitz and the Famous Flight, The Life, Times and Legacy of Thomas Prior - Founder of the RDS, Laois Lives* and *One Hundred Years of Laois GAA*. He is currently Chairman of Laois Heritage Society and a member of Laois County Development Board.

Marie Langton, Group Communications Development Manager with Glanbia plc, was an advisor to the research and editorial team.

Project Steering Committee
John Miller (Chairman), Spink; Martin Keane, Donaghmore; Tom Phelan Donaghmore; Liam Rohan, Raheen; Michael Mahon, Monasterevin; Chris Horan, Mountmellick; Billy Flynn, Clonaslee; Ronnie Bryant, North Offaly; Colm Eustace, Glanbia Agribusiness.

The editorial team: Ger Lawlor, Seán Hearn (Chairman), Michael Igoe and Teddy Fennelly.

Donaghmore – the Acorn from which the Giant Oak Grew

A message from Mr. Joe Walsh, T.D., Minister for Agriculture and Food

It gives me great pleasure as Minister for Agriculture and Food to introduce this excellent publication on the history of the Donaghmore Co-operative Creamery. The importance of co-operatives in the development of agriculture in Ireland cannot be understated. There is a long tradition of association with my Department. Sir Horace Plunkett, who, in 1899, became the first Vice-President of the Department of Agriculture and Technical Instruction, introduced the first co-operative into Ireland, when at the age of 24, he formed the Dunsany Co-operative Society and, in 1899, he started a co-operative store at Doneraile in County Cork.

They have played a major role in the transformation of rural Ireland from a landscape of peasant farmers producing primarily for local consumption at the turn of the century to the situation today, of large organisations operating on international markets trading premium Irish products. The ethos of co-operation was central in the development and growth of the Irish agriculture industry and, in particular, the expansion of the Irish dairy processing industry.

Donaghmore Co-operative Creamery is a good example of this development, having amalgamated into Avonmore in 1973, which subsequently merged with Waterford to form Glanbia plc.

Donaghmore can be considered to be the acorn from which that great oak, Glanbia, was sown. Glanbia PLC has grown and developed to become one of Ireland's most important food companies today. It is the largest dairy processor in Ireland and holds the premier position for consumer dairy products. With over 7,500 staff worldwide and operations in Ireland, Europe and the United States, Glanbia is among the world's leading dairy businesses and holds strong international market positions in the making of cheese and nutritional dairy products.

This book is a fascinating insight into the growth of a small, local co-operative. I would like to congratulate all those associated with this fine publication.

JOE WALSH, T.D.
Minister for Agriculture and Food

A Message from the Chairman

I t gives me great pleasure to have the opportunity to offer my congratulations to Donaghmore Co-operative Society as they celebrate 75 years of success in the co-operative movement.

It is indeed a great tribute to the founders, past officers and former management, to whom we owe a great debt of gratitude for their courage and commitment. Those pioneers of the co-operative movement who displayed such foresight and vision were ahead of their time as they planned ahead towards a better future for their farmers and members.

Today's multi-million euro industry, of which Glanbia is an integral part, should never lose sight of the humble beginnings of the past, seventy-five to one hundred years ago when a number of creameries were established across the country, including Donaghmore, and was the starting point of later amalgamations and development.

We should also keep foremost in our minds Sir Horace Plunkett, the founding father of modern Irish agriculture, who preached the gospel of co-operation right across the country.

Donaghmore Co-op Creamery was destined to be part of Avonmore, being one of the twenty-one creameries that came together in 1973 to form Avonmore Creameries Limited. I am confident that this loyal association with Avonmore, which benefited all, will continue to strengthen in its support for Glanbia now and in the future. In that regard I would like to wish the present management, staff and representatives from the Donaghmore Region every success.

Since the formation of Avonmore, and later Glanbia, Donaghmore has been well served by its representatives on the Board and Council: George Galbraith, Robert Bennett, John Miller, Richard Lalor-Fitzpatrick, Christopher Horan, William Delaney, Hugh Cole, Martin Keane, Liam Rohan and John McEvoy.

Finally, I would like, on behalf of my colleagues on the Board and Management, to thank the farmers and suppliers, without whose support all would be in vain. As we look forward, we should always remember the co-operation of the past, but not dwell in the past as we plan our future. President John F. Kennedy once said and I quote: "Change is the law of life and those who look only to the past or the present are certain to miss the future".

Once again congratulations to Donaghmore.

TOM CORCORAN
Chairman, Glanbia plc

Background to the Irish Co-operative Movement

The practice of Irish farmers of pooling their labour and resources for the common good can be traced back to the pre Christian era. The Gaelic Irish termed this system of co-operation "Meitheal" and there are references to it in the Brehon Laws of the old Irish clans.

The "Meitheal" tradition persisted through the centuries despite long periods of bloody conquest and persecution. Apart from the oral tradition which testifies to the practice being alive and well in 19th century Ireland, there are ample official reports and documents to verify that testimony.

Rural Ireland was still a land largely owned by a landlord class, in whose midst were those imbued with a passion to milk the country dry and extract the last penny and the last ounce of energy from their underlings, the hard-pressed tenant farmer and the even more impoverished farm labourer. The Great Famine had devastated the country in mid-century and social and political unrest was a feature of the ensuing decades. More than one million people died of starvation and disease and another million emigrated. The country's population in 1845 was around 8.5 million. By the turn of the century the population had almost halved. The British Government and the landlords had failed the Irish people in their darkest hour.

It was a Laoisman, James Fintan Lalor, whose writings sparked the revolution which eventually forced the British Government to reform the land laws which resulted in the overthrow of the landlord system. He passionately preached "the land of Ireland for the people of Ireland". Social and political radicals of the future sang his praises. Michael Davitt, James Connolly and Padraig Pearse all quoted him freely in their writings. Pearse wrote before the Rising of 1916, "Tone sounded the gallant reveille of democracy in Ireland. The man who gave it its battle-cries was James Fintan Lalor."

Lalor set out his stall quite clearly on behalf of the tenant farmer. "Our fair share of Ireland, our fair share of the earth, a house to live in that no one can tumble down, a happy home, the necessaries of life, the comforts and decencies of life, all those things without which the world is worthless and existence itself a misery – these we must have and the security for all these."

Harrowing stories of evictions and rampant famine and disease stalking the countryside fuelled resentment against the landlord which as Bolger put it, "was always a powder keg awaiting only the torch of an economic recession to bring about an explosion of agrarian violence".

Recession struck with a vengeance in the late 1870s and successive harvest failures aggravated the already dire situation in which, as ever, the poor were hardest hit. The landlord system had yet again been seen to fail the people. The Government had shown themselves, as in the years of the Great Famine during which a quarter of Ireland's population either died or emigrated, unable or unwilling to adequately respond.

The Land War

Enter Michael Davitt. He took up the rallying cry of James Fintan Lalor, "The Land for the People", and he whisked up support through platform appearances around the country. In August 1879 in Castlebar in his native Mayo, Davitt set up the Land League. He enlisted the backing of Charles Stewart Parnell, who commanded huge public and political esteem, and together they launched a great national movement a few months later. The League's main aims were to protect tenants from rack-renting and unjust evictions and, in the longer term, to make them owners of their own farms.

The National Land League grew in strength and confidence in the years that followed. It was a mass movement that shook landlordism to its foundations and forced the Government to introduce radical rural reform. Davitt was the visionary and the activist rather than the politician. Bolger sums up his achievements. "He (Davitt) deflected the militants from their policy of futile insurrection, shook the National Party out of its preoccupation with sterile constitutional argument and directed it to constructive agrarian reform. It is to his credit that in so doing, this angry and rigid patriot often submerged his own cherished personal ideals for the sake of unity."

The exploited rural working classes had just received a lesson in strength in numbers and in unity of purpose. Co-operation yields better results than individual effort.

That is the basic principle of the co-operative movement. The co-operative revolution was well-established and thriving in Britain, in Europe and in America before it took root in Ireland in the closing decades of the 19th century. The founding father of the movement in Ireland, Horace Plunkett, acknowledged the work of Davitt and the Land League as vital to the success story of the Irish co-operative movement.

The elevation to ownership of the land they worked was the fulfilment of a dream deeply held for centuries by countless generations of Irish tenant farmers. Under a series of land acts between 1885 and 1903, 60,000 tenant farmers bought their own land and after the Wyndham Act of 1903 another 250,000 gained ownership of their holdings. By 1908 almost half the farms of the country were owner occupied. The power of the landlord was broken by these land reforms and it was weakened further by local government reform. However when land ownership was secured, the problems of poverty and exploitation that the tenants had encountered on a daily basis under the landlord system did not suddenly disappear. Far from it. Their economic and social conditions remained appalling.

Agricultural exports, particularly to the British market, were the lifeblood of the country's health, and butter was one of the main products exported. The sale of home-made butter was the income mainstay of the teeming thousands of peasant farmers.

In the 1880s, the butter market had all but collapsed. What sales took place were mostly at the low end of the market where it was competing with margarine and margarine butter mixtures imported from the continent. The wealthier landowners in the lush grassland counties, such as Meath, could still export and command good prices for their cattle. The hard-pressed smallholders were, however, dependent on their butter sales and bore the brunt of the downturn in the British demand for Irish produce. The British consumer refused to buy the traditional Irish-made hard salted butter and opted for the mild cured and consistent all year round quality of continental imports instead. Irish butter simply could not compete. The Danes and other European farmers were better organised. With the establishment of farming co-operatives they had introduced modern machinery and scientific production methods ensuring consistency in quality and presentation of their product. There were no quick-fix solutions for the Irish quality problem. Butter, in the commercial creamery as well as in the home, was still being made by primitive methods. Lots for sale frequently contained layers of produce of varying age, flavours, colours, textures and aromas. Efforts to tackle the question of grading and standardisation of produce proved futile.

The newly liberated smallholders also encountered major problems at the input end of the business. Effectively they had to take what they got without question and had no control over availability, quality or price of seeds or other essential supplies. Commanding minimal bargaining power they were left at the whim of the middleman, not a new phenomenon in Irish history.

Politics offered little respite to the difficulties of the smallholder. The country was in the grip of Home Rule frenzy, which gathered new momentum following the spectacular success of the Land War. But for Home Rulers the fight was a political one, not an economic one. Indeed, certain politicians believed that securing better conditions for the masses in the shorter term would thwart the argument, and hence obstruct the campaign, for self-determination. Not surprisingly there was widespread support among smallholders for this patriotic ideal, thus compounding the difficulties facing the economic and social reformers of the period.

Horace Plunkett

It was into this maelstrom of nationalistic fervour and economic and social adversity that an unlikely patriot and champion of the oppressed arrived. Horace Curzon Plunkett was born in 1854 to an Anglo-Irish landed gentry family. The son of Lord Dunsany, he was a man of frail appearance with a slight stoop and dogged with ill health throughout his life. Neither was he helped by poor public speaking skills. As Bolger commented: " ... in a loquacious country and in an age of oratory he was a poor public speaker. He could attract and hold the loyalty of the few but could not draw crowds."[1]

Yet Horace Plunkett overcame his physical and personal shortcomings, as well as public misgivings from both sides of the political and religious spectrum, to establish himself as a

Horace Plunkett

1. *The Irish Co-operative Movement: Its History and Development* by P. Bolger. (The Institute of Public Administration, Dublin, 1977).

key figure in the emergence of the modern Ireland. He was born and educated in England, yet his aristocratic upbringing did not deter him from becoming a pioneer for social and economic reform. Although a Unionist he supported many non-Unionist causes during his lifetime, including the Gaelic Athletic Association, the Gaelic League and the campaign for a Catholic University. He was familiar with the work of the Rochdale Pioneers and had observed with keen interest the growth of the British co-operative movement, which was centred on urban consumer needs.[2] Plunkett could see the potential for an Irish model but was convinced from an early stage that it would only work if applied to Ireland's main economic activity, agriculture. His experiences at Oxford University confirmed in him the need for social reform and the vital role of the co-operative movement in achieving that aim. He experimented in co-operation in a practical way on leaving college by opening a small co-operative store in Dunsany, Co Meath in 1878. Ill health forced him to close the shop and he moved on doctor's advice to warmer climes in the USA.

From an early stage Plunkett recognised that the greatest need for co-operation in Ireland was among the peasant farmers, still using outdated farming methods and machinery and exploited on all sides, from the purchase of essential supplies to the selling of their produce. On his return from the States he seriously set about converting his theories into practical working models.

Plunkett's mission was one fraught with pitfalls and dangers of self-destruction. He was, after all, from the landlord class, detested by the Irish peasants and supportive of the Union. If the mostly Catholic and only recently liberated smallholders had reason to be sceptical of his sincerity in throwing in his lot with them, his establishment brethren were somewhat bewildered too by what they considered, at best, his eccentricity and, at worst, his betrayal of his own class and creed.

Plunkett was a determined and resilient man and sought support from wherever he might get it. He preached the doctrine of co-operation as the best way forward and asked the smallholders and sympathisers with his mission for Ireland to follow his gospel. He travelled the length and breadth of the country telling the farmers that they must take control of the means of production and come together to develop an effective marketing strategy. He was one of the establishment class which held the reins of power and influence in Ireland and he spared no effort in converting his aristocratic friends to his co-operative philosophy and enlisting their support. He also sought the best talent to drive the movement. Apart from Anderson, who became chief organiser, Plunkett forged a close bond with George Russell, better recognised under his pen name, AE, one of the foremost figures in the Irish literary renaissance at the close of the 19th century. Another brilliant recruit was Fr. Tom Finlay, an energetic, middle-aged Jesuit priest recommended by Bishop O'Dwyer as "the ablest man in Ireland". Fr. Finlay and Russell combined their talents to whip up support for Plunkett and his crusade. Together they scripted and edited the *Irish Homestead*, the official publication of the co-operative movement, later called the *Irish Statesman* (1906-1930).

Criticism of the Movement

The agricultural-based co-operative movement had a profound effect on the

2. The modern co-operative movement began with the Rochdale Society of Equitable Pioneers, formed in 1844 in order to reduce what was seen as the exploitation of consumers by the capitalist system. The emergence of the Co-operative Wholesale Society in Britain, the largest in the world, formed in 1863, traces its origins to the Rochdale Pioneers.

economic and social life of rural Ireland. Its tentacles spread out into community and into the homes through the local co-operative society. Naturally there were those who were not happy with what was happening in the towns and in the countryside. The traders and suppliers who had enriched themselves from the needs and industry of the vulnerable individual farmer soon realised that this new movement posed a great threat to their traditional business. So too the buyers of butter and other farm produce, who had bought the produce directly from the farmer at rock-bottom prices and made big profits when selling on, now found that their margins were much tighter.

The supplier or trader who lost business because the days of exploiting the vulnerability of the peasant farmer had run their course, had every reason to resist the growth of farmer co-operation. But there were others too who were sceptical about the benefits derived from the growth of the movement and especially the proliferation of co-op creameries. The late Raymond Smith, in his excellent book on the history of the Centenary Co-operative Creamery Society, instances articles published in the Cork Herald which indicted the creamery system on numerous counts. One of the claims was that the creameries "had had the direct effect of reducing the opportunities for employment on the farms and in the farmhouses, thereby encouraging emigration to such an extent that in one district alone – the Kilmallock district – at least 500 dairymaids have been forced to find employment elsewhere". It was also argued that the dairy and farm workers of the old regime "have been replaced by drivers of carts, of both sexes, whose idle sojourn day after day at the gates of the creameries, are not for the moral advantage of either". It was also claimed that the towns too had suffered through the loss of butter-markets and that coopers, blacksmiths, shoemakers and other artisans had disappeared.

These criticisms were firmly refuted in the Irish Homestead magazine, whose writer contended that jobs were not lost on the farm or in towns. Not alone that but the article contended that the life of the farmer's wife had been made easier now because the creamery had taken over one of her traditional onerous tasks of butter-making.

Referring to the butter-markets the writer asked was it not better for the profits to be retained by the farmer rather than the butter-buyer. The article dismissed the argument that the towns were suffering. "The creamery system had put more money into farmers' pockets and consequently farmers had more to spend. It was the shopkeepers who had benefited from the spending."

On the charges of idleness and moral dangers of daily sojourns "at the gates of creameries", the writer contended that the situation was far worse in the days of the old butter-markets. Whatever the dangers, perceived or otherwise, the regular impromptu meetings at the creameries developed into important social occasions for rural folk, where all the local news and gossip was traded and there were long chats about the big hurling match as well as intense debates on matters of profound national and international importance. The advent of the creameries brought many thousands of country folk out of their drab isolation and added a little colour and enrichment to their daily lives.

A more potent criticism of the creamery system that was overlooked was the negative impact it had on the independence of the farmer's wife. This drastic downgrading of the woman in the home was brought about not because she was no longer the butter-maker but because she had traditionally brought a welcome added income into the home from the sale of the butter and other farmyard produce such as eggs, a role now taken over by the creameries. To compound the indignity for the woman, it was usually the man who received the cheque and had the control over the spending.

Plunkett's plan of campaign for the co-operative movement was nurtured on his visits to Doneraile, County Cork, to see and discuss the topics of the day with his friends, Alexis Roche and Bernard Fitzpatrick.[3] He had spent ten years ranching in Wyoming, USA, at the foot of the Rocky Mountains with Roche and both retained business interests in the States. While in the States, he developed a close friendship with Theodore Roosevelt, the US Republican statesman and, later, 26th President of the USA (1901-'09). Fitzpatrick, second Lord Castletown, who succeeded to his title in 1883, had family connections in County Laois dating back to the Norman invasion and beyond. He owned estates in County Laois at Granston Manor and Abbeyleix as well as Doneraile Court. It was here that Plunkett first met R. A. Anderson, an employee of Lord Castletown. Anderson was to become a close and trusted ally of Plunkett and, his name, like that of his mentor was to become synonymous with the foundation and early growth of the co-operative movement in Ireland.

They first experimented with the co-operative concept in Doneraile before directing their attentions further afield. It is estimated that Plunkett and Anderson held as many as fifty meetings before recruits to the movement were finally taken on board. Progress was slow and it was a giant leap forward for the movement when the first dairy co-operative was formed in 1889 in the County Limerick village of Drumcollogher, made famous in song by Percy French.

There was a hostile reaction from shopkeepers and traders who viewed the co-operatives as a threat to their business. The owners of the private creameries were also outraged at the idea of farmers clubbing together to demand a better price from them for their milk.

There was not a single new co-operative enlisted during 1889 and '90. Yet Plunkett and Anderson soldiered on. Perseverance paid rich dividends and in 1891 another 16 new societies were formed. Now things were really advancing. The bulge in numbers gave the movement some muscle. It was time to test their new-found strength.

Farmers were still experiencing difficulties in securing essential supplies. This led in 1893 to the formation of the co-operatives own wholesale arm, the Irish Co-operative Agency Society Ltd (ICASL). This co-op of co-ops, with an initial share capital of £137, concentrated its efforts on marketing the butter and in addressing the problems of supply.

The emphasis on creamery, rather than consumer, co-ops by Plunkett's movement angered many in the British Co-operative Union. The British Co-operative Wholesale Society (CWS) was a large buyer of Irish butter in the latter half of the nineteenth century. One third of its total trade was in butter bought through its

3. The Hon. Bernard Fitzpatrick, 2nd and last Lord Castletown, 4th Earl of Upper Ossory (Titular) and M.P. for Portarlington 1880-'83. In 1907, on the visit of King Edward VII to Ireland he was conferred with the Knighthood of St. Patrick. He was appointed a Privy Councillor in the following year. He was a member of the first County Council for Queen's County (now County Laois) in 1899. An ardent supporter of the Gaelic League, he was a personal friend of Dr. Douglas Hyde. He preferred to be addressed as MacGiolla Phadraig and signed his name as such. (*The M.P.s for Laois and Offaly - Queen's and King's Counties 1801-1918* by Patrick F. Meehan. The Leinster Express, 1983.)

depots in Ireland. With the growth in the Irish creamery co-operatives, which had the interest of the supplier at heart rather than the consumer, tension mounted between the British and the Irish movements. This escalated into a bitter milk war as the proprietary creameries battled with their co-operative rivals to get more milk suppliers on their books. It was a long drawn-out conflict which persisted until 1912 when the CWS finally decided that their "war" was lost to the Irish and they transferred thirty-four main creameries and fifty-one auxiliaries into the hands of the local societies. Despite the opposition from the proprietary creameries, the numbers of co-operative creameries had risen to thirty by 1893. This necessitated the need for a coordinating body to spearhead the development of the movement. The IAOS was established in a building in Great Brunswick Street (now Pearse Street) in 1894. Plunkett promised that the new organisation would be "strictly economic, and no political or sectarian ends shall be promoted by word or deed. The more business you introduce to politics, and the less politics in business, the better for both."

The vexed question of supply of seeds, fertilisers and other essentials at input stage came to the fore once again in the spring of 1896. A group of five agricultural societies in the Thurles area arranged a conference amongst themselves to address the issue. First secretary of the IAOS, Robert A. Anderson, was in attendance. It was agreed that the group should bulk their orders and seek tenders for the supply of fertiliser. There was much at stake for the farmer with overall savings estimated at forty per cent. The response was swift and sharp as the local suppliers united and put pressure on the manufacturers to delay delivery for a month. The suppliers believed that this action would bring the farmers to their knees and force them to beg for a swift delivery of fertiliser at the high prices as before. But the farmers held firm and it was the traders who first broke rank when two of their number decided to deal with the societies. This was a major boost to the practice and concept of farmers co-operating. Anderson acknowledged that it was "one of the biggest things ever accomplished by our movement".[4]

As the movement continued to expand a committee of the IAOS concluded in 1897 that there was a need for a new agency to concentrate on the agricultural supply end of the business and allow the ICASL to concentrate on its core activity, the marketing of butter and dairy supplies. The Irish Co-operative Agency Society soon blossomed to become the Irish Agricultural Wholesale Society (IAWS) with Plunkett as its first chairman.

New Department for Agriculture
In 1892 Plunkett had been elected Unionist MP for South Dublin a seat he held for eight years. While at Westminster, he saw a gaping need for a separate government department for agriculture to coordinate the functions carried out at the time by a diverse number of departments and boards. During a break in Parliament in 1895, he initiated the Recess Committee to study the matter. He managed to bring together Unionist and Nationalist MPs, a rare achievement, by convincing both groups that each side would benefit by a joint approach to the British Governments for the creation of a new department to handle agricultural issues. The Committee's hard-hitting report led to the introduction of the Department of Agriculture and Technical Instruction in 1899.

4. *The Centenary Co-operative Creamery Society 1898-1998* by Raymond Smith. (Mount Cross Publishers, Dublin, 1998).

Bolger underlines the importance of what Plunkett had accomplished by getting the representatives of both traditions on the island working together in their common interest: "Plunkett had effectively taken an important Irish issue outside the British Parliament and had united his countrymen in a clear-cut demand for a considerable measure of Irish control in a specific sector. Although many Irish nationalists persisted in seeing it as a distraction, shrewd English politicians saw it as a more subtle approach than the blanket demand for total Home Rule at once, and much more difficult to oppose."[5]

Plunkett was appointed Vice-President of the new department, equivalent of a ministerial portfolio in the government of today. That appointment surprised none. Plunkett seemed the natural choice. But the appointment of the Secretary to the Department had deep repercussions in political circles and in the co-operative movement. R. A. Anderson appeared the ideal candidate for the position and it seemed a foregone conclusion that he would have the full backing of his close friend and co-operative movement ally, Horace Plunkett. He was urged to seek the job by his family and by friends in the IAOS. While Plunkett told him he could have the job if he so wished, Anderson sensed reservations in the offer. Plunkett warned him that it would mean a huge change from the work he was so capably doing for the IAOS. He explained that working with the Department would involve having to negotiate with such as the Catholic bishops and various other interests determined in pursuing their own agendas. Anderson confronted him on the matter and asked him frankly had he someone else in mind. Plunkett told him that he felt that another man, T. P. Gill, would be more suited for the job. He tried to ease the blow for his friend by praising him for his work for the co-operative movement and reminding him how badly he was needed to continue his good work for the movement. " ... What would the IAOS do without you? You have made it what it is today", said Plunkett. Anderson stepped aside and never regretted his decision but Plunkett lost his parliamentary seat as a result. The appointment of Gill, a former Nationalist MP enraged his Unionist supporters. A second Unionist candidate was put forward in the South Dublin constituency and Plunkett narrowly lost his seat on a split vote.

In 1904, Plunkett published *Ireland in the New Century* which got mixed reviews. In the book, he made some controversial references to the influence of the Roman Catholic religion, which went down like a lead balloon with the Catholic clergy and laity alike. From this time on, his popularity and influence took a downward spiral. The Liberals swept back into power in 1905. While they were strong supporters of the co-operative movement in Britain, they had little sympathy for the Irish movement. Despite his Unionist background and calls for his dismissal, Plunkett continued his role as head of the Department. But he eventually found the job untenable as pressure mounted for his removal. He resigned in 1907 and was replaced by Thomas Wallace Russell, a man with a thorough dislike for the co-operative movement.

After leaving his job at the Department of Agriculture and Technical Instruction, Plunkett continued to work diligently for the co-operative movement and turned down some lucrative appointments so that he could devote more time to his great mission in life. He backed the Free State Government after independence and accepted a nomination to the Senate from President of the Executive Council of the Irish Free State, William T. Cosgrave.

5. *The Irish Co-operative Movement: Its History and Development* by P. Bolger. (The Institute of Public Administration, Dublin, 1977).

Plunkett's relentless work for the co-operative movement which transcended all political, religious and social barriers, allied to the tremendous impact for good that the movement has had on the country, has installed him as an icon of the modern Ireland. He is widely acclaimed as the father of modern Irish agriculture, the man who inspired a movement which brought Ireland's biggest industry out of the dark ages and which was responsible for improving dramatically living conditions in rural Ireland, particularly that of the smallholder.

There are few happy endings to stories from Irish history. Plunkett's final brush with Ireland was certainly no exception. Despite living out the Christian ethic of loving thy neighbour, his courageous qualities of ecumenism and straight talking instead served the purpose of offending people on both sides of the political and religious divide. How ironic it was then for this great man, who had done so much for Ireland, when opponents burned his house to the ground, destroying almost all his possessions, during the Civil War. Although he spent his last years in England he remained as President of the IAOS until 1931. He died in Weybridge the following year at the age of 78. "He had shown, in a most practical way, how effectively Irishmen could work together, and had left a vision for the island which is far from realised."[6]

Russell did everything he could to weaken the power and position of the co-operative movement, firstly by discontinuing grants to the IAOS. He supported the traders in demanding that the societies cease carrying on non-agricultural business. He also denounced the Credit Banks Co-operative System, which concentrated its operations in the poorer districts, especially in the west and north-west, as "rotten and indefensible". The co-op movement felt the pain of Russell's resentment. More than 100 societies were dissolved in 1909 alone.

Russell's interventions, however, created even greater resolve in the IAOS and in the societies, to become more efficient and more effective. The old proverb tells us that "it's an ill wind that blows nobody any good". That was certainly the case for Irish agriculture and the co-operative movement, in particular, when war engulfed the world in 1914.

Years of Boom and Gloom

The outbreak of hostilities in the First World War ushered in a six-year boom period for Irish farmers, during which there was a huge demand for Irish dairying products and foodstuffs. Creameries played the major role in these years of phenomenal growth. In 1907 there had been 900 co-operatives with a turnover of £2 million. By 1913 the number had grown to almost 1,000 with the turnover up by almost 50 per cent. By 1920 the turnover had rocketed to over £14.5 million.

The good times came to an abrupt end, however, in the early 1920s. With a post-war economic recession in Britain, resulting in a sharp drop in consumer spending, the bottom fell out of Ireland's main market. Increased competition emanating from the resumption of international shipping and trade also hit Irish exports. If external matters were not bad enough, things were certainly not helped by the political turmoil at home. The War of Independence had a particularly harmful effect on the co-operative movement. Creameries were the main target of reprisals by the British Army for attacks on their forces by the freedom fighters. Dozens of creameries were burnt down by the Black and Tans and many others were ordered

---

6. Quote used by Trevor West in his essay, "The Development of Horace Plunkett's Thought" in the book, *Plunkett and Co-operatives, Past, Present and Future*, edited by Carla Keating. (U.C.C. Bank of Ireland Centre for Co-operative Studies, 1983).

to shut down. Civil War followed the founding of the Free State and the partition of the country in 1922. The creameries were fully operational again but business was not helped by the disruption in communications, the blowing up of roads, railway lines and bridges and the commandeering of transport vehicles used to service the creameries. This was the start of a prolonged period of economic slump, which continued in different guises more or less until the 1960s.

With Britain a no-go area for Irish exports and a stagnant economy at home, farming produce prices hit the floor. Many farmers were forced out of dairying and reverted to home butter-making for an income. A bitter all-out milk war ensued as the creameries battled for the diminishing amount of milk available. Logic and reason went out the door as the rival co-operative and privately owned businesses went at each other with a terrifying intensity. The fierce battle for milk supplies proved a costly exercise for both sides and threatened the survival of the dairy industry. The Dairy Produce Act 1924 was a comprehensive piece of legislation relating to the production and manufacture of dairy produce. The new regulations, focusing on the suitability of premises and equipment and on the employment of trained staff, were a welcome step towards standardisation in quality, but the legislation did not stop the war. By 1926 there were 580 central and auxiliary creameries in the Irish Free State, of which 400 were co-operatives. Of the 180 proprietary creameries, 114 were now controlled by the Condensed Milk Company which, unlike the co-ops, had valuable retail outlets in Britain. But even this privileged group was feeling the pinch because of the price they were being forced to pay for their milk.

In July 1926, as the milk war waged on, the IAOS appointed a new chief executive, Dr. Henry Kennedy, who was an astute economist and agricultural reformer. He could see plainly that the creameries were racing down the road to self-destruction. The milk war had to be stopped before it was too late. He put forward a strategy to rationalise the dairying sector. This involved doing a deal with the Condensed Milk Company with a view to purchasing their creameries and allied businesses. He enlisted the support of his brother-in-law, Michael Hogan, the Minister for Agriculture. The Dairy Disposal Company was established in 1927 to manage the newly acquired creameries with a view to their integration into the co-operative system.

The rationalisation of creameries in the traditional big dairying regions, involved closures, which was a painful exercise and caused much local resentment in the areas affected. Kennedy's plans extended to establishing new creameries in areas not previously served, such as the midlands. The growth of the creameries had concentrated on Munster and Ulster. In 1905, for instance, there were 121 creameries in Tipperary, 112 in Limerick, 31 in Kilkenny, only two in Laois and none at all in Counties, Offaly, Kildare or Carlow. The establishment of the Dairy Disposal Company was followed by the Creamery Act 1928 which introduced a system of licensing and empowered the Minister to control the establishment of new creameries.

It was during this period of reform of the creamery system that Donaghmore Co-operative Creamery was founded in 1927. It was born out of crisis and faced many fresh crises in the years ahead. But Donaghmore Creamery went on to play a vital role in the further development of the co-operative movement and impacted on the daily lives of thousands of farmers, workers and consumers in County Laois and its wider catchment area for many years to come.

SECTION ONE

PART ONE

In the Beginning

CHAPTER ONE

The Seed Takes Sprout

Although there were unsuccessful attempts to set up a co-operative society at Donaghmore by local clergy and farmers some years earlier, the seed that finally took sprout was contained in a letter dated 18 July 1924 to the Secretary, IAOS, Plunkett House, Dublin from William Menton of William J. Menton, Solicitors, Castle Street, Roscrea. It read:

"Dear Sir,

We have been consulted by some local farmers etc. with reference to the need for a Co-operative Dairy Society in Donaghmore Workhouse for the use of the local dairy farmers. We understand that the project was mooted before but, owing to a certain amount of apathy at the time, the idea never fructified and no definite move was made.

There are quite a few dairy farmers in the neighbourhood and the district is one that should lend itself to the formation of a Society. A number of the local clergy are interested in the matter and one of them, the Rev. Father Heneberry, C.C., Killiesmiesthia (sic), Ballybrophy, has displayed a good deal of energy in the matter and has interviewed the local farmers about the scheme. He informs us that the idea has been well received and that he is promised considerable support, and we think it would be an excellent arrangement if an inspection were made of the premises and one of your inspectors interviewed Father Heneberry with a view to sending down an organiser.

In our opinion it would be advisable to have this matter kept private for the present.

Faithfully yours,

W. Menton."

There was a hasty response from the IAOS. A form requiring completion was sent the following day. The IAOS explained that this information was required as a preliminary to sending an organiser "whose expenses would have to be guaranteed in advance". It was also stated that an inspection of the old workhouse could be arranged by the 'Creamery Expert', whose expenses he reminded them would also have to be met. A preliminary affiliation fee of 3d per share would have to be paid by the Society. "This was usually obtained by making a levy on the share applicants at the time they sign the forms, or whenever they are paying their first instalment", the IAOS letter explained.

Matters appeared to have rested for almost two years. The next relevant correspondence (in the IAOS archives) is a letter from the IAOS to Mr. D. Loughman, Killadooly, Donaghmore, Ballybrophy, dated 8 June 1926:

"Dear Sir,

Mr. Quinn, Manager, Thurles Co-operative Creamery, rang me up on the telephone today to say that a meeting would be held in your district on Sunday next, 13th inst., in connection with the proposed formation of a co-operative creamery and asked that a representative from this Society should attend it. I regret I cannot say at the moment if anyone will be free on that particular day but in any case it is optional for our staff to attend meetings on Sundays as they are working full time and more every day."

Mr. Loughman replied on 9 June.

"Dear Sir,

I shall have the forms filled in on Sunday next at the meeting after which we trust you will send down an organiser. In the meantime I would be glad if you would send us some literature on the matter.

Yours sincerely,

Denis Loughman."

Mr. Loughman advised the IAOS that a motor-car would be available at Ballybrophy railway station if necessary to convey the IAOS representative to the meeting. In a memo from the IAOS organiser in Limerick, Mr. W. O'Brien, to the IAOS headquarters in Dublin, he informed the secretary that he could not attend. "In any case they ought to fix some other day than Sunday", he stated. The assistant secretary promptly wrote to Mr. Loughman advising him not to arrange meetings for Sundays as the organisers may not be able to attend. Mr. O'Brien wrote to Mr. Loughman informing him that he was arranging to send a Mr. Langford to meet him and others the following week.

Aerial photograph of Donaghmore Creamery.

The assistant secretary of the IAOS was critical of the decision to send Mr. Langford to meet Loughman *et al* before the forms were returned and the project evaluated.[1] He wrote: "Possibly the visit on Thursday will be useful but we cannot afford to incur expense upon projects whose chances of success are doubtful. It is not a creamery district, and in any case, we must avoid travelling expenses on chancy propositions."

The initial recorded meeting that set the ball rolling for the establishment of a creamery co-operative at Donaghmore eventually took place in the Donaghmore Union buildings on 2 July 1926. There were thirty-five farmers present and local curate, Rev. J. Larkin, presided. There was no IAOS official at the meeting but the Department of Agriculture was represented by Mr. McAuliffe, who outlined the ways and means of establishing a Co-operative Dairy Society. He emphasised the need for working capital so that Government grants and bank loans could be obtained. The Department official estimated the minimum amount of capital needed was £1,000 and he assured those present that, provided this sum could be guaranteed, the services of an organiser and an engineer would be secured free of charge.

Two important motions were passed at that first meeting: (1) that a Co-operative Creamery be established in Donaghmore Union buildings to be opened on March 1st, 1927 and (2) that £1-10-0 per share be collected in three instalments before January 1st, 1927. An organising committee representing the parishes of Rathdowney, Galmoy, Borris-in-Ossory and Aghaboe was elected.

J.P. Kelly, Secretary of the Society for 37 years.

At a meeting on 15 July, at which Herbert Thompson took the chair, there were fifty farmers present. Mr. O'Brien stressed that dairying was the one system of farming that had been profitable over the previous five years and he believed that it would continue to be so. One farmer, John Dunphy, raised objections to the price of shares but his was a lone voice. There was a resounding reaffirmation of the price and applications for 142 shares (£213) were signed by an enthusiastic gathering. This had risen to 486 shares (£729) by the time of the next meeting, nine days later. Twenty-five farmers turned up and the meeting was chaired by Rev. T. Henebry, C.C., who was to play a key role in the establishment of the creamery at Donaghmore.

In a letter from Mr. O'Brien, dated 21 July 1926, to J.P. Kelly, he said that he was "now hopeful that the

1. Letter of 14 June 1926 from the IAOS to Mr. O'Brien. (National Archives).

Fr. Henebry, Chairman of the Committee of Management of the Society, 1927-'29.

project will materialise even tho' it may take some time". This is the first mention I found of Mr. Kelly, who was to occupy the pivotal role of secretary to the Society and was its main driving force for almost forty years.

Responding to an application for an organiser, the IAOS pointed out that the success of the project depended, as the Department official, Mr. McAuliffe, had already indicated, on a strong financial backing from the farmers themselves. This backing was clearly forthcoming with three-quarters of the target set by Mr. McAuliffe achieved within two weeks. An all-out effort was made to get more farmers on board, so that the target figure could be speedily achieved and surpassed. Organising parties were formed to go out to the regions and sell shares to the farmers. The minutes for the meeting on 24 July 1926 records the details: Rathdowney Brewery – Messrs Quigley, Phelan and Delaney; Rathdowney, Errill and Donaghmore – Messrs Kirwan, Thompson, Loughman and Bennett; Errill/Grogan area – Bennett, Treacy, Campion and Kelly; Pike/Castletown/Coolrain – Kirwan, Walpole and Jestin; Kilcoke/Kilpurcell/Glebe – Campion, Moylan and Kelly.

Possibly unknown to Fr. Henebry or the other interested parties in the Donaghmore project, serious doubts were still being harboured about its viability by the IAOS. In a letter to Mr. Kelly, addressed to his home at Ballymeelish Park, Ballybrophy, Queen's County (now Laois) on 23 July, 1926, the newly appointed secretary (effectively the chief executive) of the IAOS, Dr. Henry Kennedy, intimated that he was expecting members "to shoulder a considerable proportion of the financial responsibility involved or else they may find it extremely hard to form a Society". He added: "It is not easy just now to obtain advances from joint stock banks or from any other source for creamery business and it would be therefore important – assuming farmers of the district are convinced of the advisability of forming a Society and assuming further that the local conditions point towards dairying as a successful mode of farming – that the shareholdings should be undertaken on a more considerable scale. The farmers would require to show their confidence in the project by giving it strong financial backing if it is to succeed."

Doubts persist

If one could detect some doubts prevailing in Plunkett House about the Donaghmore project in the language used in that letter, an internal IAOS memo from the Waterford organiser, Patrick Courtney, leaves no doubt about the negative vibes in circulation. "The prospects for this district are not good for a creamery. I don't believe you can get enough cows for an auxiliary in a five mile radius and if a creamery is to be started, unless cows are available, it will in all probability be a second Barrowvale. The districts are similar – bullocks and tillage."

A letter from Courtney to the IAOS secretary, dated 27 July 1926, expanded on this assessment. "I know the Ballybrophy district well and am quite convinced that 400 cows are not available within a reasonable radius, for a creamery at the old workhouse buildings. On the Lisduff side the farmers are nearly all engaged in tillage and have very few cows. Between Ballybrophy and Rathdowney there are a few big ranches covering the best of the land. I have never seen anything on these ranches but bullocks, and I doubt very much if there are many cows on the Roscrea side. Whatever chance there is for this place as an Auxiliary to some Central, it would be very risky proceeding to start it as a Central Creamery having in view the results of similar such undertakings at Barrowvale and Castlelyons. We were promised big supplies of milk in both those places and today it is questionable if they can exist from want of milk.

"Store cattle and tillage are doing badly at present and there is a desire on the part of farmers in this kind of farming to change to dairying. I think it would be a fatal mistake to erect the Creamery until these men have definitely got into cows."

Courtney then addressed the question of finance. "I know the workhouse buildings and have visited them with Mr. Fant (the engineer) on a previous occasion when an attempt was made to organise a Society and they are not suitable, without a good deal of alteration, for a modern creamery because they are too narrow and will need a substantial outlay to put them up in order to comply with the Dairy Produce Act … Under present circumstances, on the 50/50 basis of overdrafts, the local people would need to put up nearly £2,000 in cash. For these reasons I think the IAOS should not, without very careful further enquiry as to the sufficiency of cows available and more hopeful prospects of financing, register a Creamery for the district.

"With reference to a Credit Society, one already exists at Errill which is not far from the proposed Creamery Centre and, if a Credit Society is needed, this should answer the purpose."

In answer to a query from O'Brien as to whether he or Courtney should proceed with the project, the IAOS asst. secretary, Mr. Riddell, on 30 July replied: 'In view of what Mr. Courtney has said about this project, I doubt whether the IAOS would be warranted in incurring the cost of sending Mr. Langford to the district for a week. Mr. Courtney states that the cows are not in the district and if that is so, no amount of organising will create them. Had we not better leave these people to show themselves what they are capable of? If Mr. Langford were to spend the time suggested in endeavouring to secure the necessary number of cows and failed, it would be so much time and money wasted for which we would not even get thanks …"

James Fant, IAOS engineer, noted his response on his copy of the above memo, which he returned to the IAOS secretary. He advised some caution in the manner in which the Donaghmore quest was being processed: "In order that we may have written material to answer any questions that may arise regarding this and similar projects, is it not better to get the Form from them (that informs us) of the numbers of cows and also to have evidence of any actions or inactions of ours if called upon."

Courtney remarked on his copy of the same memo: "As Ballybrophy is in my district I naturally would have taken up the organisation of this Society quickly if I thought the time ripe. I would again ask you to consider two things, (a) cows and (b) finance. Let these people show they have both and then the Society can be formed. Ask that the preliminary form first be signed. There's no immediate hurry at this time of year."

The Donaghmore group seemed blissfully unaware of the negative vibes within the IAOS and remained very determined to get the project off the ground. Their next step was to secure a lease on the old workhouse premises. This was the main item discussed at a meeting on 2 August, 1926, which thirty farmers attended. Fr. Henebry was in the chair. A deputation consisting of Messrs P.J. Dunphy, Murphy, Quigley and J.P. Kelly, who was now acting secretary, was appointed to meet the Board of Health "for a lease of a reasonable portion of the buildings and the entire right to the water supply".

At a meeting a week later, which only twelve people attended, (due to bad weather), Kelly reported that the Board of Health had passed a resolution "in accordance with the deputation's application". A letter was sent to the Board thanking them for the "very favourable manner" in which they received the deputation. It was also noted at the meeting that applications had been received for 646 shares amounting to £969, close to the target set by the Department. The organising committee knew there were many other potential shareholders among the farming community still to be enlisted and a fresh campaign was mounted. Members were exhorted to canvass their own areas and Mr. Courtney, of the IAOS, addressed local gatherings on successive days from 10 to 13 September at Knock, Rathdowney, Clough, Borris-in-Ossory and Errill as well as Donaghmore.

O'Brien wrote to Kelly on 5 August: "You state that these 646 shares are valued at £969 but this cannot be correct as the shares are valued at £1 each. It was understood at the meeting which I attended that each applicant would sign for three shares for two cows which would mean £1-10-0 per cow but it must be understood that the shares are valued at £1 each. I do not think it will be possible, nor indeed advisable, to let the promoters have the services of an organiser at this stage and with the inrush of work we have on hands at present I am afraid that neither I nor Mr. Langford can spend a week in Ballybrophy for some time to come. I need not tell you that the £969 would not go very far in reconstructing the workhouse buildings. The promoters should, I believe, try to get a sum of between £2,000 and £3,000 by way of share capital before we can recommend them to go on with the project, unless there is a possibility of getting capital from an outside source on reasonable terms which is rather unlikely ... "

O'Brien, however wrote to the IAOS secretary on the same day: "If the promoters can get a guarantee of supply for, say, 1,000 cows, I think we might then recommend them to go on with the project, providing also that they can get a reasonable amount of share capital. If we let the matter drop, I believe that they will seek assistance elsewhere as they seem serious about the project."

The Donaghmore group were very serious indeed in their determination to build and operate a creamery. This was the message communicated by Mr. Kelly to the IAOS secretary on 4 August: "I was not aware that you sent Mr. Loughman a form. It could have been filled up a month ago. (I am) now returning it ... My committee are determined to start some sort of creamery without borrowing one penny. The consideration of the type of creamery has been postponed until such time as the district has been thoroughly organised and all applications for shares have been handed in. Then only will my committee be in a position to start central churning or an independent auxiliary."

Fr. Henebry wrote to Courtney (care of Mr. White of the Granville Arms, Waterford), on 8 August, seeking a meeting with him and suggested Aird's Hotel, Maryborough (now Portlaoise) as the venue. Fr. Henebry had met Courtney some years previously, when an earlier attempt had been made to form a Co-operative Society at Donaghmore. His Reverence figured that a friendly approach and some subtle flattery might not go astray in this instance. He wrote: "I am very glad we come in your jurisdiction; it will be a renewal of old acquaintance again, and a chance of doing something for an industry with which you have been long identified."

Courtney reported to the IAOS secretary in advance of that meeting: "I mentioned casually that I did not think there were cows enough and he stated that there were 500 cows within a two mile radius. He also mentioned that it was Mr. Kelly and himself who had made out the list on the form sent. On looking over the list, I find that out of a total of 536 cows, 60 are five miles away, 35 are 4½ miles and 77 are 4 miles, making 172. The milk of these cows is unlikely to continue being brought to the Creamery owing to this distance and the small number of cows kept by each farmer. Unless there are a few districts outlying from which milk can be carted co-operatively a central Creamery in this district is a very risky project. I am in entire agreement with Mr. O'Brien's comments and I think the IAOS should seriously consider taking some action which would put a stop to the premature organising efforts of men who, if a creamery is started and fails, will have no responsibility in the matter. If the statements attributed to Mr. McAuliffe are true, we ought to know where we are before we take on organising a creamery, where somebody has 'queered' the pitch in advance. It is not good enough that the farmers should be given to understand without previous investigation that they can have a creamery in a district by holding a meeting and signing share forms. The law states that the shares are nominally £1 each and is it possible that Mr. McAuliffe has told these people that the value of the shares could be £1-10-0. Fr. Henebry is evidently determined to have a creamery here but it will be a much more difficult job now to organise one on proper lines after what has transpired."

Courtney suggested that a conference of the IAOS staff be called immediately to lay down guidelines, which they could follow, on the starting of co-operative societies. He mentioned the £1 for £1 idea referred to by Mr. O'Brien and said there was an opinion afloat that the Government is giving money away: "At present there are demands for Societies all over the country by people who seem to know very little and care less about co-operation and the interest of the farmers. They seem to be more concerned in using the co-operative movement for other purposes. I find instances of that in this case, (as well as) in that of proposed credit societies in County Cork and in connection with beet growers. It would be much better to have a consistent policy which we could all carry out."

Major problems to surmount

The local organising committee had major problems to surmount, therefore, before they would achieve their objective of opening a creamery. The minutes indicate, however, that less momentous matters often took up most of the time and energy at their meetings. It was on the rather mundane issue of sending out notices for meetings that the first sign of tension or rancour within the committee reared its head. At a meeting of 31 August, 1926, Mr. Phelan alleged that Canon Brennan, P.P., Rathdowney, and Mr. Quigley had received notice to attend a meeting on Sunday, 15 August, which they duly did, only to discover that the "invitation to the meeting was a fabrication". Mr. Phelan said that it was an insult "to these gentlemen" and demanded an explanation. The secretary stated that no invitations had been issued to anyone to attend a meeting on 15 August. After a lengthy discussion the matter was adjourned to a special meeting on Friday, 3 September. It turned out to be a bottle of smoke. The chairman, Rev. Henebry, informed the special meeting that it appeared that Canon Brennan had misplaced his invitation to the committee meeting held on 15 July. The elusive card 'turned up' a few days previous to 15 August and the Canon assumed that it had just come in the post. The Canon had simply got his dates wrong and the matter was considered closed.

There is nothing to be found in the Donaghmore minutes or in the IAOS archives on the meeting between Fr. Henebry and Courtney or of any other development that was likely to change the IAOS stance on the issue. But surprisingly they remained on board the project, despite their misgivings. In a letter to the secretary of the IAOS, Courtney explained that he has seen the premises and thought them very suitable. These were in the centre of the workhouse, he revealed, and were formerly used as a Catholic Church for the inmates. He mentioned calling on the aforementioned Canon Brennan, the Rathdowney parish priest, whom he said "was rather opposed than otherwise to the project". The Canon was concerned with the news that a number of creameries were in difficulties. Courtney explained that the reasons they were in trouble was because "the barley was unsaleable and the bullock trade unprofitable". He warned the Canon that if the farmers in the district did not have a creamery they would "go out of business". He also reminded him that nine years previously the Canon himself had been "advocating a creamery in the very same place".

The Canon was eventually convinced of the need for a creamery in the area and promised to support the project at the next meeting. Courtney stated that he had also visited the invalided Fr. Dillon, in Borris-in-Ossory, who regretted that he could not attend the proposed meeting but assured him of his support. The IAOS official reported that, at the meeting on 20 September, Canon Brennan backed the proposal as he had promised. The Canon told the meeting that he had been informed that agriculture was undergoing a necessary change in Ireland and that farmers should change their methods in that district "as at present they were hard set to make ends meet". He proposed Fr. Walsh to chair the meeting. Fr. Walsh referred to the success of the creamery at Kilmacow where he had served and the improvements in living conditions for farmers in that area. Courtney also reported on the very positive contribution of Mr. Quigley, a local auctioneer and trader, who advised farmers "to turn their barley into milk instead of porter and they would be better off". Courtney advised the IAOS secretary that he had attended meetings at Knock, "just over the Tipperary border". He had also attended a meeting at Clough, which was poorly attended. He explained that the reasons for the apathy at Clough[2] were

2. A farmers co-op shop operated in Clough, Ballacolla, for a short period at the end of the 19th and beginning of the 20th centuries. The Aghaboe Agricultural and Dairy Society Ltd was registered under the Industrial and Provident Societies Act, 1893, on 10 February, 1897. The committee of management consisted of Martin Carroll, Dairyhill, James Brennan, Kilmonfoyle, John

because it was a long way from Donaghmore and that a small co-operative store located there in the past had failed.

J.P. Kelly wrote to Courtney on 29 September telling him of a "very successful and business-like meeting" held the previous Monday and sought the IAOS organiser's advice on some matters. Courtney reported to the IAOS secretary on the October meeting of the Donaghmore organising committee which he attended. He was still obviously annoyed over the early intervention of Mr. McAuliffe, the Department official. But he was now in a much more positive frame of mind about the project. He wrote: "Some of the farmers who had signed £1-10-0[3] shares refused to alter them and others cut down their amount, knocking out the odd 10s. It was a great mistake that this blunder was made first. However, there will be 500 cows signed for and some of the farmers are getting in-calf heifers. There are 150 cows in the Rathdowney area still unsigned and some of the shopkeepers, who are afraid of a store, are trying to keep the farmers from signing. The talk about the creameries in Abbeyfeale being sued by the Bank also has had a bad effect. It was decided to make a further canvass of the Rathdowney/Errill areas and notices were ordered to be sent out for payment of 5s per share on or before November 1st. Until 10s per cow is in, I do not propose to register the Society. Mr. Fant is wanted down anytime to inspect the buildings and the fact of this visiting should quell a lot of rumours that the Co-operative Creamery is not going ahead."

Mr. Fant, the engineer, duly paid a visit and expressed his "entire satisfaction" with the suitability of the buildings at Donaghmore for use as a creamery. Applications for fresh shares kept rolling in. Messrs M. Kirwan, R.F. Bennett and Stephen Campion were appointed to canvass the Donaghmore area.

Minutes of a meeting on 12 November 1926 noted the death of Rev. John Larkin, the organising group's first chairman and letters of sympathy were sent to his family and his parish priest. The rules of the IAOS were read and adopted at that meeting and the secretary was instructed to make a formal application for affiliation to that body. J.P. Kelly sent a cheque for £5 as a preliminary affiliation fee. That cheque, drawn on the Munster and Leinster Bank, Rathdowney was signed by the secretary and Mr. R.F. Bennett.

Hyland, Bordwell, Timothy Phelan, Chapel Hill, James Delaney, Ballyinode, Thomas Phelan, Cuffsboro, Edward Kavanagh, Springfield, and John Bolger, Cuffsboro, who was secretary. Among the shareholders were Nicholas Hyland and Pat Hyland of Bordwell, Matt Connor, Shanavaughey, Tom Brennan, Coolbally, Mick Rafter, Boherard, Tom Rafter, Kyledellig and Bill Connor, Chapel Hill. The shop, which was operated by the Dunphys of Whitepark, retailed farming goods, feed, utensils and hardware. It went into debt and was forced to close. The farmers/shareholders had to settle the liabilities. Mary Phelan, Chapel Hill, Clough, Ballacolla, a grand-daughter of one of the founders, Timothy Phelan, furnished a copy of the original rules of the Aghaboe Society while John Hyland, a retired farmer in his eighties, who lives in Clough village, supplied extra information. He is son of the afore-mentioned, Nicholas Hyland, and grandson of John Hyland, a member of the original committee.

3. In the old Irish currency 12 pence (d.) = 1 shilling (s.) and 20 shillings = 1 pound (£). An example of how the currency was represented: One shilling = 1/-; two shillings and three pence = 2/3; Ten pounds, two shillings and three pence = £10-2-3. Decimalisation of old currency took place on 15 February 1971. In old currency 240 pence = £1. In new currency 100 pence = £1. (i.e. one new penny = 2.4 old pence.) The Irish pound broke with Sterling on 31 March 1979. The Irish pound became known as the punt. A new exchange rate for the punt was introduced on 2 April 1979. The Euro replaced Irish currency on 1 January 2002. The exchange rate was set at 1 punt = 1.2698 Euro; 1 Euro = £0.787564.

On 20 December, 1926, Kelly wrote to the IAOS advising them that there were now 975 shares signed up and the first call on payment had brought in £169 to date. He again wrote to the IAOS on the 30 December, asking about registration. The IAOS replied advising him that registration "must be delayed again". The letter, dated 31 December, (New Year's Eve), which must have come as a severe blow to the rising hopes of the Donaghmore committee, stated: "… the Durrow and Coolrain farmers in their respective areas … would impinge upon the district mapped out for proposed Donaghmore Society. We should be sure beforehand that the interests of all concerned are served in best possible way and the relation between the several creamery centres properly defined."

Kelly replied two days later and suggested that Coolrain and Durrow become auxiliaries of Donaghmore. The IAOS agreed to this suggestion and added that Roscrea and Durrow were "moving towards creameries and might also become auxiliaries".[4]

Milking the old-fashioned way.

4. Letter from the IAOS dated 29 January, 1927 (National Archives).

CHAPTER TWO

First AGM and
Setting up the Auxiliaries

This was an era when motorised road transport was still in its infancy; farmers depended on horses and donkeys for their transport needs. Because milk is such a perishable commodity and the transport methods of the day were so painfully slow, the Donaghmore committee were aware from the start that, if their venture was to be successful, they had to have access to a large part of County Laois for their milk supply. To achieve this, auxiliaries in outlying areas were essential. They acted quickly in ensuring that rival creameries would not be created. The first area targeted was Coolrain, ten miles distant from Donaghmore.

At a meeting on 14 March 1927, the secretary reported that the committee had "succeeded in interesting the farmers of Coolrain district in the creamery project with a view to establishing an auxiliary in that area. They had already a promise of almost 500 cows". A suitable site was located at Coolrain but the committee felt the asking price of £25 was a little beyond their means. At a meeting on 22 April 1927, the chairman, Rev. Henebry, proposed and Mr. Loughman seconded a motion to the effect that the secretary write to Mr. Sheeran, who was negotiating the deal, that "taking into consideration their weak financial position the committee consider that £20 is the utmost penny they could afford to pay for this or any other site". At the next meeting a week later, a letter in reply from Mr. Sheeran was read informing the committee that "Mr. Steele, the owner, would not accept a smaller sum than £25 for one Irish rood of his field". The letter was marked read. But at the first meeting of the newly elected committee, following the statutory general meeting of the Society on 5 May, it was agreed to pay the price demanded on the proposal of Mr. Dwyer, seconded by Mr. Sheeran.

On Courtney's advice, the committee started collecting the first instalments on shares. By mid-January 1927, there had been only £23 outstanding on first calls. In March, there was still £19 outstanding, representing seventy-six defaulters. However, by the following month, the amount due had fallen to £7-10-0. By this time 1,028 shares had been issued and the financial situation was well in hand.

Although the committee had been assured that the Health Board had no problems with the creamery project, the lease on the Donaghmore buildings was still not forthcoming. Concerns were expressed at what was seen as an inexplicable delay and the TDs for the area were asked to intervene to expedite the signing of the contracts. A memo from Mr. Fant to the IAOS reveals that in February 1927, Dr. Kennedy, secretary – and effectively chief executive – of the IAOS, met Mr. McCarron of the Department of Local Government on the matter. A provisional alternative site was being considered if the application for use of the workhouse failed. Mr. Fant stated that he agreed fully with Mr. Courtney that "if building selected is not granted, then it means a new creamery near (Ballybrophy) station". It was noted at a meeting on 11 April, that "the engineer and architect visited both Donaghmore and Coolrain since the last meeting but the plans have not yet materialised". The plans and specifications were forthcoming by 22 April and the secretary informed the meeting that he had advertised for a contractor "in all the local papers". The plan, specification and estimate for the 'Milk Delivery' were also examined at this meeting. Rev. Henebry concluded that the plans were "altogether too elaborate" and he instructed the secretary "to get in communication with the engineer with a view to arriving at an alternative scheme".

In March 1927, the IAOS confirmed that an application for a proposed creamery in Roscrea had been received.[1] The area claimed by Roscrea infringed very much on Donaghmore's area and included part of the area to be occupied by Donaghmore creamery itself. The IAOS secretary also thought that it included the area where Mr. Kelly lived. Mr. Kelly in his reply confirmed that the area claimed did include the Union buildings "which, of course, is ludicrous".[2] In April the vexed question of boundaries between Roscrea and Donaghmore became an issue and the IAOS attempted to resolve the situation. The Donaghmore area was fixed as follows:

the electoral division of Timoney in Co. Tipperary;
the whole of Roscrea No. 111 Rural District;
a five mile radius from both Donaghmore and Coolrain in the Rural Districts of Mountmellick and Abbeyleix and all in the County of Leix.

A proposal submitted by the secretary, J.P. Kelly, at a meeting on 29 April "that the committee desires that any employment, that they may have, should be given as far as possible to shareholders whose names appear on the books of the Society previous to this date" found unanimous approval. A tender for the supply and delivery of gravel for the Donaghmore site was shared between Mr. Stanley and Mr. Phelan of Kilcoke, at a price including delivery, of 4/6 per cubic yard. Robert McKelvey was employed to prepare the roadway for the gravel at a wage of £1.9.0 per week of six days.

Sixty-nine members attended the first annual general meeting of Donaghmore Creamery Society on 5 May, 1927, chaired by Rev. Henebry. Charles Coates (Charlie) Riddell, the assistant secretary, and R. Langford, represented the IAOS. It was decided that the committee should consist of twelve members, eight from Donaghmore and four from Coolrain. Those elected were: James Dwyer, Moneymore, Borris-in-Ossory, Michael Kirwan, Donaghmore, R.F. Bennett, Glebe House, Ballybrophy, John Treacy, Ballyquade, Rev. T. Henebry, C.C., Killesmeestia, Ballybrophy, Herbert Thompson, Beckfield, Rathdowney, Michael Phelan, Donaghmore, P.J. Murphy, Borris-in-Ossory, Joseph Cooper, Coolrain Glebe, Edward Sheeran, Coolrain, James Carroll, Mannin, Rushall and Jacob Thompson, Clonoughill, Coolrain. Mr. Riddell spoke "at considerable length" on the prospects of the dairying industry on co-operative lines. The committee were empowered to borrow a sum not exceeding £4,000.

1. Letter from the IAOS to Mr. Kelly on 28 March 1927 (National Archives).
2. J.P. Kelly's letter dated 29 March 1927 (National Archives).

The first meeting of the newly-elected committee was held immediately following the AGM. Rev. Henebry was unanimously elected chairman on the proposal of P.J. Murphy, seconded by James Dwyer. J.P. Kelly was elected as secretary on the motion of Rev. Henebry, seconded by Dwyer. The Munster and Leinster Bank, Rathdowney, was appointed as Treasurers for the Society and Mr. Edward Ryan, Rathdowney, was appointed as the Society's solicitor. Tenders for the alteration of the workhouse were discussed. Thomas Fogarty's tender was lowest at £355, which was £55 higher than the architect's estimate. Mr. Fogarty was invited to meet the architect and see if "some unnecessary details could be struck out of the specifications" to enable him bring his tender within the estimate. He was also informed that the committee wished to have the milk delivery included in the contract. Six days later it was agreed to accept the tender of Mr. Fogarty "according to the plans and specifications shown to him" for the sum of £430. The contract was to be completed in two calendar months from the date of signing or in default a penalty of £3 per week was set.

In a letter to Mr. Kelly on 6 May, the day following the AGM which he had attended, the most pressing concern of Mr. Riddell was his missing umbrella. "I am afraid I left my umbrella at Ballymeelish (where Mr. Kelly lived) or at Donaghmore last night and, if it is not too much trouble to you, I should be greatly obliged if you would be good enough to send it to me, or if you should happen to be coming to town next week perhaps you would bring it along. I am sorry for bothering you about this little matter but the umbrella may be useful to me if the weather breaks, as is prophesied – a very safe prophecy at any time in this country. If you should be in town next week, I should be glad if you would call on me in any case … Many thanks to you and Mrs. Kelly for your very kind hospitality to Mr. Langford and myself."

The increased volume of work undertaken by the secretary was acknowledged at a meeting on 11 May when he was handed out a remuneration "at the rate of two guineas a week to date from the General Meeting until such time as the Manager was appointed".

Tenders for the erection of the auxiliary at Coolrain were discussed. Three were received: Messrs Graves, £773; Thomas Fogarty, £800 and Charles Breen, £848-10-0. There was also a tender submitted from Messrs. Graves Ltd., for the erection of the skeleton and roof only for the amount of £201. The latter tender was accepted and it was decided to invite tenders for the completion of the work at a later date. The work on the skeleton and roof progressed slowly. This becomes clear from the content of a letter dated 21 July from Mr. Kelly to Mr Fant, the IAOS engineer: " … Messrs Graves' erector has been on the premises for over a week and yet work is not progressing as it should. He is an old man and almost past his labour. Apparently he is under no supervision. I wonder could anything be done to hurry up the job."

The committee were very unhappy about telephone services and on 6 June they wrote a letter of complaint to the secretary of the Department of Posts and Telegraphs: "There is no public telephone at Ballybrophy Railway Station. The community have to travel a distance of 3½ miles from Ballybrophy to Borris-in-Ossory in order to use the telephone. At the latter place it is most inefficient for long distance calls. The Box is obsolete, so much so, that people standing at the office counter can hear every word spoken in the Box. We request the erection of a public telephone on the railway premises at Ballybrophy. In the course of time it is hoped to have a direct line to our premises."

The letter also complained of the unsatisfactory telegram service and the tri-weekly postal delivery service. They demanded a daily delivery. This request bore a swift response. The July meeting heard that the Postmaster at Roscrea had informed the Society that there would be a daily delivery service of mail and parcels to the creamery. The committee requested Mr. Dwyer, TD, to use his influence to have the unsatisfactory situation relating to telegrams and telephones improved.

The Department of Posts and Telegraphs consented to deliver telegrams to the creamery at a porterage charge of 6d each but this was not acceptable. The cost for the installation of a telephone at the creamery was investigated and in September the committee gave the green light to have one installed.

At a meeting on 17 June 1927, it was decided to apply for membership of the Irish Associated Creameries Ltd. (IAC) and the Society nominated Mr. P. Courtney as a director of that body. The formation of the IAC was an attempt to co-ordinate the marketing of butter but it was ultimately to fail a mere three years later, for want of support from the individual creameries. Mr. Lynn, from the IAOS, addressed the June meeting relative to the machinery available to the Society from the redundant creameries of the Condensed Milk Co. He informed the committee that an engine and boiler (intended for Donaghmore) had been resold to Callan Creamery in error. Mr. McGowan, representing the IAWS, submitted a tender of £320 for the dismantling, transport, and re-erection of the machinery. The meeting was adjourned until the following morning so that Mr. Fant, of the IAOS, could be in attendance to explain how the mistake was made regarding the machinery intended for Donaghmore. The latter reported on the following day that it was the duty of the 'Holding Body' to find an engine and boiler as good as the machinery in dispute and he assured members that he and Mr. Lynn would make sure that they did so.

The secretary was instructed to write to Mr. McAuliffe, of the Department of Agriculture, demanding to be supplied with full details, including the price, of all the machinery purchased for the Society. He was also directed to request Mr. McAuliffe "to at once order the closure of the Knockulty group of creameries, in order that the machinery therein be made available immediately for this Society". A meeting on 27 June 1927 was told by the secretary that, in default of a reply from Mr. McAuliffe, he decided to go to Dublin to talk to him personally. Mr. Kelly stated that he had succeeded in getting an inventory of all the machinery from Mr. McAuliffe and that the price was £950. Mr. McAuliffe had advised him that the deal was conditional on the IAWS getting the contract for taking down the machinery, its transport and setting it up again at Donaghmore. The work was not open to competition, he had clearly stated. The secretary told the June meeting that the IAWS had since tendered for the work at a price of £495. The tender was accepted by the committee. At this meeting, it was also decided to appoint a manager and staff at Donaghmore and that job applications should be considered as soon as possible.

Mr. Kelly expressed great concern to Dr. Kennedy about the slowness in securing a lease on the Donaghmore premises: "I have had no communication from the Local Government Department … Surely it is time we got some title on the premises. When we have the Creamery equipped and in working order, it might then be very difficult to extract a title from the authorities. There is also the possibility of a change of Government and I have absolutely nothing to show in writing that the authorities have consented to grant a lease."[3]

At a meeting on 8 July, Mr. Phelan objected to the minutes of the previous

3. Letter dated 27 June 1927 (National Archives).

meeting being approved and expressed reservations about the wording of the advertisement for manager and staff. Fr. Henebry supported him and enquired by whose orders were the committee compelled to appoint officials from the redundant creameries only. The secretary said that the wording had been approved by the committee at a previous meeting. He added that the stipulation on staff was one of the conditions laid down by the Department. The chairman asked to see the conditions in writing and the secretary hastily produced a letter from the IAOS, in which the clause was specially mentioned.[4] The minutes were then approved and signed.

Manager appointed

Fourteen applications had been received for the job of manager, eleven for the post of fireman and one for buttermaker. It was decided to ask the IAOS to short-list the applications and then go ahead with interviews. The names of the six candidates on the short-list were read at the meeting of 18 July. The meeting decided to appoint William Grogan, aged 43 and late of the Bruree Creamery, at a salary of £300 per annum. Grogan, in his application, had indicated that the salary he expected was £360. Of the applications, only two applicants had higher salary expectations. The

William Grogan, Creamery Manager at Donaghmore 1927-'46.

new manager was given accommodation at the north end of the creamery and the "necessary alterations and repairs to same" were duly approved.

Tenders were received for the completion of the building at the Coolrain auxiliary as follows: Patrick Cordial, £690; Thomas Fogarty, £525 and Charles Breen, £469-10-0. The four Coolrain members of the committee were asked to have a word with Mr. Breen with a view to reducing his tender to £440 or less. Mr. Breen agreed to reduce the tender by £10 and this was accepted. Mr. Fogarty, who had been awarded the contract of "sinking a dug well", informed the committee that he could not see his way to execute the contract, having failed to secure the larger contract.

4. Letter dated 23 June 1927 (National Archives).

The secretary reported that a very successful meeting had been held in Raheen on 29 June 1927, which Messrs Courtney and Lynn of the IAOS attended. The meeting was told that there were 560 cows in that district inside a four-mile radius. The lease on the premises at Donaghmore had not yet been finalised.[5] A letter from the IAOS dated 26 July, was scathing of the Department's slowness in framing a lease agreement: "The matter might have been fixed up long ago but Government Departments take about ten times longer than anybody else to come to the simplest little decision. There seems to be more red tape in the country than ever before." Mr. Kelly was instructed to call on Dr. Kennedy with a view to expediting the matter. Kelly wrote to Riddell: "I take it we can do nothing … until we have a proper title … and we cannot produce this until we obtain a lease."[6]

Apart from delays with the lease, the Department were not in a hurry to decide on paying the proposed loan of £2,250. In a letter to the IAOS, dated 29 July 1927, the Department secretary questioned Donaghmore Society's ability to come up with their share of the necessary capital: "… I am desired to enquire whether a loan in this case is recommended by your Society. It is observed that the share capital subscribed by the members of the Creamery together with the additional capital does not quite cover the estimated expense. It will be necessary to have an assurance of your Society that the total expense will be fully covered by subscribed capital." The Department continued to have their reservations but they eventually agreed to pay out £1,500 as a first instalment.[7]

A Miss Walpole was appointed to the position of dairymaid, pending the sanction of the Department of Agriculture but the minutes of the following week's meeting show that a Miss Hoey was appointed, from five applications, to that position at a salary of £2-10-0 per week. Correspondence between the Society and the IAOS explains why Miss Walpole was not retained. She had been highly recommended by the manager, Mr. Grogan, and by Mr. Kelly; "(Miss Walpole) is of a very respectable Quaker family residing in the area. She has qualified at the Harper-Adams Agricultural College and holds their certificate. She is a good worker and for many reasons we are of the opinion that her appointment would be most desirable." But the Department were not impressed with her qualifications, as the reply from the IAOS dated 27 August reveals: "I have made enquiries at the Department and I find that the certificate of the Harper-Adams College is not regarded as sufficient qualification by that body. In addition the lady must have five months experience in a recognised creamery."

In response to a letter from a buttermaker relating to wages, read at a meeting on 19 August, the committee advised the applicant that "for a suitable buttermaker (male) the wages would be £2-15-0 with accommodation". In the absence of "a suitable candidate" from the redundant creameries, it was decided to appoint John Aherne from Templemore to the position of fireman, at a salary of £2 per week without accommodation. The Department was also unhappy with this appointment, seemingly unaware that the Society had trawled through lists from the closed creameries for a suitable candidate. The Department secretary wrote to Mr. Riddell on 30 August: "… as to say the action of the Society in appointing a fireman otherwise than from the staffs of the redundant creameries cannot be let pass."

5. See reference to lease in chapter on Donaghmore Workhouse and Museum.
6. In a letter to IAOS assistant secretary on 29 July 1927. (National Archives).
7. In a letter to the IAOS, dated 30 September 1927 (National Archives).

The *Leinster Express* published a progress report on the Donaghmore project, particularly relating to Coolrain, in its issue of 20 August, 1927:

> *The work on erecting the creamery at Coolrain is proceeding and should be complete in a couple of months by the contractor, Mr. Breen, Paddock, Mountrath. This is intended to be an auxiliary creamery and worked in conjunction with the central creamery at Donaghmore. The site is conveniently situated, adjoining the village and covers an area of one rood of land. Farmers and others interested in dairying industry feel confident that the enterprise will be successful, and that it will make a source of considerable profits, as in other districts, some of which are not as favourably situated as Coolrain. The central and auxiliary creameries should be ready to begin operations before the winter sets in. They will cater for a very large portion of Leix, and the people who have become shareholders are looking forward to the working of a system which has proved such a success in other counties.*

Parts of the puzzle falling into place

In fact, the project was further advanced than the local newspaper had reported. All the parts of the puzzle were falling into place and by the end of August 1927, Fr. Henebry suggested a formal opening for which the committee "should be responsible for the expenses incurred in entertaining the invited guests". Mr. Kirwan proposed, presumably in jest, that the chairman's suggestion be adopted regarding the luncheon expenses but that the committee felt "that it was usual for the chairman to put up the champagne on all such occasions". This resolution was seconded by Mr. Bennett and "passed with acclamation". Messrs Phelan and Kirwan, with the assistance of Mr. R.T. Jones, were assigned to make arrangements for the luncheon. The minutes do not make any reference to the proceedings or attendance at the official opening other than recording that apologies were received from Raheen P.P., Fr. Coyne, regretting his inability to attend. The official opening took place on Monday, 5 September 1927, at midday. Dr. Henry Kennedy, secretary of the IAOS, attended and gave a comprehensive talk on the co-operative movement, the work of creameries and the state of agriculture and the economy.

Rev. Christopher Coyne P.P., Raheen, on the occasion of the blessing of the grotto, erected by the parishioners of Raheen, to mark his 60 years in the priesthood in 1953. Fr. Coyne was one of the founding fathers of Raheen Creamery.

The Donaghmore committee were very annoyed with the condition of the boiler taken from the Mullinahone Creamery and intended for Coolrain. Mr. Kelly was quite blunt in his summation: "... The article was earmarked for Coolrain. It is almost twenty years old and looks more. We had our doubts about it and got the engineer from the General Accident Insurance Company to examine it ... I took the responsibility of holding them up (the IAWS fitters) pending the receipt of the report ... There is a good boiler at Springfield and we suggest that you will make application for it on our behalf to the Holding Body ... My committee will not consent to have this heap of scrap erected at Coolrain."[8]

In mid-September, the committee were informed by the IAOS that the Department of Local Government were finally prepared to lease the entire premises at a rent of £45 per year. Messrs. Swaine and Brown were appointed auditors. The Creamery was up and running at this stage and a sub-committee consisting of the chairman, secretary, and Messrs. Bennett and Kirwan, was appointed. They were instructed to meet weekly to examine the books of the Society and "generally be responsible for the conduct of the business until the usual monthly meeting".

A rate of 0.75d per gallon had been agreed by the committee for the transfer of milk but milk carter, Mr. H. Thompson, attended the October meeting to complain that he could not make ends meet at that price. He said he had to travel 33 to 36 miles per day and only earned 6/- per day. The committee decided to pay him 11/- per day and, any day his earnings fell short of that figure, they would make up the difference. However, if his earnings on any day were in excess of 11/- they would be entitled to recoup the excess.

The transport of milk was on the agenda of every meeting since July and would continue to feature in discussions at the monthly meetings for many years to come. Mr. Kelly reported to the IAOS that cartage was costing 1.5d per gallon and that the committee felt that it was not economic at that price. He responded to a complaint received by the IAOS that the milk collection lorry was not servicing some farmers, by requesting to know the area affected. "We will endeavour to make arrangements for the transport of the milk whatever the cost may be", he wrote. In reply, the IAOS informed him that the complaint in question came from people living on the road from Borris-in-Ossory to Roscrea.

The secretary reported that quotations from Brooks Thomas for piping and fittings were 10 to 70 per cent cheaper than the prices tendered by the IAWS. The IAOS had been advised of the situation. Mr. Fant was asked to inspect the Brooks Thomas goods before an order was to be placed. Kelly also complained of the high telephone rental costs of £10-5-0 per annum. The manager reported at the December meeting that "the Roscrea cream was being sent for manufacture to this creamery since the 1st inst". By the end of 1927, the Creamery was already functioning successfully.

The *Leinster Express* also reported some good news on the creamery and the editor was impressed with the early progress made:

> The committee and staff of the Donaghmore Creamery Ltd are to be congratulated on obtaining fourth place in the Free State at the recent surprise inspection by the Department of Agriculture. There were 180 creameries competing, and Donaghmore, which had only begun work a month ago, succeeded in obtaining the excellent marks of 96 out of a possible 100.
>
> This is certainly a very creditable performance and augurs well for the dairy industry in Leix. Mindful of their own interests of the county generally, the farmers would do well to lose no time having the bullocks replaced by dairy

8. In a letter of 19 September 1927 to the IAOS (National Archives).

cows. A splendid opportunity is offered them now by sharing and co-operating in this great go-ahead concern since its establishment. Donaghmore Creamery is making steady and satisfactory progress, there being a substantial increase in the supply of milk each week.

A special meeting on Monday, 12 December, agreed that the Society should purchase a second-hand lorry for James Bergin of Borris-in-Ossory for a sum not exceeding £50, for the purpose of collecting milk for the Creamery. Mr. Bergin was to repay the outlay at not less than £1 per week and the interest was pitched at five per cent. A special general meeting four days later was called to adopt two resolutions. One provided for getting clearance for drawing down a loan to the Society of £2,550 to be secured by a mortgage on the premises and share capital. The other resolution directed that any loan from the Department constitute "a first and paramount charge upon the uncalled balance of the ordinary share capital of the Society". The resolutions, which were explained to members by Mr. O'Brien of the IAOS, were adopted on the proposal of Mr. R.F. Bennett and seconded by Mr. Dwyer.

The IAOS were updated on progress at Raheen by their representative. Mr. P. Hickey writing from Duggan's Hotel, Scariff, Co. Clare in October 1927, informed the secretary that signatures for 333 cows had been received but that Fr. Coyne had a long way to go to make his target. The Raheen P.P. was calling for at least 1,500 to 1,600 shares to be taken. Mr. Hickey stated that Raheen was "a great tillage district" and that Fr. Coyne would do well to get in 1,200 shares. By January 1928, there were 1,311 shares subscribed representing 437 cows. There was also a promise from Mr. McAuliffe, the Department official, that he would arrange to supply the auxiliary with machinery at no cost. There was mention of the "willingness of the Raheen people to level the site and cart stones, sand and so on to it". The IAOS people were impressed. Their secretary wrote that "it would be a great pity not to go ahead … after all the work done there and the difficulty in doing it. If it does not materialise this season after all the work done, I feel it will be no easy matter, if it should be done at all, to get it going again".[9]

9. In a letter to Donaghmore, dated 17 January 1928 (National Archives).

CHAPTER THREE

Teething Troubles

The management sub-committee agreed to give Mr. Robert Mitchell a bonus of £1-10-0 per month for the first three months of 1928 for milk delivery. The fireman, John Aherne, or as he was referred to in the minutes of 6 February 1928, the engine-driver, was allocated "suitable apartments in the Female Ward, comprising of two rooms at a weekly rent of two shillings to be deducted from his wages". The sub-committee also recommended that the cost of the monthly cheque be deducted from the payment to suppliers. The manager's bond was set at £400, which was to be paid jointly by the Society and the manager.

Kilcotton GAA, the local hurling club,[1] had an application for milk as a prize in their whist drive turned down in February. The committee ruled that they had no power to make donations of the suppliers' property. Individual members, however, subscribed the cash to purchase the milk and instructed the secretary to attend to the matter. It was ordered that a charge of 2d be made for the monthly cheque of each supplier. The manager was given the discretion to decide on the smallest amount that should be paid by cheque. The green light was given by the IAOS for the Raheen project and the secretary was instructed to put the work in hand immediately.

Miss Sophie Loughman was appointed as the buttermaker's apprentice. Sophie was later, as buttermaker, to marry J.P. Kelly – one of the myriad romances and marriages that blossomed over the years at Donaghmore Creamery.

At the March 1928 meeting, the price of separated milk was settled at 1d per gallon to suppliers and at 2d for non-suppliers. The amount of separated milk a supplier was entitled to purchase could not be greater than his average daily supply of new milk.

With the level of activity at the Society growing all the time, especially due to the Coolrain auxiliary, the workload of the secretary was again causing strain. Kelly told the committee that he had to employ another man to do the work at home and on his farm and that now, with the Raheen auxiliary in the course of construction, he felt he could no longer carry on in the position. The minutes noted that he had received remuneration of 'two guineas' a week for a short period up to the appointment of a manager at Donaghmore in the previous year. This time (March 1928) it was decided to pay him a salary of £2-2-0 (exactly two guineas) a week, retrospective to 6 February, until Raheen was opened.

The sub-committee reported a big increase in the demand for butter rolls. The daily output was close on 400 and, with the daily increase in the supply of cream,

---

1. Kilcotton GAA is a hurling club with a famous history. The club won numerous senior county titles in the early decades of the 20th century and its long-time captain, Jack Carroll, led the Laois hurling team defeated by Clare in the All-Ireland final of 1914. Donaghmore is located in the traditional catchment area of the club.

Raheen Creamery circa 1928 (l. to r.): Tom Mitchell, George Galbraith, Billy Bergin (Committee members), Tim Kelleher (Manager), Joe Conroy (Driver), Johnny Lalor (Staff).

the dairymaid would have to devote almost all her time to churnings. She would not, therefore, be able to cope with the demand for rolls nor give sufficient attention to their neatness and finish. The manager was instructed to purchase a Lister roll-making machine.

The Coolrain auxiliary was opened on 19 March, 1928. The IAOS short-listed three candidates from a total of fifteen applications for the position of manager. Callaghan McCarthy was appointed at a salary of £2-10-0 per week. There were seventeen applications for the position of fireman at salaries requested from £1 to £3-15-0. William Nixon was appointed at a salary of £1 per week. Two months later, this was increased to £1-4-0 per week. The committee ordered that the Coolrain lorry be paid at the rate of 10/- for bringing the cream to Donaghmore and taking back butter and that 3/- extra be paid for taking back coal.

Meanwhile, work was progressing on the Raheen project. Messrs. Graves agreed a contract with Fr. Coyne for the erection of the skeleton and roof for a sum of £107-10-0. Eighty-four applicants from the Raheen district, amounting to 1341 shares, were admitted as members. Co-opted to the management committee from Raheen were John Tynan, George Galbraith, William Bergin and Peter Salter. It was agreed that work on Raheen should proceed with direct labour and the secretary was instructed to look after all details. Kelly along with Fr. Henebry and Mr. Thompson were appointed to a deputation to visit Raheen and put matters on a working basis.

The chairman and the secretary were appointed, at the April 1928 meeting, as delegates to the IAOS conference, with a view to having one of the Society's members elected on the IAOS committee. It was decided that some entries of butter were to be sent to the Royal Dublin Society's Spring Show. An application was received from the supervisor of the Castletown Cow Testing Association requesting that the Creamery should collect amounts due by members of the Association by deductions from the suppliers' monthly cheque. It was decided to adjourn the matter for twelve months.

The AGM was held in the Society's office on 27 April, 1928. Mr. O'Brien represented the IAOS and Mr. Grogan, manager at Donaghmore, and Mr. McCarthy, manager at Coolrain, were also in attendance. One successful motion increased the number of committee members from 12 to 16, to cater for the four Raheen representatives, while another stipulated that one fourth of the committee should retire each year "and these members shall be the ones who have the smallest number of attendances during the year". Rev. Henebry was re-elected chairman at the first meeting of the new committee which followed.

Four applications were received for the position of manager at Raheen with the job going to Corkman, Tim Kelleher. John Lalor, of nearby Corbally, was appointed engineman at a salary of £1 per week. It was decided that the Raheen lorry be employed to take milk from Raheen and Ballacolla areas to Donaghmore until such time as Raheen would be operational. The expenditure of £37-10-0 was sanctioned for the purchase of a flat skin cooler for Raheen. It was agreed to pay Mr. Salter £20 for the site, made up of eighteen fully paid shares in the Society and a cheque for £2.

At the June meeting, the chairman, Rev. Henebry, proposed that the committee should not consider an application for an increase in wages from any employee who had not at least six months service with the Society. The motion was carried, but later in the same meeting the committee agreed to an increase of 7/6 in John Aherne's wages. The manager was given free residence, and "sanitary accommodation" was to be supplied. Regarding the proposed sub-letting of a portion of the Donaghmore premises, the committee ruled at the July meeting that the applicant, Mr. Maher, should pay all the rates on the land and three-eighths of the rates on the buildings. Arising out of a report from Mr. Commane and the manager, relating to the condition of the churn, it was decided to erect a new churn. The Dairy Supply Company's tender was accepted. Most suppliers, it was noted, were now reliant on their monthly cheque from the creamery. The rate of payment was determined by the health of the estimates for the following month, which were discussed and decided at every monthly meeting of the management committee. The price of butterfat was fixed at 16d per lb and of butter to suppliers at 17d per lb. In August, the price of both commodities was raised by a halfpenny. This left the Society with a net profit of £82, which the committee considered very satisfactory. The price paid for butterfat over the following decade generally ranged from 9d to 12d or slightly more and well below the 1928 levels. In June 1936, it hit a low of 4d per gallon and dipped fractionally lower still in the succeeding months. James Dwyer, TD,[2] resigned from the committee in August 1928 and was replaced by John Loughman. The secretary's remuneration was fixed at £1-10-0 per week.

2. James Dwyer (1891-1932) was born at Newtown, Roscrea, Co. Tipperary. An extensive farmer he was a Director of Roscrea Bacon Factory and Vice-Chairman of the Ossory Agricultural Society. For a time he was Chairman of Roscrea Rural District Council and Vice-Chairman of Laois County Council. He was elected Cumann na nGaedhal TD for Laois-Offaly in the first election of 1927 (there were two general elections in that year) and held the seat until 1932 (*T.D.s and Senators for Laois & Offaly (1921-1986)* by Patrick F. Meehan (Leinster Express, 1987).

The September meeting of 1928 heard complaints relating to shortages in separated milk. Lorry drivers were to be informed that they could not purchase and retail separated milk. The price of butter wash to non-suppliers was raised to 2d.

The question of the insurance of lorries under the Workman's Compensation and the Employers Liability Act was discussed. Counsel's opinion had been received and the committee decided to request the IAOS to open a subscription list with a view to funding a test case on the question of employers' liability in the High Court. IAOS inspector, Mr. D. Barry, after making a visit to Donaghmore with Mr. Courtney in September, reported that "having regard to small supply of milk being dealt with, the Central Creamery appears to be over-staffed". He recommended reducing staff numbers, starting with the office staff. He stated that there were three people employed, the manager, secretary and a "girl assistant". He suggested that the committee should consider getting the manager to take on the duties of the other two as well as his own. This would realise a saving of £2 per week, he estimated, reminding the reader that in several creameries the manager "fulfils the dual position of manager and secretary without any extra salary". He suggested cutbacks in the cartage costs, which amounted to £38 per month and which was "a very high figure". He also recommended "where possible" that surplus money in the current account be transferred to a deposit account, where it would accrue interest. Barry reported in October that "the girl in the office had been let go" and that had effected some saving. He also stated that there were some savings on cartage but cautioned that the proposal to purchase a lorry "requires very careful consideration". He also stated that he had recommended the letting off of "the extra hand in the dairy".

Individual members of the committee were to be issued with a list of defaulters from October and each person in default was to be approached by one or more members. It was felt that a number of those who owed money would not pay up until they "were made" to do so. Pending the results of the interviews, the secretary was instructed to send out final notices to those still in default. Also discussed were the terms of sub-letting to Messrs. Maher and McGaughy. The committee approved of the sub-committee's decision to sublet a room for an Irish class on one night a week for one shilling and sixpence per night.

Department's loan

The cash-flow situation was a constant worry for the secretary and the management committee throughout 1928. The second part of the loan from the Department amounting to £550, although sanctioned, was still unpaid and was badly needed to keep the wheels turning. Kelly kept pressure on the IAOS, and the IAOS kept pressure on the Department in turn, to pay the outstanding amount. The Department official, Mr. McAuliffe, continued to use the loan as a lever to ensure Donaghmore met his requirements on the appointment of staff from the redundant creameries. Mr. Fant advised Kelly that "if your Society promises in writing to engage the staffs for Coolrain and Raheen from among the disengaged staffs at closed creameries, the loan will be sent to you immediately".[3]

Mr. McAuliffe wrote to the IAOS expressing some scepticism regarding the number of shares claimed as sold by Donaghmore. J.P. Kelly, already agitated at the Department's refusal to make the final payment, was further enraged that his figures had been brought into question. He wrote to Riddell: "Mr. McAuliffe either

3. IAOS letter dated 8 March 1928 (National Archives).

discredits our statement re Share Capital or is of the opinion that we have inflated some through the medium of some philanthropic American capitalist. On various occasions some months ago I have given you and Mr. McAuliffe an assurance that the Share Capital of the Society would be sufficient to cover our capital expenditure within a reasonable time. Now, when this has been achieved, the Department are incredulous and require, what we consider, most unnecessary details. I trust Mr. McAuliffe will not receive a severe shock when you inform him that our share capital now amounts to £4,146 made up as follows: Donaghmore Central £1,894; Coolrain £913; Raheen £1,339. All suppliers have now signed for three shares per cow and in Raheen the shares were also signed on this basis. Will you please get this loan negotiated with all possible speed. Our (cash flow) position is getting serious on account of the Raheen expenditure."[4] There were further exchanges of correspondence before the Paying Order for £550 was finally issued by the Department on 29 May 1928.

Chief State Solicitor's fees

While Fr. Henebry mentioned Kelly's fury at the reference by the IAOS inspector to the proposed sacking of a worker in the dairy, it seems from the correspondence that the secretary was far more concerned about other matters – being exploited by the Chief State Solicitor, for instance, for fees relating to the lease on the premises from the Department of Local Government. He wrote to Riddell, with the Bill of Costs enclosed, on 5 October 1928: "I take it that the Chief State Solicitor is a salaried official and I think that it is iniquitous that we should be burdened with his fees. We have no objection to paying his out-of-pocket expenses amounting to £4-1-3 but it is an entirely different matter with regard to the £18-7-3. I think if the matter was put before the Minister in question, he would not allow a salaried Government official to pile on fees to a struggling co-operative society."

Riddell appeared surprised at the amount demanded: "I am inclined to think that your best course would be to remit only the out-of-pocket costs. It is news to me that the Chief State Solicitor should charge the ordinary solicitor's fees for work done on behalf of the Local Government Department. I have had a little personal experience of solicitors and have found that they are apt to 'try it on' but when they are not on very secure ground they do not like to press their clients too far … Will see what I can do … As you know one Government servant will generally back up another."

Riddell went to the trouble of finding out the extent to which the Chief State Solicitor's Office was funded: "I note from Thom's Directory that the Oireachtas vote for the CSS Department for the year 1927/28 was £9,500, for a staff of seven officers and eleven clerks, including typists and messenger. At the same time the Department may be entitled to the amounts they have charged to your Society." That ominous message contained in the final sentence was reinforced in a further letter from Riddell dated 15 December 1928. The IAOS official had, obviously, second thoughts about the propriety of the fees demanded: "Seemingly you have no alternative to paying the costs … I cannot suggest any unless you get one of the TDs to pursue the matter … I thought the Chief State Solicitor should not charge more than out-of-pocket expenses but seemingly he is entitled to charge according to the ordinary prescribed scale judging from the fact that he has charged according to it, which he would hardly have done had he not been entitled to do so." Game, set and match to the Chief State Solicitor.

4. Letter to Mr. Riddell, dated 2 May 1928 (National Archives).

CHAPTER FOUR

Depressed Prices a Constant Concern

There was a constant exchange of correspondence between Donaghmore, the IAOS and the Department of Agriculture, relating to the delays in the payment of approved loans and the manner in which repayments should be made. The outspoken Donaghmore secretary was far from impressed by the Department of Agriculture's performance. Kelly complained to Mr. Riddell that he had written to the Department on 1 January 1929 requesting a statement of account, only to receive in return what he termed 'the usual unbusinesslike acknowledgement'. He added simply: "Motto – Never do today what you can put off until the morrow".[1]

Kelly was in plaintive mood again on 16 March. This time his criticism was directed at the RDS. He was not at all happy with the location of the butter exhibit at the Spring Show. The butter was on display for days under the direct rays of the sun and the dust raised in the Central Hall beneath was deposited on the exhibits. He said he did not believe that 10% of visitors who passed through the turnstiles saw the exhibit or knew where it was staged. He asked the IAOS to take up the matter with the RDS and the Dairy Branch of the Department. He suggested that the RDS be asked to devote a cool area in the East Hall or in some other suitable area. "Surely there is no comparison in the importance or magnitude of our industry with the picturesque and pretty exhibits staged in these areas', he stated. The Department reply did not come until two months later. Their letter to the IAOS intimated that Mr. Kelly's suggestion about finding a cool corner for the exhibits was impractical. It stated that the RDS were well aware of the problems and intended to bring a balcony in use for that purpose. They hoped that a new hall would be introduced in time that would be suitable but in the meantime Mr. Kelly and other exhibitors would have 'to bear with the Society".

In February 1929, two lorry owners, Messrs. Bergin and Riordan, complained about the price paid for the cartage of milk. The secretary confirmed that the contract with Bergin was legally binding and the committee had decided to honour the contract up until September. In Riordan's case, the matter was left in the hands of the sub-committee. The secretary felt that a compromise might be agreed, whereby Riordan would lower his price to 12s or 14s a trip. No concession was to be given to Bergin regarding the payment of instalments under the purchase agreement for his truck.

Mr Galbraith and J.P. Kelly were appointed delegates to attend a special meeting of the Irish Associated Creameries on 12 April, 1929. On the question of the remuneration of directors, the delegates were instructed to vote that the chairman

1. Letter of 5 February 1929 (National Archives).

receive £5-5-0 and the other directors £3-3-0 for each meeting attended, but the discretion of the delegates was allowed.

The depressed economic situation and, particularly, the poor prices for creamery butter were a constant concern for the Donaghmore committee as the 1920s turned into the 1930s. At the May meeting in 1929, the secretary pointed out that the price had fallen over 30/- per cwt (50kg) since the previous March. The suppliers too were complaining of the price they were being charged by the Creamery for butter. The manager was instructed to find out what neighbouring creameries were charging. At the June meeting it was reported that the price charged to suppliers was in line with other creameries and was the average wholesale price. No change was made. In March 1930, it came to light that a number of traders, who were also suppliers, were obtaining butter at suppliers' price and making an extra profit as a consequence. The committee ruled that suppliers be given the amount of butter their milk would produce at the special price but that they would be charged the retail price for quantities in excess of that amount.

A complaint was heard at the July 1929 meeting "of the filthy condition in which butter was received by suppliers per lorries". The committee decided that butter supplied for delivery by lorries be wrapped in brown paper. The manager at Donaghmore also complained about the late delivery of milk. An order was made that notices be put up in each creamery stating that the milk must be delivered before 10.30am.

At the same meeting, the committee discussed a request from the IAOS seeking a special subscription. It was not the best of times to come with such a request from the young struggling Society. A motion was passed stating that "in view of the anaemic state of our bank account a subscription of £5 be sent to the IAOS with our apologies".

The issue of credit to suppliers and the repayment of loans became a regular feature on the committee's agenda. At a special general meeting in March 1929, it had been decided that the committee should be empowered to borrow £2,000 under the ACC scheme to enable them make loans available for farmers. In August, it was decided that the repayment of principal due on ACC loans be collected by deductions from the suppliers' milk accounts and that there be an option of either six or twelve payments over the year. There were eight applications for loans at the first meeting of the credit committee. Three were allowed, three more adjourned and two disallowed, although the committee agreed to adjourn one of these to allow the applicant to get better guarantors. In February 1930, five applications came before the credit committee of which two were successful. But, when one of the successful applicants for loans was interviewed by the committee, it was revealed that he was not a milk supplier, had no intention of becoming one and that neither of his guarantors were milk suppliers.

The scheme operated successfully for a year or so but the economic situation eventually forced a rethink and at the May meeting in 1930, Mr. Galbraith proposed that the working of the Agricultural Credit Corporation Scheme be suspended until the year end. He cited two reasons for his proposal:

1. the bad price for butter which would, in consequence, make suppliers' cheques very small without additional deductions;
2. the Society had now close on £1,000 out on loan and he thought the

Society would be wise in waiting to see how the instalments of principal and interest would be paid this year before advancing further sums.

A letter from the IAOS, dated 26 September, regretted that Donaghmore "have had to take measures in court to recover share calls. This is not a good thing to do as it generally makes a man an enemy of the Society for his lifetime". Kelly replied: "Please don't imagine for an instant that the committee decided on the course they are taking with their eyes shut or without consideration. This action is only being taken in a limited number of cases but, if these men were not made pay 20/- in the £1 now, it might have disastrous consequences in a few years time. It would be unfair to other shareholders if these men were not made to pay and allowed to boast around the country that they could not be made to do so. My committee have hesitated to take this drastic step for the past eleven months but they feel they would be lacking in their duty to the shareholders, if they did not nip in the bud this Bolshevistic tendency on the part of a few 'wasters'." The IAOS acknowledged that the Donaghmore committee were not taking the prosecutions without good reason. Courtney of the IAOS stressed in a letter to Kelly, dated 30 September, that he "did not mean to imply that you are fond of law but these cases seldom have good effect. I note you are taking certain individuals who have been doing harm and I am glad you have selected them in that manner." A few days later Kelly confirmed that decrees had been obtained "in both cases".

The issue of leases

In February 1929, Messrs. Maher and McGaughy had met with the management committee to discuss the sub-letting of a part of the Union premises. They stated that they required a 25 year lease at a rent of £15. After some discussion, it was agreed to allow a 20 year lease, at a rent of £17, subject to the sanction of the Department of Local Government. In April, a letter was read from the Department refusing to allow the sub-letting to the applicants.

A motion was passed "that this Society asks the Local Government Department for legal possession of these premises". Mr. Riddell, of the IAOS, accompanied Kelly and Herbert Thompson, to a meeting with a Mr. McArdle at the Department of Local Government on 1 May to sort out the lease situation. Kelly also mentioned the sum of £300 that had been awarded by the British Military authorities for the restoration of the Donaghmore premises, arising out of damage resulting from their occupation by the British military during the War of Independence. Mr. Riddell in a memo to Dr. Kennedy on 2 May commented: "It appears the money is lodged with the County Council and that it goes with the premises. The Society is entitled to it if it wishes to get it".

The Department had a letter pertaining to the leases before the meeting at Donaghmore on 10 June, 1929. The Society's solicitor, E.J. Ryan, had been asked to be present at the meeting but did not attend. Some members felt that, by his absence, Mr. Ryan "was treating the committee very badly". But, a week later, Mr. Ryan was present and explained the legal position of the Donaghmore leases to the chairman and the seven members present. Mr. Ryan was instructed to take all necessary steps and actions forthwith to get possession of those parts of the Union's buildings and land occupied by Messrs. Maher and McGaughy. The committee decided that, having issued proceedings, Mr. Ryan would be at liberty to settle, providing that Maher and McGaughy paid their costs and agreed to new terms on the sub-leases. These consisted of a sub-lease on the private dwelling at £5 per year for five years and for £15 for five years in respect of the business premises and land, as was defined in the map in possession of Mr. Ryan or alternatively to yearly leases at the same rates. The following January, Maher asked the committee to meet him halfway on costs or to remit six months' rent. On a show of hands it took the chairman, Herbert Thompson's casting vote to carry the motion that Maher be given £5 towards costs.

Kelly's interest in co-operatives was not confined to Donaghmore. He wrote to Dr. Kennedy on 5 November, advising him that the farmers in the Ardee area of Co. Louth were "again anxious for a creamery". He advised the IAOS chief executive that he felt that Ardee was an ideal place for a creamery. "The land is suitable, the cows are there and there is quite a sprinkling of large farmers, who could afford to put in 30 or 40 cows each. Lastly it is a tillage area and they would be sure of a winter supply. I told them to write to you and you would send down an organiser." Kennedy replied on the following day: "I think the place is quite suitable. One of the difficulties would be the fact that a number of farmers from the area are supplying milk to Dublin. I am still awaiting a communication from the district before taking any action."

Kelly, in a letter to the IAOS, dated 6 November, complained of the high price being paid in the local markets by Cork Butter Merchants for farmers' butter. In 1926, the price was 6d to 8d, in 1927 it was 9d to 11d, in 1928 the top price was 1/2 and now at this time it was 1/6 per lb. "We cannot see that the price of creamery butter has fluctuated 100 per cent during this period … It is now apparent to us that the formation of a creamery here has merely created a market for farmers' butter … Our position becomes very serious if this state of things is allowed to exist … We ask you to take up this matter strongly with the Minister, with a view to giving the sale of farmers' butter, in this area at least, the supervision to which it is entitled, under the Dairy Produce Act."

Privately, IAOS officials were still far from convinced of the ability of Donaghmore to survive in the face of so many problems. The Dairy Produce inspectors were pushing the Society into providing a cold store for butter but Dr. Kennedy feared that the cost of its provision could bring the struggling creamery to its knees. He asked Mr. Fant to estimate the cost of a freezing machine and of the cold store itself. He noted "it is not at all clear to me that there is a future for Donaghmore as a churning centre". In a memo to Langford dated 14 November, Dr. Kennedy referred to the proposal of making the existence of a cold store at a creamery a condition for giving it a national brand. A decision was deferred pending further experiments on the chilling of butter during the following season. "By the time the necessity will arise over the national brand, the future of the Donaghmore creamery will be more apparent and you should oppose any development in that direction for the present. If the prospects are not better at the end of the coming year, we must face the situation of making it an Auxiliary to Roscrea."

J.P. Kelly, despite his earlier pessimism, relating particularly to the impact that the home buttermakers' activities were having on the Creamery, wrote to Dr. Kennedy on 21 November in a more upbeat mood regarding the Society's future: "I cannot see that the financial situation here is as bad as it is painted. Certainly it is not as bad as others! With reference to the milk supply, I have just compared the figures for the months July to October with those of the corresponding months in 1928 and find an average increase of 18 per cent on the 1928 figures. Would you call this bad? My (recent) letter was sent you on Mr. Fant's request and dealt with one of the causes of milk being manufactured at home in this area.

"Another reason why every farmer is not supplying milk … is because my committee insist on every new supplier taking three shares per cow. This policy is more inclined to hamper than help our milk supply … The prospects for the supply in 1930 are bright. One farmer here, who kept four cows last year, has now installed a milking machine and intends to run 40 or 50 cows. His example can, and will, be followed by others. In 1931, when the export of farmers' butter is controlled, our prospects will be brighter still."

The Donaghmore secretary missed the December 1929 meeting. This was a rare happening. He had a good reason for his absence; his mother had just died. Messages of sympathy were sent from the committee and the meeting was adjourned as a mark of respect.

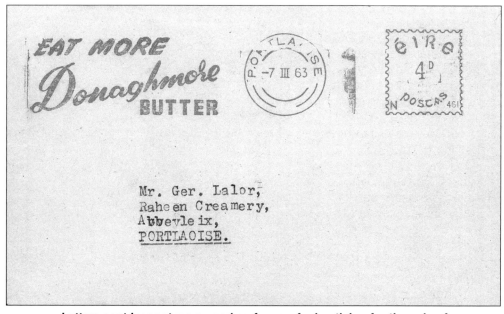

Letters sent by post were used as forms of advertising for the sale of Donaghmore butter.

CHAPTER FIVE

National Health Insurance

The committee were far from happy with the hasty departure in April 1929 of the engineman at Donaghmore, John Aherne. The secretary told the committee that he had received less than a week's notice. Edward Fox was appointed to the position at a wage of £2-2-0 per week, but his appointment caused some concerns. Mr. Loughman asked what attitude the Insurance Company might take in the case of a claim by Fox, an ex-soldier, for a defective knee under the Workman's Compensation Act. The secretary reported that an ex-soldier was entitled to employment on the same rate as an ordinary civilian and that the Workman's Compensation risk would be covered. Mr. Kelly informed Mr. Riddell that all the Donaghmore employees, except one, were insured under the National Health and Unemployment schemes and their cards were kept stamped up to date.[1] The exception, he stated was Mr. Fox, "an ex-soldier who was through the European War, was wounded and has a pension from the War Office." He advised Riddell that Fox's National Health Insurance card was stamped to date but said that Fox had informed him that, being an ex-soldier, he needed no Unemployment Card as he would not be entitled to any benefits. This, however, had caused problems when "an inspector under the Acts blew in and kicked up a row. He agrees that Fox can never benefit but insists on his card being stamped, the arrears of which amount to close on £8." Kelly asked Riddell if there was any way by which payment of the arrears could be avoided.

The Donaghmore secretary also examined the wider picture of workers' insurance. "Could creamery employees be termed persons employed in agriculture and thus be exempted under the Act? I don't think it would need a very great stretch of the imagination to do this. The £8 referred to, caused me to do a little thinking. We are paying £50 a year in Unemployment Insurance. No member of the staff ever obtained any benefits under the Act and I don't suppose ever will. If this £50 was subscribed in the same manner and lodged in a bank each year! What a nice foundation it would make, with interest accumulating, for a Superannuation Fund after 20 years. The employees would then have an interest in the Society and consequently give better service. There are, of course, other advantages too numerous to mention. If we have to pay £50 per annum in Unemployment Insurance the figure for the remainder of the creameries in the Free State must be in the neighbourhood of £7,000.

"Probably this idea has all been discussed and argued before now but I would be glad to hear your views. It has been calculated that only about 33 per cent of the money paid in Unemployment Insurance is paid out again to the workers. Most of the balance goes in administration expenses. My idea is that the workers should

1. Letter to the IAOS, dated 9 October 1929 (National Archives).

get 100 per cent. A scale of Superannuation could be drawn up, having regard to the years of service rendered and so forth. In this manner the employees would be very careful to protect the interests of the Society and their own."

Mr. Riddell, in his reply, stated that there must have been some misunderstanding in Fox's case because, as he was in receipt of a pension, that did not put him in any inferior position under the Act. A senior Department official had advised Riddell that Fox might get a certificate of exemption so far as his own portion of the contribution was concerned, but there would be no possibility of exemption for the employer. With regards to the question of the classification of creamery workers as agricultural employees, Mr. Riddell stated that he had spoken to the Minister for Industry and Commerce, who said that he could not agree to the exemption as he was bound by the Act. Riddell also revealed that he had spoken to the Deputy Chief Inspector who told him that the amending bill does not contain any provision for altering the status of creamery workers. The IAOS official added that he was taking up this point "with one or two influential people".

Engineman's persistence

The engineman at Coolrain, William Grady, figures prominently in the minutes for these early years. The first mention relates to a request from him for a raise at a meeting on 8 October 1928. The request was refused. He had another letter before the November meeting, in which he requested to be paid the week's wages which was withheld since his application for a wage increase. The committee ordered the wages to be paid but sent a shot over Grady's bows by insisting that he sign an agreement to give fourteen days notice in writing of his intention to leave the employment.

Grady must have felt a degree of satisfaction when in April 1929 both he and the engineman at Raheen were allowed a bonus of £1-10-0 per month. But he was nothing if not persistent. Instead of counting his blessings, he had another request for a wage increase before the July 1929 meeting. The committee decided that "as his present wages with the bonus amounted to 29/6 per week, he should wait until his bonus ceased to make his application". Yet another similar letter was read at the August meeting and with the same response. His persistency finally paid dividends when, at the November meeting, his salary was increased to £1-5-0 per week.

Grady's name again appears in the minutes of the monthly meeting in the following April but for a different reason. Committee members heard the bad news that the Coolrain engineman had met with an accident through the bursting of the water gauge glass. Grady had a letter before the meeting asking was he insured. At the May 1930 meeting, inevitably there was yet another request for a raise, now seeking £1-10-0 per week. This time, the minutes note, that his request was 'unanimously refused'. It was similar in June. In August 1930, Grady applied for a bonus and also payment for two days wages which were stopped from him "owing to absence from duty". This time Grady appeared in person before the committee and argued his case. A motion was passed "that no bonus be given, that his wages remain at £1-5-0 all year round and that no further application from him shall be considered". He did receive, however, payment for the two days he had missed work, for which the committee's permission had been granted. From the minutes, one can sense the growing impatience of the committee with Grady's non-stop campaign for improved wages. Grady obviously sensed it too and he does not figure in the minutes again until April 1932. In a letter to the committee, he demanded an explanation as to why he had not been appointed to a vacant position for which he had applied. The letter was marked read and the secretary was instructed not to send a reply.

Coolrain manager saga

In September 1928, there was an application from the manager at Coolrain for an increase in salary but this got short shrift. Mr. Murphy proposed, and Mr. Cooper seconded, the motion "that owing to the season of the year and the not too favourable reports which have been received about Coolrain from the Department's inspector, the committee cannot see their way to accede to Mr. McCarthy's request".

If the Coolrain manager felt poorly treated when denied a salary rise a few months previously, it was his very job that was on the line at the meeting on 5 November, 1928. The minutes record the reasons: "The secretary made a very unfavourable report in reference to the management of Coolrain auxiliary. He pointed out that the books were being kept in a very careless manner and that the testing had also been done carelessly." The committee examined the books referred to and, after some discussion, Rev. Henebry proposed … "that we censure the manager for his unpardonable carelessness and, if the next report we receive is unfavourable, we will take such action as is necessary to protect the interest of the suppliers." The manager was ordered to attend a special meeting eight days later.

The manager survived the first attack. Indeed things were looking up when McCarthy was given an increase of 5s per week in April 1929. But in June 1929 another crisis arose. The secretary reported that:

1. the creamery was locked but the keys were left in the blacksmith's forge;
2. the cream pipe was dirty;
3. the Inspector's reports were not forwarded to Central (Donaghmore) as instructed.

The committee were infuriated and Mr. McCarthy was told bluntly in a letter from the committee "to mend his ways or send in his resignation".

The Coolrain manager had survived once again. His problems, however, were far from over. Indeed there was more trouble for him just around the corner. Two letters from the manager were read at the July meeting relating to the "unsatisfactory" way in which a lorry driver was doing his job. Some members of the committee remarked that if the manager had been doing his job these complaints would not have arisen. The minutes noted ominously that "at every meeting of the committee there was some row or complaint about Coolrain but there was never a word about Raheen". Various complaints about bad management were put forward and, after a lengthy discussion, a motion was carried calling for Mr. McCarthy to send in his resignation. The secretary was instructed to advertise the position on receipt of the resignation and the sub-committee were asked to examine the applications. But at the August meeting the secretary reported that, when he visited Coolrain on 1 August, he had found a great improvement both inside and outside. The place was clean and tidy and the manager's testing of the composite samples had been done accurately. The motion requesting the manager's resignation was rescinded. Round Three to McCarthy. But his luck was running out.

The Coolrain manager saga continued into the spring of 1930. McCarthy had a letter before the April meeting, requesting an increase of salary to £3 per week "free of insurance". The application was refused. The matter finally reached a conclusion at the management committee meeting of 12 May 1930. The secretary reported that he had received further complaints concerning Mr. McCarthy. There had been a shortage of separated milk on three occasions and it was claimed that the manager had manufactured replacement by emptying cream into the tank and adding water to it. The secretary also reported that the machinery in Coolrain was not receiving the attention required and that "repairs to the separator were costing about £1 per month at least". A motion was passed requesting McCarthy to hand in his resignation. The secretary was instructed to advertise the position. A letter from McCarthy seeking a withdrawal of the demand for his resignation was read at a meeting two weeks later and it was accompanied by a "memorial signed by some Coolrain suppliers" asking the committee to reconsider their decision. The appeal was rejected without discussion and a new appointment was made. Daniel O'Sullivan was given the job at a salary of £2-12-6 per week for the first six months and £2-15-0 thereafter.

Michael Kirwan and George Galbraith – the longest serving members of the Committee of Management.

CHAPTER SIX

A Stormy End to Fr. Henebry's Chairmanship

The committee had been informed, at the October 1928 meeting, of the transfer of Fr. Henebry to the nearby parish of Galmoy. He was warmly praised for the work he had done for the Society. "Mr. Murphy proposed a vote of thanks to the Rev. Chairman for the manner in which he had conducted the destinies of the Society since its inception. He paid a special tribute to the Rev. Chairman's capability and perseverance and he said he was sure that every member of the committee had learned with regret of his departure to another parish. The Rev. Chairman thanked Mr. Murphy and the committee. He said that anything he had done for the Society was a labour of love. He would continue to take a deep interest in the affairs and would retain the chairmanship at the committee's pleasure. The statement was greeted with applause."

Rev. Henebry carried on as chairman for some time, despite his transfer. He wrote to Dr. Kennedy[1] expressing his "disgust" with Barry's report (*see* Chapter 3). He said that he would bring the matter before the committee on the following Monday night. He complained that the statement that he (Barry) had recommended letting off the extra hand in the dairy was untrue. "The truth is that Mr. Kelly is furious with me and Mr. Barry". Kelly had informed him that the extra hand "was only employed on working days and that his service would be dispensed with at the end of the present month". Rev. Henebry requested that Barry should advise him "of the date and hour of his next visit to Donaghmore Creamery".

Fr. Henebry addressed another letter to Dr. Kennedy on the following day. In it, he strongly recommended the opening of an auxiliary in his new parish of Galmoy. "This place is one of the finest centres in Ireland to put an auxiliary …", he wrote. Both letters were passed on to Mr P. Courtney who replied: " … am not nearly so much hung with proposal at present as you are. Donaghmore would want to improve their position considerably before taking on further responsibility; the milk supply has not gone up at Central or auxiliaries and the manager should be devoted to getting an economic supply in each of his areas before taking on a further area." He emphasised that he was not against the idea. He felt that it would be a wise move provided Freshford Creamery was bought out by the Dairy Disposal Company. One of the units could be closed and the other transferred as an auxiliary to a neighbouring creamery. He said that that would do away with cartage and warned that until cartage were done away with in Galmoy and Johnstown areas it would be very foolish for Donaghmore to enter into competition

1. Letter from Rev. Henebry to Dr. Kennedy of the IAOS on 7 December 1928. (National Archives).

with Freshford for the milk. Courtney also replied to the criticisms of Barry: "I should like to point out that Mr. Barry is a well trained and competent creamery manager and when he criticises the working of Donaghmore he knows what he is talking about. I happened to be with him on one of his visits and I cannot see anything amiss in his reports." He closed his letter with some personal good wishes: "I am pleased that you have not been sent very far away from Donaghmore so that your influence and your help will be still available for the Society. I hope, as a start, you will get as much milk as possible from your present district to Donaghmore rather than put up a creamery there immediately."

Fr. Henebry was incensed, not so much, perhaps, with the content of the reply as with the manner in which Kennedy, the IAOS chief, had passed his letters down the line. He took up his pen once more on 11 December and his letter was again addressed to Mr. Kennedy: "I expected a letter from you and not from Mr. Courtney. In view of Mr. Courtney's letter I can no longer remain chairman of Donaghmore. But before taking the final step, I will ask you to give Mr. Courtney, Mr. Kelly, secretary, and myself an audience in Jury's Hotel on Thursday night at 8.30pm. Faithfully yours, Thomas Henebry C.C.". I failed to find any response from Mr. Kennedy, nor could I locate any reference in the minutes or archives to any such meeting taking place.

At the AGM held on 11 March 1929, at which 47 members were present, Fr. Henebry was re-elected chairman. He had rarely missed a meeting during the time that he was associated with Donaghmore Society and he continued to take a keen interest in proceedings throughout his final year. The minutes record that the last meeting he attended was on 11 November of that year. But the final three months of his stewardship proved a very difficult time for him. His troubles began when, at the meeting on 5 August, Mr. Murphy proposed that the Agricultural Credit account be opened in the Royal Bank of Ireland. Mr. Kirwan seconded the motion. Fr. Henebry proposed that the second account be opened in the Munster and Leinster Bank and this was seconded by Mr. Loughman. Fr. Henebry's proposal was defeated by six votes to five. He did not let the matter rest, however. He had a notice of motion before the September meeting calling on the committee to rescind the resolution made at the previous meeting. In a lengthy speech, he questioned the legality of the motion passed at the August meeting on the grounds that it had not been on the agenda. The secretary explained that the matter was discussed "at every angle" by the sub-committee and it arose with other matters under the secretary's report. He pointed out that, in making the recommendation, the sub-committee had chiefly in view clause 4 of the Society's agreement with the ACC and were not acting from any personal motives whatsoever. Mr. Loughman seconded the motion and Mr. Murphy proposed a direct negative. On Mr. Galbraith seconding the amendment, the matter went to a vote once again and on a show of hands the motion was declared lost by 7 votes to 5.

As far as the Rev. Chairman was concerned the matter was far from resolved. It was his contention that a two thirds majority was needed to defeat his motion. There were notices of motion from both Fr. Henebry and Mr. Murphy on the issue before the October meeting. The situation was explosive and J.P. Kelly appealed to the IAOS for help.[2] He asked Langford to bring pressure to bear on Fr. Henebry to withdraw his motion. It was, he believed, "the only way that can save this unfortunate Society from a faction split. It is deplorable. If you want to save it you must act without delay". He felt that the IAOS was the competent authority to decide a

2. In a letter, dated 18 September, from J.P. Kelly to Mr. Langford (National Archives).

matter of this kind. "I am aware that anyone with an ounce of common sense could decide it. But which tribunal can it be referred to", he asked? Langford wrote immediately to Fr. Henebry, telling him that his interpretation of the rules was wrong and that the committee were correct and entitled to act as they did. He appealed to the Donaghmore chairman for unity and asked him to lead by example. He explained that it was in the absence of Dr. Kennedy, who was out of the country on business, that he was making the appeal.

The appeal fell on deaf ears and both motions duly appeared on the agenda for the October meeting. The chairman ruled that his motion should be considered first. It read: "that the resolution empowering the committee of Donaghmore Creamery Ltd. to open an ACC account in the Royal Bank Ltd., Rathdowney be inoperative until the procedure whereby the said resolution was carried is proved in order". Mr. Langford of the IAOS stated that it was his duty to point out that both the Credit Corporation and the IAOS were in favour "of having the accounts of societies, who were working the scheme, in different banks from their current accounts".

There was also legal opinion from Arthur Cox, Solicitors. In it, Mr. Cox stated that "it must be realised that there is no power in the committee of management to repudiate or revoke anything that has already been duly done under, or by virtue of, a previous resolution". Subject to certain observations, which he noted, Mr. Cox said that there was nothing to prevent the committee of management revoking a resolution which had been passed by them provided nothing had been done in the meantime. "The answer, therefore to your query is that, in our opinion, the committee cannot pass a resolution of its own dictating what majority of the committee must be necessary in the future, or in some future transaction of any kind or nature whatsoever."

Fr. Henebry went ahead and argued his case strongly, however. He refused to take any amendments. Mr. Galbraith finally called for a vote by ballot as between the two banks and this motion was seconded by Mr. Cooper. Mr. Langford was appointed scrutineer. The ballot papers were distributed and collected by him and he declared the vote as follows: 10 for the Royal Bank; 5 for the Munster and Leinster Bank. Mr. Murphy then moved his motion: "that any decision of the committee of management of this creamery shall be final and no decision arrived at by the said committee can be altered unless by a vote of two-thirds of the meeting at which the motion to rescind is considered". This motion was seconded by Mr. Mitchell and passed unanimously.

It was a very disgruntled Fr. Henebry who took the chair as usual at a very tense November meeting. The secretary read the minutes but the chairman refused to sign them. He proceeded to give his reasons for doing so. His primary complaint was that the committee disregarded his opinion on the banks issue. He claimed he was "ignominiously insulted" by them. The minutes record: "The chairman resumed his seat and silence prevailed for some minutes. The chairman refused to go on with the business even omitting to sign the minutes but he eventually agreed to do so if the committee would discuss the matter at their next meeting."

That was the last meeting Fr. Henebry attended at Donaghmore. He wrote to Kelly on 15 November advising him of his reasons for not signing the minutes. They were incomplete, he complained, because Mr. Sheeran's notice of motion requesting the motion in question to be rescinded, was not stated. He also asked the meaning on one particular sentence in the minutes. Kelly responded on

18 November. The secretary made his own position, and that of the Society, quite clear. It was, as usual, a business-like letter, and there were no punches pulled. Kelly first dealt with Fr. Henebry's letter. He said he regretted that, through an error in copying the minutes from the book, he had neglected to insert four words which made the meaning of one sentence unclear. Regarding Mr. Sheeran's motion he said that when the matter was discussed by the committee it would appear verbatim in the minutes of that meeting. "Minute books are not kept to give vent to the speeches of the chairman or any individual member of the committee. They should briefly contain the facts of what actually takes place at meetings. With much respect I submit that it is not for you, alone, to state that the minutes are incomplete. This is a matter on which the committee are quite competent to give a decision. If the committee find that I have not clearly set out the facts or mis-stated them in any way I will endeavour to re-marshal them to their liking, but I absolutely refuse to do so on your request."

Kelly was only warming up to his task: "I had hoped that by this time you would have been ashamed of the disgraceful scene you created at the last meeting; and that the sooner it would have been forgotten the better for all concerned; but apparently this is not your intention just now.

"The attitude you have chosen to adopt in this matter is absolutely deplorable. Because at a previous meeting a two to one majority of the committee voted against a motion of yours you endeavoured to hold up the business of the Society by making the statements that 'there was a conspiracy against the Chair' – that you were 'ignominiously insulted, utterly routed' and so forth. It is you and you alone, who had cast an insult. You have insulted the intelligence of the other members of the committee. In other words you have told them that they are not competent to give an opinion on any subject arising at the meetings, and that they must conform to your views every time otherwise they insult you. Was ever such an attitude adopted by the chairman of fifteen intelligent farmers? Certainly not by a layman and I imagine it is without precedent. Why did the General Meeting elect sixteen men to transact their business for them if you alone were capable of doing it?

"You speak of 'a conspiracy'. You refuse to conform to Majority Rule and when the majority of the committee will not give way to the minority you allege 'a conspiracy against you'. Did anyone ever hear a more ridiculous statement from an educated man?

"I cannot understand your attitude in this matter, though I have tried, and tried hard. Perhaps you have some ulterior motive? Certainly you have stooped to practices unworthy of your high calling in order to attain your ends. You have discussed the private affairs of the committee with outsiders. You even went so far as to bring the Bank Manager to use his influence on members of the committee. Why all this? "I ask you is this upholding the 'dignity of the Chair' of which you have so often spoken? Does it contain the true 'spirit of Co-operation? Is it for the material welfare of the Society? I am exceedingly sorry that I find it necessary to address you in this tone, but I at least, have the interests of our little Society at heart and I will uphold them whatever the cost. Yours faithfully, J.P. Kelly, Secretary."

I could not find any letter in reply. Was it even possible for Fr. Henebry to summon up a credible response to such a focused and damning attack? It was J.P. at his best, a straight-talking man of high principles and impeccable honesty, doing what he felt he had to do for the Society, "whatever the cost".

It was quite rare to find a lay Catholic addressing a priest in such forthright manner in the 1920s, as indeed it was up to the 1960s and beyond. To do so carried a risk of a clerical backlash which could seriously damage a person's standing in society, could jeopardise his job or business interests and cause huge embarrassment to one's family.

Kelly was clearly upset and disgusted with Fr. Henebry's behaviour. But, perhaps, had it been another man, he would have relented, thus allowing the chairman to resume his position, had he admitted to the error of his ways. As far as the IAOS were concerned, however, they had just enough of Fr. Henebry's vagaries. Dr. Kennedy demanded an immediate report from Mr. Langford on the situation. "I will be glad if you will inform me if it means that the chairman is able to impose his will on the shareholders notwithstanding their convictions. If I understand it rightly, he refused to carry on business until the motion was rescinded. If that interpretation is correct, I would certainly convey the whole story to his Bishop", wrote Kennedy.

Having received confirmation of the situation, he took up the matter with Canon Phelan, the parish priest at Piltown, County Kilkenny, who was a member of the IAOS committee. "We are in a very serious difficulty with regard to the Donaghmore Creamery owing to the attitude taken up by the chairman, Fr. Henebry. I enclose copy of report from Mr. Langford on recent proceedings and, from what I gather from personal discussion with Mr. Langford and other members of the staff, the report is worded in very mild terms having regard to the facts. At the last meeting, Fr. Henebry refused to sign minutes or to allow the meeting to proceed to business, unless the motion referred to was rescinded. The Donaghmore Society gives us much concern and it can only be regarded as struggling for existence so far and, instead of the cleavages for which the chairman is responsible, the united efforts of all concerned will be needed to develop the Creamery on a sound basis. You are quite aware that the only alternative to having Fr. Henebry removed from the chairmanship and, if possible, from the district is that a General Meeting should be called to remove him from the committee and, therefore, from the Chair. You will understand how objectionable such a procedure would be from every point of view. I see no alternative but to put the matter before the Lord Bishop so that he may adopt whatever disciplinary measures as may seem good to him. I write to you for your views in the matter. It occurred to me that you as a Canon of the Diocese and a member of this committee, might more effectively approach the Bishop on the matter than I could. Hoping you are in good health. With kind regards. Yours sincerely, Secretary."

There was relief all round when Fr. Henebry[3] announced his resignation in a letter to J.P. Kelly, dated 27 November 1929. In it, he wrote: "It is my wish that no discussion should follow this resignation. This will best serve the interests of the

3. Rev. Thomas Henebry, a native of Condonstown, Hugginstown, Co. Kilkenny, studied at St. Kieran's College and was ordained at St. Mary's Cathedral, Newcastle-on-Tyne, on 7 May, 1911. He served for some years on a temporary mission in the Diocese of Hexham and Newcastle, England, before returning to an appointment in Dunnamaggin, Co. Kilkenny. He was appointed C.C. in Borris-Ossory on 16 April, 1923. On 24 September, 1928, he was transferred as C.C. in Galmoy. On 1 December, 1930, he was appointed as Chaplain in Belmount Park. Three years later he was appointed curate in Conahy, Co. Kilkenny from where he was transferred in 1937 to minister at the De La Salle College in Castletown. He spent eleven years there before retiring. He took up a brief appointment as C.C. in Clogh, Castlecomer, but after a three month illness he died at the Burlington Clinic, Dublin on 17 January, 1954 (details supplied by John Phelan, Borris-in-Ossory).

creamery which now, as always, I have much at heart. Wishing you well." In a brief note, dated 29 November 1929, to Fr. Henebry, acknowledging his letter of resignation, Kelly wrote: "On account of old associations I am very sorry that you have found it advisable to adopt this course; however, I will see that your wishes in the matter are carried out. Yours faithfully, J.P. Kelly, Secretary." At the December meeting a proposal that Fr. Henebry's resignation "be accepted with regret" was made by Mr. Galbraith and seconded by Mr. Murphy. There was no discussion. The founding chairman's name was rarely ever again to appear in the minutes. A brief mention was made at the time of his death in 1954 regretting his passing.

SECTION ONE

PART TWO

The 1930s

INTRODUCTION

The Economic War and Self-Sufficiency

Economic depression deepened with each passing year in the Ireland of the 1920s. The infant Irish Free State struggled with its independence. The Wall Street Crash in 1929 hastened the Great Depression in the USA and its nasty tremors rocked economies throughout the world. Industry was badly hit and this caused rampant unemployment in Europe including Britain, Ireland's main export market.

The Irish dairy industry was already suffering from a slump in demand for its dairy products abroad, particularly in Britain, due to quality problems as well as increased competition not only from the Danes and the Dutch but also from Commonwealth countries. The coming to power of the de Valera led Fianna Fail government in 1932, compounded the Irish exports problems when an economic war developed between Britain and the Free State following de Valera's abolition of the oath of allegiance and his refusal to pay the land annuities, which had been agreed by the Cumann na nGaedheal administrations. An incensed British government imposed 20% duties on Irish cattle and dairy produce to recover the money being withheld. Irish retaliation was swift. The government put a twenty per cent duty on imports from Britain including machinery, electrical goods, iron and steel and cement as well as five shillings a ton on British coal.

Because of the troubled international economic situation most countries were adopting protective policies on trade. The Irish Free State was not, therefore, completely out of line with the international trend. Exports to Britain had fallen from £47 million in 1929 to £36 million in 1931, half of which came from the export of cattle. Two years later the export of cattle yielded a mere £7 million and there was a seething anger and unrest among farmers in the worst hit districts of Munster and Leinster. By 1934 total exports were down to £18 million. De Valera, however, did not see this worsening trade situation as the economic disaster it was portrayed by others. Far from it. He came to power on the rallying cry of self-sufficiency and now the Irish were forced to hasten in that direction, whether they liked it or not.

Despite a tense political situation with the emergence of a more militant and threatening opposition force, the O'Duffy-led Blueshirts, de Valera continued to promote his ideal of self-sufficiency. The huge number of small farmers created by the break-up of the landlords' estates was a key element in Fianna Fail's support base and, to help keep them on side, he promised them increased financial support for their produce in the run-up to the elections, a promise he delivered by introducing subsidies to help exports of their butter and bacon. The growing of wheat was encouraged with guaranteed prices. A major campaign was launched in 1933 to promote the crop. Every Post Office, Garda Station and National School had a poster showing a laughing farmer with wheat in his hand above a caption which read: 'A guaranteed market and price'. Farmers could not afford to import animal feed and found themselves obliged to use home-produced grain instead. With cattle virtually unsaleable, farmers were encouraged to cull their herds. Calves were sold for a shilling or slaughtered and fed to dogs. There was a bounty of 10/- put on calf skins. Old cows were sent to Roscrea where they were slaughtered and converted into meat and bone meal.

The sugar-beet industry, which had its base at the Carlow factory, was nationalised and expanded. New factories were constructed at Thurles, Mallow and Tuam, as de Valera extended his self-sufficiency strategy to industry. Tariffs, quotas and licences restricted imports greatly while ownership of resources here was largely limited to Irish involvement. With private capital in short supply, the government themselves initiated a number of development agencies and enterprises. The ESB had been established in 1927 and now Fianna Fail set up thirteen new state-sponsored bodies including the ACC, Aer Lingus and Bord Failte. Ireland's industrial base expanded throughout the 1930s but one continuing problem for the sector was the lack of raw materials and spare parts for machinery, which were very costly and difficult to access because of the trade war and the high tariffs.

With the warming once more of relations between Ireland and the United Kingdom, restrictions and tariffs on certain commodities eased as the decade progressed. A first tangible sign of a thaw in the Economic War was the 'coal for beef' pact in 1937 which allowed cattle into Britain. With the threat of a major war on the horizon a new agreement was signed in 1938 covering almost all types of food which Ireland could produce.

Despite the rush to self-sufficiency the plight of the Irish man and woman in the street improved little, if at all, during the 1930s. Poverty remained a major problem. In 1931 the average Irish income was three-fifths of that in Britain; by 1939 it was just below fifty per cent. As Irish men and women became relatively poorer, the level of emigration resumed on an upward spiral.

CHAPTER ONE

Overzealous Health Inspectors

As early as September 1927, the secretary, J.P. Kelly, had reported that a Department inspector had visited the Donaghmore premises and had insisted on the sewage being piped to the river. Mr. Kelly reckoned that Department inspectors could be put to better uses. He complained to the IAOS: "Now that we are about to start a creamery here, would not the time be opportune for the Department of Agriculture to send a vigorous inspector to Rathdowney Butter Market to deal with the filth sold there every week."[1] The IAOS secretary noted in reply that he was going to "hint" to the Department regarding the inspection of butter at Rathdowney.

The issue had provoked another strong letter from Kelly to the IAOS in January 1928. He wrote: "Recently a newly appointed and rather busy Inspector of Dairies and Cowsheds for Roscrea No.111 Rural District called at the Creamery and demanded a list of names and addresses of suppliers. We refused the information and explained that we did not buy the new milk nor sell same for consumption. We merely bought the butterfat of the milk, which was pasteurised. We feel that this gentleman will cause trouble (underlined) if possible and certainly if he goes round and condemns a number of cowsheds of suppliers, the Creamery will be ruined."

He added: "We cannot see why the suppliers to a creamery should be subjected to such annoyances when those who make butter under the worst conditions at home and market it in a primitive manner are allowed to go free of any Inspector whatever. I am not cognisant with the regulations but if it transpires that the official concerned is overstepping his duty, I would ask you to request the Department of Agriculture to inform him of same."

The IAOS passed on the complaint to the Department but there was no satisfaction to be had for Donaghmore Creamery. The Department responded: "There are no grounds for supposing that the Local Authority and their officers are unduly exacting in enforcing the provisions of the Dairies Cowsheds and Milkshops Order, which are recognised as beneficial to the trade and not calculated to injure a person in the dairy business."[2]

Fr. Henebry, at the October 1928 meeting, had added his weight to Kelly's criticisms as to the manner in which the dairying regulations were being implemented. His tabled a motion which was passed unanimously. It read: "… it appears to this committee that the Minister of Lands and Agriculture is not putting in force the Dairy Produce Act 1924 except in so far as it is operable to the Registered Creameries. While the Act has our heartfelt approval and support, we feel that a grave injustice is being enacted on creameries by its incomplete operation. It has

1. In a letter to the IAOS, dated 12 September 1927 (National Archives).
2. In a letter to the IAOS on 20 April 1928 (National Archives).

come to our notice that shareholders are withholding their milk from the creamery because of the risk of prosecution under the Act. They are at liberty to sell in local towns and markets, milk and butter of any description without running such a risk.

"We call upon the Minister to forthwith put into operation sections 41-43 of the Act and to insist on their rigid enforcement. We are aware that the blending of creamery with farmers' butter is still in general practice and we are of the opinion that every effort should be made to prohibit this noxious custom.

"It is further our considered opinion that very serious injury is being done to the trade for creamery butter across channel by the marked similarity of the packages in which creamery and factory butter is exported. We suggest that the Minister should use the powers conferred upon him by section 29 of the Dairy Produce Act to define more clearly a difference in shape or colour of the packages used for the export of factory butter." Copies of the resolution were sent to the Minister and to the local TDs.

A letter was read from the secretary of Leix (Laois) Board of Health requesting that they be furnished with a list of suppliers of milk in Roscrea No. 3 area. The secretary stated that he had ignored the letter and the committee approved of his action.

The enforcement of the Dairy and Cowsheds Order was a continuing cause of concern during the summer of 1930 and in the years that followed. After considering a report from the Leix Board of Health relating to the operation of the Order, the secretary was instructed to write to Mr. Gorry, TD for Laois/Offaly,[3] "to find the best way of obviating, or if necessary, resisting the order". Milk supplies were being badly affected by the order and with farmers now finding themselves better off by selling their milk direct to consumers, the situation for the creameries was approaching critical.

At the October 1930 meeting in Donaghmore, J.P. Kelly advised the committee that milk would only be received on four days a week. With butter prices at rock bottom, the manager, William Grogan, suggested that the Society "sell a limited quantity of new milk as the price of such at the moment was more remunerative than making butter". He was empowered to sell any quantity of new milk which he thought desirable and was to find a market for same in Dublin. Grogan estimated that selling the milk left the Society £0-1-7 per lb for the butter which it would produce. After a discussion it was agreed:

1. that only 75% of the separated milk be returned to suppliers;
2. that three halfpence per gallon be allowed to suppliers per gallon for their separated milk and
3. that the manager be instructed to purchase all the new cans necessary for the milk trade.

The 'wretched state' of the butter market finally forced the chairman, Mr. Sheeran, to ask staff to agree to a 10% reduction in wages. The manager and other members of staff agreed with the request and it was decided to make the cuts from 1 November. Whatever about the state of the market, the quality of the

3. Patrick J. Gorry, a native of Kilcavan, Co. Laois, was elected a Fianna Fail TD for Laois/Offaly in 1927. He lost his seat in 1933 but regained it in 1937 and held it until 1951. He was a senator from 1951 to 1954. He died in October 1965, "T.D.s and Senators for Laois & Offaly (1921-1986)" by Patrick F. Meehan (*Leinster Express*, 1987).

butter being produced at Donaghmore received a further boost when it was announced at the December meeting that the Society had obtained first place at a recent surprise inspection.

At the December meeting in 1930, the committee "viewed with dismay the resolution passed at a meeting of the Leix Board of Health insisting that the Order be made applicable to creamery suppliers". A motion was passed which read: "If the Inspector of Dairies and Cowsheds is allowed to carry on the inspection of creamery suppliers' premises and ignore the premises of home buttermakers, the result without any doubt will be that all, or nearly all, the suppliers to these creameries will cease to supply their milk and turn to home buttermaking thus causing the creameries to shut down. Apart from the serious financial loss that this procedure would mean to the district, it would render the Society unable to discharge its liabilities to the Department of Agriculture, the Credit Corporation and the Local Government Department."

Langford reported the grim situation facing Donaghmore to the IAOS. He estimated a reduction of over 15,000 gallons in the milk supply for November as compared with the same month in the previous year and attributed the drop directly to the Board of Health inspections. He was particularly concerned at the zeal applied by one particular inspector in carrying out his work. Many suppliers had stopped supplying the creamery and returned to home butter-making, he stated.

The IAOS passed on the complaint to the Department. In a letter dated 6 December, marked personal, to H.G. Smith, LL.D., Asst. Secretary, Department of Agriculture, Riddell wrote: "Dear Smith (sic), our organiser for the midlands reports a case of excess of duty on the part of a certain Food and Drugs Inspector, named Kenny, who it is stated in the course of his inspection work has thought it fit to disparage creamery butter in comparison with home-made butter. I do not know whether Mr. Kenny is on your Department's staff or not, but we would like him instructed not to air his private views officially and especially when his private view is diametrically opposed to the official view. If you think it is worthwhile, I will inform you more particularly in the matter, but I think it is perhaps sufficient to draw your attention to it thus briefly, in the first instance, as I do not know to whom the Foods and Drugs Inspectors are directly responsible …" The IAOS also sent a letter to P.J. Gorry, TD, at Leinster House, asking him to deal with the issue.

Donaghmore was not the only creamery attracting the attention of health officials. The Order was being diligently applied in many other areas too and despite a spirited resistance from the creameries, the operation continued one year after another. So much so that a meeting was called for the Courthouse in Portlaoise on 20 June 1931 by creameries in Offaly, Wicklow, Kildare, Carlow and North Tipperary, as well as Laois. Mr. Gorry was in the chair. A motion was passed that "this meeting views with dismay and consternation the attempt of the Boards of Health to enforce the … Order against creamery suppliers". This provoked a letter from Mr. P. Murray, Secretary of the Department of Agriculture, outlining the Government's view on the matter. It read: "The Local Government Department consider it essential from a public health point of view that creamery suppliers throughout the country should be brought within scope of the Order. Outbreaks of serious diseases have sometimes been, and may again be, attributed to the use of creamery butter and supplies of a number of farmers. It becomes necessary for public health officers to be in a position to inspect without delay the premises of cow-keepers supplying milk to the creameries. This can only be done if the names and addresses of the suppliers are registered with the local authority. The Minister is satisfied that this (cost to farmers) is a mistaken notion and that there is no reason to assume that creameries suppliers will be worse affected than other farmers."

Another letter from the Leix Board of Health was read at the June 1931 meeting, asking for a list of milk suppliers but the committee ordered that managers and lorry drivers be instructed not to give the names of milk suppliers to anyone, and that the letter be marked 'read'.

Some relief was given to the long suffering creameries when the government introduced subsidies for creamery butter produced by the 'scheduled' societies, of which Donaghmore was one, in the spring of 1932. But the Minister introduced some amendments a few months later including the withdrawal of the special concession of 14/- per cwt. for butter manufactured. J.P. Kelly complained to the IAOS that the new proposals issued by the Minister on butter prices would swing the advantage once again back to the home butter-maker.[4] He stated that the benefits accruing from the introduction in April of that year of the Dairy Produce Act on prices to the scheduled societies was only beginning to take effect. But recent amendments had given the advantage back to the home butter-maker, he claimed. "The Government last April considered that the creameries included in the scheduled list required protection to a certain degree. Their position has not been materially altered in the past twelve weeks. I trust that this is merely an oversight ..." The Department secretary advised the Society that "a sanction has now been obtained for continuing, by means of grants out of public funds, financial advantages equivalent to the special concessions which were accorded to Scheduled Societies under the ... Act and terminated on 1 August last by an Order made under that Act".[5] Kelly, not satisfied with the Department's response, went to Dublin to see Dr. Kennedy to whom he expressed great disappointment.

At the May meeting of 1933 in Donaghmore, the secretary read a cutting from a local newspaper which stated that the Leix Board of Health had decided to enforce the Dairy Cowsheds and Milkshops Order rigorously against creamery suppliers. It was agreed that no new milk be sold, and that no information be given to any inspector who might call, as the committee still firmly believed that creamery suppliers were exempt from inspection. Correspondence at the IAOS confirms that the local Board of Health were, indeed, determined to enforce the regulations. Donaghmore's vice-chairman, George Galbraith, Corbally, was one milk supplier to receive a letter of warning.[6] It read: "... The Board desires to draw attention to the seriousness of being engaged in such trade without complying with the terms of the Order. It is their intention to enforce the Order effectively throughout the district".

The issue was taken up again with the IAOS who made representations to the Department on behalf of midland suppliers. "It seems strange that apparently it is only the creameries in the Midlands, all of which have been comparatively recently established, which are affected by the ... (1928) Order. Not only is this so, but creameries here have to compete with the home-made butter market which is not supervised to anything like the same extent to which creameries generally are

4. In a letter dated 29 July 1930 (National Archives).
5. In a letter to the Donaghmore manager, dated 23 November, 1932. (National Archives)
6. Letter dated 19 May 1933, and signed by Leix Board of Health secretary, T. O'Reilly (National Archives).

Edward Sheeran, Chairman of Committee of Management 1930-'40.

subjected to supervision, under the Dairy Produce Act, 1924. These creameries are practically fighting for their lives and it is not the opinion of the IAOS that the condition of their suppliers' milk is inferior to that of farmers in other parts of the country where the Order is not enforced."

A delegation from the Midland Creameries Conference, of which J.P. Kelly was secretary, met the Minister of Agriculture, to impress on him the need for making the provisions of the Creamery Act 1928 operative against home buttermakers and taking steps to collect levies from these producers. They also raised the issue of increased subsidies (or bounties as they were known). The Minister told them, there was no money in the kitty for such increases.

There was scant mention of subsidies again for some years but in September 1939, a letter from Department of Agriculture was read notifying the Committee that a special subsidy of 8/- per cwt would be paid on all butter manufactured in August of that year. Different levels of subsidies were applied each month thereafter for a few years.

Headaches aplenty

If the infant Irish Free State had entered a bleak economic climate, Donaghmore Creamery had headaches aplenty of its own. The country's problems were often their problems too. Yet, despite all the difficulties, the Creamery struggled on. Edward Sheeran had been appointed interim chairman at the monthly committee meeting in February 1930 and at the AGM on 10 March, at which the members of the press were admitted for the first time, the Coolrain man had his appointment confirmed unanimously. R.F. Bennett was elected vice-chairman. In his address to the meeting, at which twenty members attended, Mr. Sheeran boasted that the quality of the Society's butter was among the best in the world. "At the recent Olympia Industries Fair, Donaghmore butter represented Ireland and that was a great compliment", he said.

The committee, now known as the management committee, continued to meet at least monthly and the minutes reflect just how busy the members were in dealing with a wide range of pressing matters in a fast growing business. These issues related to staff, wages, transport, discipline, quality of product, and all topics relating to the running of the Creamery at Donaghmore and its auxiliaries at Raheen and particularly at Coolrain, which was a constant cause for concern due to indifferent management there.

There was always the problem of defining the boundaries and protecting the milk supply from scavenging neighbouring creameries. The Donaghmore committee, in 1930, were looking particularly at Timahoe, at Galmoy, where Fr. Henebry was now ministering, and at Timogue, situated between Timahoe and Stradbally. George Galbraith said that he, or his committee, had no wish to prevent a creamery being erected in Timahoe or Timogue, provided that they did not interfere with the Raheen supply.

A press report of the AGM of the Roscrea Co-operative Creamery, which appeared in the Midland Tribune, stung J.P. Kelly. His cause for complaint related to some comparisons between the Roscrea and Donaghmore operations which showed Donaghmore in bad light. He enquired of the IAOS "if such biased comparisons as were prepared for the meeting are in the best interests of co-operation?" He also asked if Roscrea's actions had the approval of the IAOS. "I suggest it is against the first principles of co-operation," he declared.

Kelly was aware that the IAOS retained grave doubts about the viability of Donaghmore in the short to medium term and he may have also found out from his contacts within the IAOS that, in the event of Donaghmore failing, the parent body envisaged it becoming an auxiliary of Roscrea. On 11 April, Kelly called on the IAOS to censure the Roscrea action in the strongest terms. The IAOS replied on 12 April: "You may take it that the grounds for your complaint will not recur ... Has your committee, by the way, protested against the publication in question?"

In March 1930, the manager, William Grogan, advised the committee that the Creamery "would shortly be working every day in the week". Extra activity at the Creamery meant an extra workload for the hard-pressed secretary. Kelly reluctantly took on the extra work and was awarded an extra 12/- per week in his honorarium.

The "recent success" at the Spring Show was noted at the May meeting in 1930. On the suggestion of Mr. Murphy, it was agreed that the Society's name should appear on enamel signs, with nine inch white lettering on a blue background, to be erected outside all premises owned by the Society.

The practice of non-suppliers sending dirty oil-cans for separated milk was brought to the committee's attention in September 1930. The manager was instructed to give the offending parties a fortnight's notice, during which time they would have to procure proper vessels for the milk.

Bit off more than he could chew

Senior head-office IAOS official, Charlie Riddell, bit off more than he could chew when tackling the Donaghmore secretary on the issue of payment of the special subscription required from creameries to keep the parent organisation afloat. Riddell's letter of 29 August 1930, appeared a reasonable request for early payment: " ... We are in need of money to defray some pressing liabilities and expect, in the circumstances, your Society will come to our aid by subscribing as generously as possible. You are, no doubt, aware that the expenses incurred by the IAOS are solely in the interest of co-operatives and that it is reasonable to ask that they in turn will come to our assistance by subscribing an amount that will enable us defray our expenses. May we rely, therefore, on your generous response in this important and urgent matter." Kelly informed Riddell that the matter had been on the agenda of their previous two meetings but that its consideration was adjourned on each occasion for Mr. Langford's 'wise counsel and advice'.[7]

7. In a letter dated 1 Septmber 1930 (National Archives).

Riddell assumed this was a case of delaying tactics and he was not having any of it. He responded with more fire than usual on 2 September: "… I do not think the special sub or the payment of any contribution to the funds of the IAOS require the attendance of an organiser, so far as your Society is concerned. Surely the matter is one upon which your committee can come to a satisfactory conclusion, both for themselves and for the IAOS, without any prompting. You are well aware of services provided … The cost of sending an organiser to any society for the purpose of explaining affiliation with parent organisation, without some other object, is hardly warranted. You can readily see cost must come out of resulting contribution and, where this occurs, the contribution is greatly lessened. Is Mr. Langford's attendance necessary at your meeting of the 8th inst."

The exchange of letters continued on an almost daily basis as the war of words threatened to boil over. Kelly wrote to Langford telling him that he was not required at the next meeting. Instead of this having a cooling effect, it puzzled Riddell further. The IAOS official noted, in a letter dated 4 September, that the Donaghmore committee did not now require the attendance of Langford at their meeting. "This, however, does not answer my letter. I do not wish to withhold Mr. Langford's services if you consider them absolutely necessary. But it does not appear to me, on the face of it, to be reasonable to expect an organiser to visit a society at comparatively great expense merely for the purpose of explaining the reasons why the Society should support its parent organisation. I should like to have an understanding with you about this before it is definitely decided as to whether Mr. Langford should attend your meeting or not."

This prompted an irate response from Kelly, who felt it was time to call a spade a spade. Kelly wrote: "You appear to be labouring under the delusion that my committee has requested the IAOS to send Mr. Langford to its meeting of the 8th inst solely for the purpose (to borrow your own expression) 'of explaining the reason why this Society should support its parent organisation'. Please get rid of it! (underlined). It is not a fact! (underlined). This Society has no desire whatever to put any additional or unnecessary expense on the 'parent organisation'. Some twelve months ago, Mr. Langford told me that he was deputed to keep an eye on the new societies in the area. He told me it was his intention to attend each meeting of the committee whenever possible and accordingly I promised to send him notices of each meeting. I have done so and he has attended frequently. His presence at the meetings was much esteemed and his sound advice in matters of finance was greatly appreciated by every member of the committee and staff.

"Regarding question of now withholding his services, this is purely a matter for you to decide. You sent him here voluntarily and not on the request of the Society. The circular letter of the IAOS dated 2 July, number 4/30 came before my committee on 7 July. As no resolution was passed at the General Meeting empowering the committee to make a levy on milk suppliers as suggested and as it was considered that the addition of a further deduction from the accounts of milk suppliers to the existing ones for shares, Credit Corporation loans and cartage would have a detrimental effect on milk supply, it was decided that a Special Sub should be paid from Society funds. The consideration of the amount was adjourned as already explained in my letter of 1st inst. I have nothing further to add thereto. Yours faithfully, J.P. Kelly."[8]

8. In a letter dated 4 September 1930 (National Archives).

Riddell knew it was time to cut his losses in the face of such a powerful adversary and such a focused response. His reply of 6 September opened with an admission that he had misunderstood the situation. "We have never wished to withhold his (Langford's) services from your Society. But we were under the impression that it was not necessary for him to visit you so frequently now as formerly was the case when your Society was naturally only getting on its feet. Mr. Langford will be with you on Monday." Langford duly attended the meeting of 8 September, 1930. The committee 'decided unanimously' to increase the special sub from £5 to £10, which was handed over to the IAOS organiser on the night.

Manager seeks positions elsewhere

The Central manager, Mr. Grogan, was not, apparently, feeling quite at home in the idyllic surroundings of Donaghmore. He made a number of determined efforts to transfer himself and his family elsewhere during 1930 and in the following years. In April 1930, he applied for the job of manager at the Glen of Aherlow Creamery. Never one to allow the outcome to be decided on a simple application, he tried to enlist the support of the influential Dr. Kennedy. In a letter of 10 April, he informed the IAOS chief that he was a native of the district and that his brother was a supplier to the Tipperary creamery. "I can say I would have the full confidence of every supplier. If the appointment is referred to you I ask the favour of a very kind consideration. As you know I agreeably fell in with the suggestion to leave Bruree and although promised to be recouped of any losses, I did not get anything. I am of the opinion Glen of Aherlow would suit me better than here, hence my request. Thanking you for past favours, I am, Yours faithfully, W. Grogan."

Kennedy's response was not very reassuring for Grogan. Dated 10 April (the same date as Grogan's letter), the IAOS chief's reply read: "I could not advise you to go for the Glen of Aherlow position. In our opinion, the position there is quite serious and I think it is foolish in the extreme to continue to run it as an independent creamery. As you are aware, the Dairy Disposal Company have been in negotiations with the Glen of Aherlow for some time and the logical position is that it should merge with the DDC creamery at Tipperary. If, however, the people of Aherlow do not accept our views in the matter, and if they ask our opinion with regard to a manager, you may be assured that your application will get fair consideration."

Grogan's next attempt to transfer came in June. This time he went through Pat Courtney in the hope of enlisting support for his application. On 23 June, 1930, he wrote: "I have applied for Thurles Creamery and I write asking that you would do whatever you can for me … You know that Thurles town offers fine facilities for educating children, hence I am applying." Courtney's reply was brief: "The Thurles vacancy was decided about a week ago. The Boherlahan manager has got the job. Yours sincerely, P.C."

In August, Grogan decided that Kennedy might, after all, be his best bet. He asked Kennedy to support him for the vacant manager's job at Tullamore. In his letter of 1 August, he wrote: "… I have five childen aged 3½ to 13½ and I consider the facilities afforded at Tullamore for education very good indeed. Nearest school of any description to here is 2½ miles, church the same, so the difference is very obvious. I would do my utmost to keep Tullamore up to Mr. Lane's standards and beat it if possible. Donaghmore is in a sound position … Yours in anticipation, I am, Yours faithfully, W. Grogan." There is no reply to be found in the IAOS papers.

The Donaghmore manager laid low for a little while before reactivating his plans for a transfer. The next recorded attempt came in a letter to Mr. Courtney dated 4 January 1932: "I am applying for vacancy at Black Abbey Co-op Adar (sic). In all likelihood, the appointment will be referred to the IAOS. I will be very much obliged to you if you could see your way to get my name before the committee. By doing this I will always be grateful. You know I have a thorough knowledge of everything in connection with a Central and auxiliaries. I have got the highest class butter twice out here and at Bruree, so if appointed you need never regret it." Grogan wrote a similar letter to Dr. Kennedy on the same day. Kennedy replied: "If our advice is asked we shall, of course, give your application fair consideration. It is quite apparent that there is going to be a very big field."

Grogan did not leave it at that. On 6 January he acknowledged Kennedy's letter: "… I beg to thank you for your kind reply … I wonder would I presume too much if I asked you to inform me (in advance) in the event of I being selected to be put before the committee. I can do a canvass with a few of the committee. Needless to say I deprecate a manager doing an indiscriminate canvass." There was no further correspondence and Grogan remained reluctantly, no doubt, at Donaghmore.

CHAPTER TWO

Electrification

T he advent of the ESB and rural electrification changed the face of Ireland. It was the Quiet Revolution. It lit up a dark country, brightened people's lives and was a tremendous innovation in factories, on farms and in the home. J.P. Kelly, forever seeking improved working methods, was quick to grasp the impact this new mass energy supply would have on industry. He could visualise the benefits of electrical power in the creamery. He wanted a supply for the Creamery – he wanted it at the right price and he wanted it immediately. Kelly was not in the business of being ripped off by the ESB or anyone else. Nor was he one to hang around.

The first mention of electrification for Donaghmore appears early in 1930 with a letter from Dr. Kennedy to the ESB, seeking estimates for a connection of power to the Creamery. In a hand-written reply from Thomas A. McLoughlin, Managing Director of the ESB, a figure of £448 was given as the cost of supply.[1] Kelly was appalled at the quote and expressed his doubts to the IAOS about the Creamery showing any further interest in the proposal. "Does it not appear absolutely ludicrous?" he asked. "… let us assume that my Society was foolish enough to pay the sum demanded and the lines were brought to the Creamery – a number of local residents, three publicans in the village and possibly the mill, would at once avail of the supply at our expense, not to mention Ballybrophy Station, 1½ miles distant. At Ballybrophy, the company manufacture their own gas in an obsolete plant and all trains stop for water. If a supply of electricity was available there, I have no doubt that the company would make a considerable saving in the cost of lighting and pumping alone.

"My committee had this letter from the ESB under consideration at their last meeting and they decided to abandon the idea of electricity for power purposes. We are at present in negotiation with a firm for a crude oil plant. The cost of this would be about the same as the cost for erection of five motors, wiring and so on for electricity but the running cost of the crude oil plant would be much the lower. At the same time the electricity has many advantages and it seems a pity to abandon the idea altogether. Can nothing really be done before 12th proximo when this matter of a crude oil plant will be decided? Would you … see if they are in earnest about this transmission line cost." It was apparent that Kelly wanted an electrical supply but not at any price.

On 13 September 1930, Mr. McLoughlin gave a fresh quote. "We are now prepared to give the extension if the committee pays £150 and gives a guarantee (of) a minimum revenue of £150 for five years." After further representations the guaranteed minimum revenue was dropped to £120 for five years and no capital cost.

Kelly had negotiated a very attractive package for the Society and it was only

1. Dated 13 March to the Manager at Donaghmore (National Archives).

then that he presented the proposal to his committee. The first mention of electrification in the minutes was at the meeting of 6 October, 1930. The secretary explained in detail the proposed scheme. He estimated that electrification of the plant would result in a saving of £70 per annum minimum on coal alone, while there would be other savings on oil, belting and wear-and-tear to machinery. The IAOS engineer, Mr. Fant, presented a report to the meeting and, after a lengthy discussion, Mr. Murphy proposed and Mr. Treacy seconded the motion to proceed with the scheme. The chairman, Mr. Sheeran, proposed that the Electricity Supply Board tender of £320 to erect the necessary motors be accepted. Mr. Cooper seconded and all agreed. Mr. Langford was asked to get Dr. Kennedy to use his influence with the ESB, with a view to arranging that the 10KV transmission line be laid via Donaghmore village. Kelly was particularly anxious about the date of completion. He informed the IAOS that he knew of one creamery whose contract was given to the ESB in January and the work had not yet been completed. "I should not like anything approaching this to happen in our case," he wrote.

Also at the October 1930 meeting, consideration was given to the erection of a mill to grind corn grown locally. The IAOS had outlined the advantages of having such a mill. These included its convenience to the general public, the absorption of local labour on non-working days at the creamery and the consumption of electric current to ensure that the cost of the amount consumed in a twelve month period would reach the required amount of £120. The tender for the erection of a 15 hp motor for driving the mill was £42. The purchase of a new mill of the type recommended would cost up to £90 and there would be a £10 cost in alterations.

It was at this point that the secretary made a very generous gesture. He told the committee that if they did not wish to risk the outlay on a new mill, he would provide a mill, free of charge for one year, together with a 'good No. 4.C. Bamford' motor. If after a year they decided not to proceed with the idea, he would take back the mill without any obligation to the Society. If they did decide to continue grinding, he would sell the mill at any valuation which a valuator appointed by the committee would fix on it. Furthermore he said that he would not ask for payment thereof until such time as the mill had earned its own cost and the cost of the motor for driving it. It was agreed to proceed with the project and an ESB tender of £42 for a motor to drive the mill was accepted. In September, 1931, Mr. Fant was asked to put a value on the mill. He came back with a price of £35, which was agreed by both sides.

Fish kill

Kelly wrote to Riddell, of the IAOS, on 27 January 1930, advising him that they were "having trouble with fishery people". He enclosed the solicitor's letter of complaint and an analyst's report. Kelly, in his report, stated that Donaghmore could not possibly have been responsible for the pollution. It was his view that the fish kill was the consequence of activities at a mill in Donaghmore village, over a mile away, owned by a man named Walpole. He accused Walpole of implicating the Creamery, by informing the Garda on false information to take the suspicion away from himself.

Solicitors for the IAOS, on reading Kelly's account of the incident, felt that any prosecution in the case would fail adding: "In any case I think issue should be contested as it would be a dangerous precedent to admit that creamery effluent is injurious to fish. This might lead to similar cases all over the country."

A copy of the letter was sent to Mr. Fant, who wisely felt that the Department should examine the whole question of sewage disposal immediately and that the IAOS should get their considered opinion before taking other steps. "The Department have investigated this matter for about 25 years and so should be able to advise as to what is the right course." Dr. Kennedy did not agree. "I am inclined to think that this is part of our function and that it is not advisable to hand over responsibility for it to the Department." Regional organiser, Langford, in a report to the IAOS, judged the problem from a different angle again. "The question is, will the financial position of the Society be good enough to undergo legal proceedings which may prove costly." Langford suggested that Donaghmore should send a delegation to the IAOS solicitors and discuss all aspects of the case.

The fish kill issue (although not identified as such in the minutes) was first brought to the attention of the committee at the meeting of 10 February 1930. The secretary read "all the correspondence to date in the alleged poisoning of fish". He was directed to investigate the complaint and "bring the matter to a head if necessary".

Dr. Kennedy wrote to Kelly, which was followed up with a letter from Riddell to Kelly dated 13 February. "You will, no doubt, have received Dr. Kennedy's letter of the 10th inst., in which he suggests a solution of the trouble without recourse to litigation. Law is the pugilism of disputes and is therefore the refuge of the weak … It (litigation) should only be used in the event of your failing to find a means of settlement out of court. …"

CHAPTER THREE

Drop in Milk Supply a Major Worry

At the AGM held on 9 March 1931, Mr. Sheeran, who was re-elected chairman, stated that consistent with supplies, Donaghmore Creamery paid the highest price of any creamery in Ireland. He also informed members that electrification of the Creamery had led to an estimated savings of £100 per year. IAOS organiser, Mr. Langford, expressed concern about the drop in the milk supply. At the conclusion of the AGM, an informal meeting was held at which Mr. Galbraith called upon the Government "to immediately proceed with the de-rating of agricultural lands". He addressed the meeting on the worrying position in which the farmers all over the country were placed and said that "unless relief in some form was forthcoming, matters would be very serious indeed in twelve months time".

In May 1931, an offer by the Department relating to loans to co-ops on very favourable terms for the erection and equipping of cold stores was considered. An application was made to the Minister for some relief in respect of the payment of the instalment of loan due on 1 October. The June meeting heard, however, the Department's inability to accede to the loan remission request. In January 1932, two Department inspectors called to Donaghmore and spent the day going through the accounts of the Society since its inception. In March 1932, payment of interest due was requested and "copious details from the Share Ledger" were also sought. The committee considered these demands "rather superfluous" and the secretary was instructed to ask Mr. Riddell of the IAOS to approach the Department with a view to having "their requirements mitigated".

The Society was coming under increasing financial pressure as 1931 wore on. This did not, however, stop them from giving the secretary 12/- per week for extra office work done by him. No one knew, better than Kelly, the critical nature of the situation. He wrote: "Things are bad. Dam (sic) bad … Loss for month: £38. We are back 900 gallons per day compared with last year. On top of it all we had applications from three lorry drivers for increased remuneration. Tullamore are undercutting our price in Athlone (by) a halfpenny per lb. Our trade for meal is the only end that shows an improvement."[1]

Mr. Langford alerted the IAOS secretary that "with small suppliers the carters earnings are correspondingly low and they are getting very discontented. It will soon be necessary to review their situation once again". He advised of the grim details of the drop in supply of milk in the Donaghmore franchise. He contrasted the June 1931 situation with the same month in the previous year. The daily performance was as follows:

---

1. In a letter to Mr. Langford on 6 June 1931 (National Archives).

June 1931: Donaghmore 690 gals, Coolrain 386, Raheen 448;
Total 1,524 gals.; No. of suppliers 211.

June 1930: Donaghmore 1130 gals, Coolrain 534, Raheen 708;
Total 2,372 gals.; No. of suppliers 278.
This represented a drop of over one third from the previous year.

The balance sheet showed a loss of £40-18-5 for the month.

Income: June 1931:
Skim milk: £20-14-0
Cream: 2-2-6
Butter: 1037-17-5
Profit on millstuff: 20-0-0
Total: **£1070-13-11**

Expenditure: June 1931
Est. expenses: £404-1-6
Butterfat (paid for) 667-12-0
Reduction in stocks: 39-18-10
Total: **£1,111-12-4**

The audited accounts for the six months ended 30 June 1931, showed a loss of £391-6-5 with bad debts totalling £39-12-8. After allowing for profit brought forward from 1930 of £261-16-4, liabilities exceeded assets by £171-4-9.

At the August meeting, the chairman proposed support for the tough action of the sub-committee in the collection of share instalments due. The secretary was also authorised "to proceed with the collection of £0-2-6 (half a crown) per share on the uncalled for share capital". There were several letters from shareholders before the September meeting, asking for more time to pay. The secretary was told to instruct the Society's solicitor to "take immediate action in some cases to be selected by the sub-committee" and that shareholders, who have asked for reasonable time to pay, be granted it. Mr. Riddell of the IAOS intimated that he had received a telephone call from the Donaghmore secretary relating to the status of certain share forms.[2]

Kelly complained that he had written several letters to Mr. McCarthy, the former manager at Coolrain, now in charge of the Mourne Abbey Creamery auxiliary at Glenville, enquiring about certain forms witnessed by him. But McCarthy had not replied. Riddell informed Langford that legal proceedings were being considered in some cases and that McCarthy could be a material witness. He surmised that the fact that McCarthy had been dismissed by Donaghmore may have been the reason for his failure to reply to Kelly. "Mr. Kelly thinks that you may be able to persuade McCarthy to reply. He believes you had something to say in his getting his present position", said Mr. Riddell.

Kelly wrote to the IAOS on 26 November, complaining that the ESB was overcharging. He explained that Mr. Fant (IAOS) and ESB officials had informed him that the charge for current would be 2d per unit for first 2,500 units, 1.5d for the next 1,000 units and .8d for any greater amount. The ESB had charged them 2.5d

2. In an internal memo to Mr. Langford dated 14 October 1931 (National Archives).

for 6,500 units, 1.5d for the next 2,000 and 1d for the remaining 3,381 units used. Kelly said that he, unfortunately, had not got any agreement in writing on the charges. He was informed a few days later that the ESB had, obviously, made an error and that Donaghmore should pay at the rate agreed.

A plan for the marketing of butter drafted by the ICMA was explained at the September meeting by the secretary but it was decided 'to have nothing to do with the scheme'. The secretary was instructed to collect three pence per share from milk suppliers for the month of August making a total deduction for the year to date of one shilling and three pence.

CHAPTER FOUR

Wage Cuts All Round

Kelly advised Langford that despite the drop in milk supply from 517,937 gallons in 1930 to 318,410 in 1931, the profit for the year was £315, an increase of £54 on the previous year. This was due mainly to the reduction in milk price from 4.95d to 3.93d per gallon. But the installation of electrification had had also contributed to the improved profit for 1931. The estimated saving on coal was £280 and on oil was £20. The cost of electricity was £120, leaving a saving of £180.[1]

In February, 1932, Mr. Kirwan put forward a plan aimed at increasing the milk supply without seeking out new suppliers. He suggested that the Society should lease a suitable piece of land adjacent to the Creamery, purchase 10 or 12 cows and milk them for the benefit of the Society. R.P. Bennett supported the proposal and it was passed unanimously. Messrs. Kirwan, Bennett and Thompson were authorised to procure around 20 acres of land on the eleven month system.

Despite the profit recorded for 1931, the backs were still to the wall at Donaghmore, in financial terms, and action had to be taken. Staff-related cost-cutting measures were adopted at the March meeting. In November 1930, the manager and staff had all agreed to a 10% wage cut in the interest of keeping the operation afloat. Now, as the minutes reveal, the swing of the axe took a wider sweep:

1. Coolrain: To dispense with the services of the engineman. Manager to run the creamery as a one-man auxiliary with the aid of a boy to deliver the separated milk @ 2/- per working day. Estimated saving £39.
2. Raheen: Dispense with manager's services. Engineman to weigh and sample milk. Testing to be done by Central manager. Give engineman 4/- or 5/- extra and a boy to assist as in Coolrain @ 2/- per working day. Estimated saving £89.
3. Central: Dispense with services of engineman as a regular employee. Give him preference of occasional work such as grinding and box-making @ 30/- per week. Estimated savings £75.
4. Reduce by 10% from 1 March, the salary of the secretary, all managers and the dairymaid. Estimated saving £61.

Despite the wage cuts, however, viability was still threatened by the continuing fall in milk supply. At the AGM held on March 6, 1932, Mr. Sheeran warned members that, if the decrease continued, the committee would be forced to recommend the closure of the Creamery. The price paid for butterfat during the year was low but he stressed that it was the utmost that could be paid 'consistent with good

---

1. In a letter dated 14 January 1932 (National Archives).

finance'. He told members that the installation of electricity was the cause of 'putting £400 in the pockets of suppliers which would not otherwise have been possible'. This shows a difference of £220 from the estimated savings reported in January, but there is no explanation as to how the figures differed so much. In the Report of the Committee to the AGM, members were told that joining the ESB grid "had proven an unqualified success … Your milling venture, which in reality is a side issue of the installation of electricity, has also proved successful and remunerative beyond our expectations."

The amazing attention to detail which the management committee applied to their business is borne out by an item in the minutes for September 1930: 'the manager in his report mentioned that the Society had recently purchased a long ladder and he anticipated that a number of people would require the loan of it. The committee ruled that the ladder not be leased'. This ruling was tested in May, 1932, however, when a request for a loan of the ladder was received from Rev. C. Bergin. The committee showed their flexibility by giving their assent to the request.

The April meeting had heard of the resignation of the dairymaid, Miss Hoey. The resignation had been accepted, as also was her application for a refund for £1-10-0, which she had spent on electrical installation. At the June meeting, it was the turn of the Coolrain manager, D.F. O'Sullivan, to announce his resignation. It was a move that, obviously, had been signalled in advance because the chairman, Mr. Sheeran, was able to announce at the same meeting that Thomas Brosnan of Cahir, was to replace him at a salary of £2-5-0 per week.

Loans to members, price of butterfat, milk supply, shares and membership issues, purchases, IAOS correspondence and cartage matters were issues that were aired at most meetings for the period. At the February 1932 meeting, it had been noted that a carter, Mr. Mitchell, had asked the Society to purchase his lorry. The sub-committee were empowered to negotiate the price fixed at £70 with discretion to spend a further £8-£10.

At the June 1932 meeting, a list of ten borrowers was submitted by the secretary of those who were not supplying milk to the Society. It was ordered that the borrowers be advised that the loans would be called in forthwith, unless they supplied their milk to the Society.

The IAOS auditor, Henry Ribton, as a result of a visit to Donaghmore in August reported that "the prospects of collecting further calls for 21 shareholders are bad; 4 members representing 78 shares have made no payments, 2 with 9 shares have left the country, one member has died and 11 others with 88 shares are not able to pay". He also reported that ICAS, a company in liquidation, owed the Society £144. Donaghmore had received goods to the full amount owed but the liquidator objected to the account being treated on a contra basis and threatened legal proceedings unless the account was settled.

The manager, William Grogan, stated at the December meeting that Dowdall O'Mahony were selling (factory) butter in Athlone called 'Golden Harvest' at a price of 10d per lb. He complained that the Department allowed this competition because these factories "are strictly keeping within the letter of the law, but that the general public are being deceived into thinking that the butter in question is creamery".

Kelly informed the committee in September that he had purchased 150 barrels of oats and 40 barrels of barley. Members felt that he should purchase more barley. In December, he reported that reminders sent to non-supplying members in relation to share instalments, had met with little success. The share calls had yielded only £5 or £6 and that in the neighbourhood of £100 was still outstanding from over eighty members. Kelly said that most of the defaulters were well able to pay. He was instructed to get a solicitor on the job but was advised to get an estimate of costs before issuing instructions.

CHAPTER FIVE

"Must Get Help to Survive"

A letter from the assistant secretary of the IAOS to its representative in the midland area, Mr. Whelan, dated 16 January, 1933, queried the difference in price being paid for milk to suppliers by Roscrea and Donaghmore. Roscrea paid 11½d per gallon for its milk in December 1932 while Donaghmore paid only 11d. The price difference was probably the reason why Roscrea accounts showed a loss of £60 for the month while Donaghmore had shown a profit of £9-7-11.

It was a matter of cutting your coat according to your cloth and this was a key tactic in Donaghmore's survival during this testing period. A meeting of the management committee on 6 March was told by the chairman, Edward Sheeran, that "if your creameries are to survive they must get milk". He noted that the milk supplies had shown a further decline of 39,700 gallons in 1932 – a drop of 20% on 1931. The position was still satisfactory though due to the help of Department's subsidies and good housekeeping which resulted in a reduction in expenses of £517 for 1932".

Other creameries were not as astute in cutting their cloth and found themselves in an even more precarious position because of the depression in prices. Michael Quill of the Midlands Co-operative Creameries based in Tullamore, with branches at Belmont, Clonaslee and Kilcavan wrote to Mr. Kelly on 16 February, relating a tale of woe. He pointed out that Roscrea had lost 30,000 gallons in supplies in 1932, Athy was closed, nothing was heard from Scariff and surmised that "things are none too rosy with you either". He called for another meeting of the Conference of Creameries and it was felt to be an urgent matter. "You know how everyone you approach in our line is so slow to move and unless some good move is made by 1 April, God help us … I want to know ere that date if anybody will lift a hand to save us. We fellows here put all that is in us into our creamery but we must get help to survive. The odds are too great." He asked Mr. Kelly to invite "all the usual" including Scarrif, Carlow and Campile and also "to try to get (Dr.) Kennedy; failing him Riddell".

The Conference was duly called but fate intervened. A snowstorm caused havoc and confusion. Kelly related his own difficulties in trying to get to Maryborough (Portlaoise) for the meeting to Riddell: "I had intended going by road but that was out of the question owing to drifts. Walked 4½ miles to Creamery and tried to get you on phone but it was out of action. Then decided to go by train in case you would come and after waiting 1½ hours at Ballybrophy I learned the train would not arrive for another hour. Sent telegram to you at Courthouse, Maryborough, but was told by the post office that delivery was not effected up to noon on Saturday. I hope you had the good sense not to travel. I'm sure nobody else could turn up. Still snowbound here. Practically all the roads are impassible."[1]

1. In a letter to Riddell dated 28 February 1933 (National Archives).

The AGM for 1933 was held on 6 March which twenty members attended.[2] Mr. Whelan of the IAOS, as well as Mr. Redmond and Mr. Kilmartin "of Dublin" were also present. Mr. Whelan expressed his disappointment with the small number of members present at the AGM. The chairman expressed the hope that "the year 1932 would be the worst year which the present generation of farmers would have to meet". An application from Mr. Conroy to be appointed the Society's agent in Dublin was accepted. Mr. Redmond expressed his confidence "in the boy and promised that he would supervise his work" in the capital.

The transport of milk to Coolrain and of cream to the central was the main item on the agenda for the April meeting. The chairman informed the meeting that it was the wish of Coolrain suppliers that Mr. Pratt be given the contract. His offer of 9/- per day for delivery of cream was considered satisfactory and he agreed to accept 5/6 per day for collecting the milk.

The issue of accepting milk from non-shareholders was discussed at the June meeting. This was happening in the Timahoe area and the suppliers in question were shareholders with the Kildare and Leix Creamery which had been closed for a period but was open again. It was decided that milk supplied by non-shareholders should not be refused on any account but that there should be an effort made "to get such persons to take shares for at least one cow". It was agreed that James Bennett be allowed cartage on any milk he brought to the creamery for his neighbours. A loan of £10 was approved for a woman in Camross for the purchase of a cow. Joseph Moloney was advanced £5 for the purchase of a cart. It was agreed to make a special subscription of £15 to the IAOS.

At the August meeting, a letter from the Department was read refusing any reduction in the rent. At the same meeting, an application was received from sub-tenants, Maher and McGaughy, requesting a reduction of £10 in their rent for 1932. A reduction of £5 was agreed. A long discussion took place on the question of the price the creamery should charge for butter sold to suppliers. The Department insisted on 1/3 but the committee felt that this price would damage milk supplies and settled for 1/- instead.

Correspondence between Kelly and the IAOS reflect the widespread confusion caused by the complexities of the import tariffs imposed by the Irish government as the economic war with the UK geared up. The IAOS wrote to Kelly: 'They (the Department) say they have a clerk working specially on the matter as they get a great many inquiries and it is more or less an expert's job to tell what is dutiable and what is not'.

Sourcing vital equipment and spare parts for the creamery was an important function and this aspect of operations, like all other operational matters, was left in the ever-capable hands of the resourceful and multi-talented secretary. This often meant shopping around. Apart from his many useful contacts in the IAOS and the Department, and despite the tangled web of tariff regulations, Mr. Kelly was well capable of doing his own shopping. This meant dealing direct with machinery firms in the UK and on the continent. In August 1933, he was engaged in correspondence with a German firm with a view to purchasing a new hoist. What was required was quite an innovative piece of equipment that could be employed for

2. Those present were: Edward Sheeran (chairman), Rev. C. Bergin C.C., William Bergin, R.F. Bennett, J.S. Cooper, P. Fitzpatrick, Timothy Fitzpatrick, John Delaney, George Galbraith, John Hennessy, R.C. Howard, Michael Kirwan, John Maher, William Moynan, Thomas Mitchell, John Rohan, H. Thompson, Jacob Thompson, J. Walpole and Richard Wall.

specific tasks in the creamery. There were also the questions of price and transport. These issues together with the technical data were addressed in letters signed by J.P., written not in English but in German.

Also in August 1933, the Department of Industry and Commerce wrote to the IAOS conveying a request from a Charles Fitzpatrick, an employee of the Great Southern Railway (GSR) and employed at Ballybrophy Station, to send an inspector to the district to explore the potential of establishing a Turf Co-operative Society there. It was noted that Mr. Fitzpatrick was secretary of the local Fianna Fail Cumann. A list of turf suppliers was included. A letter from the IAOS on the issue was discussed at the September meeting. It was agreed that the Society would support the plan but the opinion of the committee was that little or no turf would be offered to them for sale. In a letter to Dr. Kennedy of the IAOS, Mr. Kelly indicated that the feeling of the committee was that producers would not be inclined to dispose of their turf under the Government scheme while they were able to obtain prices from 16/- to £4 per ton in local towns and villages. However less than twelve months later, on 12 July 1934, the Donaghmore Turf Society was formally registered. This was confirmed in a letter from the IAOS, dated 19 July 1934, to Sean Casey, secretary of the Society, with an address at Ballykerwick, Donaghmore.

The secretary told the September 1933 meeting that the Society had been appointed as agents for the purchase of grain for Messrs. Bannatyne and Sons. The committee fully backed Kelly's initiative and promised their "individual" support. At the October meeting he stated that they had handled 8,800 barrels and earned a net commission of £202. The excellent service rendered by Joe Bergin in this regard was favourably noted and the committee showed their appreciation for the "boy" with a gratuity of £5. The secretary was given a gratuity of £10 for his work.

Although constantly under cash-flow pressure, the committee boldly decided to purchase fifty 'A' Preference shares and twenty-five Ordinary shares in Ranks Ltd., an English company. Mr. Fletcher, on a vote, was appointed the Society's solicitor. It was estimated that the quantity of milk used by home buttermakers in the area covered by Donaghmore was three times greater that the amount supplied to the creamery. Because the supply of milk to the auxiliaries on Sunday was low, it was ordered that they be closed on that day. Mr. Kelly said he was "pleased to report that every penny of tax paid on interest paid to the Department had been rebated".

At the December 1933 meeting, it was decided to go ahead with the construction of a cold store. It was costed at £395 and a loan of £200 for the purpose was sanctioned by the Department. The refrigerated unit was built by direct labour and completed in May 1934, at a cost of £280, representing a saving of over £100 on the contract price. In recognition of the secretary's initiative in keeping costs down, he was given a bonus of £20.

CHAPTER SIX

Manager, Chairman and Secretary – "a Good Team"

Only four members turned up for the first meeting of 1934 and the chairman, Mr. Sheeran, decided to call it to a premature halt for lack of a quorum – the first time such a decision had to be taken, although it was to happen many times into the future. It was usual to discuss urgent business at such meetings and refer decisions taken to the next committee meeting for ratification.

The AGM was held on 5 March and twenty members attended.[1] The chairman reported an increased turnover of almost £4,000 and a profit of £227. He said that the price paid for milk was "better than that paid in any creamery in the Free State". There was an increase in milk supply of 25% (79,000 gallons) which, according to the chairman, was a remarkable achievement. The purchase of grain had turned what would have been a trading loss into a profit on the year's working and enhanced considerably the Society's prestige, he added.

Pat Courtney said that he recalled his first visit to Donaghmore in 1915. He came with Fr. Dillon, P.P., to organise a creamery. Although the farmers were too polite to say it, it was his opinion that they didn't believe a word of what he had told them. He said he came again in 1922 and at that time he was told it would be madness to start a creamery. He was very glad to come back now after twelve years and find things in such a flourishing condition. He pointed out that if the Society were to go into liquidation at that time they would be in a position to pay all their debts and have £524 to distribute among shareholders. He praised the work of the manager, chairman and secretary and said they were 'a good team'. He concluded by saying that his organisation "will always continue to help those people who count, namely the men who pull the cows' tits and carry the rest of the country on their backs".

The secretary was directed at the April meeting to purchase fifty Cumulative Preference shares and twenty five Ordinary shares in Ranks (Ireland) Ltd. After a discussion, it was decided to hold on to their investments in both the English and Irish companies.

Samuel Pratt had an application before the May 1934 meeting for an increase of 1/- per day in his cartage contract. He was allowed 9d. A later application from him for 9/- per day was turned down. A similar application from John Shanahan

---

1. Mr. Sheeran was in the chair, Mr. P. Courtney represented the IAOS and the following members were present: Rev. C. Bergin C.C., R.F. Bennett, Stephen Campion, J.S. Cooper, John Delaney, George Galbraith, John Hennessy, R.C. Howard, Patrick Kavanagh, Michael Kirwan, Thomas Mitchell, Robert Mitchell, P.J. Murphy, John Rohan, Herbert Thompson, John Thompson, Jacob Thompson, John Treacy and Richard Wallace.

was fixed at 8/9 per day. At the May meeting this was increased to 11/6 per day, however.

The IAOS suggested that "certain Scheduled Creameries should take common action with a view to having the levy of 2.75d per lb on production reduced or not collected at all". They pointed out that Slaney Valley had lost well over £500 in the previous year, Kildare and Leix Creamery, as well as Carlow Creamery, were all shut down and Edenderry and Shelburne were in a precarious state. "There seems a case for special consideration", he concluded.[2]

In May, Mr. Galbraith informed the committee of the increased volume of work at Raheen and proposed a bonus of 10/- per month for Gerald Quinn and Joe Butler until November of that year. The secretary mentioned that the engineman, Power, had been married in recent days. He had been with the Society for seven years and he thought that the committee might like to mark the occasion in some manner. Power was given a wedding gift of two guineas.

Mr. Kelly told the meeting that the Society was now in a position to pay some of the loan due to the Department. They had £1,000 on deposit at 2% interest while the interest on the loan was 5½%.

There was also somewhat alarming news that the grain company, with which they had dealt previously, had now made "other arrangements" for the purchase of native grain. Mr. Kelly said that there was a possibility that the contract might yet be saved 'through influence' but he said he was not at liberty to tell the committee how he proposed to proceed. If they were able to trust him sufficiently and made it worthwhile, he would do his utmost, he said. If he failed, it would not cost them a penny. But if he succeeded he would ask the committee to give him 50% of the net commission which the business would earn. He was given a free hand in the matter. The secretary reported to the September meeting that he had made final arrangements for the purchase of grain in various centres. He had appointed loading agents who would look after the loading, consigning, and the issue and return of sacks. The chief centres were Roscrea, Maryborough and Ardee and the remuneration was 1/6 per ton in each case.

At a special meeting called on 18 June 1934, the eight members present discussed the engineer's report on the local mill at Donaghmore, which could be taken over. It would cost £150 to place the mill buildings in a suitable state and a further £150 to renovate existing machinery. The proposition was regarded as 'too big a one for the Society'. The following alternatives were examined:

(1) to install an improved plant capable of turning out maize meal in three grades;
(2) to install a pinhead oatmeal plant; or
(3) to install both.

The secretary reported to the July meeting on a visit that he and two IAOS officials had made to Castlecomer to inspect machinery. He was instructed to go to Cork and inspect more machines on offer.

Mr. Galbraith proposed three motions at the July meeting which were supported:

(1) that any member of the staffs passing any religious or political remark to a supplier be instantly dismissed;

2. In a letter to Donaghmore dated 11 May 1934 (National Archives).

(2) that it shall be the duty of the staffs to see that no person whether a supplier or otherwise be allowed on separated milk platforms or lofts;

(3) that all milk pass books be handed to the attendants weighing out separated milk and that no milk be sold until suppliers have obtained their requirements.

Mr. Kelly advised Mr. Riddell of the IAOS, that there was little doubt but that the Society had benefited considerably by being included on the list of Scheduled Creameries under the Act. He quoted figures to prove his point:

From 1 October 1931 to 30 September 1932 the total was 269,556 gallons. For the similar period 1932-'33 the total was 351,875 and for 1933-'34 the total was 390,289. The number of suppliers had also grown correspondingly.[3]

Flooding at Raheen

A meeting of the Raheen Branch under the chairmanship of Fr. Coyne, P.P., in early 1934, heard of numerous protests to Leix (Laois) County Council relating to frequent flooding of the road at Coole, Raheen, during the previous year. The road had been impassable on a number of occasions. The IAOS were asked to bring the matter to the attention of the Minister for Local Government. A covering memo to the resolution sent by Mr. Kelly to the IAOS noted: 'Hope you will be able to get a move on Feeney (sic) without much further delay'. This must have been a reference to Malachy Feehan who was County Surveyor at the time.

Mr. Feehan explained the causes of the flooding: "Two year ago the GSR Co. cleaned certain damns (sic) on the line and Mr. Dowling's lands were flooded (as a result). Mr. Dowling turned this water on to the public road thus causing the flooding. There was no way for the water to escape except over the land of Mr. Salter who stopped the water. There had been no flooding here previous to the action of the persons concerned." He added: "I may note that this matter is in the hands of the Co. Co.'s solicitor".[4]

George Galbraith, who was party to the complaint from the Raheen Branch, was not satisfied with this reply. In a letter to Kelly, he wrote: "It matters not who caused the flooding. Our only concern is to see that the road is open to our suppliers without having to try and swim through about ten perch of water about three feet deep in the centre. I think it is the Co. Co.'s business to see that this is not allowed to occur. Secondly if the matter is only now in the hands of the Co. Co.'s solicitor – after fourteen months – it looks as if something might be done about it by 1940". Having recounted the litany of letters he had sent to the County Council he added a warning: "Sooner or later, someone with too much liquor will be drowned in it and then some notice will be taken to remedy it". He urged Mr. Kelly to "get Dr. Kennedy to stir up the Co. Co.".

3. In a letter dated 4 December 1934 (National Archives).
4. In a letter to the Department of Local Government dated 14 April 1934 (National Archives).

CHAPTER SEVEN

Opening of Spink Branch

The issue of milk supplies in the Spink area was discussed at the June meeting of 1934. The committee were aware that Ballyragget Society, which was in considerable financial difficulties, was planning to start an auxiliary there. The consensus was that if the cows were there, Donaghmore should seriously consider the erection of a milk separating station in the area. Mr. Galbraith and Mr. Mitchell agreed to investigate the area. Pat Whelan, of the IAOS, reported on a survey he had done on the Spink area. He estimated that there were 700 cows in the area owned by 70 farmers, the owner of the old creamery was prepared to let it out at a nominal rent and that the machinery for the unit would cost £500. At a meeting on 13 July 1934, two letters from Dr. Kennedy, of the IAOS, were read. The IAOS chief executive disapproved of the Society "having anything to do with Spink without obtaining share capital in the area". However there was also a letter from the Department which intimated that they had no objection to granting a licence. The committee discussed the issue at length before deciding to go ahead with the installation of a cold separating unit at Spink.

In a report to the IAOS secretary, dated 24 July 1934, Mr. Fant, the engineer, indicated that the owner of the old creamery intended keeping a portion of the building for his own use. He intended retailing millstuffs and similar goods. "This of course precludes Donaghmore Society doing business other than separated milk and will prevent shareholders and suppliers of future Spink branch from receiving the same service by way of purchases of millstuffs. There is the possibility of friction in this arrangement", he wrote. The Donaghmore committee were satisfied with the arrangement, however. A lease of the premises was proposed at £24 per annum with a provision to sublet the portion not required back to the owner, Mr. McDonnell. Mr. Fant advised Mr. Kelly that the well at Spink had been sunk about the year 1902 and that it was deepened to 28 feet in the following year. Attempts to get an increase in water from the well had failed.

The milk supply from the Donaghmore fringe areas was but part of Ballyragget Creameries' problems. Its very viability was at issue. Pat Courtney advised the IAOS of a meeting he had had with Mr. Hayes, manager of Castlecomer Creamery.[1] Apparently Mr. Courtney had posed the question of Castlecomer acquiring Ballyragget. Mr. Hayes stated definitively that he would not take "a present" of Ballyragget should the Dairy Disposal Co. buy it from the Society and offer it for sale. There was not sufficient milk for Ballyragget and if the Department gave a licence to Donaghmore to open an auxiliary at Spink, the Ballyragget situation would be hopeless. Courtney also related that Mr. Hayes was very resentful "at Donaghmore people coming into his district and blames the IAOS for not

1. In a letter dated 10 September 1934 (National Archives).

acquainting him in time and for not opposing the licence". Courtney added: "Although he paid me special sub, he stated that when the Donaghmore people put a creamery at Spink, he would cart away every gallon of milk which he could obtain in the district to his own creameries. I understand his committee are even holding stronger views". The IAOS apologised to Castlecomer Society for not advising them of the Spink licence application in a letter to Capt. R.H. Wandesforde, Castlecomer House, dated 17 September 1934.

Courtney reported that he had also called at Freshford. Neither the president, Very Rev. Canon Bowe, nor the manager, Mr. Maher, had shown any interest in acquiring Ballyragget until he informed them that Kilkenny would likely buy it in any case. Kilkenny was not interested but Courtney advised the IAOS secretary that "I believe the only possibility of selling Ballyragget is by trading on the rivalry between Freshford and Kilkenny".

The manager, Mr. Grogan, reported to the October 1934 meeting that Mr. Courtney of the IAOS together with a member of the Ballyragget committee had visited him recently, keen to discuss the proposed development at Spink. The Donaghmore committee was not in the mood for a parley, however, and decided once again to go ahead with the project. At the November meeting, there was a proposal from Mr. Kirwan to postpone the project for some months "to see how the prospects in the dairy industry would fare in that time". Most members felt, however, that the Spink project should go ahead in the interest of protecting Raheen.

Although the Society had sealed the lease on the Spink premises in the spring of 1935, work on alteration was halted because of a dispute over who was to be responsible for the repairs and upkeep of the roof. It was proposed that the lessor, Mr. McDonnell, should be solely responsible for the first ten years of occupation, after which time the responsibility was to be shared equally by McDonnell and the Society.

There were 'numerous replies' to the advertisement placed in the newspapers for the manager's position at Spink, the April 1935 meeting was informed. Three names were short-listed by the committee and following comments on the applications from the IAOS, the final selection was left with Mr. Galbraith and Mr. Kelly.

The appointment of Mr. O'Leary was confirmed at the May meeting. His salary was pitched at 45/- per week. Orders were given to open the Spink branch on Monday, 13 May. The appointment of a helper there was left in the hands of the committee members from the Raheen area. Mr. Galbraith told the May meeting of a provisional agreement with Spink suppliers that they would not be charged more than a halfpenny per gallon for cartage as this was the price charged by Ballyragget. A resolution was passed at the June meeting, thanking W.J. Hande, P.J. Wall, John Seale and S. Copely "for the splendid assistance they have given in organising a milk supply for our Spink branch". At the August meeting, Bernard (Ben) Moran was appointed helper at Spink at the rate of 2/6 "per working day". For the following forty years, he was to play a key role in shaping the future of Spink branch.

The Ballyragget boundary affair

Allegations that Ballyragget Creamery was "poaching" milk supplies from the Raheen area was the cause of considerable friction throughout the early thirties. In May 1933, the IAOS had relayed a complaint from the Ballyragget Creamery of poaching by Donaghmore. Kelly responded on 12 June: 'In case any misunderstanding should arise ... I wish to point out our lorry did not collect any milk outside our registered area. I am unable to vouch for Ballyragget in this regard'.

The June 1934 meeting heard of encroachment by Ballyragget Creamery in the Raheen area. Mr. Galbraith had complained in a letter to Kelly that Ballyragget was collecting milk from four non-shareholders and charging them less for cartage. This was an unfair advantage, he pointed out.

In 1935, hostilities broke out again and this time the IAOS was caught up in the cross-fire. The rivalry between the creameries was spurred on, no doubt, by the decision of Donaghmore to open an auxiliary in Spink. In March, Mr. Galbraith informed the meeting that Ballyragget Creamery was sending a lorry to collect milk within three miles of Raheen. He said that such persons as supply them with milk should not be asked to become shareholders with Donaghmore.

The issue provoked a long discussion at the August 1935 meeting. The IAOS came in for heavy criticism and the question of payment of their subscription was raised. The IAOS official, in his report, explained: "One member of the committee, Mr. Herbert Thompson, wanted to know what were the functions of the IAOS and of what use was this body to Donaghmore Society. Another member (Mr. Howard) read a draft letter he was thinking of sending to the Dublin papers complaining of the Department's system of levying creameries (who are not large exporters of butter) ... the conclusion of the letter being in the nature of a query inquiring what the IAOS and the ICMA were doing to remedy things (the exorbitant price charged for butter and the uneconomic prices to suppliers of milk). Mr. Galbraith indulged in an attack on the IAOS for not compelling Ballyragget to discontinue what he termed poaching and canvassing for milk in the Raheen Auxiliary areas; further that the IAOS was giving every assistance to Ballyragget Creamery and none to Donaghmore." In proof of this, he quoted press reports of the Ballyragget AGM (which noted) votes of thanks (to the IAOS) "for assistance rendered".

Ballyragget Co-operative Creamery raised the temperature of the debate in a letter to the IAOS intimating that a resolution had been unanimously passed at a special general meeting which read as follows: "The following townslands be included in the Society's registered area – Moate, Boolabeg, Spink, Graigue, Graigueahown, Garryglass, Derryfore and Boolahown. The Society has requested that the IAOS be asked to put same in order."[2]

The IAOS responded as follows: "I am doubtful whether meeting of 12 August was in order. (Pity we were not consulted). Consent of the IAOS must be obtained. I need not remind you that the question of area, as it affects your Society, arises out of a certain degree of competition between Ballyragget and Donaghmore Societies and apart altogether from the regularity of the meeting ... it now falls to IAOS to decide whether your Society's registered area shall be amended in the manner desired or otherwise."[3]

The letter also sought a meeting between the belligerent parties to agree on common ground. The Donaghmore committee had agreed to such a meeting and suggested Maryborough as the venue at their August meeting. This suggestion was dismissed by Ballyragget in a reply dated 18 November 1935: "The Society

2. Signed by the Ballyragget Co-op secretary, Michael O'Reilly, on 10 October 1935. (National Archives).
3. The assistant secretary of the IAOS in a letter to Ballyragget on the 16 October 1935 (National Archives).

are of the opinion that this procedure should have been resorted to last year before Spink branch was erected by Donaghmore. The committee have also intimated that they are not prepared to give up the very considerable milk supply which is drawn from the Spink area. I am to state further that my committee would be willing to meet Donaghmore Society with a view to acquiring the Spink auxiliary as this Society very strongly objects to same being within their rightful area."

The IAOS came under fire again at a meeting in Donaghmore in November. Mr. Whelan, of the IAOS, felt let down by the criticism, and especially because of lack of support for the IAOS from J.P. Kelly. In his report he said: "I pointed out that IAOS had no physical power to prevent an alleged poaching and that an amicable solution of the troubles between the two societies was turned down by Ballyragget. Furthermore, as I had to attend the Ballyragget AGM I had to bear the brunt of the attack on IAOS for what members stated was permitting Donaghmore to erect the auxiliary at Spink. The return of thanks to IAOS had no connection with above. I mentioned IAOS had declined to sanction the partial amendment of Ballyragget rules on the grounds that the amendment would overlap areas already registered in Donaghmore rules, a fact of which Mr. Kelly was already well aware. Mr. Kelly was very silent during the discussion and I felt he could have supported the IAOS." Mr. Whelan also reported that it was decided to pay a £10 subscription. The IAOS representative pointed out that Roscrea Co-operative contributed £33. He thought Donaghmore should pay at least £15.

Other matters

The secretary told the January 1935 meeting that he had paid the principle of the Department loan in full but had withheld the interest portion, pending receipt of the Department's decision on the Society's application for a reduction. A letter from the ACC requesting information on the results of a decision to institute legal proceedings against borrowers who owed more that £10 on 30 November 1934 to the Society, was read by the secretary. Mr. Kelly said he did not impart the information. After a lengthy debate, Mr. Thompson proposed: "that this committee desires to place on record their entire disapproval of the action of officials in communicating to outside sources the private transactions of the committee without its authority".

An increase in milk supplies of 12% over the previous year was reported for 1934. The proceeds of the farmers' grinding amounted to £105 for the year. If signs of an upturn in fortunes existed at Donaghmore, they were not evident in many other creameries in the south Leinster area. In a letter to the Department in February 1935, the IAOS revealed that five creameries, included among those listed on the Schedule, had closed for business because of the inadequacy of milk supplies. These were Athy, Stradbally, Carlow, Baltinglass and Edenderry. Athy belonged to the Kildare and Leix Society, which was now in liquidation. A deputation from the Scheduled Creameries met the Minister for Agriculture on 21 February. Mr. Kelly, as secretary of the Group, read the deputation's address. The Minister advised that the scheduling of creameries would not be re-enacted. In an effort to meet some of their demands, however, he assured his visitors that it was his intention to pool levies on both creamery and home-made butter, and that the Government would formulate plans to prevent escape for anyone in the production or selling of butter. He promised that he would not collect any levies on exported butter.

The AGM was held on 11 March 1935. Mr. Sheeran was in the chair. Mr. P.

Whelan represented the IAOS and fourteen members, including the secretary attended. The chairman expressed disappointment, not for the first time, at the small attendance. The balance sheet showed a healthy surplus of £483. The bad debt reserve was increased by £100.

In March, the secretary reported on his talks with the directors of Ranks Ltd. He stated that they, in conjunction with other millers, had decided not to purchase any more grain on commission. They decided that salaried officials would do this work in the future. Mr. Kelly said he had been offered, and had accepted, one of these positions. The work would run from June to January but it would not preclude him from giving a portion of his time to the Society.

Mr. Galbraith proposed that the Society supply manures to beet growers under contract and for cash. On a recommendation from the Department it was decided to provide cold storage at Coolrain. It was ordered that a new milk pump be installed for the purpose.

There was correspondence from the IAOS complaining of alleged encroachment of Donaghmore on Castlecomer Society's area. It was decided to send a deputation to meet Castlecomer representatives at Ballinakill to sort out the problem. Copies of agreement between both creameries on the boundaries issue were signed at the June meeting.

At the April meeting, Mr. Thompson raised the question of the sale of artificial manures. He pointed out that it was a violation of a promise which he and another member had given to certain traders in Rathdowney in 1926 when canvassing for shares. The secretary informed the meeting that most of the business was done in the Abbeyleix area and that sales were comparatively small. Mr. Thompson felt, that if an undertaking was given not to sell manures south of Donaghmore, it would satisfy the merchants. Mr. Kelly said that he saw no difficulty with that.

The buttermaker, Sophie Loughman, a little later in the year to become Mrs. J.P. Kelly, had a letter of resignation before the meeting. The committee voted her a £5 bonus for her dedicated service. A vote of sympathy was passed with Dr. Kennedy 'on the great loss he has sustained by the death of his wife'.

It was decided to put Mr. Butler in charge of Raheen at a wage of 3/- per day. Michael Lalor, whose brother John, had resigned and left for England, was appointed his assistant at 2/6 per day. Both men were to receive a bonus of 10/- per month from May to November. The secretary informed the meeting that he had sold the Society's car for £55, which the committee approved. Mr. Galbraith told members that Mr. Kelly would be working for Ranks Ltd. in the near future and would be unable to cope with all the work of the Society. The secretary was given permission to employ and pay a person to help him when needed.

A letter from one of the founders of the co-operative movement in Ireland and close associate of Horace Plunkett, Mr. R.A. Anderson, informed the committee of his new book, *With Horace Plunkett in Ireland.* Mr. Murphy proposed and Mr. Galbraith seconded a motion permitting the secretary to buy one copy. A Stephen Morrissey was appointed buttermaker at a salary of £2 per week. A vote of sympathy was passed, once again with Dr. Kennedy, this time on the death of his brother, the late John Kennedy.

The secretary read the regulations regarding the Department's scheme for marketing butter and emphasised that those creameries who participated were obtaining 3/- per cwt. more for their butter on an increased bounty. The manager, Mr. Grogan, reported that seventeen boxes of butter had been refused export owing to loose moisture. The secretary, Mr. Kelly, was presented with a cheque (amount not disclosed) on the occasion of his recent marriage.

There was a letter before the November meeting from the Department demanding payment of principal and interest on loans due to the sum of £618-5-1. It was ordered that the principal be paid when monies due from the beet manure and seed wheat schemes were received.

Numerous applications from shareholders asking for time to pay their instalments were received for the December meeting. Sympathy was expressed with the family of the late Mr. Collier, who had been an agent for the creamery. Mr. John Cavanagh, Derryduff, Coolrain, was appointed in his place.

The annual report for 1935 showed that supplies of milk to Donaghmore and Coolrain were down while the Raheen branch showed a marked increase from the 1934 figure. Price for milk at 4.5d per gallon was a slight improvement on the previous year although they received a halfpenny per lb less for butter returned. The prices were regarded as satisfactory and bore favourable comparison 'with any creamery in the Saorstat working under similar conditions'. The report indicated that a small meal and manure store was in the course of construction at Raheen. It was also reported that the steam engine at Coolrain was being replaced by a modern crude oil engine and it was estimated that the "renewal will save its cost in four years". The minutes noted that there was an attendance of 9.3 persons at each meeting during the year.

The old mill in Donaghmore village.

CHAPTER EIGHT

Raheen and Spink
Proving their Worth

The AGM on 9 March 1936 heard that the Society had handled 464,000 gallons of milk in 1935, an increase of 64,000 on the previous year, the chairman reported.[1] The new Spink auxiliary was already proving its worth, while there was also an increase in supply of milk at Raheen. Mr. Riddell commented on the liquid assets of the Society which exceeded the liabilities by £300, thus showing a healthy position. He was pleased to note that the committee had always adopted a conservative policy regarding prices paid and had a sound financial position. He stressed that any profits made in the Society were for the benefit of the suppliers and shareholders. A committee of management meeting was then held and Mr. Sheeran was unanimously re-elected chairman for 1936-37. Mr. Galbraith was elected vice-chairman. Mr. Sheeran, expressed regret that he had been unable to attend all meetings in 1935 but expressed appreciation to Mr Galbraith for his dedication – "he even cycled 16 miles to a meeting in the middle of winter". Following a letter from the IAOS, it was decided to subscribe one guinea to the memorial to the memory of George Russell (AE).

At the November 1936 meeting a letter from the IAOS explained why carriers' plates were being refused to private individuals: "… The underlying principle of the Road Traffic Act is to divert traffic to the Railway Company. Where the Railway Co. offer a service at a reasonable rate, the Minister will not issue a licence to anyone else in competition with the Company, unless by agreement with the Company. I understand that the Railway Co. has offered to cart milk for your Society at the rate of one penny per gallon, and I take it that this would be a satisfactory arrangement. But at some later date the Railway Company may say that they cannot make the business pay at that rate and raise it. In such a case there would be a good case for consideration by the Minister (for issuing a carrier's plate to a private operator). While the Act is intended to help the Railway Co., it is not intended to give the Company a monopoly at any cost."[2]

Mr. Galbraith, at the January 1937 meeting, presented his findings on cartage costs at the different branches. It was apparent that the cost of collecting milk at Donaghmore and Coolrain was excessive and, with this in mind, he proposed "the

1. Chairman Mr. Edward Sheeran presided. The following members were present:- Rev. C. Bergin, C.C., Mr. George Galbraith, P.J. Murphy, Michael Kirwan, Joseph Bergin, R.C. Howard, John Treacy, J.S. Cooper, Timothy Fitzpatrick, Richard Wallace, R.F. Bennett, John Hennessy, Michael Hogan, William Bergin, Roderick McEvoy, Thomas Mitchell, Patrick Kavanagh, John Delaney, Stephen Campion and John Morahan. Mr. C.C. Riddell of the IAOS was in attendance.
2. In a letter from the IAOS to Donaghmore Co-op dated 11 December 1936 (National Archives).

Joe Butler was manager at Raheen Creamery from early 1930s.

carters at present delivering milk to Donaghmore on a fixed daily rate be given the option of continuing there at the rate of one penny per gallon. If they do not accept the figure, the secretary is hereby instructed to approach the Railway Co. with a view to getting the work done at a price not exceeding one penny per gallon and to make all necessary arrangements. This would apply to Coolrain also on the expiry of the Society's existing contract with Mr. Pratt."

At the February meeting it was noted that the carters Mitchell and Shanahan had been "warned by the guards" of the likelihood of an early prosecution for carting milk to Donaghmore.

A letter from the Railway Company was read at the March 1938 meeting which indicated that it was uneconomic for them to collect milk from the Spink area. They proposed working on a mileage basis but the committee heard that this would increase the cost to the Society by 100%. It was decided to discuss matters with officials at Kingsbridge and, if not successful, they would bring the matter to the attention of the Minister for Industry and Commerce.

In May, the Railway Co. informed the Society that they would be charging 8d per mile for the collection of milk from 27 June and demanded £4-15-0 for Sunday work. The committee felt it would make more sense to operate their own transport and purchased a lorry for £322. Joseph Duigan of Barney was appointed driver. He was strictly forbidden from carrying passengers and other rules were drawn up.

The meeting was told that the Spink supply could be increased by 100 gallons per day if haulage arrangements were made. It was decided to purchase a second lorry to accommodate this. The purchase of the lorry was financed through the sale of a portion of the Society's holdings in Rank's Ltd and Rank's Ireland Ltd. Preference shares in Rank's Ltd were sold for £69-13-0. They had been purchased for £65. The second lorry was duly purchased and earned a profit of over £1 per day on each of the first 7 days of its use.

Milling, Store and Grain Trade Vital to Survival

The annual report for the year ending December 1936 revealed that assets exceeded liabilities by £472. Milk supplies showed a decline of 127,637 gallons. In the previous year, supplies had been down by 30,000 which was a situation that was deplored at the time. "Comment on our part, therefore (on this year's returns) is futile. The price paid for milk was 4.25d per gallon, which was the highest price since 1930. The modern diesel engine at Coolrain had accounted for a saving of £50 and it was the intention of the committee to make similar alterations at Raheen."

The report commented: "Without the milling, store and grain trade it would be utterly impossible for us to carry on the creamery side of the business ..." There was an appeal for more support from members. Cash flow, in the short-term, was a problem. The secretary was instructed to obtain an overdraft on the Society's current account not exceeding £1000. With regard to the collection of share money, it was agreed that legal action be taken against any person refusing to pay money due on shares.

The February 1937 meeting heard that the estimated cost of alterations and additions to machinery at Raheen was £200. It was decided that the scheme of improvements there be carried out. However, on the recommendation of the Inspector a few weeks later, the work was deferred until the end of the year.

A special meeting was held on 8 March 1937 to discuss costs at the different branches. Following a long discussion, it was decided to dispense with the services of the manager at Coolrain, Mr. Brennan. That auxiliary was to be worked on the same basis as Raheen. The committee also examined the possibility of the Society purchasing pigs on a commission basis.

The AGM was held on the same day, 8 March, at which Mr. Sheeran presided.[3] The auditor's report stressed the fact that, if all the Society's debts were paid and all accounts due to the Society collected, there would be £620 remaining to give back to the shareholders (excluding the value of machinery and buildings). Taking everything into consideration, he complimented the committee, the secretary and the manager "on the position achieved since the Society's inception 10 years ago". He added: "Many creameries started about the same time have gone down with the tide, while Donaghmore has flown the flag of success and flown it high. But were it not for the activities of the Society other than the handling of milk, the position would not be so satisfactory." He alluded to the turnover in agricultural goods and milling and appealed to all present and all the milk suppliers to purchase their seeds and manures and sell their grain through the Society.

The secretary complained that matters discussed at committee meetings were being broadcast to the general public. He regretted that there was not a greater spirit of loyalty among members.

At the March 1937 meeting, one of the topics of debate was an application from the local Fianna Fail cumann to hold a dance on the premises. The secretary was instructed to ascertain from the Parish Priest whether the Committee would be liable to incur the censure of the ecclesiastical authority by their action in allowing the dance to go ahead. The response was revealed at the April meeting. The committee were advised that allowing such a function on the premises "would indeed incur the censure of the local clergy".

Interim accounts showed a loss of £172 for the period to August 1937. Mr

3. Those in attendance were Messrs R F Bennett, Joseph Bergin, Stephen Campion, Timothy Fitzpatrick, George Galbraith, John Hennessy, R C Howard, Patrick Kavanagh, Thomas Mitchell, P.J. Murphy, Roderick McEvoy, Joseph Thompson, John Treacy and Richard Wallace. Mr. P. Whelan represented the IAOS.

Phelan said that the area that needed the most attention was the question of credit, which was too high with regard to store goods. He suggested that the committee keep the bank overdraft as low as possible, and emphasised that the balance sheet at the end of the year should show a profit, even if it was only a small one.

Two cases of faulty seed wheat, which was supplied by the Society to growers, Bennett and Austin, were reported. The Society contacted the importer, who refused responsibility. The secretary advised the committee that the Society could not compensate the grower and recover from the importer without a Court Order. The claim was passed on to Warnocks who offered £8 in settlement of Austin's claim for faulty seed. Austin would not accept the offer and subsequently Warnock's withdrew their offer completely. At the December 1938 meeting, the secretary expressed appreciation for the way IAWS dealt with the compensation for faulty 'Red Marvel' seed that had been supplied by them.

In February 1938, a summons was received from the Chief State Solicitor for the non-payment of £1,084-12-8 due on foot of loans of £3,576 from the Department. The secretary recommended an immediate payment of £169 (£100 for principal and £69 for interest) and a similar payment in the following month. This was endorsed by the committee and the IAOS were informed. The IAOS pleaded with the Department to accept the offer: "As you are aware, the Society has been carrying on under considerable difficulty and I would suggest that you give a favourable consideration to these proposals." The Department relented and said they would withdraw the threat of prosecution, providing the Society made an immediate payment of £169 and a further £200 by June 1938.[4] It was agreed to accept these conditions. There were further demands from the Department and new arrangements agreed in the years that followed.

Coolrain Closed

The annual audit was completed in time for the February 1938 meeting. The balance sheet showed a profit of £119 for 1937 on a turnover of £8,271 for dairy produce and £4,712 for other business.

At the AGM, Mr. Sheeran commented that the price paid for milk was higher than in any year since 1930 but, despite this, the supply had fallen. The Society's position was difficult in that a large percentage of the milk supply had to be carted by hired transport and this cost had to be borne by suppliers and the Society.[5]

The importance of the store business was once again stressed, especially the grinding of corn, and members were asked to give their continued and increasing support for these operations. "Without the milling store and the grain trade, it would be utterly impossible for us to carry on the creamery side of the business on present supplies," the chairman stated.

In July 1938, it was agreed to take in wheat at the Donaghmore premises and it was to be paid for by the Society at the increased commission of 6d per barrel. An overdraft of a further £1000 was arranged to purchase the grain.

4. In a letter dated 28 February 1938 (National Archives).
5. At the Annual General Meeting on 7 March 1938, Edward Sheeran presided and the following members were in attendance: Messrs R.C. Howard, Joseph Bergin, P. Kavanagh, John Hennessy, G. Galbraith, W. Bergin, R. McEvoy, T. Mitchell, M. Kirwan, S. Campion, T. Fitzpatrick, Jacob Thompson and P.J. Murphy. Mr. P. Whelan of the IAOS, the manager and the secretary were also in attendance. The balance sheet showed that the liquid assets exceeded liabilities by £1000. At the committee meeting which followed the AGM, Mr. Sheeran was re-appointed chairman and Mr. Galbraith re-appointed vice-chairman.

In June 1938, it was decided to suspend the separation of milk at Coolrain and that the lorry should go to Prescott's Cross to receive milk from the suppliers for transmission to Donaghmore. The services of the employees at the Branch were terminated on 18 November. In May 1939, the question of re-opening Coolrain branch was discussed but the decision was adjourned.

At the September 1939 meeting, the committee decided to close Coolrain as and from 16th of the month and issued instructions that no further collection of milk from the area take place. The oil engine was to be removed from Coolrain and brought to Raheen. Mr. Fant reported to the IAOS that he regretted the decision to close the auxiliary. He felt that there was good land around the area which, he believed, should be capable of producing a milk supply for the Branch.

Fall in Milk Supplies a Continuing Worry

Only two members, J. Bergin and P. Kavanagh, turned up for the usual monthly meeting on 9 January 1939. Pat Whelan of the IAOS was also present. Despite the lack of a quorum, the secretary insisted on fixing the milk price. It was settled at 6d per gallon.

In February. the secretary was selected to represent the Society at an IAOS conference and he was asked to seek a better price for butter. Suggestions were to be made to the Agricultural Commission by way of the IAOS to include:

1. a stop in the export of in-calf heifers and cows,
2. more attention be paid by the Department to ravages being caused by Contagious Abortion and
3. that the subsidy on fertilisers be increased to 25% of their cost ex factory.

The question of an extension to Raheen store was discussed. It was said that great trade could be done in coal if the accommodation was available.

At the AGM in March, Mr. Ribton of the IAOS dwelt forcibly on the fall in milk supplies and asked members to do everything in their power to increase the supply.[6]

At the July l939 meeting, the secretary referred to the purchase of grain for the coming season. He also said that the existing method of elevating grain was too slow. He suggested the employment of an accountant for the 12 to 14 weeks of the grain season. It was decided to leave the arrangements in the hands of the secretary and manager.

At the August meeting, it was decided to contribute two guineas to the R.A. Anderson (IAOS President) Testimonial. An examination of the Society's accounts for the 7 months "found everything to be satisfactory". A loss of £217-10-0 was recorded for the first six months of the year.

Mr. Kelly wrote to Mr. Fant seeking information on the purchase and installation of an electric hoist. He required to know the lifting capacity, the type of goods compatible for use with the hoist and details of the electric current required to operate the hoist. Information was received in September that electric pulley blocks,

---

6. At the Annual General Meeting on 6 March 1939, Edward Sheeran presided and the following were in attendance:- M/s P. J. Murphy, M. Kirwan, Jacob Thompson, Joseph Bergin, Patrick Kavanagh, John Hennessy, Martin Carroll, S. Campion, Thomas Mitchell, T. McDonald, George Galbraith, R. McEvoy. Mr. Ribton of the IAOS was also in attendance. At the committee meeting which followed, Mr. Sheeran was re-elected chairman for the coming year while Mr Galbraith was re-elected vice chairman.

required for the hoist in the grain store, were held up in Dublin Docks due to "the situation in Europe", and awaiting the necessary paperwork to be completed.[7] The "situation in Europe" referred to was, of course, the outbreak of World War II.

The difficulty of trading in war conditions was explained by the secretary at the December meeting. He dealt especially with the necessity of acquiring stocks of certain goods on a cash basis. This would lead to the depletion of cash at hand at the bank, he said. It was decided to seek an overdraft at the bank to a maximum of £2,200.

Secretary's plan for wheat purchase

At the August 1939 meeting, a report was presented by the secretary, J.P. Kelly, regarding the whole question of wheat purchase. "… I have come into possession of certain information which may seriously affect the status of this Society. I learn that it is the ultimate intention of the Millers' Association to place the buying of the entire wheat crop in the hands of about a dozen large firms throughout the country. This change may come next year or in 1941, but my informant assures me that come it will."

"For reasons, which must be obvious to you, I do not wish this information to be broadcast throughout the country nor to have my name mentioned as its author. It is most useful information and to be forewarned is to be forearmed … The only effective way of dealing with the situation is to throw our weight about and say we are going to be one of these twelve firms. How can we do it? By increasing our quantity to 20,000 barrels or thereabouts … In my position, I have the control of large quantities of wheat. I can put as much of this wheat, as I possibly can, through the Society's book whether it be 5,000 or 12,000 barrels; it must be definitely understood, here and now, that the Society is not entitled to the commission which will be paid on such quantity.

"I am responsible for the various charges in connection with the purchase of this wheat … Working on this system, if nothing very unforeseen occurs, I hope to be able to make the Society's figures far above those of any registered dealer hereabouts." Kelly asked for a resolution to be passed to confirm the Society's agreement to his terms. It was unanimously decided that the scheme outlined by the secretary be adopted.

7. Letter from an R.S. White dated 6 September, to the IAOS (National Archives).

SECTION ONE

PART THREE

The 1940s

INTRODUCTION

The Emergency and its Aftermath

The uneasy political situation that had ignited into military conflict in 1939, quickly engulfed Europe and, soon, the world was at war. This country remained neutral, the war years in Ireland becoming known as the "Emergency". These were years of special enabling legislation, of scarcity of every conceivable item of use in the home, farm or factory.

To add to the misery of the rural community, there was a Foot-and-Mouth outbreak in 1941, which severely restricted movement not only of livestock but also of people. There was a scarcity of motor fuel, which cut down vehicle movements. And even the use of a bicycle, with the shortage of tyres and spare parts, became a luxury.

The shortage of food was, however, an even bigger problem than mobility. Bread was rationed, as were most other foodstuffs, including butter, tea and sugar. Regulations were issued for compulsory tillage, which created particular difficulties for farmers in non-arable areas where suitable implements and expertise were lacking. What became apparent was that the people who prepared the legislation knew little about soil fertility or the cropping potential of land. A huge area of land (over 600,000 acres) was set aside for wheat and yields were often no more than 0.5 ton per acre. The produce was low quality and the resulting bread almost inedible. The health of the population deteriorated and, by 1946, tuberculosis had reached epidemic proportions.

Apart from the horrific bloodshed of World War II, international trade had been brought almost to a halt and economic activity languished in the trail of the military and political turmoil. Ireland was slowly getting on the move again when another disaster struck – and with great speed. This time, it was Mother Nature that struck the heavy blows, hitting particularly the already hard-pressed farming community. The arctic conditions that descended upon the country in the early months of 1947 were unprecedented in their length and intensity. These months of ice and snow were followed by the worst summer in living memory. It was another national emergency as city and town folk joined hands with their country cousins in a desperate bid to save the crops and salvage the harvest.

Creameries struggled to survive as milk supplies dipped. Donaghmore was hit similarly to elsewhere but the biggest challenge faced by the Society there was in keeping the hatchery sufficiently warm during the long arctic spell which caused havoc with the electric current on which the operation depended. Management and staff improvised ways and means of keeping the incubations warm and the thousands of fragile chicks therein safe. It was another instance of the remarkable adaptability and durability of the personnel that sustained Donaghmore over so many critical periods in its colourful history.

The dairy industry was slow to regain the export market it had lost in the difficult war years. The dreadful weather of 1947 was an added setback. Although milk supplies remained low in the immediate post-war years, it was during this time, however, that the base was laid for a recovery in dairy exports in the years that followed. Improved livestock breeds, and more concentrated use of fertiliser on pasture land, eventually helped to reap the dividends of improved milk supply and, by the end of the decade, supplies began to increase rapidly.

Rapid progress was also made in rural electrification after 1948. The advent of electricity to rural homes and farmyards opened up a new future for the long-pressed farmer. It facilitated the use of milking machines on a widespread scale and led to increased efficiency, particularly on dairy farms.

CHAPTER ONE

Store Trade Keeps Creamery Alive

At the AGM in March 1940, the auditor's report pointed out that, were it not for the store trade, which had been substantially increased, there would be no creamery because of the very small milk supply.[1] The figures verify how important the store trade now was to the Society. Dairy products accounted for £6,647 in turnover for 1939, compared to £80,648 in store trade.

W.J. Ryan, of Fitzsimon and Ryan Solicitors, Abbeyleix, was formally appointed solicitor to the Society in place of Mr. T. J. Fletcher, who had retired.

The secretary wrote to Mr. Ebrill of the IAOS on 2 July regarding the installation of a Bamford Grinder at Raheen. Ebrill replied that he had heard that there was no Bamford 4C Mill in the country but he understood delivery would be almost guaranteed within 14 days "Hitler Volente".

There was a notice of resignation from P.J. O'Leary, manager of the Spink branch, before the July meeting. Billy Wallis was appointed in his place at the August meeting. His pay was fixed at 50/- per week. Mr. Wallis was later to become general manager of Donaghmore Co-op and was the person responsible for managing the development of the shops and stores business, which were becoming such a major contributor to the overall operation.

At the August meeting, it was decided to test the old gas tanks before refilling them. In September, an application was received from Supt. Keyes seeking permission to use Coolrain Creamery for the purpose of lectures for the Local Security Force (LSF) in the area and an application for similar use of premises at Donaghmore. The request for Coolrain was acceded to, but Donaghmore was refused as the premises were in use. Regarding an application from the Timahoe LSF for use of lorry to carry passengers to Stradbally, the secretary advised members that their insurance would not allow it. It was decided to introduce a levy of half a penny per gallon of milk carted at Spink. In his report of the meeting to the IAOS, Mr. Whelan confirmed the employment of a lady Creamery Manager (Miss Fitzgerald) at Central to assist temporarily during the grain season. A resolution was read from Mitchelstown Creamery regarding the use of grain for animal feed rather than for human consumption.

---

1. The Annual General Meeting of 1940 was held on 11 March. Edward Sheeran presided and others present included M/s Joseph Bergin, Galbraith, Howard, Hennessy, Kirwan, Kavanagh, Murphy, McEvoy, Thompson, Treacy, J Moylan, Campion, McGaughy and J. Carroll. Mr. P. Whelan represented the IAOS. The chairman expressed his regret at having to close Coolrain but pointed out that there was little or no milk available in the area. He also pointed out the difficulty of trading under war conditions but said that all concerned had done well. Mr. O'Leary, Spink was specially thanked for his work through the year. Mr. Sheeran was re-elected chairman and Mr. Galbraith was returned as vice chairman.

At the October 1940 meeting, a discussion took place on the conserving of butter supplies. It was decided to leave the matter in the hands of the manager and secretary. In November, it was decided to supply millstuffs and other goods to Spink suppliers direct from Raheen. Sub-committees, to work in conjunction with the managers, were formed at Donaghmore and Raheen with P. Kavanagh and J. Bergin appointed at Donaghmore and G. Galbraith and R. McEvoy at Raheen.

IAOS praise

The assistant secretary of the IAOS, in February 1941, acknowledged the contribution of £10 from Donaghmore. The letter was addressed to W. Grogan, Manager, Donaghmore, and not to the secretary, J.P. Kelly, to whom correspondence was usually addressed. It read: "…It is very gratifying for us to receive the committee's expression of appreciation of the services rendered to the Society by the IAOS. Your Society's loyalty and support are no less appreciated by the IAOS. This mutual feeling of goodwill is just as it should be between the parent organisation and one of its members. Were this only more widespread, if not universal, the co-operative movement in the country would be in a much stronger position, not only financially but morally. We congratulate you on the result of your work for 1940. You have done consistently well for the Donaghmore Society, whose success and present position are so largely due to your efforts and devotion to duty …"

Because of the difficulty in obtaining coal supplies, it was decided in February 1941 to restrict sales and to sell to regular customers only. Due to petrol restrictions and the difficulty in forming a quorum at meetings because of the fuel shortage, it was decided that members from Raheen should hire one car to take them to meetings.

At the AGM of 1941, the chairman spoke of the previous year's trading, which he described as a difficult one.[2] In spite of reduced milk supplies and the difficulty in obtaining most of their agricultural requisites, the Society had a successful year. At the committee meeting that followed the AGM, Mr Galbraith was appointed Chairman after a vote against Mr. Sheeran on a result of 7 to 5. Mr. Sheeran was offered vice-chairmanship but declined to accept the position. Mr. Treacy was appointed vice-chairman. The secretary said that, in view of serious position regarding petrol supplies, he had provisionally ordered a Producer Gas Plant of the Sentinel type for the Raheen lorry at a cost of £150.

Turf shortage

There was a discussion on turf shortage at the April 1941 meeting. It was decided to write to Bord na Mona, Clonsast, for information and to collect local data on the turf situation. The milk price was set at 7d per gallon. The secretary reported that Ben Moran had resigned from his position in Spink because, it seemed that, the money he was earning was less than his family had to pay another worker to work in his place at home. It was decided to offer Moran 4/- per day. The meeting was told that the Producer Gas Plant was held up at Liverpool, owing to an embargo against their export – but there was still a possibility of getting it through.

2. The Annual General Meeting of 1941 was held on 10 March. Mr. Sheeran presided and the members present were Messrs. Bennett, Wm Bergin, Joseph Bergin, George Galbraith, T. Mitchell, S. Campion, John Moylan, John Doherty, Martin Brennan, R. McEvoy, P. McDonald and John Treacy. Mr. Whelan, representing the IAOS, was also present.

It finally arrived in June. The Society was currently receiving enough petrol to run lorries for three days a week. This ration would not be increased in the months ahead, which would mean that it would be very difficult for the Society to operate during the summer period, the secretary warned.

The question of turf shortage was again discussed at the May 1941 meeting. Four loads had been purchased. Four perches had been allotted to the creamery adjacent to Raheen at 5/- per perch. It was agreed to purchase 50 tons of turf at the lowest possible price under 35/- per ton delivered to the creamery. To conserve petrol, the secretary had personally brought the cream from the auxiliaries on several occasions, thus saving two gallons of petrol per day. He was commended for his work. There was a report of the alleged discovery of the forge, which had been stolen from Coolrain thirteen years previously. Identification was the difficulty.

Foot-and-Mouth disease had now a firm hold in Laois, and Spink Creamery was closed for a short time to enable certain precautionary measures to be carried out. The premises were re-opened on 4 August.

In July, it was revealed that 120 tons of turf had been saved on the bog at Raheen. It was proposed that the purchase of turf be left in the hands of the secretary and the manager. It was also suggested that members of staff be supplied with lorry loads of turf at a little over cost price plus transport. It was ordered that no coal be sold and that turf be sold only to old coal customers.

A letter from the Munster and Leinster Bank was read at the September meeting, notifying members of an increase in their half-yearly charge by 3000%. The minutes record that "deep indignation was felt at this iniquitous proceeding". The secretary reported on the grain position and it was proposed that the Society join the Irish Grain Traders Association and pay the entrance fee of £2-2-0.

At the October meeting in 1941, it was decided that a letting agreement should be drawn up with the LDF in Coolrain. It was decided to let the premises at 5/- per week for two nights weekly. Following a meeting with the LDF, it was further agreed to allow them to make certain internal alterations to the building, including the removal of an internal partition. The secretary said he felt that the purchase of another lorry for grain traffic had been warranted and accordingly had purchased one for £160. This was approved. The use of the lorry would net the Society £12 in earnings weekly, it was estimated.

In November, the secretary stated that it would be necessary to increase the Society's overdraft in the bank, as the Society was currently holding increased stocks including wheat, butter, fuel and sundry other items. It was agreed to write to the bank seeking an increase of £1000 on the overdraft. As Foot-and-Mouth disease regulations had been suspended, it was expected that the Society would have a large quantity of turf for sale. It was noted that the Parish Council had obtained a grant for the repair of the bog road. The question of Sutton's flour quota was discussed and the manager was instructed to demand ration cards from Sutton's customers before supplying them with flour.

CHAPTER TWO

Pressures from the Bank

The secretary had reported at the December 1941 meeting that the Society had gone over its bank overdraft level by £938 and that the bank manager "was making things unpleasant". It had been decided to look into other banks and see if the Society could get an overdraft of £4000 for six months and £2200 for the remaining six months.

Mr. Whelan reported to the IAOS in February 1942, that the overdraft at the bank at 31 December 1941 was £3,757 as compared to £1,440 for the end of December 1940. £1,800 of this was, however, a temporary overdraft for the purchase of grain. The overdraft limit was £4,000 and the bank manager was pressing for a substantial lodgement. He also reported that a member of the committee had stated that the bank manager "in a recent conversation, which was supposed to be private, criticised working expenses, the small profits returned and the general activities of the Society, meaning, it is believed, the store business, which is envied by the shopkeepers of Rathdowney". Whelan revealed that J.P. Kelly had been in touch with the National Bank at Athy about accepting the Society's account, and about security if required. He also noted: "I understand the directors of the Royal Bank of Ireland turned down the application put through by their manager of the Rathdowney branch, who by the way was in favour of securing the account."

On receipt of correspondence from the Munster and Leinster Bank, the secretary was instructed, at the May meeting, to apply for an overdraft accommodation of £2200 until 1 November and £4000 from 1 November to 30 April. At the June meeting, it was decided to write to the Bank Manager requesting overdraft arrangements to be made in advance as the current situation with the bank was considered unsatisfactory.

A deal was agreed with Miss Dugdale, in January 1942, for the purchase of her interest in the mill buildings, as well as the yards and houses adjoining, for the sum of £150. With regard to the utilisation of the mill premises, it was decided to dismantle and sell the premises at the far side of the river.

The committee heard of problems with the Raheen gas lorry which seemed to be giving an inordinate amount of trouble. However, it was reported at the February 1942 meeting that the lorry was working much more satisfactorily and that there had been no more breakdowns. The lorry driver, Brennan, resigned and Michael Lalor was appointed in his stead on probation. Drivers were warned regarding the carrying of passengers and taking intoxicating drink.

With regard to the distribution of manure, it was ordered that all purchases of manure be made out according to the 1940 level and from thence an equitable distribution of the quota be made. A sub-committee of chairman, secretary and manager, along with P. Kavanagh and J. Bergin was set up to look after distribution.

The Society was advised that it was entitled to 15 tons of artificial manure. The distribution of this was to be left in the hands of the sub-committee.

At the AGM for 1942,[1] the secretary suggested that it would be a good idea to accept deposits from members generally. The Society could pay up to 4% interest as opposed to 1% at the bank and the Society would have the use of the money at 2% under the bank rate. The motion was passed unanimously.

With regard to the need for a clerical assistant for the office, the committee heard that for some time the secretary has been paying for assistance out of his own pocket (30/- per week in winter and £2 per week in summer). Miss Gretta Grogan had been working for him for 6 to 7 years and he felt that she deserved more than the 15/- a week he had been giving her out of his salary. Some members were surprised at the situation and proposed the secretary should be relieved of paying Miss Grogan and that she should be employed as an office assistant at £1 per week.

Copies of 'Agricultural Ireland' were posted to members. In his report to the IAOS, Mr. Whelan noted that the secretary had praised the journal and had said that the articles were "so well and lucidly written that he, a non-farmer, could follow them with interest". Mr. Whelan also commented on the success of the store and grain business. "Without these, there would be no creamery", he stated bluntly.

There was a letter from Department of Agriculture relating to the cold storage of butter. It was decided to apply for permission to store 600 boxes.

In September 1942, the secretary reported of a visit from two Department Inspectors and of their having impounded seed oats and barley. A letter followed from the Department stating that were refusing to issue a barley dealer's licence to the Society. By January 1943, however, members heard that the barley and oats had been released and the licence problem had been resolved.

Proceeds of an auction realised £320 (the minutes were not clear as to what was auctioned, possibly some machinery in the mill premises). The manager explained, at the October 1942 meeting, that the price of butter had been increased by 28/- per cwt and, in addition, 24/4 per cwt by way of subsidy. The milk price was set at 8.75d per gallon. The price of butter to suppliers was fixed at 1/9 per pound.

Kelly's views on the ideal candidate

A letter from Ranks Ltd. was read at the November 1942 meeting, intimating that, on the instructions of the Department of Industry and Commerce, they would supply the Society with a flour quota until after the Emergency.

A letter of resignation was received, in December, from Miss Gretta Grogan of the office staff. She was given £5 as a wedding present. Her sister, Kitty, applied for the position. It was decided that a male clerk be appointed at a wage of £2 per week and the position was to be advertised. The secretary, writing from Fruitlawn, Abbeyleix, to Whelan advised him of the situation. The committee wished Mr.

1. At the Annual General Meeting on 9 March 1942, chairman, Mr. Galbraith, presided and the following were also in attendance: Messrs. William Bergin, T. Mitchell, P. McDonald, R. McEvoy, J. Moylan, Michael Kirwan, R. Mitchell, J. Carroll, P. Kavanagh, S. Campion, John Doherty, John Hennessy, J. Treacy and J. Rudd. Mr. P. Whelan of the IAOS was also in attendance. The Auditor's report showed that the position of the Society was good after fifteen years in operation and that the liquid assets exceeded the liabilities by more that £1200. At the committee meeting which followed, Mr. Galbraith was re-elected chairman and Mr. Kavanagh was appointed vice-chairman.

Whelan to examine the candidates and pick one. "Nice job that!" he remarked. Kelly suggested that the IAOS official should come early on the day of the next meeting, 4 January 1943, examine the boys in the afternoon and report that evening. Kelly expressed his own views on the ideal candidate: "Apart from their clerical abilities, I consider that the following general marks should be allowed for the following items – 1. Breeding; 2. Manner; 3. Appearance; 4. General Knowledge."

In January 1943, the secretary was delegated to attend the AGM and Dinner of the Irish Native Grain Traders Association. It was decided to increase the manager's salary by £50 per annum by way of bonuses and that a weekly or monthly tenancy agreement be drawn up, whereby the Society leases him his residence at a nominal rent of £1 per annum while in the Society's employment. The tenancy agreement was sealed and witnessed at the February meeting.

It was agreed to contribute £30 to the IAOS Golden Jubilee Trust Fund. Sympathy was extended to the IAOS on the death of its president Mr. R. A. Anderson.

The February meeting heard that the profit for 1942 amounted to £811, which was seen as very satisfactory. Necessary improvements such as the partitioning of office space to which the public could have access without interfering with office work, the erection of sheds to house lorries, the erection of a small office at Raheen and the provision of a more reliable turf burning stove for Donaghmore office were approved.

At the AGM, the committee was reduced from 16 to 12 as there had been four members representing Coolrain, which was now defunct.[2]

The secretary wrote to Mr. Riddell on 2 April, advising him of an item in Stubbs' Gazette relating to the formation of a new company under the name of 'Donaghmore Dairy Co. Ltd'. The query was passed on to the Department who replied on 16 June. The reply stated that the new company referred to intended to confine its dairying business to the production and sale of liquid milk and the development of a trade in the highest grade milk. It noted that the company owns a farm at Donaghmore, near Ashbourne, Co. Meath, hence the name chosen for the company.

In April, a discussion took place on the petrol supply. The secretary informed the meeting that, for the current month, they had only been issued one quarter of their usual ration. The secretary and manager were empowered to make whatever arrangements they could in the event of there being a cessation of supply. The petrol situation had eased somewhat by July, however, and normal supplies were anticipated for a month or two.

There was a letter from the IAOS regarding the Livestock Act and its effect on milk supplies. The secretary pointed that the export of the best type of cows and heifers and retention of the "weeds" was responsible for the low milk yields around the country.

The purchase of a tractor, binder and plough for the purpose of hiring them out to farmers was approved by the committee. The cost was £340.

2. At the Annual General Meeting on 8 March 1943, Mr. Galbraith, presided with the following in attendance: William Bergin, Joseph Bergin, S. Campion, J. Doherty, P. Kavanagh, M. Kirwan, J. Hennessy, John Moylan, Joe Moylan, R. Mitchell, P. McDonald, R. McEvoy, J. Rudd and J. Treacy. Mr. Whelan of the IAOS was also in attendance. He dealt with the auditor's report and congratulated the Society on its successful working as evidenced by the sound financial position. Mr. Galbraith was re-appointed chairman and Mr. Kavanagh, vice-chairman.

The secretary reported to the July meeting that the cab of the gas lorry was in a dangerous condition and that other repairs amounting to some £200 would also have to be made. The secretary and manager decided to purchase a Fordson lorry in very good repair and have it fitted with a modern producer gas plant. They could use the old lorry for spare parts. This decision was approved by the Committee.

In September, Branch managers, Butler and Wallis, were granted an increase in wages (bonus) of 5/- per week "subject to the sanction of the Department of Industry and Commerce". John Galbraith also applied for an increase in wages. After a discussion – for which his father, George Galbraith vacated the chair – it was decided to increase his wages by £1 per week to cover overtime and extra work during the harvest season.

Rationing of butter caused concerns at the November meeting. The Government was considering introducing a rationing of butter to ½ lb per head per household per week. The minutes note that "if this goes ahead there will be a threat to supplies".

In December, the secretary brought up the question relating to the lighting of the Mill road. He said he had talked to Mr. Loughran, Assistant Engineer of the IAOS, who had given him an unofficial quotation for erecting 14 lights at a cost of approximately £50.

Following the absence without notice of an employee, it was decided in future that if an employee absented himself without the permission of the manager or secretary, he/she will be dismissed forthwith.

Labour Unrest

Union agitation was becoming a serious issue for management and the committee. A letter from the ITGWU seeking a bonus for all employees was discussed at the meeting of 5 September 1943. The secretary said that the committee could not tolerate any interference from the Transport Union in the management of a co-operative society and would not pay any attention to any communication received from that body. "The committee will, of course, deal sympathetically with applications formally made by the employees", the secretary noted.

The problem of confidentiality at meetings was raised at the October meeting. J.P. Kelly pointed out that matters discussed at meetings should be kept private and not discussed outside of meetings. There was a strong feeling among committee members that at least one from among their ranks was passing on information with the intention of stirring up trouble. It was believed that this was central to the union unrest and there were also some nasty undercurrents of a religious nature. Kelly declined to say who had spoken out of turn and a heated controversy took place at which chairman, Mr. Galbraith, said that "persons had been going around saying that the place was turned into a Protestant show". As the meeting got out of control, the chairman threatened to resign. He walked out but was followed by other members of the committee who persuaded him to return.

Among the contentious issues discussed was a letter from the ITGWU relating to holiday pay for employees. The secretary informed the meeting that he had looked up the legislation and, despite their co-operative statutes, they were compelled to give a week's holiday with pay to their employees. Therefore employees were due a week's holiday pay for every year since May 1939. It was proposed to pay employees their entitlements.

There was another controversial holiday pay problem on the agenda for the

November meeting. An employee, Stephen Morrissey, had refused to accept his wages as he had not been paid for a Church holy day on which he did not work. The committee ruled that there was to be no payment for Church holy days unless work was done. Because of the rise in the number of labour-related disputes, a sub-committee consisting of the chairman, Messrs. Kavanagh, Kirwan, Hennessy and Joe Bergin was set up to deal with problems as they arose.

In November 1943, Mr. Whelan advised the IAOS that he had cautioned Kelly on the unions and the possibility of strike action.[3] He named the committee member whom he believed was stirring up the trouble. "The member, Stephen Campion, who is causing some trouble in the affairs of the Society, did not come in until meeting was well through, having been at the Fair in Rathdowney. Just as the meeting was finished, he asked for an apology from the chairman for a remark passed at the last meeting. Mr. Galbraith assured Mr. Campion he was under a misapprehension as to what was said. Members asked Mr. Campion to overlook imaginary grievances. According to Kelly, Campion had discussed Society's affairs with a local shopkeeper who is not friendly disposed to the Society. Mr. Campion was blamed for transmitting information to some of the workers in their agitation for more wages and other demands."

It was a long winter of discontent. Bill Davin, TD,[4] wrote to Dr. Kennedy on 1 November, enclosing a letter of complaint about activities at Donaghmore from a Mr. McEvoy. Among the contentious issues raised by McEvoy were the alleged wrongful dismissal of his son, which the management claimed was a resignation, and also the refusal to sell skimmed milk to his daughter. Davin asked Kennedy to sort out the problem. "As you are, no doubt, aware this Creamery is situated in my native area and I am anxious to see the best possible relations existing between the management and workers."

Pat Courtney visited Donaghmore to investigate the complaint on 30 December 1943. In his report, Courtney claimed that "young McEvoy" was insubordinate. Kelly had found this out, however, only after McEvoy resigned as a result of a disagreement with the manager, Mr. Grogan. The manager had apparently told the Station Master at Ballybrophy not to send McEvoy on the railway lorry to cart corn for the Society. The facts of the case are somewhat vague but what is certain is that Kelly was furious with Grogan over the incident. The report tells more about the working relationship of the manager and the secretary than it does about the grounds for the McEvoy complaint. "Kelly severely reprimanded Grogan and told him not to do such a thing again unless ordered to do so by the committee. The only reason why Miss McEvoy was refused buttermilk was because none was available. Kelly said that he was not aware that McEvoy Snr. had interfered and that the Society had no connection with him. As far as Kelly was concerned, there was no vindictiveness but Grogan was bitter by nature and possibly he has been vindictive. Kelly told me but for his intervention, Grogan would have fallen foul of even committee members and has done so in one case recently.

3. In Pat Whelan's report of the meeting on 8 November 1943 to the IAOS (National Archives).
4. William (Bill) Davin was born at Grogan, Rathdowney, in 1890. He joined the clerical staff of the RMS Railway Co. in 1908 and became Harbour Master at Dun Laoghaire in 1921. In 1943 he was appointed Station Controller at the North Wall, a position he held until he retired in 1953. In the general electon of 1922, he easily headed the poll, to become a TD for Laois/Offaly. He held his seat until his death on 1 March 1956. In the second government of John A. Costello, he was appointed Parliamentary Secretary in the Department of Local Government in 1954 (*T.D.s and Senators for Laois & Offaly (1921-1986)* by Patrick F. Meehan, Leinster Express, 1987).

"(The) Society has acquired a mill in the village of Donaghmore and has bought considerable quantity of corn for millers and seed. (It has a) very good kiln. Kelly responsible for corn buying and candidly, I believe, that only for him the Society would have long since had to go into liquidation. Grogan is simply a creamery man and nothing else. Kelly is afraid that when Grogan resigns he will get his son appointed. Kelly says he doesn't want to see another Grogan in the job.

"McEvoy Snr. has been known as a private organiser for labour[5] for years and it is just possible he was inciting the son to start a branch of the union at the creamery."

Area organiser, Mr. Whelan, on the refusal to give Miss McEvoy buttermilk as usual reported: "… Manager said that it was because of lady's family connection in recent labour troubles. This lady is neither shareholder nor supplier. Normally gets six to eight gallons. Instructions (were issued) to supply her with not more than a 'sweet-can full' (about one gallon) for making of bread. The townspeople get small supplies of buttermilk and, of course, suppliers are entitled to preference."[6]

Good price being paid for milk

At the 1944 AGM, Pat Whelan, IAOS, in congratulating the committee and management, said that the price being paid for milk compared very favourably to that being paid by creameries with four or five times greater supplies.[7]

The secretary stated, at the January 1944 meeting, that he had arranged with the ESB for 13 lights in the mill at a cost of £30. This was approved. It was decided to send £30 to the IAOS as the Society's contribution to the Golden Jubilee Trust Fund. There was a letter from the Department of Agriculture stating that Production Allowances were being increased by £3 1s 8d per cwt. It was ordered that the Society's seal be affixed to a document forwarded by the Munster and Leinster Bank aimed at indemnifying them against claims arising out of the use of a form of receipt on the back of certain cheques. The milk price was fixed at 1/-. The price of butter to suppliers was fixed at 2/2 per pound.

At the April meeting, it was agreed that the chairman and secretary were to represent the Society at the IAOS AGM and Golden Jubilee Dinner along with Mr. Kavanagh. The question of the remuneration of the secretary arose and, in his absence, it was unanimously agreed to pay him £150 per annum.

There was a letter from the Irish Red Cross read at the May meeting relating to their scheme for farmers to grow one extra perch of potatoes for them and asking for the Society's co-operation. Committee members felt that this would not work but made the suggestion that farmers be asked to donate one barrel of potatoes to the Red Cross at harvest time. It was decided to apply to the Munster and Leinster Bank for an overdraft of £6,000.

In June, Mr Ebrill suggested the re-construction of the coal shed as a new office premises. This was agreed to. Regarding the appointment of an accountant, it was felt that a salary per week should be about £5 or £6. The quotation from the GPO

5. Probably relates to the Labour Party, to which Mr. Davin was affiliated.
6. Report to the IAOS on 12 January, 1944 (National Archives).
7. At the Annual General Meeting on 13 March 1944, the chairman, Mr. Galbraith, presided and the following were in attendance: Messrs. Michael Kirwan, S. Campion, Joe Bergin, John Doherty, Philip Campion, Michael Phelan, John Moylay, Pat Kavanagh, Thomas Mitchell, George McKelvey, Anthony McKelvey, William Bergin, Jerome Shortall, John Hennessy, R. McEvoy, P. McDonald and John Treacy. Mr. Galbraith was re-elected chairman while Mr. Kavanagh was re-elected vice-chairman.

relating to the telephone installation at the mill was considered excessive and it was decided not to proceed with the project. The manager and secretary were instructed to advertise any old machinery or iron not required and to sell it at the list price.

Work on the new office was held up due to difficulty in obtaining permits for cement and timber, the August meeting was told. The chairman pointed out, at the September meeting, that there would be a very big increase in the charges for railway lorries for the current year. It was unanimously agreed to purchase an Austin lorry for £535. The butter ration to milk suppliers was to be curtailed to 10oz per head per week.

The committee acknowledged that work in connection with the grain business was progressing more smoothly than in any previous year, and that this was due in no small part to the work done by Mr. Wallis. The drying of the seed was proceeding well and shifts for 24 hours had been organised so that over 500 barrels per week were being dried instead of 180 as heretofore. Mr. Wallis was congratulated for his good work and was granted a bonus of £10 as a 'thank you'. Mr. Whelan in his report to the IAOS commented: "Only trouble is short supply of railway wagons which seems to be general. The carrying of grain gets only 6th preference by railway company. Should be given at least 2nd preference in place of beet."

In November, the committee gave permission to Midland Co-op to use Donaghmore, Raheen and Spink premises for the purposes of holding turkey markets. But there was a letter from Mr. McDonnell, Abbeyleix, before the December meeting, complaining that Midland Co-op was buying turkeys at Spink. Because McDonnell was their landlord at Spink, the secretary said he would write to Midland telling them not to buy turkeys there. It was noted that "they pay good prices and people in Donaghmore area are very satisfied".

An "undignified" job for a young scholar

The minutes of the meeting of 7 October 1944 record that a committee member objected to his son being asked to do degrading shift-work on the kiln. The secretary found it difficult to understand how such work could be degrading and said that the arrangements had already been made and could not be changed. The organiser, Mr. Whelan's, report reveals somewhat more about the issue. "Mr. X, a member of the committee, complained that his son was transferred to an 'undignified' position in the Mill at Donaghmore which was not in keeping with the boy's scholastic attainments viz. Leaving Cert. with Honours 'fit for entrance to University'. (He) referred to exam for a male clerk which I held in January '43 and stated that I was not an 'independent' person to conduct such an exam. I took exception to these remarks and demanded an apology which the committee insisted upon. Ultimately, Mr. X apologised when Mr. Kelly pointed out that, in spite of a special notice sent to his son in reference to exam, he didn't turn up. It would appear the boy was subsequently taken into the Society's employment and, according to Kelly and Grogan, Mr. X was not satisfied in some of the jobs assigned. Finally, Mr. X was told that if he was not satisfied with his son's present position which carried a wage of 5/- extra per week, he could keep him at home. Mr. X left the meeting."

CHAPTER THREE

Spink's Errant Manager

At the meeting on 9 April, 1945, D.F. O'Sullivan, formerly manager of Coolrain, was appointed manager of Spink in a temporary capacity for three months at £3-10-0 per week. The next mention of Mr. O'Sullivan in the minutes was nine months later. The secretary told the meeting on 7 January 1946, that he had found that Mr. O'Sullivan, manager at Spink, had been neglecting his duties due to drink problems, and that he had suspended him from work. Kelly was given discretionary powers as to what future action was to be taken in the matter.

In his report to the IAOS, Pat Whelan, gave more details of the problem: "… It would appear that O'Sullivan was drinking heavily for some time past and, during the Christmas holidays, Mr. Kelly and the chairman checked up on the accounts. They found three ghost milk suppliers against whom were debited butter. I made an audit and found a shock deficiency of 281 lbs. of butter @ 2/4 = £32-15-8 plus cash not accounted for – Total £40-1-4. O'Sullivan was formerly manager at Lissarda Creamery, where he did **not** distinguish himself." In a letter of 18 January 1946, Whelan informed the IAOS that O'Sullivan had, in fact, been dismissed and that he had now applied for the Pettigo vacancy.

In March 1946, John Keane, from Kells, Co. Kilkenny, was appointed manager of Spink at a salary of £3-10-0. Mr. O'Sullivan wrote to the committee seeking a wage of £5 per week for his work as temporary manager (normal wage for temporary managers) and requested that the money, that he was due, be issued to him. The committee agreed to give him the £10-10-0 that was in dispute.

Key appointments

John Galbraith was appointed as office assistant in a temporary capacity from 1 February 1945 to the conclusion of the 1945 audit. Mr. Galbraith was soon promoted to bookkeeper/cashier at the rate of 70/- per week. His contract was up on the completion of the audit in March 1946 but it was decided to make the appointment permanent at £4-5-0 per week. Chairman, George Galbraith, left the room during all discussions on matters relating to his son.

Mr. Wallis was appointed store manager in February at a wage of 65/- per week, an increase of 4/- on his present wage. However, Mr. Wallis asked the committee to reconsider their wage increase to him. It was then decided to fix his salary at 67/6 per week and to allow him commission at the rate of 1/- per acre on all grass seed orders taken by him, to be payable only when accounts were collected. There was another application for a wage increase to 90/- per week from Mr. Wallis discussed at the November meeting. He informed members that he had had an interview for Ballingarry Co-op. It was agreed to pay him 85/- per week.

In January 1945, it was decided to advertise for the appointment of a manager at Spink. The February 1945 meeting heard that only four replies had been received for the vacant managership at Spink and that none of those were suitable. It was decided to re-advertise in March when a number of young men would become qualified.

At the committee meeting which followed the AGM, Messrs. Galbraith and Kavanagh were re-appointed chairman and vice-chairman respectively.[1]

The question of the revision of the amounts of the bonds of auxiliary managers came up for revision in April 1945. It was decided that the Spink manager's bond should be £50 and that of the Raheen manager, £100. The accountant's bond was fixed at £300.

At the June 1945 meeting, it was decided to put an asbestos cement roof on the structure erected at Raheen for turf. A letter from the Minister for Defence was read relative to the re-employment of demobilised men. Attention was drawn to the need for having horse sprayers for hire and the necessity of having a seeding machine that could be loaned to customers.

In October an offer of £100 for the purchase of the premises at Coolrain was refused. It was agreed that the lowest figure which would be accepted would be £150. In January 1946, however, instructions were given to the secretary to get the best bargain he could for the property. The secretary revealed, in February 1946, that the offer for the property had been increased to £125 and that this had been accepted.

An application was received from Mr. Hoare, Instructor in Agriculture and Science, for the use of a room in the Society's premises for the purpose of starting up a Young Farmers' Club. This was agreed to, provided that there was no objection from the Insurance Company.

The secretary reported, in January 1946, that he had purchased a new 5-ton Austin truck at a price of £630 and his decision was unanimously approved by the committee. A bonus of £10 was paid to Harry Moynan whose work during the year had been deserving of special consideration. Kelly was instructed to purchase a safe for the Raheen Creamery. It was decided not to purchase fire extinguishers.

At the meeting on 7 June 1946, a previous decision not to appoint a vice-chairman was rescinded and both Mr. Kavanagh and Mr. Walsh were nominated for the position. The latter withdrew and Mr. Kavanagh was declared elected.

On reviewing the half-yearly accounts, some members felt that the Society was giving out too much in credit; others felt it was necessary to do so to hold on to trade. The secretary refused to take responsibility for employing extra clerical staff for the harvest season, following criticisms, made at the AGM, about overstaffing. The committee agreed to take responsibility and instructed the secretary to employ extra office staff as was necessary.

The price of wheat was fixed at 55/- per barrel, owing to the increased cost of saving the harvest due to poor weather conditions and the fact that the wheat would not be up to the standard of previous years. The secretary reported that the wheat received would amount to 20% less than the previous year.

It was decided, in December 1946, to go ahead with the project of planting oziers, which would be used for the basket-making industry being set up in Raheen. A pension scheme for co-operative employees was being investigated.

---

1. At the Annual General Meeting on 12 March 1945, Mr. Galbraith presided and the following were present: Messrs. Joseph Bergin, William Bergin, Stephen Campion, John Doherty, John Hennessy, Patrick Kavanagh, John Moylan, John Treacy and J.P. Kelly, secretary. Mr P. Whelan of the IAOS was also present. The auditor's report stated that the Society was in a very satisfactory position.

CHAPTER FOUR

Row over Appointment of a Manager

If committee members were shocked, in January 1946, at the fraud perpetrated at the Spink branch, there was an even bigger shock in store for them before the end of the month. This was the sudden death of the Donaghmore manager, William Grogan. Mr. Riddell of the IAOS, on hearing the news, immediately sent a letter of condolence to the Donaghmore committee. This was acknowledged by Kelly: "Being here for 19 years without a break, we will miss him a lot. Collapsed and died at mass on Sunday."

A Special Meeting was called for 28 January. The following resolution was proposed: "That we were deeply grieved and shocked to learn of the sudden death of our manager and that we tender to Mrs. Grogan and family our very sincere sympathy in their great trial and sorrow." It was also resolved "that the secretary be empowered to make temporary arrangements for the conduct of the Society's business pending the appointment of a new manager".

With regard to the position of manager, the chairman, Mr. Galbraith said he felt that the dairy business was now a mere sideline of the Society's operations. He suggested that a junior manager should be appointed to hold responsibility for the Dairy and the development of the Egg and Poultry trade only. He favoured Mr. Wallis being left in charge of the Store and Grain business. The rest of committee was 'mostly' in agreement, according to the minutes. The secretary was instructed to advertise the position. The advertisement was for a manager, not a junior manager.

A special meeting was called on 4 March 1946, for the purpose of making the appointment. A fidelity bond for £400 was set for the manager. Twenty-five applications were received for the position. These had been forwarded to the IAOS, who in turn sent back the names to Donaghmore of five candidates they recommended for interview. Three were interviewed and two names were brought to the committee for consideration, Mr. Sugrue who looked for a salary of £275 per annum, and Donal Grogan, son of the late manager, who sought a salary of £300 per annum.

Grogan Jr., solicited the support of an influential player in the dairying industry, Edward Roche, manager at Mitchelstown Creamery. He asked Mr. Roche to put in a word for him "to secure the position". He wrote: "Now (I am) the only support of my mother and brother, at present in St. Kieran's (College) studying for the priesthood ... Only way I can keep the old home in Donaghmore open for them is to get my father's job ... Trusting you will do your best, I remain dear Mr. Roche, Respectfully yours, Donal F. Grogan." Roche sent the letter to Mr. Fant of the IAOS, who passed it on to Mr. Riddell, and he passed it on, in turn, to Mr. Whelan.

The letter did not have the desired effect, however. A ballot was held at the special meeting in Donaghmore, which resulted in 6 votes for Sugrue and 5 for Grogan. Mr. Sugrue was declared elected. Messrs. Kirwan, Treacy and Campion protested vehemently against the appointment saying that Grogan would have to be appointed. A discussion ensued which led to raised voices and an absence of order. Chairman, George Galbraith, ruled that the matter was not up for discussion, as the appointment had been made by ballot. Before any change could be made, Sugrue would have to be dismissed, he ruled.

A number of members left the room and a suggestion was made by the chairman to Mr. Kirwan that the IAOS be asked to arbitrate. The secretary then asked Kirwan that if the IAOS decision was not in favour of his candidate, would he abide by their decision. Kirwan said that he would not agree to this and further arguments followed. The meeting was in uproar. Outside the building, a small crowd had gathered shouting their support for Grogan. Some climbed up to a window to watch the proceedings inside and so as to exert maximum pressure on the committee members present.[1]

The chairman left the chair and the meeting, having first asked the vice-chairman, Mr. Kavanagh, to take over. J. Bergin then proposed that Donal Grogan be appointed manager. Kirwan seconded and there being no amendment, Grogan was given the job.

The secretary, J.P. Kelly, was not convinced of the legal standing of the manner of Grogan's appointment and sought advice from the IAOS. Arthur Cox, solicitors for the IAOS, were of the opinion that the first appointment was valid. They advised that Sugrue would have to be offered a contract to sign. The only way that he could be dismissed was by a two-third committee majority.

Riddell informed Whelan that Kelly and Galbraith wanted him (Riddell) to attend the next meeting (the AGM) at Donaghmore.[2] It would be a difficult meeting, he believed. In a letter to Kelly on the same day, Riddell informed the Donaghmore secretary of a telephone call he had received from Grogan. The latter had given a different account of the meeting, he said. Grogan claimed that there had been two ballots and the chairman had given the casting vote. The row split the Society almost down the middle and, for some time at least, there was a grave danger that it might not survive the repercussions.

Chairman, George Galbraith presided at the Annual General Meeting on 11 March 1946.[3] A vote of sympathy was extended to the family of the late Mr. Grogan. This was immediately followed by the early salvos of the war that was to follow. The chairman was challenged as to the validity of his membership of the committee. Some members claimed that since he was an Agent of the Society this invalidated him from holding such a position. The minutes record that various questions were asked about the small profit on turnover[4] and some members felt that there was a superfluous number of office staff. The question of the appointment of the manager

1. As recalled by Bobby Bennett in an interview.
2. In an internal IAOS memo dated 9 March 1946 (National Archives).
3. Present were: Messrs. M. Kirwan, J. Treacy, J. Bergin, W. Bergin, P. Kavanagh, John Hennessy, Rody McEvoy, Pat McDonald, S. Campion, Michael Walsh, Joseph Keyes, Denis Breen, John Carroll, James Whelan, Jer Devin, M. Maher, James Kelly, H. Moynan, John Cahill, Michael Phelan, Pat Campion, A. Marshall, L. Campion, J. Moylan, William Brophy, James Brophy, Michael Houlihan, John Bergin, Phil Campion, S. Loughman and R. McKelvey.
4. Turnover for 1945 was as follows: Dairy produce, £16,968; Agricultural goods, £137,599. Total £154,567. Net Profit: £1,650.

was raised and, although the chairman felt that this was not the place to air the matter, a long and heated discussion took place. Mr. Galbraith eventually managed to move on to other items on the agenda.

Mr. Riddell acted as chairman at the committee meeting which immediately followed the AGM and the election of the chairman for the coming year took place. Messrs. Kirwan, Kavanagh, Bergin and Galbraith were all proposed. Both Mr. Kavanagh and Mr. Galbraith withdrew their names. Mr. Kirwan eventually accepted the chair. The question of Mr. Galbraith acting as a member of the committee whilst being an Agent for the Society again arose. Mr. Galbraith offered his resignation but, on being pressed, he agreed to remain on the committee until September. Mr. Kavanagh declined to become vice-chairman and, on the proposition of Mr. J. Bergin, it was agreed that no vice-chairman be appointed. The milk price was set at 1/- per gallon. On the question of the position of manager, the secretary said that neither of the two candidates had been appointed, as the legal position was not clear, and he informed those present that he had sent a copy of the minutes to the IAOS for their advice. Mr. Kavanagh said that, in order to test the legality of the issue, he proposed that Donal Grogan be appointed manager. This was seconded and passed without opposition. Mr. Kavanagh then tendered his resignation but it was ruled out of order. In his report of the meeting, Riddell commented that "Grogan's supporters were determined to have their way, one way or another".

In April, Mr. Wallis asked the committee to have his duties properly defined and his position clarified. The chairman was authorised to sign the manager's agreement and it was agreed that the new manager, Donal Grogan, be given the use of the residence and quarters formerly occupied by his late father. The Society's seal was affixed to the letting agreement.

In April, Mr. Kavanagh wrote, resigning his membership of the committee, because of malicious accusations circulating relating to him. Mr. Galbraith pointed out the seriousness of losing Kavanagh and his resignation was refused. Kavanagh was not the only committee man troubled by vicious rumours. The secretary challenged members if they had any charges to make against him, as he had been hearing of issues relating to his activities being discussed in local pubs. He refuted any allegations made against him and formally tendered his resignation. Kelly was asked to reconsider his decision, but refused, saying that he would remain on until the next meeting when the committee should appoint a successor.

The IAOS representative, Mr. Kelly, in his report of the meeting expanded on some of these rumours. "He (the secretary) was supposed to be making money at the expense of the Society and to be running it largely to suit his own purposes. In many statements, he was linked to Mr. Galbraith and his son. (He) refutes all charges. Chairman (Mr. Kirwan) advised the secretary not to heed malicious gossip and pleaded with him to reconsider his resigning." Mr. Galbraith wrote to Riddell telling him of the "filthy accusations" and of the secretary's resignation. Riddell replied on 16 April, stating that he hoped Kelly would continue in office "as it would be only serving the purpose of the trouble-makers if he were to resign and might result in the disintegration of the Society, which would be a calamity for farmers in the district who are not generally a party to the differences which have arisen".

There were appeals again, at the May meeting, to J.P. Kelly to reconsider his resignation. The secretary felt unable to accede to this request as he had already undertaken to do other work, which would occupy his time for a number of months. Committee members suggested that the secretary could delegate some of his work. Kelly eventually agreed to these conditions providing that he be allowed to take a drop in salary to reflect his reduced workload.

A clear sense of unease continued to prevail at the Creamery. Galbraith told Riddell, in a letter of 16 May, that there was "still trouble in the air". He added: "I understand the trouble is due to a lack of understanding between the manager and the secretary. I think if the manager consulted Mr. Kelly a bit, it would make all the difference, but I'm afraid other influences are at work advising him to the contrary." The other Mr. Kelly, in his report to the IAOS, confirmed that there was still a problem. "Kelly withdrew his resignation after unanimous appeal. Danger to this arrangement arises out of a likelihood of a clash of opinions between Grogan and Kelly. If this can be avoided, the backwash from the last stormy few months will subside in time."

The duties of the manager and store manager were clarified, at the May meeting, as follows: manager was responsible for writing up of the stock-book and checking the stocks monthly, completion of all returns to Government Departments and Cement Company, supervision of tractor work, responsibility for employees working in connection with lorries and store; manager and store manager jointly responsible for fixing prices of cereals, manures and seeds, purchasing of cereals and store goods, responsibility for work and for employees at the mill, checking goods inwards and outwards; store manager was responsible for fixing prices of hardware, purchasing turf, employment and dismissal of temporary labour and had responsibility for planning of work in advance for the Society's lorries.

At the July meeting, a letter was received from George Galbraith tendering his resignation. A discussion followed, from which Galbraith absented himself. The huge amount of voluntary work done by Galbraith was acknowledged by committee members and it was felt he would be a huge loss to the Society. It was decided to discuss the matter further at the August meeting.

At the August meeting, it was decided to ask Mr. Galbraith to reconsider his decision. In order to facilitate him in doing so, the chairman proposed "that the secretary be instructed to revert to the practice and manner of paying Grain Commissions that obtained in the years 1939-1940." Mr. Galbraith was called into the room and, under these conditions, he withdrew his resignation.

The appointment of a charge-hand for the new incubator and hatchery came before the meeting of 11 December. There was a direct clash once again between Kelly and Grogan. Grogan pressed for his sister's appointment but Kelly did not concur. The secretary felt that a Miss O'Neill from Clonakilty was better qualified. The manager felt that his sister was equally qualified. Mr. Whelan, in his report to the IAOS, fills in the details: "Mr. Kelly pointed out that Miss O'Neill held the necessary certificates for testing eggs which Miss Grogan did not. He saw no difficulty, at least for some time, to prevent the one person manage the egg store and supervise the hatchery. Mr. Grogan said the appointment of his sister would be the most economical for the moment. His sister, all agreed, was capable of managing the hatchery but was not qualified to test eggs. The manager and secretary were asked could they not agree. They couldn't. Miss O'Neill was appointed. Mr. S. Campion proposed that Miss Grogan be appointed to the hatchery, but there was no seconder. The chairman was embarrassed and asked for guidance. It was decided that, if an assistant was to be appointed in future, Miss Grogan would get preference." Whelan noted that the meeting was a marathon one, running for 3.5 hours and that the meeting before that had lasted for 4 hours. Mr. Galbraith also advised Riddell of the meeting, to which the IAOS assistant secretary replied: "Now that problem has been resolved, I trust that the affairs of Donaghmore will now proceed smoothly without interruption. Am glad to note your interest in it has not waned in the slightest and I trust you will be spared for many a long day to give the Society the benefit of your good counsel.'

Tensions at the Creamery were strained further when Mr. Wallis sent in his resignation in December 1946. This was accepted with reluctance by the committee who rewarded him with a cheque for £10-10-0 as a token of esteem. There was a poor response to the advertisement for his replacement. It was proposed to appoint James Fitzpatrick "at as low a salary as possible". He had sought £5-10-0 weekly but had to settle for 5/- less. Fitzpatrick resigned in May and Billy Wallis was asked to reconsider resuming in his old job. He agreed under certain conditions. His salary was set at £6-10-0 weekly.

Receipt written by William Grogan, first manager in Donaghmore.

CHAPTER FIVE

New Hatchery

The secretary, J.P. Kelly, reported to the meeting on 10 December 1945, that he had had discussions with Mr. Philpott, Chief Poultry Inspector of the Department of Agriculture, regarding the starting of a poultry farm at Donaghmore. Pedigree birds were required. There would be a market for the chickens and eggs. Kelly was asked to go to Barryroe, Lisavaird and Drinagh hatcheries and report his findings.

In February 1946, following a visit to a hatchery and further discussions with Mr. Philpot, it was decided, after a lengthy discussion, to go ahead with the hatchery scheme. Members were told that this would necessitate employing a person with the Department's Certificate for Egg Grading. It was agreed that the Society should apply for an Egg Exporters licence. Following a visit by Mr. Philpott to Donaghmore, he advised that the salt store was suitable for the installation of an electric incubator, with an 8,000 eggs capacity for the sale of one-day-old chicks of pure-bred strain, preferably Rhode Island Reds. It was agreed to acquire the Board Room premises for an egg store and to organise the poultry stations. A sub-committee was formed to manage the hatchery, consisting of the chairman, secretary, John Hennessy, J. Bergin, M. Walsh and William Bergin.

In May 1946, it was decided that the Society should subsidise the cost of cockerels for the first year of the Poultry and Egg Scheme to the equivalent of one third of the invoice price. Denis McGaughy agreed to surrender possession of the Board Room, which he held on lease. His rent for the remainder of the premises was fixed at £10 per annum and a fresh agreement was drafted.

The secretary reported, in July, that the hatchery building was almost complete and that the incubator had been installed. It was decided to leave all details in connection with the hatchery in the hands of the sub-committee.

Messrs. Kirwan, J. Bergin, W Bergin, Hennessy, Kavanagh and Walsh along with Miss Doyle were present at a hatchery sub-committee meeting on 21 August. The price of eggs was fixed at 6/- per dozen for the months of January to March. It was agreed that penalties would be imposed on flock owners, where more than 25% of the eggs supplied proved infertile. The Society would supply the cases on loan for the delivery of eggs and the suppliers would pay for freight on their eggs or send their eggs to meet the Society's lorries.

In October 1946, it was decided that the appointment of a suitable manager for the hatchery and egg business be left in the hands of the manager and secretary.

In December, the secretary reported that the trial hatch in the incubator was fairly successful and that eggs from two of the established stations had produced 80%. It was decided to go ahead and manufacture a chicken mash and to pack it in suitable cotton sacks. The secretary informed the meeting that it would be necessary to get a licence to produce chicken mash and it was decided to apply for one.

Spink Loses Another Manager

The manager of Spink, Mr. Keane, resigned having received a position with Ballingarry Co-op. He had only taken up the position ten months previously. Mr. Cahill of Piltown was appointed in his place at a salary of £4-10-0 per week but when he turned down the job, it was re-advertised. The May meeting heard that a Mr. Connellan had been appointed. In July, Grogan commented on the unsatisfactory work being done by Connellan at Spink. It was decided to ask him to hand in his resignation. Connellan duly obliged. Grogan stated that he had received verbal complaints from Senior Dairy Produce Inspector Power about the cleansing facilities at Spink which he deemed inadequate. The appointment of Mr. O'Driscoll as manager at Spink at a salary of £5 per week was confirmed at the November meeting. He would leave the position by the following May.

A good year's trading

There was general satisfaction at the reading of the auditor's report, which showed a good year's trading. The committee advised caution in dealing with customers in view of the imminent worldwide depression. Mr. R. P. (Bobby) Bennett was co-opted onto the committee in place of Mr. Doherty. The chairman and secretary were asked to investigate what improvements would be needed to provide shop windows at Raheen and Central.

At the committee meeting, which followed the AGM,[1] Messrs. Kirwan (outgoing), Galbraith and Kavanagh were nominated for the position of chairman. Mr. Galbraith withdrew and, on a show of hands, Mr. Kavanagh was elected. Mr. Hennessy was appointed vice-chairman. A discussion took place on the necessary improvements at the various premises. Some of the improvements included installing an electric hoist for the elevation of grain at Central and the provision of grain cleaning equipment. The secretary and manager were asked to investigate more modern accounting practices.

At the April meeting, Ben Moran asked for extra remuneration in consideration of his increased duties while acting in the capacity of temporary manager at Spink. It was agreed to pay him an extra £1 per week. Work was to be executed at Spink to overcome a flooding problem. It was decided to try and secure a piece of land adjoining Raheen premises for the purpose of building extra stores, which were badly needed. In a review of wages, the manager was given a bonus of £26 and the salary of the manager at Raheen was set at £4 per week. The secretary did not apply for an increase as he felt he did not deserve it (according to the minutes, written by J.P. Kelly himself).

1. At the Annual General Meeting on 12 March 1947, chairman Michael Kirwan presided and the following were in attendance: Messrs. J. Bergin, W. Bergin, R.P. Bennett, S. Campion, G. Galbraith, J. Hennessy, P. Kavanagh, R. McEvoy, P. McDonald, Michael Walsh, R. Mitchell, S. Loughman, Michael Hogan, J. Walsh, M. McEvoy, J. McWey, A. Marshall, J. Kennedy, Martin Carroll, J. Butler and J. James. Mr P. Whelan of the IAOS was also in attendance. Messrs. Swain Brown were re-appointed auditors. It was proposed and passed unanimously that the three outgoing members Bergin, Bennett and McDonald be reappointed to the committee. It was decided to increase the bad debts reserve to £500. It was decided to hold the next AGM of the Society in the Raheen/Spink area as a large amount of the Society's trade came from that area and shareholders should be afforded the opportunity to attend.

It was announced at the May meeting that Mr. Talbot had indicated that he would be willing to sell land adjacent to the Raheen premises. Mr. Galbraith was asked "to approach the man casually" to see what kind of price he would be asking rather than rush into the situation.

There was general dissatisfaction at delays in commencing the egg business and the purchase of eggs. The manager was urged to concentrate on its rapid development. The IAOS wrote requesting a substantial increase in the financial support from Societies. After discussion, it was agreed to forward £40. The committee decided to allocate monetary prizes for three special classes in the poultry section of the Ossory Agricultural Society's annual show for pullets reared from chicks supplied by Donaghmore Hatchery.

Prizes awarded at London Dairy Shows and Royal Dublin Society's Spring Show.

TELEGRAMS: "CREAMERY, BALLYBROPHY."   TELEPHONE: DONAGHMORE 3.

RAILWAY STATION: BALLYBROPHY.

DONAGHMORE CO-OPERATIVE CREAMERY, LTD.

BUTTER MANUFACTURERS — — GRAIN & SEED MERCHANTS

Our Ref. *R P Bennett Esq*

Glebe Ho

Donaghmore

Nº - 478

BRANCHES AT—
RAHEEN AND SPINK

BALLYBROPHY

LEIX

14th Feby 1947

Pure Creamery Butter - 1-lb. rolls a speciality - Regd. No. C348.
Buyers of Wheat, Oats, Barley, etc. - All Corn Seed Kiln Dried.

Dear Bob,

At a meeting of my Committee on 12th inst you were unanimously co-opted a member in room of Mr John Doherty who has not attended for many months.

I trust that you will be able to accept office and take an active interest in the Society.

Yours truly

J P Kelly
Secretary

Letter from J.P. Kelly advising Bobby Bennett of his co-option to the Donaghmore Committee of Management in 1947.

The secretary was directed to procure 'proper' grain cleaning equipment. It was revealed that new cleaning equipment would not be delivered for two years but it was decided to go ahead and order it, nevertheless. In December, members heard that Department Inspector O'Keane had visited Central and had stressed the necessity of procuring a proper cleaning plant immediately.

The manager, Donal Grogan, sought an increase in wages. His wage had been £300 per annum and a free house. It was raised to £350 per annum.

The Department of Agriculture was insisting that the millers make payment directly to the growers for the 1947 wheat crop. It was proposed to call a protest meeting in Kilkenny on 14 July and Mr. Galbraith was unanimously selected to attend.

In December 1947, it was decided to proceed with the work of transferring the proposed shop site from the building adjoining the egg store to that adjoining the mill in order to relieve office congestion. A Bamford (Grinding) Mill was to be acquired for Spink if possible. A 10 cwt truck had been delivered and was taxed as from the start of the month. The Ford V5 truck and the Austin were no longer viable. Mr. Bennett proposed that the two old trucks should be sold and replaced by a new 5 and 2 ton truck.

A discussion on the credit given to customers took place and it was agreed that 'as far as possible, all non-agricultural goods should be sold on a strictly cash or monthly account basis.'

CHAPTER SIX

Too Valuable to Lose

A letter of resignation was received from John Galbraith in January 1948. It was decided to ask him to attend next meeting to see if they could get him to reconsider as he was too valuable an employee to lose. Mr. Galbraith was present at the February meeting and explained the difficult conditions under which he was trying to work. A number of improvements were sanctioned including the procurement of modern office equipment, extra office accommodation, and an additional girl was to be employed in the office until everything was up to date. It was also agreed to increase Mr. Galbraith's remuneration to £6-10-0 per week.

Following an application from the County Registrar, it was agreed, at the January 1948 meeting, that the outer room of the egg store be given for use as a polling station during the coming Dail election. Fire and light was to be provided. The committee ruled that "any orders given to employees by either the manager or Mr. Wallis should be implicitly carried out and, in the event of refusal, such employee be instantly dismissed". Miss Moriarty was appointed to the hatchery position at a wage of 70/- weekly.

There was a discussion, at the February meeting, on the affiliation and special subscription fees paid to the IAOS which, under new rules, could be as much as £70 to £80 for the year. It was decided to levy the cost of the special subscription from milk suppliers. A fee of £50 was agreed at the March meeting.

A letter of resignation was received from Ben Moran, Spink, in February 1948 but a further letter from the same man pointed out the possibilities of developing the store trade in the area. The general feeling was in favour of Moran being appointed as store manager but it was pointed out by the secretary that before any change was made in Moran's status a suitable store premises would have to be acquired. The following month Moran was offered a wage of £3 per week, which he accepted.

The secretary pointed out the need to extend the hatchery stating that they could probably get a grant of £500. It was agreed to procure and install a 12,000 egg incubator. A discussion took place on egg production, which resulted in the Manager being urged to obtain an export permit without delay. It was also decided to obtain an egg dealer's licence for the Raheen premises.

The completed audit showed a profit figure of slightly over £1000. The auditor pointed out the large amount of overdue accounts and suggested charging interest on them. It was agreed to charge 5% interest per annum.

Members heard at the April meeting that the cream vat had been sold for £150. The secretary reported a difficulty in the fact that there were some big bills to pay and that the current overdraft would not cover this. He also had difficulty with the attitude of the bank manager. The secretary was asked to discuss the Society's financial position with Mr. Riddell of the IAOS.

At the AGM, which was held in Raheen School, the chairman, Mr. Kavanagh, referred to the decline in milk supplies and the necessity of getting into other lines to keep the Society afloat.[1] He appealed to Raheen and Spink members to increase milk supplies. Mr. Whelan of the IAOS referred to the particularly high price paid for milk to the suppliers, stating that it was far higher than a number of other Societies.

Work on the shop premises at Spink was completed by May 1948 and the shop was in operation, members were told. A salary increase for Miss Moriarty from £3 to £4-10-0 was awarded in June, in case she "was lured away by other hatcheries".

Deputy Oliver J. Flanagan,[2] responding to a request from the Society, informed the July 1948 meeting that Ben Moran would not be approved by the Department of Agriculture for the position as manager at Spink. The matter was left in the hands of the manager and secretary. Mr. Whelan, in his report in September, revealed that the position of manager at Spink remained unfilled. "Mr. Kelly had written to Henry Spring, Ballyheigue, Tralee, who applied last April at a wage of £5-10-0 per week. Spring in his reply asked for £5-15-0. The committee decided that this wage was too high," he wrote. Mr Wallis was re-appointed Manager of Spink at the December meeting and it was hoped that it would receive the Department sanction.

At the September 1948 meeting, it was agreed to purchase a manure distributor for the Raheen and Spink areas at a cost of £75. A small charge would be made for the use of the machine. Members heard that the grain cleaning machine had been erected in Raheen. On the question of credit for household and hardware items, it was decided, at the October meeting, to use discretion in individual cases.

At the November meeting, it was decided to put the details of the Federal Superannuation Scheme before the employees for their consideration. At the December meeting, it was moved "that due to the lack of unanimity among the employees as to its acceptance and to the very high cost of the scheme to the Society, its adoption be not considered at present".

The problem of accommodation for the female employees at the hatchery was raised at the December 1948 meeting. Miss Moriarty sought a flat on the Society's premises or alternatively to be driven to and from her lodgings or, failing this, to

1. The Annual General Meeting took place on 14 April. Mr P Kavanagh presided and the following were in attendance: Messrs. R.P. Bennett, J. Bergin, T. Whelan, Thomas Wilkinson, Michael Kirwan, John Kilbride, James Ryan, John Treacy, T. Mitchell, J. McWey, G. Galbraith, P. Lalor, J. Moylan, John Hennessy, James J. Moffatt, J. Ryan, John Lalor (Ring), George Porter, Michael Walsh, J. Butler, R. Galbraith, R. McEvoy, Michael Whelan, Thomas McDonald and Pat McDonald. Mr. P. Whelan of the IAOS was also present. M/s Swain Brown were re-appointed auditors for the coming year. Of the three retiring members of the Committee Messrs. J. Bergin and P. McDonald were re-appointed and Mr. McWey was appointed in place of Mr Willie Bergin. John Treacy Jnr. was elected in place in his late father. Thanks were extended to Fr Coyne PP for facilitating the AGM in Raheen School. At the committee meeting that followed the AGM, Mr. Kavanagh was re-elected Chairman while Mr. Hennessy was elected vice-chairman.

2. Oliver J. Flanagan was first elected TD for Laois/Offaly in 1943 on a Monetary Reform ticket. As an Independent in the General Election of 1948, he received 14,369 votes. In 1961, on a Fine Gael ticket, he received 15,200 votes. He held his seat continually, and was a regular poll-topper, from 1943 until his death on 28 April 1987, at which time he was the longest serving member of Dail Eireann. After holding Parliamentary portfolios in Agriculture and Fisheries (1954/57) and Local Government (1975/76), he was appointed Minister for Defence in 1976. He was awarded the Knighthood of St. Gregory by Pope Paul 1 in 1978 (*T.D.s and Senators for Laois & Offaly (1921-1986)* by Patrick F. Meehan, Leinster Express, 1987).

receive an extra 30/- weekly to hire a car to transport her. The manager pointed out that he had, on many occasions, driven her to her lodgings and volunteered that he would check the incubators at bedtime so she wouldn't have to come back. It was agreed that Miss Moriarty be allowed to go home at 6pm each day and not be subjected to night work.

Further correspondence was received from Miss Moriarty in January 1949, regarding the provision of accommodation. She informed the meeting that Mr. D. McGaughy was willing to sublet an unfurnished room to her subject to the approval of the Society. She enquired if the committee would be willing to furnish the apartment. It was decided to loan money to Miss Moriarty to furnish the apartment which would be repayable on a weekly basis, the furniture to become her property when fully paid. It was decided that legal opinion should be sought on the matter of the lease. In his report to the IAOS, Mr. Whelan commented: "I was told that this girl is 'doing a line' with a committee man's son, who lives quite near the creamery. At present, she is in digs five miles away." Miss Moriarty sent in her resignation in April 1949, but agreed to stay on to the end of the hatchery season.

Outbreak of Poultry Disease

The February 1949 meeting heard that there had been an outbreak of BWD, a poultry disease, on some supply farms although they had been tested and passed previously. It was stressed that the selection of farms, stock and blood testing was under the absolute control of the Department of Agriculture and no hatchery had any jurisdiction in the matter. The manager reported, at the March meeting, that he had ordered the removal of all poultry from the premises. He had approached Mr. Maher in the absence of McGaughy and requested their removal but Maher would not do so until he was compensated – the amount being discussed was £200.

A Special Meeting was held on 15 March to discuss what action should be taken to protect the Society's interest in view of Maher's refusal to remove his poultry from the premises without compensation, particularly in view of the fact that the Society could have lost its licence in case of failure to comply with the Act. Mr. W. J. Ryan, solicitor, was in attendance. Miss Golden had phoned, stating that she would have no option but to recommend the withdrawal of the licence if the poultry were not removed. This would mean the loss of trade for the season, the loss of a grant of approximately £500 on cost to extension of hatchery and the possible loss of all subsidies on chicks. In the solicitor's opinion, an injunction could be obtained against McGaughy on the grounds that the poultry was a nuisance. Mr. Ryan and the manager left to put the committee's viewpoint before Maher, whom they regarded as McGaughy's representative. It was also agreed that the Society's solicitor be instructed to serve notice on McGaughy of the Society's intention to terminate his agreement for the business premises on 31 December 1949. Upon their return, the solicitor and manager stated that Maher had consented to the removal of the poultry to the paddock and that this poultry would be retained for laying purposes. He said that he would have them blood-tested and if reactors occurred, he would have them terminated. It was felt that the department might accept this until the end of the season but, if not, the solicitor was instructed to institute proceedings for the recovery of his dwelling house/premises or some other such action to protect the company's interests.

Due to the difficulty in securing a male person to take charge of the egg and poultry store, it was decided to train a boy for the job at the Society's expense. The

Department refused to consider claims for compensation for eggs destroyed, holding that it was a normal risk of hatchery work.

Other issues

A letter from the Department of Agriculture was read at the January 1949 meeting, relating to the improvement of premises with particular reference to sanitary accommodation. It was decided to provide flush lavatories and that an estimate of the cost should be sought.

The secretary reported that he had placed an order for a Ford petrol engine and alternator at a cost of £220 as a standby unit for the hatchery in case of breakdown of electric current. This measure was approved.

George Galbraith proposed that a new store be provided at Raheen. He stated that the site adjacent to the Creamery had been inspected by Mr. Ebrill. It was suitable but the owner wanted £200 for the quarter of an acre site, which was more than the committee felt it was worth.

The secretary brought a time-recording machine to be inspected at the meeting. It was agreed to purchase the machine at a cost of £54 complete. On the question of employees absenting themselves during working hours, it was decided to penalise them with the loss of half a day's pay for a first offence and for a subsequent offence to dismiss them.

It was decided to sell the Ford truck at Raheen as it had outlived its usefulness and to purchase a 2-ton second-hand truck for £350. It was decided to buy a mixer for mixing the three mashes for which a licence had been received at a cost of £100, as and when it was required as renewal of the licence could be dependent on this. The secretary's salary was raised to £5 per week.

The completed audit showed figures that were not as promising as had been hoped. The profit was over £1000 but the wages bill was up by £1,300. Eggs showed a loss while the hatchery and shop showed profits.

At the AGM on 13 April 1949, Mr. Marshall questioned why there was not a copy of the financial report for all shareholders and he was told that the Society was under no legal obligation to provide these and for reasons of economy had stopped doing so. If shareholders wanted a copy prior to the AGM, they could request one.

A discussion on BWD took place and it was resolved "that we call on the Department to see that the hens that have the BWD disease be destroyed and that we are of the opinion that there should be more speed in tracing the disease".[3]

Following lengthy discussion on the matter, it was agreed to increase the Society's overdraft to £20,000 for the following twelve months to accommodate the payment of large accounts. A sub-committee was formed to meet occasionally and report on financial and other matters to the committee. It consisted of the chairman, vice-chairman, and Messrs. Bennett and Campion.

A small fire occurred in the Board Room on Easter Sunday. A decision on the procurement of fire-fighting equipment was left in the hands of the manager and secretary.

---

3. At the Annual General Meeting on 13 April, Mr. P. J. Kavanagh, presided and the following were in attendance: Messrs. S Campion, Bennett, Galbraith, McEvoy, McWee, Walsh, Treacy, M. Phelan, Kirwan, J. Devan, A. Marshall, Maher, L. Campion. Mr. P. Whelan of the IAOS was also present. At the committee meeting which followed the AGM, Mr. Kavanagh was re-elected chairman while Mr. Walsh was elected vice-chairman.

It was agreed to send Mr. Wallis to the Agricultural Show in Shrewsbury. It would be of great benefit to him, members felt, and he might make very useful contacts.

The current system of egg collection was proving very costly and it was decided to encourage some of the employees to obtain vans and collect eggs independently, if necessary the Society could assist them in securing transport for the purpose. A contribution of £20 was made to the Maynooth Fund.

In May, the manager reported that a number of people were interested in supplying milk to the creamery but none of them would consider bringing in the milk or having it carried by their neighbours. The secretary estimated that it would cost £6 per day to carry the milk and that they would need a good load to make it viable. The matter was left in the hands of the manager and secretary.

The issue of the high cost of cartage to Raheen Creamery was brought to the attention of Mr. Riddell by George Galbraith. Mr. Galbraith said that it would not be an economic proposition to put a lorry on the road or to employ CIE to do the job. "It would be for a tractor owner as he would have the tractor for a good part of the day for his own use. I understand position is similar at Donaghmore. From recent speeches of the Minister, I think he would give consideration to any reasonable proposition for collection of milk. I wonder if the IAOS would approach the Department or Minister and ask for an exemption to allow private lorries and tractors to be used for collection and delivery of milk to creameries. The exemption to be only for this purpose … it would improve butter production to extent which never seemed possible. If you want any further information I could ring at any time from Raheen Creamery (Abbeyleix 16)."[4]

The IAOS suggested a deputation to meet the Minister from all the creameries concerned. "Perhaps you and Mr. Kelly could come up for the occasion, but before I ask anyone to come up, I shall have to find out whether the Minister would be agreeable to receive a deputation."[5]

In June, the manager reported on the milk position and the general trend among farmers to get away from home butter-making and sending milk to the creamery. It was decided to charge 1d per gallon cartage to all new suppliers.

Special Meeting

A Special Meeting was called for 24 August for the purpose of discussing all matters in connection with the commercial eggs, poultry and hatchery departments. The department was running at a loss of about £15 per week. After lengthy discussion, it was decided to carry on with the trade if at all possible. The following resolutions were also passed: to purchase poultry only from dealer; Laurence Kealty appointed in charge of poultry department at a salary of £5 per week and that an egg tester be employed to assist him. It was decided to review the situation in February 1950.

At the meeting on 7 September, there was a proposal to erect a creamery at Durrow. Investigation was to be made to see if it was in the Society's registered area. The matter seems to have rested there.

Donaghmore is situated in the heart of the traditional hurling area of Laois. Most of the members of the 1915 All-Ireland winning team came from within a few miles of the Creamery. Local clubs – Kilcotton, Rathdowney, Errill and Ballygeehan – were famous names to the hurling fraternity. Yet, when Laois reached the

4. George Galbraith's letter of 31 May 1949 to Mr. Riddell (National Archives).
5. IAOS reply dated 4 June 1949 (National Archives).

All-Ireland final of 1949 against neighbours, Tipperary, there was not a mention of the achievement in the Society's minutes. The working of the Co-op was strictly business as far as the committee and management were concerned.

Notice was received from the Labour Court regarding its decision to grant a 5/- increase to all employees and also specifying that they were considering granting, in addition to seven consecutive holidays, twelve whole holidays with pay each year for creamery employees. The Society objected to the increases on the grounds that there had been no increase in the cost of living since the last wage increase and there had been no increase in the price of milk during the same period. A long discussion also took place on the interruption increased holidays would cause.

In the half-yearly report, the profit for the first six months realised £15,000. It also pointed out that there was £27,000 out in credit to farmers. This was a large amount and the Society should be careful when loaning money in the next few years, members felt. It was decided to purchase a separator from the Dairy Supply Company and quotations were to be sought for a Brine Cooler and Cream Pump. It was decided to increase the public liability policy cover for any one accident from £1,000 to £2,000. It was also decided to erect a shed at the hatchery for the purpose of washing and drying the egg trays.

The original lease on the Donaghmore property, which had been missing for some time, was still not to hand. Mr. Whelan advised the IAOS on 12 November 1949 that, when the Society was founded, a loan had been taken out from the Department to meet the cost of buildings and machinery. The lease was handed over to the Department and, although the loan had been long since repaid, the lease was not returned and could not be found. He told the IAOS that "Mr. Kelly has a copy of the lease and he is not disposed to pass it to the bankers for the purpose of claiming relief from income tax".

In December 1949, it was noted that Harry Moynan had resigned from his employment with the Society. His brother, Ed, was given the job at the weekly rate of £4 with the proviso that he be responsible for the execution of running repairs and maintenance.

A long discussion took place on the accountancy system and the meeting was informed that if they insisted on monthly statements and further departmentalisation of accounts, it would be necessary to employ another assistant in that department. It was proposed that the services of a competent person be acquired in the capacity of ledger clerk. Because of difficulties regarding the distribution of goods on working days in the dairy in Spink, it was decided to employ a "smart local apprentice".

SECTION ONE

PART FOUR

The 1950s

INTRODUCTION

Increased Output, Low Prices

I f there were glimmers of hope for the Irish economy as the 1940s came to a
close, the optimism proved to be mistaken. The 1950s were grey years for the
Irish population with jobs scarce, prospects bleak and, not for the first time, emigration proving the only outlet for droves of thousands of our young people.
Economic policy remained blinkered and inward-looking and economic activity was
stagnant. Agriculture suffered along with other sectors. To compound the situation,
unemployment and emigration were not the only two economic indicators pointing
northwards, so too were wages and inflation.

Frustration with the low prices for their milk and the lack of development in the
dairy industry led to the creation of the Irish Creamery Milk Suppliers' Association
(ICMSA) in 1950. Attempts to elicit the support of the Donaghmore Co-op management for this new and militant organisation received a mixed reception. From
the minute books, it can be judged that Donaghmore did not welcome this new
body with open arms but, similar to many Co-ops around the country, the secretary, J.P. Kelly, and management committee learned to live with it in time.

The post-war move to modernisation of farming methods continued apace during the 1950s, however, and while the benefits were slow to materialise, it eventually paid rich dividends in the 1960s and 1970s. Increased mechanisation of the
farming processes led to increased efficiency and output. The dramatic surge in
cow numbers and yield is reflected in the Donaghmore figures for the period. Milk
intake there increased five-fold to 866,000 gallons between 1948 and 1950 and
rose to over two million gallons for each of the last five years of the decade.

Exports remained low and, with the glut of supply on the home market, so too
did prices. External markets were needed to sustain the rapid growth in output. By
the end of the 1950s, the problems of the Irish dairy industry were reduced to markets and marketing.

*Spink Creamery and
petrol pump (hand
operated) late 1950s.*

CHAPTER ONE

Fowl Pest Restrictions

There was a letter from the Creamery Milk Suppliers, read at the January 1950 meeting, suggesting the formation of a suppliers' organisation embracing the whole country. The manager reported that a lot of cash would be needed for the purchase of fertiliser and seed oats in the short term and estimated that an overdraft of £25,000 would be needed for this purpose.

The operation of the Spink branch came up for discussion at the February meeting and it was found to be unsatisfactory. It was decided to appoint a new manager. The secretary was delegated to go to Cork to interview candidates at the University. A charge of 3.5d per gallon was set for all milk collected.

J.P. Kelly reported on how the Fowl Pest Restrictions affected the Society. Almost 5,000 chickens had been destroyed and a further 3,000 were to be destroyed. There was no movement of poultry or hatchery eggs permitted even though they were situated 55 miles from the outbreak.

A Special Meeting was held on 15 February for the purpose of examining the Society's position with regard to the egg and poultry trade. A six-month set of figures showed a rather substantial loss and Mr. Kealty was questioned about his management of the department. He resigned in May and it was decided to close down the department.

The secretary raised the question of the accounts of the egg and poultry department at the June meeting. He challenged members whether or not they were satisfied with them. He had heard from the son of a committee member that the accounts were not substantiated, leading to a grave reflection on himself as well as on Messrs. Galbraith and Grogan. The meeting agreed that there was no question of the accounts ever having to be substantiated.

Following a letter from the Department of Agriculture, it was resolved at the March 1950 meeting that the Milk Recording Scheme "would receive the approval and cooperation of the committee, provided that the clause that penalises farmers for not having a greater average in their herds than 400 gallons be eliminated from the scheme at its commencement and that the owner of a herd who brings his average to 600 gallons and over be paid a premium."

A discussion took place on the merits of the Social Security Scheme following the report of the delegates who had attended a conference on the issue in Thurles. It was agreed "that the Scheme would be brought to the country but neither the employers nor the state could afford it; that, while employers will be called upon to pay both their own and their employees' contributions, they would receive no benefit whatsoever." Members considered the scheme "ridiculous". The secretary was instructed to send the committee's views to the Minister for Social Welfare and to each of the TDs representing the constituency. It was also decided that all employees keep to summertime that year for work purposes.

Mr. Kelly informed the IAOS that his committee had signified its intention to pay a dividend to shareholders, provided that funds permitted.[1] He sought an outline of the procedure and asked if it was necessary to have the matter mentioned on the agenda for the AGM. In its reply, the IAOS referred to Rule 73 relating to the allocation of funds. Surplus money could be disbursed under four headings, one of which was in the form of dividends to members and employees. The letter added: "I do not consider it legally binding to call a general meeting but it would be in accordance with good custom (to do so)."

The April meeting was told that a Mr. McAdam, a native of Killeshandra and holder of the manager's diploma, had accepted position at Spink at a salary of £4 per week. Following a small net profit for the previous three months, it was decided to keep the branch going for another three months.

Disappointing profits

The accounts for the Society for the year, which showed a net profit of £700, were described as very disappointing at the AGM on 11 May 1950.[2] It was decided to extend the Society overdraft to £30,000 to allow the Society carry on until the harvest. The milk supply for June was well up on the previous year at 126,259 gallons compared to 41,144 gallons for June 1949.

The meeting on 12 July heard that there were difficulties with some milk carters who did not make alternative arrangements when they could not complete their routes. It was to be stressed that they must make alternative arrangements. The secretary reported that the office work was up to date and it was felt a reduction in staff was now warranted. On the question of Miss Moriarty, it was agreed that if she could not be usefully employed in the Dairy, she was to be given a prolonged holiday and paid a retaining fee of £2 weekly, this fee to be paid in arrears after the resumption of her normal duties in the hatchery. It was agreed that new office accommodation be constructed at Spink. The meeting was informed of the possibility of extending rural electrification to Raheen and it was agreed that the branch should seek a supply.

There was a letter from Irish Creamery Milk Suppliers Association before the August meeting, setting forth the objectives of the association and soliciting a subscription. No action was taken.

The position was unsatisfactory with regard to the payment of rents due by the various tenants. All but one of the tenants were in arrears and it took six months rent to pay rates and income tax on the holdings. It was decided that legal proceedings should be instituted against tenants who did not pay up all arrears before a given date.

A letter from Mr. Butler, manager at Raheen, was read relating to the long number of overtime hours he had to work to keep the books up to date. After a complete examination of the situation, it was decided to increase Mr. Butler's remuneration to £6 per week and that he train an assistant to relieve him of some of the duties.

The October 1950 meeting was informed of the unprecedented increase in the number of combine harvesters in operation that year and, in view of the number of

1. In a letter to the IAOS on 13 March 1950 (National Archives).
2. At the Annual General Meeting in 1950, Mr. P.J. Kavanagh, presided and the following were present: Messrs. Bennett, Campion, Galbraith, Hennessy, Kavanagh, Kirwan, McEvoy, McWey, Treacy, Walsh, Carroll, Bowe and Mitchell. Mr. P. Whelan of the IAOS was also in attendance. At the committee meeting that followed the AGM, Mr. Kavanagh was elected chairman and Mr. Michael Walsh was returned as vice-chairman.

orders already booked for the machines, it was estimated that about 50% of the grain would be harvested by this method by the following season in the area. This would necessitate the erection of an automatic drier. The secretary and manager were directed to obtain quotes and other advice.

The secretary said that some creameries were having sewage problems and that the new Health Act may require industrial concerns to cease direct entry of waste into rivers. It was suggested that a septic tank would sooner or later be required.

The opening date for the hatchery was provisionally set for 10 December and it was noted that chick orders were coming in slowly. It was decided not to alter milk intake equipment because Mountmellick Products Ltd. could not guarantee future requirements regarding milk supply.

A Special Meeting was held on 15 November 1950 for the purpose of discussing the erection of a grain dryer. The site had been chosen, members were told. It was decided to purchase a Triumph 4 ton dryer and, in the meantime, definite assurances were to be obtained from Ranks or the Department of Agriculture that dried wheat would be taken from the Society. Following a report by the secretary, it was decided to install an oil-burning furnace compatible with the installation of the new grain dryer.

Overdraft requirements

At the February 1951 meeting, it was decided to seek an overdraft accommodation of £30,000. Members heard that in normal circumstances £20,000 or £25,000 would be ample, but the Department of Agriculture insisted that all creameries lay in sufficient stocks for at least one year and such stocks were to be maintained at that level. The Society was also committed to a capital expenditure of £5,000 for the replacement of dairy machinery on the instruction of the Department of Agriculture.

The Department of Social Welfare pointed out that coal supplies would be unobtainable and suggested that arrangements be made for the production of the Society's own supply of turf. It was decided to procure fuel supplies by direct purchase. The secretary informed the meeting that a 1000 gallon fuel oil-tank had been ordered as had an additional storage tank.

At a finance sub-committee meeting on 5 March, it was noted that there were overdue accounts amounting to approximately £2,000. It was requested that the supply of goods on credit terms to debtors be discontinued.

The committee heard at the March meeting that the bank had postponed consideration of the overdraft extension pending the receipt of a printed copy of the accounts of the Society. It was decided to purchase a new 1,100 gallon separator to accommodate the milk supply in the summer. The old separator had a capacity of 660 gallons.

At the AGM a net profit of £3,322 was recorded for the year.[3] The meeting was

3. The Annual General Meeting on 11 April 1951, was held at Raheen National School. Mr. P. Kavanagh presided and the following were in attendance: Messrs. J. Ryan, John Kilbride, M. McWey, Jer Shiel, James Ryan, Pat Holland, R. Galbraith, T. Mitchell, R. Bennett, J. Bergin, S. Campion, G. Galbraith, J. Hennessy, M. Kirwan, W. McWey, R. McEvoy, J. Treacy, P. Shiel, M. Walsh. A loss of £385 was noted on the handling of dead poultry. Following the approval of the auditor's report it was decided that the Society pay a dividend of 5% on all fully paid up shares. All retiring members of the committee were re-elected. Thanks were extended to Fr Coyne for the use of the school for the meeting. At the committee meeting that followed the AGM, Mr. Kavanagh was re-elected chairman. Mr. Walsh was appointed vice-chairman.

informed that the bank had acceded to the request for an overdraft not to exceed £30,000. It was decided to build a strong room following the auditors' recommendation that one was necessary for security reasons.

Mr. Kelly wrote to Dr. Kennedy of the IAOS on 16 April enquiring about rural electrification for the Errill, Grogan and Borris-in-Ossory area. "I feel it would be a great boon to a large proportion of our suppliers, a number of whom are contemplating the installation of milking machines and water supplies. This year, we hope to receive one million gallons of milk. After twenty years, the district is definitely getting more cow-minded."

A meeting was held on 17 April to discuss wages for outdoor workers. Road and brewery workers had recently received an increase in wages of 7/6 and 6/- weekly. Several workers had their wages increased by 6/- weekly. Mr. Bergin received an increase to £5 weekly. The manager, Mr. Grogan's, salary was raised to £550 per annum. It was also agreed to pay a bonus of £40 to Mr. Wallis, £30 to Mr. Galbraith and £20 to Mr. Butler.

Wage increases

The May meeting heard that staff were agreeably surprised by the wage increases. However, they knew of the increases before being informed by the manager or secretary and this was seen as further evidence of information leaking from the meetings.

It was revealed at the June meeting that John Talbot had agreed to sell a quarter acre of land adjoining the Raheen premises for a price of £40. This would provide extra storage space. Miss Margaret O'Sullivan was appointed as buttermaker.

With regard to the grain dryer, the secretary informed members that it seemed impossible to construct a dual-purpose furnace and that it was considered advisable to erect twin furnaces side-by-side. Petrol and diesel tanks had been erected and filled. These units were intended for emergency use only.

It was decided that all necessary action be taken with a view to increasing the share capital of the Society, including an insistence that all milk suppliers should be members of the Society. But there was a very poor response to the appeal. It was suggested that a personal canvass would be the best option and that this should be done during the harvest or winter.

Mr. Kelly informed the IAOS that "a carter named Prior had said that he would not collect milk on Sundays."[4] He went on to explain: "The manager had told him that it was essential and that if he would not collect milk on a Sunday he need not collect it on Monday or any other day. We sent a lorry to collect milk on Monday but found Prior had collected 50% of load and took it (presumably) to Ballyragget." Within two months, however, the crux had been resolved more or less to Donaghmore's satisfaction. Mr. Whelan reported to the IAOS: "The carter, Prior, who left Donaghmore Society and influenced a number of suppliers to transfer to Ballyragget some months ago has fallen between two stools as more than 90% of the suppliers have returned."[5]

The manager, Donal Grogan, reported on a dispute between Spink and Castlecomer creameries, which he hoped to have settled amicably. Mr. Whelan termed it "some little friction".[6] He stated that Mr. Hayes of Castlecomer had

4. In a letter dated 2 July 1951 (National Archives).
5. Internal IAOS memo dated 12 September 1951 (National Archives).
6. Ibid.

complained about their suppliers "on the border line" in the townslands of Crutt and Chatsworth being approached by Donaghmore and had told him that if this matter was not amicably fixed that he would refer it to the IAOS. At the November meeting, however, it was revealed that an understanding had been reached between the two creameries.

In October, it was agreed to pay carters 2.5d per gallon for milk collected, with 2d being deducted from suppliers and 0.5d from the Society. A new accounting machine had been purchased to speed up the computing of milk payments and other matters. Department officials were dissatisfied with the layout of the Spink premises and required extensive repairs and alterations or the building of a new creamery. Mr. Ebrill was asked to make a survey and to estimate the cost of repairs prior to any decisions being made. The Society decided to subscribe for membership of the newly formed Country Merchants Association.

Members, at the November meeting, were informed that only one carter had signed for the new price arrangement. It was agreed that no more cash remuneration be paid to carters unless they duly signed the agreement.

A new sandpit was acquired but the secretary pointed out that the method of extracting and loading sand in the pit was both obsolete and expensive. A loading shovel would cost £900. It was estimated that this cost would be recovered in extra work over 12 to 18 months. It was decided to go ahead with the purchase.

Mr. Kelly received a letter from Philip Brennan, Cuffsgrange, Co. Kilkenny, secretary of the Kilkenny ICMSA, requiring the co-operation of the committee at Donaghmore in forming branches 'in County Leix'. The secretary stated that he had read some of the ICMSA literature, which had not impressed him.

In December, the finance sub-committee made recommendations relating to credit:

1. Sale of fertilisers only on credit terms to be discontinued;
2. Credit to be given for only 50% of goods, the rest to be paid in cash;
3. Sale of cement on credit to be discontinued while all millstuffs were to be sold on a strictly cash or monthly account basis.

The manager reported that he had placed an order for a new self-indicating scales and a new milk-weighing machine, the price being £207. The meeting was made aware of a proposed change in the accounting system where the branches would keep their own accounts.

John Galbraith, the accountant, gave notice of his intention to terminate his employment as soon as the audit was complete. According to Mr. Whelan, in his report to the IAOS, this news came as a "bombshell to Mr. Kelly and others." Galbraith sent in his resignation in March, 1953. There were no less that 31 applications for the job, some from qualified accountants, but the committee was anxious to hold on to Mr. Galbraith. He came before the May 1952 meeting to discuss his problems, financial and otherwise, and was awarded a salary rise of £2 per week.

STATEMENT

Telegrams: "Creamery, Ballybrophy."
Telephones { Donaghmore 3
          Abbeyleix 16.

Railway Station—Ballybrophy.
Branches—Raheen and Spink

DONAGHMORE CO-OP. CREAMERY LTD.

BALLYBROPHY, LAOIGHIS

Seeds and Manures
Fuel, Cement and Sand
Grain, Mill Stuffs and
General Hardware

*Creamery Proprietors
and General Merchants*

Butter and Cream
Poultry Appliances
Hatchery Proprietors

27/11/51.   19

M.r. H. G. Pratt,
Dealsgrove,
Kilbricken.

To A/c. Rendered		
May 16. To Trump.	3	.
July 14. 6 Pkts. Saltosan.	2 5	.
20. 4 Saltosan.	1 10	.
28. To Spraying S. Doors.	5	.
	7 10	.
	3 00	
	£ 4 10 0	

Telephone: Donaghmore 3

DONAGHMORE CO-OPERATIVE CREAMERY, LIMITED,
BALLYBROPHY, LEIX.

18725
6 . 12 . 19 57

RECEIVED from Mr. H. G. Pratt,
Dealgrove .... the sum of
Four .... Pounds
Ten Shs. ——— Pce.

WITH THANKS
£ 4 : 10 : 0 X   Butter A/c.   Goods A/c.   Chick A/c.

Invoice and receipt for purchases at Donaghmore Co-op Creamery in 1951.

CHAPTER TWO

Jubilee Year

The milk supply to Donaghmore broke the magical one million gallon mark for the first time in 1951. The intake was up 23.6% on the previous year. The committee of management report stated that "this is probably the largest supply received by any creamery in Leinster. We were waiting twenty-five years for it to reach this level. Now it is of vital importance that we concentrate on maintaining it". A record profit of £4,625 for the previous year was deemed very satisfactory. A letter from the IAOS commented, "I think ... that your Society has exceeded all expectations at the time of its formation".[1] A dividend of 5% was paid to shareholders. The secretary's salary was pitched at £300 per annum with an added bonus of £75. The manager got an increase in his salary of £100 to £650. Other executives also received increased bonuses. The silver jubilee year was, therefore, a time of quiet celebration for Donaghmore Society. It had survived many difficult years. The perseverance, adaptability and dedicated service to the cause by many committee members over the years had kept the churns turning and the doors open, when many other co-ops in similar situations had folded.

At the AGM of 1952 on 27 March, a vote of congratulations was extended to one such committee man, Mr. Kirwan, who was a founder member of the Society and who was still serving on the committee in the jubilee year. No such congratulations were noted for another man who had not alone stayed the course but whose ingenuity and leadership as captain, had steered the good ship through many turbulent storms and but for whose presence over those twenty-five years, there would not have been any silver jubilee to celebrate. That man was J.P. Kelly. J.P. was not a man to get carried away on a tide of emotion, however. He was more concerned at this time about the ongoing health of the Society and this was being damaged by the recurring problem of information leaking from committee meetings, he told members.

The huge increase in supply was stretching production facilities and the AGM considered the options available. Attentions were turned to Spink. The creamery there was originally constructed to deal with 1,000 gallons of milk per day but it had taken in 3,000 gallons per day during the previous summer. The Department of Agriculture had been alerted to the problem and the matter had, as a result, to be resolved quickly. Not alone were facilities stretched but workers there were also feeling the pressure. There was an air of discontent among the staff over the long hours they worked for a basic wage. The Department Inspector had suggested that it may be necessary, if the repairs were not carried out, that a new creamery should be built in the Timahoe/Garryglass area, which he considered was "a more central position for the present milk supply".

With reference to the renewing of the lease at Spink, the owner, Mr. McDonald,

---

1. IAOS letter from assistant secretary dated 11 March 1952 (National Archives).

said that he would not consent to any alterations to the premises which would restrict the view from his shop. The only alternative was to buy the property or to look elsewhere for accommodation. Attempts were made to purchase the property. An offer of £1,200 was made in March but McDonald's price was £3,000. Other possible sites were examined and, on McDonald again refusing to reduce his asking price, the committee decided to purchase the site owned by Mr. Tommy Lennon and "to sign all the relevant documents".

The Spink manager, Mr. McAdam, found that the job was becoming more difficult by the day and eventually resigned in June 1952. William Keane, from Listowel, was appointed in his place. The new manager met with the Department's senior inspector, Mr. Power, and his assistant, Mr. O'Connor, at the new site. The location was to their approval. A set of plans was sent to the Department in December, 1952. There appears to have been some complications with the title deed for the site, however, and a fresh sounding was made to McDonald. His asking price was first dropped by £500 and, after further negotiation, a price of £2,250 was eventually agreed in January 1953.

A new complication was added when Inspector Power informed the manager that he did not think that the Department would approve of the plans but this snag appears to have been resolved and at a special meeting on 26 January, it was decided to proceed with the building of the new creamery "on the site purchased and according to the plans submitted".

Although he had sought tenders from various parties, the secretary, J.P. Kelly, reported to the February 1953 meeting that only one tender had been received. That was from Duggan Bros., Templemore and was for £2,492, labour only. By April, however, there were more tenders to be considered. The engaging of a quantity surveyor to assess the costs of the building work was considered but the IAOS advisor, Mr. Ebrill, felt such a measure was unwarranted. He advised the committee that a quantity surveyor's fee would be 2.5% of the contract price and, even then, he would not be in a position to supply the full information needed. The management committee took matters in their own hands. After some deliberation, it was decided to give the contract on a labour only basis to Duggan Bros.

In June 1952, the chairman, George Galbraith, mentioned the 'very unsatisfactory' delivery of separated milk in the Raheen area. Suppliers also complained of the late hour of the delivery of their cans. It was noted that a lorry-load of cans was observed "at a late hour outside the Picture House in Abbeyleix".[2]

The building work at Spink was completed by the end of 1953 but the premises were not operational until 8 April 1954 because of late delivery of machinery. The all-in cost of building work came to £4,444. A new milk scales was purchased for the branch.

Secretary injured in accident

The secretary was seriously injured in an accident at the Society's new drying store at Donaghmore on 1 September 1952. Sympathy was extended to Mr. Kelly on his misfortune and he was wished a speedy recovery at the committee meeting a few days later. At the October meeting, however, the concern was more on the question of whether the Secretary was insured and whether other clerical and office staff were insured for duties other than office duties. The manager, Donal Grogan, was asked to investigate. Mr. Kelly had sufficiently recovered to attend the November

2. In a letter from the IAOS dated 11 October 1952 (National Archives).

meeting but he told members that his doctor had refused to allow him to resume his duties for some time yet. The December meeting heard that the secretary had tried to recover the costs and expenses incurred from the Industrial Appliance and Mill Engineering Company, suppliers of the machinery involved in the incident, but was informed that the contract had not been with him but with Donaghmore Co-op and that they would have to be joined in the action. An upshot from the secretary's misfortunate accident was a decision to cover certain employees in a special personal accident insurance. A quote of £29-18-6 for full 24-hour cover was accepted and a proportion of the premium was to be paid by the individual employees.

In the autumn of 1952, the Society was informed of the Department of Agriculture's intention to set up an artificial insemination (AI) centre in North Kilkenny. The creameries were to be the owners and collect the fees, while the Department would stock the centre with animals, pay a veterinary surgeon and train inseminators. In March 1953, Donaghmore decided to apply for membership of the South Eastern Cattle Breeding Society and an application was made for 866 shares at £1 each. George Galbraith and Donal Grogan attended its first AGM.

A notice from the Labour Court of its intention to increase the wage of adult dairy workers by 12/6 weekly and other dairy workers by 8/6 was not well received by the committee. There was also some concern relating to carters threatening to cease carrying milk because of changes in the conditions under which privately owned transport operated. The carters were up in arms because of a proposed road tax increase. The rate of pay for Sunday work was clarified by the IAOS. The regulations provided for a rate of 1/3 per hour for all hours worked on that day, subject to a maximum of 5/- for any one Sunday.

At the December 1952 meeting, it was noted that the bank position was £5000 better off than at the same time in the previous year. Plans were presented for a new store at Raheen but Laois County Council turned down the Society's first planning application.

Resisting ICMSA agitation

In the spring of 1953, Donaghmore resisted efforts to close its creameries in support of an ICMSA campaign for better prices for dairy produce. A deputation consisting of Messrs. Buckley, Everard (two employees of the Centenary Society) and Egan (representing the ICMSA) had come along to Donaghmore hoping to persuade the committee to close down its operations. The chairman and some other members had met them but the visitors were not invited to take part in the committee's deliberations. J.P. Kelly, again functioning as secretary, stated that he had supplied the list of suppliers' names and addresses to the ICMSA the previous year and, despite the latter's best efforts, they had failed to get any support. The manager, William Grogan, told the committee that the Centenary Creamery manager had telephoned him advising him that, because Donaghmore Creamery and its branches were in an isolated area, they would be vulnerable in the event of trouble. Mr. Galbraith said that the "Civic Guards of Maryboro" had enquired from him if any assistance was needed. Mr. Kelly left no one guessing over his stance on the issue. He stated emphatically that he would bring his milk along the following day "pickets or no pickets". It was agreed, however, to contribute £50 to the ICMSA fighting fund.

The AGM for 1953 heard that the profit for 1952 amounted to £5,520 while the milk supply figure was 1,114,000 gallons and the turnover was up to approximately

£260,000. Senior staff were rewarded with bonuses.[3] A dividend of 5% was announced. Mr. Whelan, of the IAOS, drew attention to the fact that the Society's original £1 share was now valued at £3.

The first annual outing took place in July 1953 to Ardnacrusha and to the millers, Ranks Ltd., of Limerick. The Society paid for the luncheon. The Society decided in 1953 to adopt the metric system 'with certain reservations', which were not specified. A request from Fr. Coyne to distribute letters to milk suppliers appealing for funds to help rebuild Milltown Park, which had been destroyed by fire, was given the green light by the committee. A donation of two guineas was made to the Portlaoise Church Building Fund. The committee was much more generous in their response to an appeal from the Killesmeestia Church Repair Fund in June 1954, when they donated £50 to the project.

The manager, Donal Grogan, and accountant, John Galbraith, both had their salaries increased to ten guineas per week. The secretary, J.P. Kelly, told the December 1953 meeting that the Society was losing business for day-old chicks because they were unable to supply sexed chicks. It was decided to send Mr. Grogan on a week's training course in the art of sexing. Some years later, Richard Kelly, son of J.P., who worked in the store, became the chicken sexing expert.

Earlier in 1953, part of the dairy floor had been resurfaced and the remaining section was laid down when the recently acquired second-hand Astra churn was installed. A second-hand hammer grinding mill with electric motor was purchased at a cost of £275. A seed dressing machine was also purchased.

A new accountancy system had been introduced at Raheen and Spink branches in January 1952. Two years later, it was decided to purchase a calculator after the merits of the machine were debated at a committee meeting. Later in the year, the committee discussed the purchase of a cash register.

Passing of a founding father

At the February 1954 meeting, sympathy was extended to the relatives of the late Rev. T. Henebry, the Society's first chairman.

It was mentioned at the same meeting that a Raheen lorry had been in an accident and that cream was spilled on the roadway. The lorry had to swerve to avoid a cyclist "who had fallen across the road". It was noted that damage to the truck was not serious. There was no mention of damage to the cyclist.

J.P. Kelly mentioned the "hidden reserve" of diesel oil at his premises at Ballymeelish and said that there was no longer a need to keep it hidden as, in his opinion, there was now no danger of war. The tank was removed to Raheen.

The IAOS official, Mr. Whelan, told the AGM on 25 March 1954 that the IAOS was very proud of the success of the Society, all the more so because now its activities covered practically the whole of Co. Laois. All permanent staff received an increase of 5/- per week in their wages. A 5% dividend was struck. Supplier shareholders were also awarded a halfpenny per gallon bonus on all milk supplied in 1953. This was proposed by Bobby Bennett who felt that it was right that the people who 'initiated the good work' should now be rewarded. Bonuses were also announced for senior staff members. It was decided to purchase a sack lifting machine to facilitate the loading of grain and fertiliser.

---

3. Bonuses for 1953 as follows: Donal Grogan £100, J.P. Kelly £100, Wm. Wallis £75, Joe Butler £75, John Galbraith £50, Wm. Keane £20.

A quote of £1,230, labour only, was received from Duggan Bros. for the building of a new store at Raheen. Secretary, J.P. Kelly, estimated that the labour cost should not exceed £550 and that the cost of the project would be in the region of £2,500. He also said that new offices were required at the branch. It was decided to build the store by direct labour. Agreement was reached with the ESB on the supply of three-phase electricity to Raheen. A capital payment of £600 and a guaranteed usage of £100 per annum were demanded. Installation work began in February 1955.

At the September 1954 meeting, the manager reported the loss of £200 worth of cream due to the gross carelessness of an employee, whom he dismissed "there and then". Some members complained that the onus for her dismissal and reinstatement appeared to have been put on the committee.

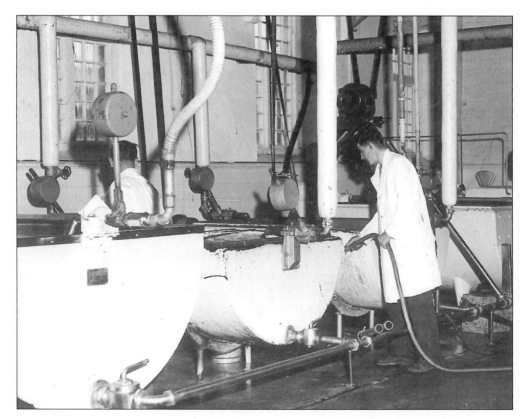

Mick Power working in the old dairy on the vats for chilling cream (1950s).

CHAPTER THREE

Butter Quality Concerns

Many complaints were noted regarding the quality of the Donaghmore butter. The manager was instructed to adopt a system whereby each pound roll when wrapped could be traced to a particular churn and date of manufacture. At the October 1954 meeting, the manager informed members that some butter had been returned by the BMC due to dirt detected in the produce. Mr. Grogan had traced the cause to decaying wood in the old churn. Quotations were to be solicited for a new churn and the faulty butter was to be sold to a butter factory.

There were also complaints made relating to one of the Society's tenants. J.P. Kelly explained: "The position is not a healthy one for the Society. In the past 8 or 9 months, Maher (the tenant in question) had built a shop and had altered the internal structure of the premises. He had built a shelter for his van outside the dairy door and his most recent effort was the erection of a privy within 10 yards of the dairy with a connection to the main drain. No permission was sought for these items. Recently while (the secretary) was ill, the yard in front of his door was rolled and covered with tarmac, contrary to instructions. To cover up his tracks, he stole several barrows of plastering sand and spread it over the patch as a blind." The committee ordered that the legal aspect be investigated.

The death of Fr. C. Coyne, P.P., Raheen, was noted with regret and the October meeting was adjourned for fifteen minutes as a mark of respect. The manager reported on a visit by Dr. McSearraigh, the county's health inspector, regarding alleged pollution of a stream by the creamery.

In a letter to the IAOS, J.P. Kelly asked that a case be made to the Fair Trade Commission regarding the price of dairy machinery. He felt that there was a cartel operating exploiting the creameries. He gave some sample prices: churn £1,530, compressor £2,300, rollmaker £195 and rolls for same £20. By publicising such prices, it might highlight the problem, he said. At the December 1954 meeting, the secretary announced that he had ordered a new Kolding churn at a cost of £1,980.

Ben Moran appointed manager at Spink

In March 1955, the Society was once again seeking a manager for Spink. The average length of tenure there was short with appointees soon disillusioned with the work, the salary or the job prospects. The manager, Donal Grogan, was sent to Cork University to interview prospective managers "with a view to seeing if one could be found who would take more interest in his work than his pay packet".

In April 1955, Edward Cronin was appointed with a salary of £400. He turned down the offer and Richard Stapleton was given the job. Less than twelve months later, the job was vacant once again. J.P. Kelly, supported by the committee, would have been very happy to appoint local man, Ben Moran, as manager there. He had proven ability but he lacked the qualification, the Diploma of Dairy Science, demanded by the Department of Agriculture. Despite several appeals by Kelly to allow Moran's appointment, the requests were turned down time and time again. In March 1956, however, a letter from the Department indicated that an examination would be held and, if Ben Moran passed the test, the Department's sanction would be forthcoming. Moran duly undertook the test and, in October 1956, news came through that he had passed it. His appointment as manager was immediately confirmed. In January 1957, his salary was increased to £8 weekly.

In February 1955, it was agreed that, in future, transport would be provided for committee members who had a difficulty in their travel arrangements for meetings at Donaghmore. The secretary was wished well, having undergone an operation. Committee eyebrows were raised with the news in April 1955 that rates on the Donaghmore premises had been increased by £90 with a corresponding increase at the branches.

In 1955, an electric petrol pump was installed at Central with the existing pump relocated to Raheen and another mechanical pump installed at Spink. A replacement five-ton Commer diesel truck was purchased. It was reckoned that the Society was losing £150 per year in interest on Production Allowances of £6,000 due from the government. By September, the amount due had risen to £7,000. A room was set aside for workers for use as a canteen. Permission was given to the office staff to have a tea and biscuit break at 4.30pm each day. Accommodation was provided for bicycles for staff members.

Having achieved an increase in profit of £800 in 1954 from the previous year, it was decided to pay the same bonuses as for 1953, with Billy Wallis and John Galbraith getting an additional £25 each. Donal Grogan felt aggrieved that his work "did not reach a standard to warrant an increase in bonus or salary". His complaint bore fruit because his salary was increased to £700 per annum from June 1955.

Manager's complaints

Grogan, earlier in 1955, had complained that he felt the committee did not trust him with regard to signing the cheques in the absence of secretary, J.P. Kelly. This was refuted by the committee and a new order was drawn up whereby the manager signed the cheques and John Galbraith was to attend to all other secretarial duties. In July, Grogan was critical of the supervision and general routine at the dairy. He suggested the appointment of a qualified assistant manager but this was refused and instead a "more reliable person than the present one", who was given instruction in the proper system of weighing and sampling milk, was appointed.

Then, in December 1955, Grogan complained bitterly about the state of his residence. The house was too large, too damp and too cold and, to make matters worse, a portion of the ceiling had fallen in. The committee replied that they were not in a position to provide alternative accommodation but were prepared to allow him an extra £100 to his salary if he could make alternative arrangements himself. In January 1956, however, he advised the committee that he had purchased a house in Rathdowney.

A cold store extension was erected and improvements were made at the dairy in the latter half of 1955. These included the installation of a pasteurising plant and changes in working arrangements were made to clear the dairy floor of congestion. Tenders received for the pasteurising equipment ranged in price from £1546 to £3400. The lowest tender was received from the Dairy Supply Company. It was approved by the Department in January 1957, which qualified Donaghmore for a grant of 50% of the cost.

Following a complaint about untidy staff in the dairy, it was agreed to supply "two brown coats to each dairy worker and one coat each year thereafter".

In November 1955, a prosecution by the Foods and Drugs Inspector over moisture levels found in a pound of Donaghmore butter purchased in Mountmellick was dismissed under the POA. The minutes noted with satisfaction that there had been no publicity about the prosecution.

The committee, however, were not so pleased over complaints from both the County Medical Officer and the Department of Fisheries relating to pollution of rivers at Donaghmore and at Spink. Remedial action was taken to avoid a recurrence.

In March 1956, it was noted that there had been a fire in the brooder room of the hatchery. It did not cause much damage but was the third such incident to occur caused by paraffin lamps. It was decided to ban the use of the lamps as, the minutes noted, "another fire might destroy the whole premises".

Bonuses for senior staff were announced at the April 1956 meeting.[1] At the AGM in May, which reviewed another profitable year, it was resolved that £1,000 be transferred to a pension fund reserve for workers. There were some complaints from shopkeepers regarding the similarity of the new butter wrappers to those used by margarine manufacturers. A number of traders insisted on obtaining the old blue wrapper.

Information leaks persist

The leaking of confidential information by committee members was again raised at the meeting of June 1956. J.P. Kelly thought it was irresponsible conduct and that such behaviour was grossly unfair to the other members. In the interests of the Society, he said that he would name the person responsible for the next leak that came to his notice.

The secretary stated that an attempt had been made in the recent past by the Workers Union of Ireland to get Donaghmore workers to join but it had failed. He wondered could there be a connection with a recent Labour Court request for information. The IAOS replied that it was "fairly certain the Labour Court had no ulterior motive in its request for information".

In October 1956, a franking machine, costing £80, and an addressing machine were requisitioned for the office. It was also decided to purchase an Alfa Laval separator and a Desco milk vat at a cost of £825 and £1010 respectively.

J.P. Kelly's role in the continuing success story was, at last, fully acknowledged. Although he had been effectively the full-time chief executive from the Co-op's foundation in 1927, he had never demanded and was never paid the salary to which he was entitled. It was now a big business and a very profitable one as well. The Society's turnover was close to £500,000 for 1956 and the profit figure was £10,900. The committee decided to show their appreciation for the man by doubling his salary from 1 January 1957 and by clearly establishing his executive functions.

His duties were redefined as follows:

---

1. Bonus payments for 1955 as follows: Donal Grogan £100, J.P. Kelly £100, John Galbraith £100, Joe Butler £75, Billy Wallis £100, Ben Moran £50 and Mr. Horsburgh £50.

1. To co-ordinate the various departments of the Society and act as liaison officer between the committee and staff.
2. To direct the policy of the Society in all matters concerning employment and administration of labour.
3. To advance all repair and reconstruction work, to direct and supervise all orders for goods, machinery and equipment.
4. Impertinence from any member of the staff to the secretary will mean their immediate dismissal.

At a special meeting on 27 February 1957, it was decided to erect a second intake platform at Donaghmore to cater for increased supplies. It was estimated that the cost would not exceed £2,000 as against an estimated costs of £10,000 for a new auxiliary. There would also be a saving in running costs.

Pictured at the petrol pump at Spink Creamery in the 1950s. (L.-r.): Peter Kelly, Pake Costigan, Tim Costigan, Pat (Junior) Lacey and Jimmy Deighton. Front: Gerard Lawler and Johnny Butler.

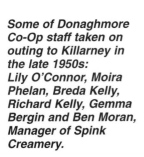

Some of Donaghmore Co-Op staff taken on outing to Killarney in the late 1950s: Lily O'Connor, Moira Phelan, Breda Kelly, Richard Kelly, Gemma Bergin and Ben Moran, Manager of Spink Creamery.

CHAPTER FOUR

Praise from the IAOS

In February 1957, it was agreed that an extra £100 be contributed to IAOS as a voluntary gratuity. This was received with great appreciation by the IAOS and it prompted a rounded acknowledgement from no less an official than its much esteemed chief executive, Dr. Kennedy. It read: "May I thank you personally, and through your committee, for the extremely generous act in allowing us to join in your prosperity this year. I am fully aware that your Society is one of the few distinguished ones that loyally follow their engagement of paying their subscription according to scale. But to add to that, this special bonus of £100 is something that revives my faith in the influence of co-operation among farmers. Sometimes in the drab routine of the Organisation's work, one begins to wonder whether our efforts are appreciated. It is all the more pleasant then, to find a Society like yours not only fully generous with regard to money but also appreciative of the little we can do for such a powerful Society such as yours. I need hardly tell you that every penny is spent most economically and that it means a great deal to the poorer societies in the less well-off districts to have the more wealthy societies giving larger subscriptions. I understand, of course, that this is merely a bonus and would not establish any precedent."

Aerial view of Raheen Creamery mid 1950s.

At the 1957 AGM,[1] a bonus of 1d per gallon was allowed to shareholders on milk supplied by them in 1956. A letter of apology was received from George Galbraith for being unable to attend; his first non-attendance in 29 years. Quotations were received for a 2200 gallon plate pasteuriser and it was decided to go with the one from the Creamery Supply Company at £2,215.

It was decided that no further issue of shares be made. Persons desiring membership must acquire shares from existing members. Two hundred shares became available for transfer from non-active members. Due to continuing problems with the carters and the delivery of milk at specified times, it was decided to impose a fine of £1 for each day any milk carter does not arrive at the creamery at the appointed time. Authorisation for the purchase of a milk meter was sanctioned by the Committee. It was decided to purchase four mechanical sack loaders for the grain lorries as a matter of necessity. John O'Callaghan of Inch was appointed assistant manager.

The Society secured first place in a surprise butter inspection in June 1957. The committee was impressed with this achievement on the part of the acting buttermaker, Michael Loughman, who received a £5 bonus for his efforts. It was hoped to have Mr Loughman certified as a qualified buttermaker but the Department of Agriculture refused his application.

In September 1957, the dairy inspector reported problems with the pasteuriser, which was unable to maintain the necessary temperature for the four-hour period of milk intake under conditions then existing. He advocated an extension of the intake facilities. Having taken into consideration the fact that milk supplies had increased by 32% in the previous five months, it was agreed, in September 1957, to proceed with the erection of a dual intake platform as had been previously proposed.

The question of starting a co-operative cattle mart was raised in the autumn of 1957. It was generally felt that it would be a good idea. Plans had been underway for the formation of a mart in Rathdowney but it was felt that it would never come about. The secretary wrote to the IAOS seeking advice about the committee's proposal to start a cattle mart in the Society's grounds.[2] A syndicate was formed to purchase a site and, after considering the option of going the co-operative route, they decided to go ahead with the project on a private basis. But the bid failed and the local branch of the NFA had to foot the bill. Donaghmore Co-op contributed £15 towards the costs.

A radio telephone was installed in the office in connection with AI calls. A demonstration of the operation of the radio telephone was given to the meeting and the members were much impressed by its efficiency. It was ordered that a receiver be installed at Raheen but the GPO demanded a fee of £25 for the extension and this delayed installation there for a short time.

Managerial functions outlined

At the committee meeting in November 1957, it was revealed that the secretary had been subject to impertinence from an employee, who was instantly dismissed.

1. The following people attended the Annual General Meeting held in Donaghmore on 27 March 1957: Messrs. J.C. Carroll, William Roe, R.P. Bennett, M. Walsh, P. Shiel, J. Butler, S. Campion, Rody McEvoy, J. Hennessy, M. McWey, W. Cassidy, J. Martin (IAWS), Michael Kilmartin, P. Kelly, Patrick Purcell, J. Moylan, Michael Kirwan, J. Galbraith, Lee Whelan, William Wallis, James Brennan, S. Bailey, Joseph Bergin, John Treacy, J. Kennedy and J. P. Kelly. Mr. P. Whelan of the IAOS was also in attendance. P.J. Kavanagh, who presided at the meeting, was re-elected chairman while Mr. Walsh was re-elected vice-chairman.
2. Letter dated 12 September 1957 (National Archives).

A customer (on extreme left), J.P. Kelly, Richard Kelly and Robert Horsburgh at the Donaghmore Shop in 1957.

Some of the office staff in 1957 as follows: Lily O'Connor (née Dowling), Moira Phelan (née Ryan), Breda Kelly, Gemma Bergin and John O'Callaghan, Assistant Manager.

The manager, Donal Grogan, was incensed by Kelly's action. He referred to the incident which had taken place in his absence and asked to know what his duties were: was he in command or not? The issue was discussed at the December meeting in the absence of both men. The following procedures were outlined:

1. Manager in charge of dairy and hatchery and responsible for the completion of all returns to government departments and large firms where much correspondence is required. He shall write up the stock book and visit the branches at least once a month, furnishing a report thereon to each monthly meeting.
2. The assistant shall be responsible for the cash and all work in connection with the books of account, bank lodgements, etc.
3. The store manager shall be responsible for the conduct of the store trade of the Society together with the grain, fertilisers and gravel pit. He shall have responsibility for the operation of all transport.
4. The secretary shall assume the status of general manager and be responsible to the committee for the coordination of all the departments. Prices of seeds and fertilisers both in purchase and sale should be discussed with him before orders or price lists are made out. He shall be consulted in dealing with all matters of major importance especially complaints from the public and the issuing of orders for any goods in excess of £100. The committee shall insist on prior consultation between the manager and secretary on all matters however small concerning the Society's affairs.
5. That the interests of the Society can be best served by the co-operation of all concerned.
6. That it must be understood that the committee are the final authority in all matters relating to the running of this.

Grogan protested that he had been appointed manager of the creamery and it now appeared that he was no longer manager. He demanded the terms of his appointment be read. It was pointed out to him that he was originally appointed to be in charge of the dairy, the hatchery and the egg and poultry store. He was told that Kelly was the general manager. On his undertaking to co-operate with the Secretary in all matters, it was agreed to 'forget the reason for the present discussion on this whole subject'.

At the January 1958 meeting, the committee voted for a £50 donation to Abbeyleix Macra na Feirme towards their hall-building fund. The secretary reported that the installation of the new Hammer Mill was nearing completion. He also revealed that electricity was now available at Spink. It was agreed to distribute a circular from the *Farmer's Journal* advocating the sale of that paper.

It was noted in April 1958 that the milk supply showed a decrease of 1360 gallons in the previous month's intake, this being the first decrease recorded for some years. The Society reported a record profit of £17,000 for 1957. The chairman stated that he would like to see all the employees reaping the reward of their good work in 1957 and he proposed that all employees, who were 12 months in the Society's employment, be given a bonus of one week's wages. This was agreed to.

Share values increase six-fold

At the AGM for 1958, Mr. Whelan of the IAOS compared the liquid assets to the liabilities of the Society and pointed out that, if the Society was wound up, the shareholders would now receive £6 for every £1 invested.

Committee members and staff on an outing to Killarney in 1958
Back: Mick Hogan, Paddy Sheil, Robert Horsburgh, Paddy Kavanagh, Paul Broughan, Joe Butler, — , John O'Callaghan, John Hennessy, Mike Kirwan.
Middle: George Galbraith, J. P. Kelly, Mrs. Grogan, Donal Grogan, Michael Walsh, Mrs. Wallis, Billy Wallis, Joe Bergin, John Galbraith, John Treacy.
Front: Richard Kelly, Murty McWey, Mrs. Kavanagh, Breda Kelly, Gemma Bergin, Bobby Bennett, Lily O'Connor, Moira Phelan (Moira Ryan), Ben Moran.

Peter Mangan (helper/driver) arriving at Spink Creamery with load of milk in the 1950s.

The County Medical Officer wrote to the Society in connection with the alleged pollution of the river at Donaghmore. It was decided to go ahead with "some sort of purification system".

The manager reported in August 1958 that it was proposed by the Irish Chick Hatchery Association to float a company who would deal with the export of chicks and eggs to Italy. It was suggested that the Society should hold £100 stock or shares in the company. Members showed an interest in the proposal but sought more information before agreeing to join.

Milk suppliers from Vicarstown who delivered their milk to Crettyard wrote to the Society asking to change their intake point to Spink. This was allowed, providing they were told that they would have to arrange their own cartage to the alternative venue.

L. to r: Jack Power and Paddy Campion employees at Donaghmore pictured on their way to Mass in Borris-in-Ossory in the 1950s. Jack Power was one of the first employees of Donaghmore Creamery.

The provision of extra grain storage space became a critical issue for the committee in the autumn of 1958. Because of lack of facilities, the grain had to be sold off and purchased later on at increased prices. Officials visited storing facilities at other locations before agreeing on a plan for Donaghmore. Mr Ebrill, of the IAOS, estimated the cost of the proposed storage facility at £25,000. After discussion, it was moved that the scheme as outlined be proceeded with and it was hoped that the modern equipment involved would expand the grain trade and reduce the selling price to members. In March 1959, two draft plans of a building for grain storage were submitted for inspection. One was for use with Grapel steel silos and the other would house a number of mass concrete silos. After discussion, it was unanimously decided to go ahead with the erection of the mass concrete silos. The secretary pointed out that they would not be ready for the following harvest as no preliminary work could be done on them until the working plans were available. A small grain drier was purchased for Raheen to save having to transport grain for drying to Donaghmore. Working plans for the granary were laid before the April 1959 meeting.

It was noted that there was a reduction of 30% in the milk supply for January 1959 compared to the previous January. Mr. Grogan reported that the hatchery was producing more chickens in 1959 than in the previous year but that weekly clearances were difficult and there was a carry-over of some breeds.

The IAOS representative, Mr. Whelan, passed along a note to the IAOS chief executive, Dr. Kennedy, in July 1959, regarding a proposed visit to Plunkett House by George Galbraith. The latter was concerned about J.P. Kelly's ill health and the difficulty that would arise if Mr. Kelly could take no further part in the Society's activities. Mr. Galbraith believed that there was no other person in the Society capable of taking over from him. An assistant to Mr. Kelly was suggested but this matter would have to be handled tactfully, Mr. Whelan advised.[3] The secretary was welcomed back after his illness at the August meeting and said he needed some assistance as the volume of his work had increased substantially.

Paul Hurley, Jimmy Phelan, John Maybury and Johnny Lalor at construction work at back of old dairy, Raheen late 1950s.

3. An IAOS internal memo dated July 1959 (National Archives).

SECTION ONE

PART FIVE

The 1960s

INTRODUCTION

A New Era Ushered In

The 1960s ushered in a new economic era. In 1959 Seán Lemass had succeeded de Valera as Fianna Fáil party leader and Taoiseach, and gave full support to the new strategy of industrial development, largely financed by inward investment. Agriculture too was to change dramatically. The emphasis was now more outward-looking. The days of self-sufficiency belonged to the past. Mechanisation and modernisation of farming methods led to a dramatic increase in farming output, particularly in the dairy sector. With export outlets limited, supply exceeded demand on the home market and prices remained low. If farmers were to reap their due rewards, overseas markets would have to be found. The emphasis on agricultural policy turned to marketing.

The establishment of An Bord Bainne in 1961 marked an important milestone for the Irish dairy industry. This semi-state enterprise replaced the old Butter Marketing Committee. It was exclusively an export organisation. The Kerrygold brand was launched on the UK market with great success. Irish butter was now marketed as a quality product, with a distinctive wrapper, which commanded a premium price. By the end of the 1960s, the Kerrygold brand had a worldwide market and exports increased dramatically from year to year.

The important home market was not neglected in this frenzied search for overseas buyers. Responsibility for the promotion of milk and dairy products at home was handed over to another new body, the National Dairy Council, founded in 1964.

Milk intake at Donaghmore trebled during the 1960s to almost seven million gallons. In the twenty years to 1969, the intake had increased almost twenty-fold. By the mid-1960s, the Donaghmore management knew that they were facing a big problem as their production facilities strained under the ever increasing milk supplies. Donaghmore shared this problem, to a lesser or greater extent, with other co-ops.

As Ireland prepared to join the EEC, policy became focused on the need for Irish industry and agriculture to be competitive in relation to other member states. In the dairy industry, amalgamations, diversification and economies of scale became the buzz-words. The dairy industry was to be transformed in a relatively short space of time from being comprised of a big number of relatively small units into an industry dominated by a small number of co-operative giants. Donaghmore found its future in one such grouping – Avonmore, later to merge with Waterford Co-op to form Glanbia.

CHAPTER ONE

Secretary's Health Causing Concern

There was concern over the secretary's health throughout 1960 and this continued to dominate proceedings at Donaghmore for the next few years. J.P. Kelly had played such a dominant role in the Society for so long, that members found it difficult to contemplate how the business could be run efficiently in his absence. There was, however, an undercurrent of unease evident at the lack of co-operation and communication among senior executives, including Kelly himself.

At the meeting in February 1960, the chairman, P.J. Kavanagh, found it necessary to advise the secretary and manager that there should be better co-operation among them, "otherwise both would be asked to resign", he said. In May of the same year, Mr. Kelly of the IAOS, suggested that there should be a weekly meeting between the secretary, the manager, the store manager and accountant to discuss problems as they arose. He further suggested that a sub-committee be appointed to delve deeper into business-related matters and become conversant with the working of the Society.

The sub-committee consisted of three members from Donaghmore and one each from Raheen and Spink. These were: Messrs. Bennett, Campion, Henry, Galbraith and Walsh with the chairman, Mr. Kavanagh an ex-officio member.

The secretary was back in hospital in December and he tendered his resignation to that month's meeting because of his illness. The committee decided not to discuss the matter until Kelly's return.

A special meeting was called for 4 August 1961 to discuss the management issue. Mr. Kelly of the IAOS pointed out that the secretary had been advised by his doctor that he would have to give up work altogether or reduce it considerably. This necessitated a change in the management of the society. Kelly agreed to take care of the Share Ledger. It was proposed that William Wallis and Donal Grogan should be made joint managers and, privately, each were asked their opinion of the proposition. Both agreed that it was in the best interests of the Society. It was unanimously decided that the initiation of the joint managership should commence on 1 September 1961 and that the secretary should look after all the legal matters relating to it. Their salaries were fixed some months later at £1,250 per annum. The constitution of the sub-committee was drawn up. It was decided that it should consist of four members, one from Raheen (G. Galbraith) and Spink (M. McWey) and two from Donaghmore (the chairman, P.J. Kavanagh, and R.P. Bennett). The decision to appoint joint managers proved to be a compromise that simply would not work. It led to friction and difficulties down the road.

Rody McEvoy had resigned from the committee after 23 years service in January 1959. His death was recorded in the minutes for September 1960. He was praised as a zealous worker on behalf of the Society.

Reg. No. C 348   1 lb. Nett.
454 G

This Butter has been automatically moulded, weighed and wrapped and has not been touched by hand during the process of manufacture or packaging.

IRISH CREAMERY BUTTER

Manufactured by

Donaghmore

Co-operative Creamery Ltd.

DONAGHMORE - LAOIGHIS

PRODUCE OF
THE REPUBLIC OF IRELAND

This Butter has been automatically moulded, weighed and wrapped and has not been touched by hand during the process of manufacture or packaging.

A Donaghmore butter wrapper of the 1960s.

Summons for river pollution

The issue of waste disposal had arisen again in the autumn of 1959 when the Society received a summons for river pollution issued by the Waterford Fishery Conservators. The case was adjourned for six months at court in November which gave the Society a little time to put matters right. The committee considered erecting what was known as an American plant at a cost of approximately £3,000. But there was a delay in sourcing this and, in any case, there was not one similar plant operational in the country which they could examine. An alternative was to purchase land and pump the waste from the creamery on it. The secretary approached local landowner, Michael Murphy, and asked him if he would sell twelve acres for this purpose. Murphy said he would sell the whole 29-acre farm at a cost of £3,000. The committee agreed to the price and the sale was completed by January 1960. Work on the pumphouse was completed during the summer but the sewage pump was not delivered until December 1960.

In May 1960, Shanahoe suppliers signified their intentions of transferring to Ballyragget. However, a settlement with them was successfully negotiated.

Roscrea NFA invited the Society to become an interested party in the erection of a branch creamery in the town. A deputation was received by a Donaghmore sub-committee on 20 October 1960. It was stated that the proposers had about 600 cows but it was ascertained that up to 75% of the cows in question were already being catered for by Centenary or Donaghmore. The secretary wrote to Roscrea NFA telling them that the Society was not interested in the project. In December 1960, there was an approach to open an auxiliary in Birr. In 1961, the IAOS informed the Society that Courtwood Society, formed in 1914, was going badly and inquired if Donaghmore would be interested in a take-over. There was no enthusiasm for getting involved. A discussion took place in November 1961 on the possibility of churning for the new creamery at Monasterevin. Members were informed that to do so would involve a capital outlay in the region of £5,000. It was decided that such expenditure would not be justified.

The store manager, Billy Wallis, informed the committee in the summer of 1960 that he was endeavouring to involve the Society in the area of grass seed production. It was hoped to get some growers interested in the sowing of Italian ryegrass. The Department of Agriculture sponsored the project and a lecture on the subject was given in November. Meetings were arranged in Rathdowney and Roscrea for the purpose of getting customers interested but little progress was made. Mr. Wallis reported that the barley was of a poor quality and in short supply. He also revealed that there were little or no oats available and that the quality of all samples offered was distinctly poor.

Changes in the Road Traffic Act

The private milk carters, who had played a very important role in operations at Donaghmore and most other creameries for many decades, were forced to cease deliveries of all goods because of changes in the Road Transport Act. The action took place as a result of a successful prosecution in November 1960 against the Society at Abbeyleix Court for using the services of a private carter, Felix Bennett, in delivering goods to farmers. The Society was fined £10 and Mr. Bennett £5.

Although their main function was in collecting milk from the suppliers and bringing it to the creamery, the carters were also engaged in delivering all items of goods ordered by the farmers from the co-op stores. They were an important link between the milk suppliers, many of whom lived in isolated rural areas, and the co-op and they performed a very useful service that was acknowledged by both the Society and the customer.

New arrangements had to be hastily made to enable the Society to make the deliveries with its own lorries. Very soon, this was seen to be both too costly and cumbersome. The store manager, Billy Wallis, was empowered to purchase a light delivery vehicle to assist the vehicles currently employed to provide an adequate service, especially to farmers in the Raheen and Spink areas, where the biggest difficulties were being experienced.

An appeal against the conviction was lost and, having sought legal opinion about a further appeal, the Society was advised that it would be injudicious of them to bring a case to the High Court because of a previous conviction. The committee felt that the widest possible publicity should be given to the operations of the Act as it related to creamery milk suppliers and to the creameries. A letter of protest was sent to the Dail representatives for the constituency and other societies were advised of their action. The Mountmellick based TD, Oliver J. Flanagan, tabled a motion highlighting the situation in the Dail. In his reply, the Minister for Transport, Mr. Childers, explained that "since there was no objection to transport of goods on

Donaghmore Committee and staff outing to Salthill, 1961

Front row: John Treacy, Michael Kirwan, Gemma Bergin, Lily O'Connor (Dowling), Breda Kelly, Noreen Whelan (Hyland).

Second row: Paddy Daly, Murty McWey, J. P. Kelly, Mrs. Sophie Kelly, Mr. and Mrs. Greg Tierney.

At back: Richard Kelly, R. P. Bennett, Mrs. K. Grogan, Wm. Wallis, Robert Horsburgh, D. F. Grogan, Paul Broughan, Paddy Kavanagh, Michael Walsh, Joe Bergin, John Hennessy, Ben Moran, George Galbraith, Stephen Campion, Paddy Sheil, Seán Reilly.

a genuine obligement basis without reward, I cannot see that there is any case for amending the law". He said the difficulty in the Donaghmore case was that the milk carriers entered into a contract that, in part consideration of the payments made to them, they would deliver goods other than empty milk churns. Any goods carried under such a contract would, he added, be deemed by the courts to be carriage for reward.

Donaghmore was not alone in its anger. Mr. Greg Tierney of the IAOS told the committee in January 1961 that Dungarvan Co-op were being prosecuted for a breach of the Act and that the outcome would probably be a case stated in the High Court. In March, the committee was advised that Castlecomer had also been subject to a prosecution. Another blow was felt a few weeks later when the Society was convicted for "aiding and abetting James Campion for the carriage of goods for reward under the Road Transport Act". The case was appealed to the High Court on this occasion. A resolution was drafted by the committee with regard to the problem for discussion at the AGM of the IAOS. There was also a question of costs. In January 1962, Greg Tierney of the IAOS advised Donaghmore that Dungarvan and Castlecomer "were prepared to contribute something to the costs" but he did not expect any other co-op to help out. J.P. Kelly took a poor view of the IAOS stance on the issue. "They promised full support to stand behind us as far as costs were concerned", he told the committee. A proposal to apportion the cost of the legal fees between the three co-ops, as advised by Mr. Tierney, was agreed by all sides the following June. The issue of the legality of milk carters' carrying goods other than milk and milk cans fizzled out in the months that followed.

John Galbraith, J.P. Kelly and Donal Grogan, pictured at Donaghmore Co-op in early 1960s.

CHAPTER TWO

All Not Well on Management Front

In March 1961, the store manager, Billy Wallis, reported on a move afoot to lower the level of the Gortnalec River and drain adjoining lands under the land reclamation scheme. The Society and 20 to 30 farmers had signed the request. It was suggested that the Society appoint a spokesperson to represent all interests.

Mr. Hennessy agreed to act in this capacity. It was proposed that the river level should be lowered from Donaghmore village and not from the bridge crossing the road near the Creamery. Mr. Wallis later confirmed that this had been agreed with the Department officials.

Donal Grogan was finally allowed to have an assistant manager in 1961. In April, it was decided to appoint Denis O'Mahony to the position but the matter was deferred when O'Mahony declined to take the job. James Somers was appointed in a temporary capacity the following month.

In the spring of 1961, the committee considered buying the Royal Ballroom in Borris-in-Ossory "for the purpose of keeping competitors away". They would buy it if any firm in the grain or seed business got involved in the bidding. On hearing that the offer had risen to £1,500 and that the interested party was a ballroom syndicate, it was decided to withdraw from the bidding. But they still had an interest in leasing the building on a temporary basis for storing grain for the 1961 season, if that was found feasible.

Tenders for a new grain store were before the June 1961 meeting. The lowest was from Hegarty's of Cork for £22,755 and it was accepted with work commencing immediately. It was also noted that the office reconstruction was now almost complete.

The joint managers, Grogan and Wallis, paid a surprise visit to Spink branch in August 1961 and found some things not to their satisfaction. Dairy utensils had not been properly cleaned and the daily record books had not been written up for two weeks. On a subsequent visit three weeks later, however, Grogan reported a big improvement.

The barley harvest for 1961 was satisfactory and the Society fulfilled its own requirements. The only difficulty was in finding storage. But there were problems with the wheat crop. The October meeting heard that one third of the acreage had still to be saved. It was reported that "all the wheat on shank is sprouting and will be classed as unmillable". Their worst fears were realised when Mr. Wallis informed the Society that practically all of the wheat sent to Limerick had been rejected for flour milling. This was a serious matter for both the farmers and the Society, he said.

All was not well on the management front. J.P. Kelly was in failing health, there was a lack of communication between the joint managers and the accountant,

John Galbraith, was not quite sure of the extent of his executive functions. J.P. wrote a "confidential" letter to Mr. Tierney on 22 November advising him that the management issue had been aggravated further by the accountant, John Galbraith, refusing to sign affidavits as to the state of accounts in default, a task he had performed for twenty years. The latter maintained that it was the manager's job. The secretary appealed to Mr. Galbraith that the "status quo" should remain. "He does not agree, saying that the status quo is gone long ago. He is being difficult."

The joint managers and Mr. Galbraith, were asked by the committee to draw up regulations for "the more orderly management" of the Spink branch. Mr. Galbraith was told to consult the joint managers when problems arose and, if this did not lead to a unanimous decision, he was then to consult the sub-committee. A meeting of the joint managers and the accountant was to take place monthly.

Clonaslee Co-op seeks support

The Provender Milling Joint Labour Committee recommended a rise of £1-1-0 a week to workers in the industry in the spring of 1962. But when the Society agreed to grant the increase to the nine workers involved, it almost led to a strike by other workers, who demanded similar increases.

Around the same time, Camross IFA wrote to Donaghmore regarding the possibility of opening a cream-separating station in Coolrain. There does not seem to have been any concerted follow-up to this suggestion. An auxiliary creamery of Donaghmore had operated in Coolrain from 1928 to 1938, when it was closed down because of the shortage of a milk supply in the area.

The manager, Donal Grogan, attended a meeting in Kilkenny at which a group of co-ops showed an interest in acquiring the powder milk factory, which was being planned for Ireland by the American concern, 'Foremost Dairies'.

In April 1962, the committee discussed a letter from Clonaslee Pig Fattening Co-op looking for support. Members were aware that Mullingar and Monasterevin creameries were canvassing Raheen suppliers in the Mountmellick/Clonaslee area. By joining forces with Clonaslee Co-op, a buffer could be created to protect the Raheen supply in the area. Bobby Bennett suggested that Donaghmore should buy £1000 of shares in Clonaslee provided that they get representation on the committee there. Messrs. Galbraith and Walsh were duly elected on Clonaslee committee in October. There was a proposal to raise a loan of £30,000 to erect accommodation for 2,000 pigs but this was considered a little adventurous by Donaghmore and, in November, a decision was taken to proceed with a more modest building, estimated at £17,000, which would accommodate up to 700 pigs.

The Clonaslee committee were invited by the Society to Donaghmore for an information visit in January 1963 and were entertained to 'high tea' in Rathdowney later that evening.

A special meeting was held on 16 May 1962 for the purpose of meeting the milk carters and working out an agreement on a number of vexed issues. The carters' representatives were Messrs. Bowe, Bennett, Kelly, Seale, Nolan and Lacey. Members of the committee present were Messrs. Bennett, Bergin, Campion, Galbraith, Hennessy, Kirwan, Reilly, Treacy and Walsh as well as the chairman, P.J. Kavanagh, and the branch managers, Joe Butler and Ben Moran. The carters put ten points before the committee for consideration. The first item was a demand for a payment of 3d per gallon of milk collected. This was refused. Other creameries were charged at 2.5d per gallon, the carters were told. There was agreement, however, on a number of issues while others remained unresolved.

Two years later, the carters, now calling themselves Donaghmore Milk Hauliers Association, were back demanding an increase in their rates. The committee agreed to an increase of 0.25d per gallon. Among a number of other issues ruled on was that the carters could not, in future, object to suppliers bringing their own milk or making arrangements with their neighbours to do so. Broad agreement was reached.

The third break-in to Society's premises was noted at the May meeting in 1964. It was decided that a night watchman be employed but the man appointed to the position only lasted two weeks in the job. He sought more pay which was turned down. The committee then examined a number of options on security including the practicality of installing an automated fire and burglary alarm system. Eventually, on 1 November, Thomas Phelan was appointed on wages of £10 for six nights and his duties included office cleaning.

There was much deliberation in the early years of the 1960s as to the best superannuation scheme that could be introduced at Donaghmore. Quotes were received from financial institutions but these were considered too expensive for the Society's needs. Greg Tierney of the IAOS investigated the possibility of the Society formulating its own scheme with the approval of the Revenue Commissioners. It was later decided, however, that the scheme submitted by National Mutual Society be adopted. The March meeting of 1962 heard that 70% of the eligible male employees had signed application forms to join the scheme. R.P. Bennett proposed that any employee who did not join the scheme before the closing date should not be allowed to do so at a later date. The motion was passed. It was later decided, due mainly to pension costs, that the age of all entries into the Society's service must be under twenty one years, unless by special permission of the committee.

Boundaries issue

The issue of boundaries got a full hearing at a meeting in Plunkett House in September 1962. Mr. Grogan and Mr. Galbraith represented Donaghmore. Grogan complained that problems had arisen with Tullamore (Westmeath Co-op) in the Clonaslee and Kilcavan areas. Mr. Landers, for Westmeath Co-op, said that boundaries with Donaghmore and Monasterevin would have to be agreed. Closer contact with the IAOS on contentious boundaries was agreed.[1]

Committee member, Mr. Hennessy, pushed for the installation of heaters in lorries operated by the Society at the January 1963 meeting. He said that the drivers and helpers were 'perished' on long journeys. Heaters were installed in two lorries by March.

Monasterevin Creamery had made soundings at Donaghmore to do the churning for them but, at the January 1963 meeting, members were informed that they had made arrangements for Castlecomer to do this work. A matter of even more immediate concern relating to Monasterevin was mentioned at the April 1964 meeting. Raheen manager, Joe Butler, said he had been reliably informed that the

---

1. The meeting was held on 25 September 1962. The six co-ops represented were: Donaghmore (Grogan and Galbraith), Monasterevin (Carter and Mahon), Castlecomer (Teehan and Graham), Barrowvale (Prendergast, Buckley and Fennelly), Athboy (O'Connell and Miggin), Westmeath (Ginnell and Landers). Patrick Kelly and Greg Tierney represented the IAOS.

Kildare-based creamery, just recently formed, intended to put transport on the road to collect milk in the Mountmellick area, which was currently served by his branch. They indicated that they would charge 2d per gallon cartage and Mr. Butler felt that this might be tempting to suppliers. Mr. Tierney of the IAOS promised to investigate the matter.

The secretary told the April 1963 meeting that he had sent a congratulatory note, on behalf of the Society, to Patrick Kelly on his appointment as secretary of the IAOS in succession to Dr. Kennedy.

J.P. Kelly advised the IAOS in May 1963 that Mullingar were underselling their butter in Portarlington. He claimed that they were charging only 4/3 per lb roll, whereas the agreed price was 4/4. "We see little sense in the farmers and the co-ops shouting for an increase in milk prices if this is allowed to go on", he stated bluntly.[2]

In August 1963, the secretary complained about the leaking of information from meetings. He said that matters in this regard had improved in recent years but he did not want to see the problem continuing. He said that "any person giving away such information was no friend of the Society". The matter arose yet again in November 1964, when the new secretary, John Galbraith, mentioned four instances of information being leaked and called for offending members to be more responsible. In December, Mr. Galbraith complained that staff knew of the committee's decision not to allow them a five days week before they had been officially informed by management.

In September 1963, there was an application before the committee for a 'cost of living' increase of £2 per week from sixteen yardmen and drivers. Members felt that the application was "totally unjustified" but agreed to reduce the working week to 46 hours. A communication from the IAOS indicated the rise in the cost of living that had occurred quoting an index of 100 for 1947, which had jumped to 160 for February 1963.

Clerical Staff of Donaghmore 1960s
Back row: **Irene Fitzgerald, Lena Delaney, Moira Ryan, Rita Nolan, Kathleen O'Gorman, Martha Ryan, Gemma Bergin, Noreen Hyland.**
Front: **Rita King, Breda Kelly, Lily Dowling.**

2. In a letter from J.P. Kelly to secretary of the IAOS dated 11 May 1963 (National Archives).

CHAPTER THREE

Credit Control a Thorny Issue

The accountant, John Galbraith, was feeling somewhat unhappy with his situation and sent in a letter of resignation in November, 1963. Mr. Galbraith's problems centred on the joint managership which, he said, was not working well. It was making it difficult for him in the circumstances, for instance, to take responsibility for restricting credit to defaulters. The whole area of credit control had become a thorny issue with the committee. Management had been warned to keep a close eye on the situation. Mr. Tierney advised that the joint managers and Mr. Galbraith should meet on the last Friday of every month to look at the credit situation. Executive functions were defined as follows: secretary, John Galbraith, was told that he had full charge of clerical employment, Donal Grogan had full charge of the dairy and hatchery while Billy Wallis had full responsibility for the shop and stores.

Tensions continued to exist at management level and, to add to the dilemma, the secretary, J.P. Kelly, announced that, on health grounds, he too was considering his position. As a temporary measure, he asked for permission to train his son, Richard, in some of his work for a period of three months. This was agreed to.

At a private meeting on 22 January 1964, however, the matter was further discussed and a decision was made to allow Mr. Kelly to resign. Vice-chairman, Mr. Walsh, read the following statement after the meeting: "The members of the committee considered the request of Mr. Kelly to resign and, while regretting his

Members of management and committee of management pictured in the 1960s
Front row (l. to r): Patrick Kavanagh, Michael Walsh, Murtagh McWey, Michael Kirwan, John Hennessy, George Galbraith, Joseph Bergin, Patrick Sheil, Seán O'Reilly.
Back row (l. to r): Stephen Campion, John Galbraith (Secretary), John Treacy, Bobby Bennett, Billy Wallis, John O'Meara and Donal Grogan (Manager).

decision, they were reluctantly forced to accept it from 18 February next." A pension of £600 per annum was announced and a request that the retirement be marked with a suitable presentation to mark his "long and honoured service on behalf of the Society". The temporary appointment of Richard Kelly, as assistant to the secretary, was rescinded from the date of resignation. Another private meeting was held on 31 January 1964 at which it was decided to appoint John Galbraith as secretary/accountant. Mr. Kelly was asked to continue to deal with legal and insurance matters when requested.

Active in retirement

Mr. Kelly may have retired but he retained a passionate interest in the Society and this brought him into conflict with management and, in particular, Mr. Grogan. A private meeting of the committee was held in July to discuss Mr. Kelly's position. At a previous meeting, he had been critical of the way the dairy was being run. He claimed that on two occasions, at least, farmers had weighed in their own milk and had recorded the weights in the books of the Society. He also claimed that there had been a pilferage of butter by members of the staff. He further claimed that the toilet facilities in the Society's premises were not being adequately cleaned and blamed Mr. Grogan, specifically for this. Mr. Grogan said the situation was intolerable in his view that the retired secretary still considered that he had duty and, indeed, authority to interfere in the administration of the Society. It was suggested that if Mr. Kelly, as a shareholder, had a complaint to make he should do it through a committee member. This was an attempt to explain to Mr. Kelly without causing offence, that in fact he had no rights at meetings of the committee. "I should point out that Mr. Kelly attends the Society's office every morning and still occupies the secretary's office with Mr. Galbraith ... Mr. Galbraith is quite happy that this situation should continue for the time being as he is not anxious to cause offence to Mr. Kelly", Mr. Tierney reported.[1]

On other fronts, Mr. Wallis reported that 1963 had been a very unsatisfactory year for wheat intake. Donaghmore showed a 16% rejection rate while at Raheen the figure was up to 25%. J.P. Kelly highlighted the amount of donations given out by the Society over the previous twelve months. He put the figure at £133. "These begging letters have now become quite a racket", he told the committee. The installation of a PA system at Donaghmore was agreed in September 1963.

Agricultural instructor

In February 1964, R.P. Bennett recommended that the Society should employ an agricultural instructor for the benefit of members only. He was strongly supported by Mr. Joyce, of the IAOS, who spoke at length on the issue at the March meeting. It was advisable, he said, provided that the appointment worked hand in glove with advisory services already existing. He spoke of the type of work which an advisor might be expected to do such as soil testing, crop inspection, determining the causes of "dirty" milk, proper cleaning of milking machines. The instructor would have to take instructions from management. Mr. Bennett proposed, and Mr. Walsh seconded, the appointment of a "degree man" with experience and ability. John C. O'Meara, an instructor with the Longford County Committee of Agriculture, was duly appointed with a salary of £1,300.

1. Internal IAOS memo from Greg Tierney for Mr. Kelly, the secretary's, attention dated 4 August 1964 (National Archives).

This was a significant innovation on the part of the Society and was a move that proved both popular and productive. It was done at a vital time when huge changes were taking place on the farming scene at national and international level and farmers were finding it increasingly difficult to keep abreast with the changes. Mr. O'Meara filled this gap for the Donaghmore fraternity of members, but there were fears that such an appointment might be seen as cutting across work already being done by the local County Committee of Agriculture. Mr. Tierney, of the IAOS, tried to allay such fears by emphasising that the appointment had been done with the full approval of the County Committee.

In March 1964, an increase in salaries of 12% was announced. The new salary scale agreed was as follows: Joint general managers, Grogan and Wallis - £1,288; secretary, J. Galbraith - £1,288; hardware manager, R. Horsburgh - £876-10-0; branch manager, J. Butler (Raheen) - £880; branch manager, B. Moran (Spink) - £608; assistant manager, J. Somers - £880; former secretary, J.P. Kelly - £672.

In March 1963, members had discussed the necessity to build a new dairy at Raheen. But extra land was needed. An offer of £500 was made to Mr. Talbot for an acre of ground at the rear of their premises. Talbot was given seven days to decide and there were to be "no tails or concessions involved in the transaction". The offer was refused. Talbot said that the Society could have the acre for £1,000 after the harvest season. The Society improved its offer to £600 and an agreement was reached.

The matter of a major investment in Raheen was allowed to rest until May 1964, when Mr. Grogan told committee members that the existing plant, especially in the branches, was not equal to the then supply of milk not to mention the anticipated increase. The problem at Raheen was, he said, particularly acute. The manager presented the committee with a list of requirements costing in the region of £30,000. A special meeting was held on 16 June to discuss the issue. Mr. Ebrill and Mr. O'Lubaigh of the IAOS were present. Mr. Ebrill felt that Grogan's estimate of the cost of works needed was low. The amount could be as much as £50,000, he stated.

Committee burn the midnight oil

Since its foundation, the business planning and decision-making at Donaghmore had emanated from the committee's monthly meetings. Because of the extent and complexity of the Society's operations by 1964, the committee members often burned the midnight oil. Mr. Hennessy raised the question of meetings running late, saying the situation had been getting steadily worse. It was decided to hold two meetings a month from August, 1964.

In that same month, a decision was made to provide a new facility at Raheen which would have mechanical intake installed capable of handling up to 12,000 gallons of milk daily. Talks with Mr. Talbot got under way again to buy a further piece of land needed for the development. In October 1964, a plot at the rear of the existing store, and adjacent to the portion acquired earlier in the year, was purchased for £300.

In view of the proposed big capital expenditure at Raheen, the Department of Agriculture sought the closure of Spink and the re-direction of the milk supply to Raheen. Donaghmore rejected this proposal claiming that Spink had a substantial store trade, which would be lost if the branch was closed. Fears of a loss of a considerable number of suppliers to Ballyragget were also expressed.[2] Instead of

2. Information is taken from an IAOS internal memo prepared by Greg Tierney dated 17 November 1964 (National Archives).

closing one of its branches, the Donaghmore committee were contemplating representations being made for the opening a new one, at Rosenallis. Mr. Grogan told them that there were complaints from some suppliers that they were too far away from the Raheen creamery. There was a "very active" parish priest there and the question of building a creamery in the area was being discussed.[3]

The April 1964 meeting was informed by Mr. Grogan of the proposed creation of a cheese factory in Kilkenny by Miloko, together with a number of co-op societies in Leinster and Munster. Mr. Tierney told of the implications for Donaghmore and he was asked to keep a watching brief on developments on behalf of the Society. He said that the Mid-Leinster Churning Federation proposal had neither faded out nor gone ahead. He advised that it would be best to see what happened with that proposal before any major capital outlay was contemplated on the Miloko proposal. Mr. Tierney also spoke on the implications of the Knapp Report which had been recently published. This recommended wholesale changes in the structure of the IAOS and the co-op movement to meet the demands of a fast-changing agricultural scene in Ireland.

Group pictured at Donaghmore in the 1960s
Front: **Donie Dowling, Jimmy Hearns, Joe Delaney, Billy Percy, Michael White.**
Back: **Mick Power, Paddy Campion, Christy Fitzpatrick.**
Extreme back: **John Fitzpatrick.**

Joe Shortt and Mick Flanagan (cap), receive the keys for two new lorries from Hino Sales reps at Dublin airport in the late 1960s.

3. Details from an IAOS internal memo prepared by Greg Tierney dated 19 November 1964 (National Archives).

CHAPTER FOUR

Federation

The establishment of a federation was an idea that emanated from a joint committee set up by Miloko and the Unigate organisation of Great Britain, through
their Cow & Gate division. As a result of their research, it became evident to
Irish members that there was a great need for milk diversification. It was felt that
the amount of milk produced could be doubled within five years, in view of the
Second Programme for Economic Expansion which had just been published by the
Government. The scheme set out by the committee and the IAOS listed two
stages:

1. The establishment of a federation to purchase all the milk of members; to
   provide central churning facilities; to collect £100,000 as share capital.
2. To provide a dried milk powder factory by 1966; to provide a cheese factory
   by 1967; to provide for other manufacturing facilities.

Capital required was estimated at £600,000. Apart from the share capital investment, the remainder was expected to come from State grants and loans from the
ICC and the banks. In September 1964, George Galbraith proposed that £10,000
be invested in the scheme provided the rules were to Donaghmore's satisfaction.
Miloko having pulled back from the project, a federation council was set up from
thirty-seven co-ops who appointed a committee of eight to coordinate the project
with the intention of linking up with Cow & Gate at a later stage. The project was
known as Avonmore Co-operatives Ltd. The federation was grouped into four
regions. Mr. Galbraith was elected to the board of management. He told a meeting
in Donaghmore in April 1965 that a site was being examined near Durrow, Co.
Laois, for the factory. He felt that this was the best site available and was confident
that, despite pressure from Kilkenny, it would be located there. This would have
been good news for County Laois but, alas, it was not to be. Political moves were
afoot to locate the facility in County Kilkenny and political expediency won the day.
The full sorry story is revealed in Part Six. At the committee meeting in June 1965,
George Galbraith confirmed the news that the site for Avonmore Creameries had
been decided for Ballycondra, Ballyragget.

A special meeting at Donaghmore was held on 9 November 1964 dealing with
the extensive capital programme now being undertaken by the Society. Members
heard that the estimate for improvements at Raheen had risen to £62,100. It was
reckoned that £10,000 was required for machinery at Spink, and £20,000 at
Donaghmore. Then there was £10,000 for the extension to the shop and store at
Donaghmore. Members felt that because of the confined space in the store, the
Society was losing customers. A similar amount was assigned for the federation

project in Kilkenny. Taking all the projects into consideration, they would absorb all their reserves which had taken many years to build up and members were not happy with this. It was decided to scale back the Raheen project.

Discussion on Raheen was top of the agenda at a number of special meetings that followed. An option between one plan costing £62,000 and another for £37,000 was put before a meeting on 2 February 1965. After a lengthy debate, lasting over three hours, the smaller project was the preferred choice. The IAOS did not agree with the Donaghmore decision, however. Mr. Kelly, of the IAOS, was not sure what the situation was in relation to grant aid for the amended project. He said that in the long run the bigger project would be the cheapest. Planning permission had been granted, a licence had been obtained from the Department and grant aid had been negotiated. If the Society went ahead with the smaller project, the whole process would have to begin again. That would mean a considerable delay and the Department might not cast a kindly eye on the revised development, Mr. Kelly pointed out. In view of such advice, the committee had a rethink on the matter and quickly came to a decision to go along with the IAOS recommendation after all.

Provender Milling

Also in January 1965, J.P. Kelly attended a meeting of the IAOS Provender Milling Company at which the establishment of a national brand of Provender Meals by co-ops engaged in the industry was discussed. It was proposed to form a federation, which would oversee the erection of a large plant capable of an output of 500,000 tons annually. The meeting, however, felt that it might be better to start in a smaller way by developing a national brand first and then consider the provision of costly buildings and plants when the market was established. By October 1965, the Donaghmore committee were cooling to the plan because of transport costs and a preference to keep their own brands and brand name. They promised to support the federation, however, by giving first preference to purchasing from the federation's facility.

Mr. Costello of the IAOS attended a special meeting in November 1965 and outlined the benefits of a federation-controlled provender milling operation. He informed members that fifty-five compounding societies were now manufacturing 12% of total consumption. It was difficult to control quality in such circumstances. By establishing a national brand, it would instil a greater degree of confidence in the product. In the Kilkenny area there were 42 societies serving a total of 14,000 farmers within a radius of 35 miles. A concentrated effort on tackling this market would pay rich dividends, he said. A sympathetic consideration would be given to societies, such as Donaghmore, who were already established in the business. The general idea was to offer the customer a complete range of products. The estimated cost of the project was £115,000. One rival group had already invested over £300,000 in extending their output. The entry of Donaghmore into the federation would give the project a huge boost, Mr. Costello said. In November 1965, R.P. Bennett said that while he felt Donaghmore would be supportive of a central mill for Kilkenny, Tipperary, Wexford and Laois areas, he was not in favour of surrendering their own established brand and trade. He called for a meeting of all interested societies so that the issue could be further discussed. A few weeks later, the Donaghmore members showed more enthusiasm for the federation and Mr. Bennett seconded George Galbraith's proposal to invest £2,500 in the project.

The meeting in April 1965 was informed that there was a move afoot to establish a pig-fattening unit in the Donaghmore area. A committee had been formed, capital was being negotiated and the project was being enthusiastically pursued.

There was a letter from Golden Vale Food Products Ltd., before the April 1965 meeting, relating to the formation of a federation of members of Golden Vale and other selected creameries for engineering and service purposes. The benefits outlined included participation in profits, provision for better service, cheaper installations, repairs for members and a voice in the management. Members felt it was an opportunity not to be missed and decided to invest £1,000 in the federation.

Lisduff limeworks

In May 1965, Billy Wallis informed the committee that Lisduff limeworks, owned by Edward Byrne, was for sale. He offered it to the Society for £22,000. Mr. Wallis said that the product was of immense value to the Society. Their agricultural advisor, Mr. O'Meara, and the Department had been advocating more use of ground limestone and, by owning the plant, they could supply their own needs, which otherwise could not be supplied locally. It was agreed to purchase the buildings, the plant and the 30-acre site. The price agreed was £20,000 and the limeworks were to be run as a separate trading department within the Society. Peter Bergin was appointed manager. By July, the limeworks were in production and orders were pouring in. It was soon producing 100 tons per day. The committee visited the site on 9 August and inspected the work being conducted there. CIE assigned one lorry to work at Lisduff, refusing to put a second at the disposal of the limeworks. An attempt was made, through talks with parliamentary secretary, Paddy Lalor, TD, to get a second licence plate for the quarry. A side-product that was being successfully developed at Lisduff was block-making. The quality of block was good and demand was growing.

Other matters that came before the committee in the spring/summer of 1965 included a proposal to participate in local efforts to start a pig-fattening unit in Rathdowney. Mr. Grogan reported that the Society had won first prize for its butter entry at the Spring Show. Daniel Whelan, Clonagooden, Borris-in-Ossory was appointed trainee milking machine serviceman. The weekly wages, which had been paid on Saturdays heretofore, were from now on to be paid on Friday nights. It was also noted that a profit of £430 for the Clonaslee unit had been returned for 1964. There was an appeal from the ICMSA for a donation to the John F. Kennedy Memorial Fund at the July meeting.

In August, on the proposal of George Galbraith, the Society supported the election of T.J. Maher, chairman of the National Dairy Committee, to Bord Bainne. It was decided to join the Federation of Irish Industries and the Ground Limestone Manufacturers Committee, on the basis of Lisduff wages bill only.

A special meeting was held on 7 September between the milk carters' representatives and the management committee. The hauliers were represented by K. Bowe, John Malone, John Nolan, Patrick Lacey and John Seale. The delegation raised a number of complaints including problems with intake and outlet points at Donaghmore and the loading and delivery of skimmed milk. Concerns were expressed over replacing the carters' role by bulk tankers and the impact that the opening of the Ballyragget facility would have on them. The management, in turn, spoke of the criticisms of the high rates being charged by the hauliers for milk collection. At a meeting two weeks later, it was estimated that the revenue of the hauliers had doubled in less than five years and a reduction of ½d per gallon was deemed appropriate.

Because of the exceptional amount of capital being spent on buildings, on machinery, on Lisduff quarry and other ventures, the bank overdraft facility was extended to £150,000.

A special meeting was held on 5 December 1965 to discuss the need for informed and educated member and public involvement in the affairs of co-ops. There was also an emphasis on getting young people interested. The IAOS felt that by starting with the youth, they could build up a feeling of confidence in the co-op movement, said Mr. O'Donoghue of the IAOS.

Committee members at opening of Raheen new dairy in 1967
Front row (l. to r.): **Michael Kirwan, George Galbraith, Bobby Bennett, Michael Walsh, John Treacy.**
Back row (l. to r.): **John Hennessy, Joseph Bergin, Patrick Sheil, Seán Reilly, Murtagh McWey and Stephen Campion.**

CHAPTER FIVE

The Sad Passing of J.P. Kelly

The final days of 1965 brought the sad news of the death of J.P. Kelly. A special meeting was called on 28 December solely to pass a resolution tendering sincere sympathy to Mrs. Kelly and the Kelly family. The Society's minutes record: "Tributes were paid by all the committee present and by the management to the late Mr. Kelly, to whose devotion to an ideal and hard work this Society owes its existence. The best tribute that could be paid to his memory was to ensure that the future of the Society was based on the example set by him."

Despite all that had gone on before to clarify areas of managerial responsibility, Donal Grogan appeared shell-shocked after being told at a committee meeting in April 1967 that he was not the overall manager of Donaghmore Co-op. In a letter addressed to the secretary, John Galbraith, Mr. Grogan wrote: "I was told in no uncertain terms that I was never appointed and never was manager of the Society as a whole and was appointed originally as creamery manager only … the position of general manager, creamery department, a position which the committee offered to me in November 1966 and which I accepted … which was supposed to come into effect on 1 January 1967 and which up to last night I thought was the latest mind of the committee … did not in fact ever exist as they abandoned this idea and reverted back to the joint general managership system. This was the first time in my 21 years employment with the Society that I really know where I stand, as I was under the impression – mistaken apparently – that I had applied for and obtained the position of manager of Donaghmore Co-op Creamery Ltd. which became vacant on the death of my father, who was the first manager of the Society."

Mr. Grogan stated that he would take no further responsibility for anything outside the limited scope of his position and sought a contract stating clearly the terms of his employment and responsibilities.

Tensions had eased again by October but the committee made contingency plans in the event of a further breakdown in relations between Grogan and Wallis. It was decided that in such an eventuality, the IAOS would immediately advertise for a general manager and the advertisement was to be so worded as to attract business people from outside the creamery industry. The salary to be offered to attract competent managers was up to £3,500.[1]

Grogan wanted to get out of Donaghmore but was finding it difficult to secure a similar job elsewhere. He had yet another complaint to make – this time to the IAOS. In a letter to Patrick Kelly, the secretary of the IAOS, dated 22 March 1968, he wrote that he had applied for the position of general manager of Black Abbey Co-op, Adare, Co. Limerick. He said that his intentions of writing to Mr. Kelly was

---

1. Internal IAOS memo from J.F. Madden to secretary of the IAOS dated 20 October 1967 (National Archives).

not to solicit his recommendation for the job but to advise him that he did not want his application to be made known to the Donaghmore chairman, his committee or any member of staff. He added: "Every time I applied for a job previously the news was given to the chairman, Mr. P.J. Kavanagh, now deceased … If I wish to change from my present position, I feel I am entitled to seek such change … without running the risk of having the whole thing told to the chairman and committee. As it happens, I do desire a change although my life and loyalty is bound up with Donaghmore Creamery. It is evident the change will not come about in my position here." In his letter, Mr. Grogan criticised the IAOS very strongly: "If an applicant cannot have confidence in the IAOS that they will respect the knowledge they obtain through such applications, then this system of screening the applications will lose any reputation it may have." Mr. Kelly replied, refuting Grogan's allegations of breach of confidentiality. He stated that the IAOS always observed confidentiality but that, once the short-list of names was passed on, his organisation could not be responsible for information leaks from the creamery committees or elsewhere.

Around the same time as Donal Grogan was making determined efforts to get out of Donaghmore in March 1968, the committee were planning ambitiously into the future. The new creamery at Raheen, one of the first with mechanical intake in Ireland, had opened in 1967 and the new creamery at Spink was also complete. But to meet the demands of further development, further share capital was needed.

The call for share capital was directed first and foremost at the milk suppliers. In his letter to suppliers, the secretary, John Galbraith, outlined the phenomenal growth in milk supplies over the years, from 176,000 gallons in 1947 to over six million gallons in 1967. This had stretched facilities at Donaghmore to the limit. The letter also outlined all the developments that had taken place at Donaghmore and the branches in the previous decade. It mentioned the investment in Avonmore Creameries and explained that developments there would absorb the surplus of milk, but a further very substantial investment would have to be made in order for the Society to fully avail of that milk outlet. There was much more to be done at Donaghmore, Raheen and Spink "to keep abreast with the ever-expanding trade and to provide the ever-expanding services which we are constantly asked to provide." The letter pointed out that the majority of farmers who were sending their milk to one or other of the Society's three creameries were non-shareholders. It appealed to non-shareholding milk suppliers and other customers and also to shareholders with a small number of shares relative to their milk supply, to buy new shares and provide new capital. As an encouragement to buy shares, the letter outlined that as from 1 May 1968, the shareholder milk suppliers would receive a half penny more per gallon for their produce than the non-shareholders.

Managerial crisis

By November 1969, the management crisis at Donaghmore was coming to an end. James Joyce of the IAOS reported to his organisation that the joint management arrangement "had obviously not worked". Mr. Bennett had told him that since the death of J.P. Kelly "there was poor coordination of staff and resources". He had also told him that Mr. Wallis was very discontented and had suggested that he might be seeking alternative employment elsewhere. This would be a severe blow to the development at Donaghmore, Mr Bennett had warned. Mr. Wallis had tried to make the joint manager arrangement work but Mr. Grogan had been unable to work under this arrangement. The other members of the sub-committee were unanimous in agreeing that Mr. Wallis should be made general manager of the Society. Mr. Joyce revealed that he had sounded out Mr. Wallis, who told him he would be interested in the position but only on very specific terms. He outlined what these were. He wanted to be secretary to the Society as well as general manager. He would appoint his own staff to all departments. His salary would have to be £3,500 and he wanted a staff car.[2]

Appointing Mr. Wallis might solve one problem; it was, however, likely to create another. What action would Mr. Grogan take in the event of Mr. Wallis' appointment? The committee decided, and the IAOS agreed, that the best option was to get Mr. Grogan to retire, even if it meant paying him something over the odds for his stepping aside.[3] A contract on the terms of the agreement was drawn up with two options and offered to Mr. Grogan. The first option was for retirement and included a clause on his immediate retirement "on health grounds"; a gratuity of £2,500, one year's salary, for loss of position; a pension of £1,500, guaranteed by the Society. The other option was if he remained working he would be responsible to the general manager and his salary would be £2,500 per annum. Mr. Grogan considered his options and, having been given explanations on a number of issues, particularly in relation to his pension, he decided to bow out.

Committee members, management team, and clergy, at opening of new dairy in Raheen, May 1967.
Front row (l. to r.): Michael Kirwan, Fr. Mahon P.P., Raheen; George Galbraith, Ben Moran, Billy Wallis, Joint Manager; Rev. Finney, John Treacy, Fr. T. Ryan P.P., Abbeyleix and Donal Grogan, Joint Manager.
Middle row (l. to r.): Bobby Bennett, Chairman; Michael Walsh.
Back row: Mr. Callaghan, Insurance Agent; John Hennessy, Joseph Bergin, Patrick Sheil, Seán Reilly, Murtagh McWey, John Galbraith, Secretary; Stephen Campion, John Delaney, Milk Manager, Raheen.

2. Internal letter from James Joyce, Commodity Section) to secretary of the IAOS dated 18 November 1969 (National Archives)
3. Letter from James C Moloney, asst. secretary, IAOS to James Joyce, IAOS dated 10 March 1970 (National Archives).

Meanwhile, the Donaghmore committee of management had successfully concluded discussions with Mrs. Bailey, the proprietor of Pims of Mountmellick, to purchase the interests of its long established business which served the local community with its farm and general household requirements. Mrs. Bailey was keen on disposing of Pims to a farming co-operative rather than put the business on the open market. The IAOS facilitated the deal with the Donaghmore Society. The deal was concluded by the autumn of 1968 and Mountmellick became a fully fledged Branch of the Donaghmore Co-op Society.

A second business opportunity in Mountmellick arose three years later when another long established general and hardware store, Smiths, came on the market. The then recently established Mountmellick area advisory committee was keen on transferring the business into co-op ownership and members agreed to go security for the bank loans required to finance the purchase. The deal was finalised in the autumn of 1971. (See Section Three – Extending the Frontiers – for a fuller account of the Mountmellick story.)

Mick Power removing butter from new vats in Donaghmore Creamery in 1969.

Jim Somers, supervising at the dairy in Donaghmore in the 1960s.

Pictured at milk intake in new dairy Raheen, May 1967 were (l. to r.) John Delaney, Tom Scully and Tom Carroll.

SECTION ONE

PART SIX

Amalgamation

TELEGRAMS: "CREAMERY, BALLYBROPHY."   TELEPHONE: DONAGHMORE 3.   RAILWAY STATION BALLYBROPHY, G.S.RLY.

PRIZES AWARDED AT :—
LONDON DAIRY SHOWS AND
ROYAL DUBLIN SOCIETY'S
SPRING SHOWS.

Donaghmore Co-Operative Creamery, Ltd.,

MANUFACTURERS OF
PURE CREAMERY BUTTER
1LB. ROLLS A SPECIALITY.
REG. NO. C. 348

BALLYBROPHY

Leix,   *16 - 1 -*   193 2

BRANCHES AT—COOLRAIN, MOUNTRATH. RAHEEN, ABBEYLEIX.

PHONES: HEAD OFFICE—RATHDOWNEY 43 & 44 & 83
Raheen Branch—ABBEYLEIX 31104   Spink Branch—ABBEYLEIX 31169

INVOICE

Donaghmore Co-operative Creamery, Ltd.
DONAGHMORE, LEIX

Samples of different style headed paper used by Donaghmore Co-op over the years.

CHAPTER ONE

Period of Rapid Modernisation

The 1960s was a period of rapid modernisation. The election of Seán Lemass as Taoiseach in 1959 heralded a new era for Ireland replacing the long stagnant economic years of de Valera's reign. Europe too was in the process of modernisation, at last shaking off the political fallout from World War II. Instead of internal political and military strife, the model was now in place for a strong unified Europe. Old war protagonists, Germany and France, were at the heart of this unstoppable movement, the European Economic Community, formed in 1957 with the objective of economic and political integration.

The Irish economy was inextricably linked with the UK and Irish entry into the EEC was dependent on the success of the UK application. French President, Charles de Gaulle, blocked all attempts by the UK to join and it was only when he departed from the political scene in 1969, that progress was made on European enlargement.

The dairy industry, so vitally important to Ireland's economic welfare, was not in good shape to meet the demands of a fast changing country and world. In 1962, the Minister for Agriculture, Paddy Smith, had set up a team of experts to analyse the situation and propose the changes needed in advance of Ireland's entry to the EEC. Their report indicated that there were too many small inefficient creameries. They recommended amalgamation, by compulsion if necessary, and the formation of larger units to effect economies of scale and to allow diversification in production and marketing.[1] The Knapp Report largely endorsed many of group's findings.[2] The IAOS was called upon to support the concept of rationalisation of the industry. Closing down creameries, many long-established and in rural areas often bereft of any other economic activity, was not an easy bullet to bite for the government or the IAOS. But unease was growing among individual co-ops, which found themselves vulnerable to developments all around them.

As early as 1950, thirty-five co-operative creameries in the Kilkenny-South Tipperary region had come together with a number of English shareholders to form a federal co-op, Miloko, and build a factory for the manufacture of chocolate crumb. It was a relatively small organisation but was hugely important and gave a useful impetus to dairying in the region. A number of co-ops in the grouping put pressure on Miloko to expand into cheese production. When Miloko pulled out of negotiations, an organising committee was set up to form a separate federation with the aim of building their own cheese factory. Donaghmore Society was one of a group

---

1. *The Irish Co-operative Movement – its history and development* by Patrick Bolger (The Institute of Public Administration; Dublin. 1977).
2. Joseph G. Knapp, *An Appraisement of Agricultural Co-operation in Ireland* (Dublin Stationery Office, 1964).

Reddy Brennan
First Group Managing Director
Avonmore Creameries

of twenty five creameries that formed the federation, which became known as Avonmore Creameries Ltd. The organising committee consisted of four creamery managers and four farmers. The chairman was Reddy Brennan, the manager at Muckalee.

Talks on a joint venture were started with Unigate, the biggest milk co-operative in England, which had already a considerable interest in cheese production in Ireland. It was decided to go ahead with the project. The joint venture of Avonmore and Unigate created Avongate. Irish creamery interests invested £154,000 in the project and Unigate invested £112,000. By various strategies, however, sixty-five per cent of the business was kept in Irish hands. Reddy Brennan believes that Unigate's presence was crucial to the success of the undertaking. "They contributed greatly to the business. Managing to bring twenty-five creameries together was a big job. The fact that we had Unigate on board gave us stability. Before the factory got going, we agreed with Unigate that they would take two containers of our produce every week. It all went over in bulk. That was a huge breakthrough and a number of other creameries were extremely jealous of the deal." Some years later, the Unigate shareholding was reduced to 22% and, in 1979, Avonmore bought them out for a relatively small consideration.

As soon as that decision was taken to build their own factory, the organising committee felt that it was imperative to appoint a general manager to spearhead the new venture. The federation had to look no further than the organising committee's chairman to find the best man for the job. Reddy Brennan was appointed in April 1966. A former Kilkenny hurler, he had made a good reputation as an innovative manager at Muckalee Creamery and his name was well-respected in the industry. But, at first, he was reluctant to accept the offer. As Reddy recalled: "I had full job satisfaction and if I wanted more money, I had only to ask for it. But the way things were shaping up, the man who was likely to get the job, in my opinion wasn't a great man manager. There was going to be a lot to do to bring people together and bring harmony with it. This man would have been in a hurry. I sat down one day and I looked at the pros and cons and decided to put my hat in the ring."

Appointing a full-time executive at such an early stage proved an inspired move and Reddy was the ideal man. He had a vision of rationalisation and diversification as the way forward and his vast experience in the role of creamery manager of a progressive creamery had given him good insight into the particular problems that small independent co-ops might face in merging with others.

Reddy moved the concept forward with great speed and resolve. Without such a concentrated focus as the Kilkenny man applied, it is unlikely that such a loose grouping as he had adopted, even with full IAOS backing, would have been able to get so many to stand behind the Avonmore banner and make the tough decisions that had to be made.

There were over thirty co-ops now on board including Nenagh, Centenary, Callan and Mullinahone creameries that later refused to amalgamate. One of Reddy's first tasks was looking for a site for the factory. A Board of Directors was formed consisting of four managers, four farmers and a couple of people from Unigate. A farm was purchased in Callan but this was soon seen as being located too close to Carrick-on-Suir, where Miloko was situated.

Reddy revealed the next move. "The site was needed further up the country. We looked at one on the Dublin Road just outside Durrow in County Laois. It was a lovely site on the main road. There happened to be a by-election in Carlow/Kilkenny at the time. Charlie Haughey was Minister for Agriculture. You had to get a licence at the time to build any sort of milk processing plant. Charlie would not give a licence for the plant unless it was in the Carlow/Kilkenny constituency. A big delegation went up from Laois to see the Minister, including George Galbraith, clergy of all persuasions and business people, but Charlie wiped the floor with them. He told them to go home.

"At that time we had a temporary office overhead in the Bank of Ireland in the Parade (in Kilkenny). It was a one-roomed office but a fairly big room. I was the first employee and soon a secretary was employed. Next we appointed a financial controller (who is still around and a great friend of mine). We got a phonecall one evening, an urgent call from the Minister. Charlie came on the phone and said 'come up and see me', just like that. I went up with John Deasy, who was secretary of the South Tipperary farmers in Clonmel, and Paddy Kelly, secretary general of the IAOS. We were put sitting down in Charlie's office. The Minister came in. His

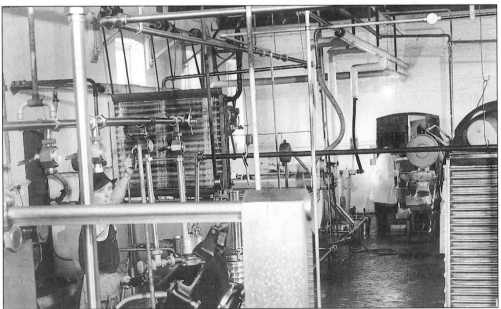

Mick Power (at back) packing butter at the old dairy in Donaghmore.
John Fitzpatrick can be seen at left foreground (1957).

first words were; 'I didn't think Kelly would be here.' I said that I had arranged with your private secretary for Kelly and Deasy to be here with me. 'I'll decide who I'll see', he said. That was a nice start.

"I made the case for the building of the factory in Durrow, but Charlie wouldn't listen to the case under any circumstance. I explained that the consultant engineers regarded it as a much better site than the one in Ballyragget, on which we had an option, or the one in Callan which we owned. 'I have no time for engineers,' he said. Needless to say Mr. Kelly made no contribution.

"We reported back to the Board. It was decided that they and the consultant engineers would have another try. An appointment was made and we all went up to the same office as before. I was asked to do the talking. We were arranged in the form of a triangle and I could see no one but Charlie. We made our case but, needless to say, the meeting did not last long. We all went over to the Shelbourne Hotel for a drink. One of the Unigate fellows sidled up to me and said: 'There is a gentleman whom I read a lot about but never met by the name of Al Capone. That gentleman we have just met reminds me very much of Al Capone'."

Reddy would have preferred the Durrow site because it was on the main Dublin-Cork road and "for advertising purposes it was there for all time". But Haughey was not for turning and Avonmore went ahead with their development at the Ballyragget site. Work started on the site in late 1966 but the first gallon of milk was not processed there until 1 May 1968.

Ballyragget Complex.

CHAPTER TWO

Federation Too Loose

At the time of the Federation only whole milk powder and cheese were sub-sidised. Butter had a fixed price but was not regarded as being subsidised. Avonmore started at a time of weak markets. The price of milk powder went down to £51 per ton and, because the price of milk was fixed at 22.70 pence per gallon at about 20% butterfat, it cost £77 to produce it. "We were heading for major losses", Reddy Brennan recalled. "Luckily we, with other manufacturers, got a skim milk stabilisation scheme going. This meant that £77 was paid out with the provision that the deficit would be taken care of in future years when the price would go up. Milk powder was the only thing we could manufacture. There was only a limited market for cheese. That came later, much later."

The cheese factory was built in time but very little of the commodity was manu-factured at Ballyragget in the first few years. A deficit built up on milk powder but it was soon brought under control when the price of the commodity rose sharply. Reddy Brennan again: "Had the low price lasted much longer, we would have been in bother. Around Ballyragget, at that time, they used to say that if Friday passed and the place didn't close, then it would close the following Friday."

By the end of the first year, Ballyragget had processed between six and seven million gallons. The balance sheet showed a loss of only £45,000 and that included the start-up costs. "That gave us huge confidence", Reddy related. "All the cream-eries in the federation were still making their own butter and, despite continued rumours of Ballyragget's imminent collapse, most were more concerned about the supply to their own plants. Within a few years, however, the demand rose rapidly for butter for export of the unsalted variety and the standards of production were set so high that independent co-ops were faced with huge capital expenditure to upgrade their facilities. In a short time, most creameries stopped making their own butter. One creamery had been making butter since 1895 but stopped the produc-tion when one of its container loads was rejected. Had another one been turned back, they would have had to close down. In a relatively short space of time, we were making all the butter and took over the butter trade of all the major towns in the region such as Kilkenny, Portlaoise and Bagenalstown. For some time the creameries continued to separate the cream and send in the cream and the skimmed milk separately. But that didn't make any great sense, so we stopped it and eventually all the milk came directly into the factory."

George Galbraith, who had played a central role in Donaghmore's progress for three decades as a member of its management committee and as its chairman from 1941 to 1945, became first chairman of the Avonmore federation and remained at the helm in the boardroom until he fell into ill health in 1971.

Donaghmore had been one of the champions of the Avonmore concept but its faith in the project was "seriously shaken" as the 1960s ebbed away. The issue that triggered the doubts about their continued close co-operation with the venture began to take root because of a perceived arrogance and lack of accountability at Ballyragget. The Society had not been given any satisfaction by Avonmore to questions relating to the apparent discrepancy in the cream returns for July 1969. Only the previous year, the committee had shown their enthusiasm for the venture by promising £13,150 towards the proposed cheese factory project. Now feeling somewhat powerless to get the answers they requested, their positive attitude to Avonmore was being closely questioned. Matters came to a head when, at a meeting in September 1969, it was decided to defer any resolutions on future policy on Avonmore and also their intended investment in the cheese factory. This decision acutely embarrassed Mr. Galbraith, because of the position he held in the federation. He seriously considered resigning from the Avonmore Board.[1] The intervention of Greg Tierney of the IAOS helped smooth out the problems that had arisen and, in a little while, Donaghmore's confidence in the Ballyragget project had been restored and Mr. Galbraith was able to continue in his role as chairman of the Avonmore federation.

By the early 1970s, Donaghmore Co-op was a countywide operation in Laois and had some interests in neighbouring counties as well. It carried on a profitable and progressive business and was in a stronger financial position than at any time in its history. Milk supply scarcity had been a constant source of concern for creameries over the years and neighbouring co-ops vied with one another over boundaries and suppliers. The scarcity even led to milk wars, which at times threatened the future of the industry. But now milk supplies were increasing rapidly each year and the problem that many creameries faced was not in scarcity of supply but in their capacity to handle the increased volume.[2] The emergence of Avonmore solved this problem. The co-ops involved in the federation had the advantages of being part of a bigger and more influential grouping in the dairy industry while fully retaining their independence. Those involved could withdraw from the federation at any time if their shareholders felt that that was the best way forward. The looseness of the membership arrangement was, however, one of the weaknesses of the federation, which had to compete against big, compact and well-organised groups in Europe and New Zealand, fully tuned to the demands of modern international business.

In 1972, a referendum resulted in an overwhelming vote in favour of Ireland joining the EEC. The country now became a member of one of the biggest economic blocks in the world. It had much to gain from becoming a member. The Common Agricultural Policy boosted Irish farming through production subsidies and higher

1. Information contained in a letter from Maurice Colbert to Greg Tierney, IAOS dated 11 September 1969. (National Archives).

2. Why did milk production rise so dramatically in the late 1960s and early 1970s? For generations farmers brought their milk into the local branch where it was separated and they brought home the skim milk. With the advent of the Common Market the skim milk became more valuable because of the protein. In the 1950s and early 1960s farmers could buy all the skim milk they liked for 1d or 2d per gallon. But then the skim milk became as valuable as the butter side and today it is, indeed, more valuable. The main use for skim milk is for skim milk powder and for casein. Although casein looks like skim milk powder, it is 80% protein compared to about 30% protein for the powder. It takes about 2,000 gallons of skim milk to make one tonne of skim milk powder but it takes 7,000 gallons to make one tonne of casein. The demand for skim milk powder is in the Third World whereas the casein market is mostly in the USA.

prices. The country's historic dependence on the British markets was now reduced and other export markets were opened to Irish producers. On the other hand, Ireland's home market was now more exposed and this brought its own problems. Producers here had no option but to change and improve their methods in order to compete in the widened market. Advantages of scale and diversification were important factors in the evolving process to make Irish farming more competitive.

There was a growing opinion within the Avonmore federation that the grouping as it stood was too unwieldy to meet the new challenges or to capitalise on the new opportunities presented by membership of the EEC. Reddy Brennan explained: "In 1971 we decided that the co-ops in the group were too small and too scattered. They each had their own independence. It did not make commercial sense. Unless we tightened up our operation it was not going to be a success. Whereas Waterford had only four or five big co-ops like Donaghmore, and they had merged in 1964, we were late in the day in coming along, both on the processing side and on the merger side."

To unlock the required investment needed for further stages of the development, a greater commitment to the Avonmore concept was demanded from the member co-ops. Attentions were now turned to amalgamation. Reddy recalled: "We spent the next two years discussing the situation and preparing the ground for amalgamation. We knew that each shareholder in each co-op would, at the end of the day, have to make the decision. By 1973, we felt that the proposal would go through. But it took a lot of persuasion before the shareholders gave the thumbs up."

Top: Sample of headed paper used by Donaghmore Co-op before amalgamation.
Bottom: After amalgamation.

CHAPTER THREE

A Big Decision

The decision to amalgamate, or not to amalgamate, was a big one for the individual co-ops to take. Amalgamation meant a diminution of their independence, a transfer of the decision-making process to a central body. On the other hand, co-ops that decided to keep their independence ran the risk of losing their competitiveness, which could lead to closure or forced amalgamation under less favourable terms than if done on a voluntary basis.

This was precisely the problem facing Donaghmore Society shareholders in the run-up to the amalgamation votes in 1973.

Donaghmore had more to lose than many others. It had a very healthy balance sheet and covered a bigger area than any other single co-op in the Avonmore area. It had also retained the co-operative ethos and the management committee structure, comprised of farmer shareholders elected by the members, who not alone made the policy decisions but also played a hands-on management role in the running of the business.

Bobby Bennett pictured in 2002 with letter from J.P. Kelly in 1947 advising him of his co-option onto the committee of management of Donaghmore Creamery.

One man who greatly influenced the shareholders' decision to vote for amalgamation was the then chairman of the Society, Bobby Bennett. "We gave up our independence because we felt that, although we were independent, we might not be able to afford to stay independent. Milk supply was growing at an enormous rate. It grew from four million gallons in 1968 to nine million in 1973. We could not afford the kind of sophisticated machinery that was needed to cater for such an increase. Even if we had the capacity we could not put it all into butter, because we had not the market. One of the attractions of amalgamating was that it made it possible to diversify from butter into cheese and many other products. The farmers knew that if we could diversify, then they could get a better price for their milk. If we stayed on our own, our price would not have been able to

194

match that of the amalgamated group, and that would have brought on fresh problems for Donaghmore. Whether we joined or not, diversification was going to happen, anyway. That's the way things were heading, and that's the way they still are heading."

What effect did the amalgamation have on Donaghmore shareholders? "There was a levy put on milk called a Capital Contribution. The purpose of this scheme was to develop Avonmore and those who contributed received shares. Every milk supplier became a shareholder, whether they liked it or not", Bobby informed.

Nenagh, Centenary, Callan and Mullinahone were all part of the federation but did not amalgamate and remained independent. They are still viable today, thirty years later. Does this not prove that amalgamation was probably an unnecessary step for Donaghmore to take? Bobby agreed that remaining independent did not seem to do those others any harm. "But", he quickly added, "they rode on our coattails. Centenary, for example, are very strong financially. They send their milk to Ballyragget, where all the investment in processing has taken place. They got shares for the money they put into the development, but they have no responsibility for the way the business is run. Donaghmore farmers have a say."

Bobby was still satisfied that shareholders made the right decision in voting for amalgamation. "You do give up your overall independence, but Avonmore is well-structured in that we still have our local committees. They are there only in an advisory capacity, but you are still in touch with what is happening and you can give advice. There are also Area Committees, which give members a feeling of independence although they are now part of a bigger group."

Understandably, not everyone associated with Donaghmore agreed with amalgamation. "There were very mixed feelings", Bobby revealed. "We had to do a lot of work to convince some of the people about it. In the initial stages the majority of us felt that we were independent and we wanted to stay independent. It took a while to convince us."

One important factor that swayed farmers to vote for the merger was the commitment pledged by Avonmore that they would keep the branches open. That was a commitment that has held firm until the present day, some thirty years later.

Bobby Bennett admitted that he was very much influenced in his decision by a very good friend, John Duggan, then chairman of South Tipperary Farmers, an amalgamation of a number of small creameries in the Clonmel area. "His group was not prepared to amalgamate with Avonmore unless Donaghmore came in. They wanted another big one in there and they felt it would damage the group if we stayed out. John was all for amalgamation. If they did not come in with Avonmore,

John Duggan
Chairman of Avonmore, 1978 to 1997,
and
Chairman of Glanbia plc, 1997 to 2000.

he was determined that South Tipp would amalgamate with Mitchelstown or some-where else."

There were meetings between people from the South Tipperary group and Donaghmore, which proved quite friendly. The whole process was pushed along by Reddy Brennan and Jim Joyce, representing ICOS. "Eventually it was decided at a meeting of the Management Committee that we would go for amalgamation", Bobby explained. "Our first job was to convince the people who didn't want it. First we had to convince ourselves that we were doing the right thing. Then we had to convince others. Some members of the committee and of management didn't want it. We had meetings all over the place to convince people and then we had two special general meetings at which we had to get a 75% majority at each meeting. It takes some doing to get a 75% majority. Only two people spoke against it at the first meeting and it got through. We had over 75% majority again at the second meeting. That was how it was done. Donaghmore was a very important part of the amalgamation plans for Avonmore."

Brendan Graham, formerly group secretary of Avonmore and later of Glanbia Ltd, who has strong Laois connections, believed that the transition from an inde-pendent co-op to the amalgamated group went smoothly due principally to people like Bobby Bennett, John Miller, John Hosey, Billy Flynn, James Costello and Harold Carter, who were "level-headed and good leaders". The smooth transition was helped by Avonmore's policy on communications and the level of capital expenditure in branches on grain facilities, milk plant, machinery and transport, he felt. Brendan said that it was also a help that Donaghmore had a regional structure in place at the time of the amalgamation, whereas other regions had to be devel-oped from many small independent creameries. He explained that Monasterevin and Donaghmore retained their separate regional committees and held separate meetings and also a num-ber of joint regional meetings up to the late 1980s, when the restructuring of the two committees took place to form the Donaghmore/Monasterevin regional com-mittee. He firmly believed that the positive influence of Macra na Feirme was also important in the changing agricultural envi-ronment brought about by the EEC and the need for rationalisation.

John Duggan remembered the talks on amalgamation and his early associations with Donaghmore. "Four co-operatives got together to form Co-op Animal Health. Donaghmore, of which Bobby Bennett was chairman, was one and South Tipperary, of which I was chairman, was another. Immediately I struck up a tremen-dous relationship with Bobby which still lasts until today. Bobby later served as vice-chairman of Avonmore during my

Brendan Graham, a native of Mountmellick, was Group Secretary of Avonmore and Glanbia plc from January 1987 to September 2000.

term as chairman. A more trustworthy and loyal man, and a more balanced and common sense man, I think it would be hard to find. Bobby and myself formed a close liaison with Barrowvale, of which Jules Logan was chairman. We were the three big ones going in and that had a huge influence on the others.

"Donaghmore was more or less equal in size to South Tipperary. But ours was a very young society because it was a merger of seven small co-operatives that had only taken place in 1967. We had a branch almost at every crossroads. Donaghmore had only four trading centres which made it quite different than us. But the volume of milk was fairly similar to ours, so we had a lot in common.

"For some reason, as a Tipperary man, I found it very easy to relate to the Laois men. Among those I got to know were George Galbraith, Jimmy Cooney and Chris Horan. I was very involved with Macra na Feirme, especially in debating circles and I debated in a national final against Fintan Phelan, the two Cleggs and Sean Finlay. Later I debated in a national semi-final against Liam Rohan and his team. I forged a friendship with these people and others from Co. Laois", John added.

"Had Donaghmore decided to stay out then I think it would have been inevitable that South Tipperary would not have come in. We had options of going to Mitchelstown or Dungarvan. The ICOS had put us in their rationalisation plan[1] in the Avonmore end of the equation and, of course, we had shareholding in Avonmore through all the creameries that existed in South Tipperary. We had a lot of linkage with Ballyragget but, at that time, Ballyragget had substantial borrowings relative to the time and it was very difficult for them to pay the top price for milk. Dungarvan and Mitchelstown were in a much stronger position to pay a decent milk price. Bill Carroll, God rest him, was president of ICOS at the time and he was an influence on me opting for Avonmore.

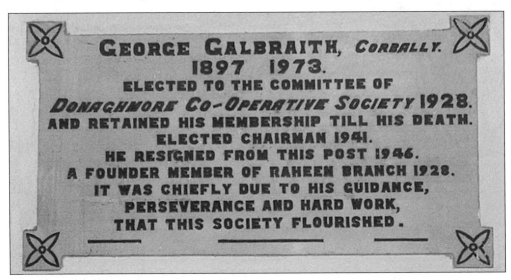

GEORGE GALBRAITH, *CORBALLY.*
1897 1973.
ELECTED TO THE COMMITTEE OF
***DONAGHMORE CO-OPERATIVE SOCIETY* 1928.**
AND RETAINED HIS MEMBERSHIP TILL HIS DEATH.
ELECTED CHAIRMAN 1941.
HE RESIGNED FROM THIS POST 1946.
A FOUNDER MEMBER OF RAHEEN BRANCH 1928.
IT WAS CHIEFLY DUE TO HIS GUIDANCE,
PERSEVERANCE AND HARD WORK,
THAT THIS SOCIETY FLOURISHED.

Plaque to the memory of George Galbraith at Raheen Creamery.

1. The IAOS issued its "Proposals for Reorganisation in the Dairy Industry" in February 1966. The rationalisation plan was based on the creation of nineteen large co-operative creamery groups through the amalgamation of existing societies and the transfer of the Dairy Disposal Company's creameries to co-operative control. The policy of rationalisation of creamery co-ops, with Government support, eventually led to the emergence of the Big 4 Dairy Co-ops, Kerry, Dairygold, Golden Vale and Glanbia. These now control the vast bulk of the national milk pool.

"I don't think anyone should underestimate the role played by the ICOS (formerly IAOS). I often thought that what they were doing at the time was quite a contradiction for their staff, because the more mergers we got the more sizeable creameries we got and, consequently, the less staff was needed in ICOS. So, to some extent, the more they went around persuading people to amalgamate, the more they were talking themselves out of a job. Jim Joyce, who was designated to the Avonmore project by ICOS, along with Reddy Brennan really burned the midnight oil and achieved what they set out to do.

"If Donaghmore and South Tipp had stayed out, I think it would have remained a federation rather than an amalgamation. The weakness I saw in a federation was that, first and foremost, theoretically the milk was locked in and you were sure of your supplies, but that would fragment over time. In amalgamation, your milk was in and there was no way of getting it out again. I think that was the stable force that put Avonmore on the map. Some of those that didn't come in took part of their milk away from us in spite of the fact that they were, allegedly, bound by rules to supply all their milk to Ballyragget plant. If Avonmore had to remain a federation, I believe it would have disintegrated over time.

"The other serious consideration for amalgamation that was very strong in my mind and, I think, also in Bobby Bennett's mind, was that we would share in the profits made at Ballyragget. At the time we were only assembling milk and sending it on to Ballyragget. The local creamery had a very poor margin on it whereas there was a fairly decent margin in the factory. Amalgamation made sense in order to get part of the profits – the factory profits, the regional profits and the store profits, all in the one pool", John Duggan concluded.

The merger took place on 1 September, 1973.

The surviving members of the last Committee of Management of the Donaghmore Co-operative Creamery Ltd. – 1973:
Back Row: John Kirwan, Frank Hyland, Hugh Cole, John C. Galbraith (Secretary), Seán Reilly and John Miller.
Front Row: Bernard Rochford, Murtagh McWey, Killian Flynn, Gerry Culliton, Laurence Phelan, Richard Lalor-Fitzpatrick.
Inset: Chris Horan and Bobby Bennett.

DONAGHMORE CO-OP CREAMERY LTD.

STATISTICS

Year	Gallons of milk received	lbs. of butter made	Produce Gals. of milk per lb. of butter	PRICES Received for butter per lb.	Paid for milk per gal.	TURNOVER Dairy Produce	Agricultural Goods	Total Expenses	Nett Loss	Nett Profit	Surplus as per Balance Sheet	Bad Debts Reserve	Other Reserves
				d.	d.	£	£	£	£	£	£	£	£
1927	39,568	19,029	2.07	18.46	6.64	2,352		494	13	—	—		
1928	403,829	180,577	2.23	18.09	6.44	22,564	—	2,986	—	359	327		
1929	575,050	261,227	2.20	17.98	6.38	20,090	—	4,587	—	93	355		
1930	517,957	233,935	2.21	14.20	4.95	15,309	—	3,930	96	—	261		
1931	318,419	142,334	2.23	13.83	3.93	9,237	2,490	3,539	—	122	315		
1932	278,702	122,564	2.25	14.39	4.09	8,220	2,308	3,058	—	71	377		
1933	358,192	161,971	2.21	13.75	4.01	9,053	5,681	2,979	—	227	489		
1934	400,847	181,163	2.21	12.31	4.08	10,848	25,798	3,052	—	63	550	100	
1935	464,130	210,405	2.20	11.86	4.12	10,879	5,058	3,244	68	—	531	200	
1936	434,025	195,461	2.22	12.07	4.20	11,853	4,109	3,169	—	104	415	200	
1937	306,388	136,868	2.23	13.68	4.22	8,271	4,712	2,847	—	119	479	200	
1938	228,712	102,402	2.23	14.97	4.76	7,614	27,463	2,774	—	260	705	200	
1939	183,088	81,172	2.26	16.87	5.14	6,547	80,648	3,252	—	268	938	200	
1940	160,311	72,148	2.22	17.27	5.78	7,642	80,012	3,137	—	526	1,462	200	
1941	185,483	84,428	2.19	18.46	6.25	6,405	83,611	3,816	—	437	1,887	200	
1942	157,335	71,422	2.20	21.27	7.69	6,700	105,429	4,371	—	811	2,688	200	
1943	161,272	72,955	2.21	24.94	9.46	9,559	112,737	5,674	—	1,176	3,613	200	
1944	187,209	84,661	2.21	29.18	10.56	14,170	138,353	6,178	—	896	4,663	200	
1945	200,707	89,664	2.23	28.33	10.72	16,968	137,599	6,668	—	1,650	6,219	200	
1946	165,097	73,795	2.24	27.98	10.80	16,776	130,735	7,140	—	1,595	7,839	200	
1947	144,468	63,426	2.28	33.25	14.42	15,438	99,484	8,358	—	1,017	8,973	500	
1948	176,075	78,611	2.24	34.55	14.57	20,719	175,406	9,789	—	1,457	10,343	500	
1949	393,212	177,300	2.21	37.46	14.54	27,748	233,910	14,787	—	789	10,889	500	
1950	866,283	396,504	2.17	38.37	14.74	53,073	156,905	15,865	—	3,323	14,267	500	
1951	1,071,317	481,607	2.22	42.47	15.925	67,118	148,509	17,529	—	4,624	18,036	480	
1952	1,114,843	496,030	2.24	42.61	16.048	85,725	164,509	22,461	—	5,530	15,531	1,000	7,000
1953	1,226,683	549,896	2.22	46.56	18.009	108,988	215,872	26,991	—	7,971	19,869	972	10,000
1954	1,500,834	670,774	2.23	47.30	18.683	130,080	234,074	32,227	—	8,730	22,950	1,500	14,000
1955	1,625,518	716,124	2.264	46.55	18.537	129,614	245,429	35,142	—	7,405	16,233	1,500	26,000
1956	2,094,015	942,658	2.218	47.26	18.641	198,131	249,977	37,257	—	10,943	18,283	1,500	33,000
1957	2,625,849	1,180,890	2.22	46.937	18.609	230,502	300,757	40,021	—	17,247	21,328	1,500	43,000
1958	2,439,620	1,128,891	2.15	48.155	18.194	230,978	279,647	45,039	—	18,461	23,800	1,500	55,000
1959	2,064,256	930,464	2.21	48.463	18.107	180,657	312,559	43,767	—	18,872	20,941	1,500	73,000
1960	2,338,397	1,061,677	2.199	49.507	19.720	239,557	340,463	45,002	—	19,062	20,052	2,000	87,000
1961	2,782,302	1,269,734	2.191	50.041	19.935	271,561	335,930	54,702	—	21,402	22,082	3,000	100,000
1962	2,941,792	1,362,111	2.160	50.068	20.077	296,493	400,797	66,687	—	20,439	18,761	3,000	115,000
1963	3,300,445	1,515,397	2.176	50.055	20.582	327,162	441,750	73,386	—	25,995	20,844	5,000	116,000
1964	4,015,738	1,804,551	2.208	50.950	22.111	393,283	540,049	93,431	—	27,423	25,227	5,000	126,000
1965	4,659,997	2,071,179	2.27	50.58	22.446	451,744	662,635	130,953	—	24,468	21,458	5,000	136,000
1966	5,229,208	2,360,583	2.215	50.62	24.177	521,964	718,739	165,799	—	15,189	11,525	5,000	116,000
1967	6,326,273	2,717,261	2.201	49.90	24.958	635,477	797,430	180,084	—	28,090	36,950	5,000	102,000
1968	7,225,241	2,976,447	2.23	50.5	25.071	733,955	912,721	208,263	—	30,903	44,487	5,000	116,000
1969	6,889,048	2,544,861	2.227	52.56	25.202	865,862	1,149,991	249,733	—	14,221	49,540	5,000	118,000
1970	6,731,560	2,379,505	2.269	53.87	26.44	897,695	1,312,682	275,329	—	5,511	47,457	5,000	116,000
1971	7,001,693	2,221,623	2.267	22.56p	12.49p	1,079,917	1,418,100	299,896	—	34,613	63,851	5,000	126,500
1972	7,522,826	1,865,095	2.134	33.32	17.65	1,480,941	1,743,336	341,573	—	60,183	138,194	5,000	126,500

Production statistics of Donaghmore Creamery from 1927 to 1972.

On the Avonmore Creameries stand during the walk on the farm of Dick Palmer, Boley, Abbeyleix (creamery milk supplier of the year in 1982) were Joe Delaney, Avonmore, Raheen (left) and Michael Kenny, Iron Mills, Ballinakill.

Discussing a piece of machinery at the Avonmore stand during the walk on the farm of Dick Palmer, Boley, Abbeyleix (creamery milk supplier of the year 1982) were (from left) – Tom Conney, Tom Shelly, Paddy Power all from Grangemockler and Timmy Finlay from Avonmore.

SECTION ONE

PART SEVEN

Post Amalgamation (1973-2003)

CHAPTER ONE

Working as a Team

Twenty-one co-op societies, including Donaghmore, amalgamated on 1 September 1973 to form Avonmore Farmers Ltd. The Board consisted of twenty-seven members, from which an executive committee, comprising of nine, was established.

Reddy Brennan was the group's first managing director. He recalled an early decision that proved vital to the success of Avonmore. "One of the first things we did was to regionalise the group, which worked out very well. We had a regional manager in each area. They had a lot of autonomy and could do their own thing. As regards capital expenditure, the Board was always very supportive. Accounts were prepared on a regional basis and it was easy to see what area was doing well and what wasn't, what sales were going up and what was the bottom line."

Traditionally, one of the fundamental functions of a creamery was in determining the price paid to suppliers for their milk. There was what was known as a monthly estimate. The manager would see how much milk was received, what the average butter fat test was, how much butter was manufactured from it and approximately what the cost was for running the business for the month. Then you knew what was left. This was divided by the number of gallons of milk in order to arrive at the price per gallon. That all changed at amalgamation. Fixing the milk price was no longer a problem for the individual creamery. The price was now fixed at Ballyragget. As Bobby Bennett once quipped, the price was now 'Reddy-made'.

Donaghmore, in this regard, was typical of other creameries in the group, according to Reddy Brennan, but it was bigger, much bigger, than most in the store business and was seen as a leader in this field. Mr. Brennan remembers it also as a leader in another field. "Donaghmore was one of the first creameries in the country to have monthly management accounts for the totality of the business. The budgets were examined against the final results. They were very progressive in this regard."

Donaghmore brought some problems along with it as well, he recalled. "They were having some trouble with the carters, who were looking for more money. When the merger came along it helped get rid of that problem. The carters were looking for compensation but they didn't have much influence on the bigger scale."

There were also some questions about profits. Donaghmore had posted record profits of over £80,000 in 1972, up from £35,000 in 1971. It had, indeed, recorded losses on only two occasions in its history. These were minimal and occurred in the early years of 1930 and 1935. But the alarm bells started ringing when the region reported a loss in its full first year under the Avonmore umbrella in 1974. A loss was also recorded for 1975. Reddy Brennan again: "The profits they were showing prior to amalgamation just weren't there. It had something to do with stock valuations.

We didn't really have problems with it, though. After a little while things were sorted out and Donaghmore has worked really well for us."

After amalgamation in 1973, there was large-scale development and a high level of investment in grain intake, drying, handling, and storage facilities at Donaghmore. Facilities there were also used for the storage of intervention grain.

Donaghmore and Monasterevin were teamed together to form a region for managerial, administrative and accounting purposes after amalgamation. However, from an advisory point of view they each retained their separate regional committees until 1986 when the committees were restructured to form one regional committee. Following the losses reported in the previous two years, in 1976 the Board expressed satisfaction at a return to profitability for the region, which went on to play a key role in Avonmore's success into the future. "It was one of the bigger regions but there were only five or six branches involved," Reddy Brennan reflects. "They gelled very well together. The regional management team became very enthusiastic. Donaghmore had 1,700 suppliers around the time of the amalgamation. They were manufacturing about 7,000 tons of feed and selling about 11,000 tons. They were taking in 6,000 tons of grain at four intake points, which was only 13% of Avonmore's total and were selling about 17,000 tons of fertiliser, which was about 27% of the total. They were also big into hardware, seed and agri-chemicals, accounting for about one third of the total. There was obvious potential in the region."

The Avonmore Group was consolidated with Avonmore Creameries Ltd. amalgamating with Avonmore Farmers Ltd. on 21 June 1976, bringing together the milk processing operations and the various other trading interests. The amalgamated Society had 8,334 individual farmer shareholders and six corporate shareholders. The total number of employees was 1,105 of which 250 were employed on a seasonal basis. Their gross wages and salaries amounted to £3.25m. Total sales amounted to £50m. and the profit returned was £1.348m. on £14m. capital employed. In 1978, Avonmore purchased all the remaining Unigate shares in the Ballyragget Milk Processing complex and from 1979 operated as a wholly owned Irish farmers co-operative. The Avonmore Fresh Milk brand was launched in 1981. In the late 1970s, Reddy Brennan realised that what was badly needed was a provender mill. "Donaghmore was manufacturing some but a lot of other areas were not producing any. There was a huge demand. As milk became more relevant, more feed was required and the animals had to have a balanced ration. Laois may not have got the creamery (which was located at Ballyragget – see chapter on Amalgamation) but it has now one of the biggest Provender Mills[1] in Ireland and,

1. The original team at the Portlaoise Provender Mill comprised of: general manager, Hugh Harkin; production manager, Pat Fealy; accountant, John Roche; accounts assistant, Tom Forbes; creditor accounts, Trudy Nealon; debtor accounts, Breda Doran (nee Cuddy); receptionist, Peig Hackett; laboratory, Ina Purcell; transport manager, Michael Barry; despatch office, Billy Hogan; bagger / packer, Kieran Hogan; forklift, Kieran O'Connell; panel operator, Tom Phelan; press operator, Peter McEvoy; additives, Tom Whelan; fitter, Michael Parish; electrician, Ray Lawlor.
Provender Mill employees in 2002: Kevin O'Shea, Tom Salmon, James Fitzpatrick, Peter McEvoy, Bernard Scully, Sean Byrne, Eamon Delaney, Willie Byrne, Willie Deegan, Aidan Kennedy, Michael Fitzpatrick, Ger Cullen, Frank Fleming, Denis Bergin, John Scannell, Tim Fahey, Hugh McCabe.
Administration: Carmel Moore, Mary Larkin, Mary Phelan, Trudy Nealon, Joan Byrne, Mary Keegan.
Management: Eamon Walshe, Sean Hearn, Dave Delaney, Martin Gorman, Seamus Greene, Donal Williams, Pat Bolger, Tom Kerr.
Bridge Street, Portlaoise – Sales & Marketing: Joe Murphy, Chris Miller, Geraldine Cullen, Gillian Doran, Colm Eustace.

Seán Power at the milk intake in Donaghmore, October 1987.

indeed, Europe. It was commissioned in 1981 with a £4 million outlay and, in its first full year in operation, feed production exceeded 100,000 tonnes. Portlaoise was the right location and it has done extremely well under the direction of Sean Hearn and his team."

Amalgamation did mean changes in the management structure at the individual creameries, including Donaghmore. This led to some creamery managers changing roles within the enlarged structure, while others opted for early retirement. Reddy believes that most managers were happy with this arrangement but admits that it did cause pain to others. "Some were individuals and would never have wanted to be part of a regional team. The day of the one-man-band was over", he explained. "We had to have a team around. We simply got on with pulling things together. I would never admit to being ruthless but some tough decisions have sometimes to be made." He summarised his philosophy of management simply – "Recruit the best people and let them get on with the job. Support them when they need support and judge them and reward them on the results".

Donaghmore received a fillip when, in 1982, Raheen milk supplier, Dick Palmer, won first prize in the Dairy Farmer of the Year competition, a prestigious national event. Reddy Brennan retired as Group Managing Director in 1983 after eighteen fruitful years in the position. He was replaced by Pat O'Neill.

John Duggan, chairman of South Tipperary Co-op at the time of amalgamation and later chairman of Avonmore Creameries for many years, recalled that it took some time for people, especially at Branch level, to adjust to the new situation. "When top management began to reshuffle the pack and decided to put some managers into different branches, there was a lot of resistance for a time. One of the things that used to annoy me was that headquarters was blamed for everything. If something went wrong at local level it was because of a policy handed down from headquarters, it was claimed. This wasn't the truth at all but it was a convenient excuse. After any amalgamation you are going to have surplus staff anyway and some people would not have a job long term. Then there was the question of a person's capacity to fit into a team situation. Reddy Brennan was a brilliant man to spot bright young people. If you were on the staff and had the potential, you got the opportunity to move up the scale.

"With Pat O'Neill and myself, and with Reddy Brennan in his time, there was no nonsense. We tried to call it as it was and we tried to call it for the common good. A number of sacrifices were made and a number of people got sacrificed in the process. But that was the price of progress. That was the price of success. One of the things that is often mixed up in relation to co-operative endeavour is that a co-op has to be commercially successful. One can mix up the social element and the commercial element as much as one likes, but if there is not a commercial success there, you have no hope at all of doing anything socially for the people."

One important factor that swayed farmers to vote for the merger was the commitment pledged by Avonmore that they would keep the branches open. "Yes", said Reddy Brennan, "in the plan we promised that we would keep all the creameries and branch creameries open. This we did and it is a feature of this part of the country that a lot of creameries and relatively small branches are still going strong. These places are well painted and decorated and are important places in their own areas. In other parts of the country they levelled them. Mitchelstown is one case in point. If you go down the road from Tipperary to Limerick there is, what used to be, a fine central creamery called Oola. Now it's gone. Clonbranna, where I worked for ten years, was a central creamery with four branches serving a population of about 70,000 in Limerick, Shannon and Ennis and now there's only a couple of sheds there. It became part of Mitchelstown and they closed it down. Mitchelstown were only interested in milk and processing cheese. They made a lot of money from cheese. But I think they made a big mistake.

"Donaghmore is still a vibrant place and so are all the branches, because of retail and diversification. There are other outlets such as Muckalee, Bennettsbridge, Ballyhale, Mullinavat, Kilmacow, Carrigeen, Castlehale, Kells and others, some of them only a couple of miles apart, and still going strong. One co-op that didn't amalgamate was Thomastown, which has long since gone 'belly-up'." John Duggan agreed that the promise to keep the branches open was a trump card for Avonmore in the amalgamation talks in the early 1970s. But he believed that it was not as contentious an issue for Donaghmore as it was for other co-ops.

L.-r.: Martin Lalor, Tim Costigan, Gerard Lawler and Michael Igoe at Spink Branch in November 2002 in connection with the 75th anniversary of Donaghmore Creamery.

"Unlike Kilkenny and South Tipperary, where you had a multiplicity of branches, there were only four in Donaghmore, and they were servicing a huge geographic area. But it was more critical in other areas. Avonmore kept branches open, some of which were only a few miles apart, and they are still making a contribution. In other places where amalgamations took place they cut down on the number of branches dramatically. You could argue in favour of either policy. But, I believe, that it is impossible to measure in pounds or euros the amount of goodwill you could lose, or the amount of damage you could do to the organisation, by closing branches. The branches today are not what they were ten or fifteen years ago and they have not as many staff as they used to. We must recognise that the forklift truck revolutionised branch creameries and the fact that bulk feed and bulk fertiliser came in. But the local man in the local area is still looked up to and they still give a great service."

The committee system within Avonmore, and later within Glanbia, has succeeded to a large extent in ensuring a satisfactory line of communication between the management and the farmers. The farmer shareholders have their Area Advisory Committees locally. The Area Committees send representatives to the Regional Committees. These feed into the Council from which the Board of Management is formed. A farmer's concerns, which have first been aired at an area committee meeting, may find their way onto the agenda of a Board meeting. Similarly the decisions and policy matters discussed at a Board meeting may be relayed down the line to the Area Committees and the local farmer.

Bobby Bennett explained how the system works in his local area. "Donaghmore has an Area Committee of 28 people made up of big and small farmers. If a smaller farmer has a problem, our Board member will bring that case before the next Board meeting. If it's something that needs urgent attention we will send in a proposal for the next meeting, John Miller is our Board member and he comes to most of our

Billy Finnane (behind counter) with customers in Donaghmore Home & Farm Shop 1980s.

Area Committee meetings. He presents a report on what is happening at Board level. If John can't come we have our own Council member, Martin Keane, who reports. I would say the big business gives shelter to the small man. If we were just a small society we would not get the same benefits at all. I also believe that Avonmore and Glanbia have always tried to be fair to the small farmer."

John Duggan has attended a lot of information meetings of shareholders in the Donaghmore region over the years. What does he think of their attitude? "You'd certainly be put through your paces and you wouldn't want to be talking a lot of nonsense. There were some cranks but I always found that if you gave a good, honest answer, no matter how thorny the question was, if the answer was straight, even if it wasn't palatable it would be accepted. I found the people on the Donaghmore committee of great integrity. They didn't just argue for the sake of arguing, they argued if they thought that there was something worth arguing about for the benefit of farmers. If you gave a good reason then they tended to accept it and row in with you. You could be sure as you left the meeting that if they said they were going to support you, that's precisely what they would do."

How important in John Duggan's view was Donaghmore to the merger. "If such a big part of the country, or of the map of Avonmore, remained out then, I think, it would have had serious consequences. I think it is worth noting that when Avonmore was formed its geographic area was two million acres. It was exactly the size of the six counties.

"When I became chairman in 1978," said John, "one of the first things I decided we should do as a Board was that we should take a trip on a bus around what we called our constituency. When I fully realised the extent and diversity of the land in our area, I remember saying to Pat O'Neill, who was deputy group managing director and group secretary at the time, that if we couldn't make a success of it, we would not make a success of anything."

John admits he was deeply impressed by Donaghmore's attitude towards amalgamation. "When they said they were coming in, they were coming in. There was no shilly-shallying. They took their time, made up their mind, but from the minute it was made up they were absolutely positive. They were in right up to their tonsils, making every effort to make a success of Avonmore. I think that Donaghmore played more than a proportionate role in ensuring that Avonmore became the success that it was and is.

"I have no doubt but that Donaghmore was, and still is, a cornerstone of Avonmore, and Glanbia now, because of its size and its open thinking. The Bobby Bennetts and the Billy Wallis' and the people like them have an awful lot to be thanked for. They did not close off any angle and whatever was possible they went for it. I think there is a legacy there today that is a tribute to all those type of people."

"Even after amalgamation, it took a lot of tedious argument before South Tipperary closed down their butter plant," John recalls. "The same thing applied in Donaghmore. When it was decided that all butter for export had to be unsalted, that forced a change of minds. Few co-ops could afford the huge capital expenditure required to update the processing operation to acceptable standards. That was a major breakthrough for Ballyragget."

On 9 November 1979, Avonmore marked a very significant milestone when it celebrated the intake of 100 million gallons of milk in the one year – the first Irish co-op to achieve that figure.

CHAPTER TWO

Avonmore Goes plc

The basic principle governing agricultural policy of the Common Market as set up in 1957 was to ensure that Europe would produce enough food to ensure self-sufficiency. This was achieved by a combination of price supports with intervention being used to deal with seasonal surpluses. The policy was very successful and eventually led to the production of ever increasing surpluses, which had to be heavily subsidised in order to compete on the world markets.

Some time after Ireland joined the Common Market (then known as the EEC and now the EU), which it did in 1973, it became apparent that it was only a matter of time before production would have to be curtailed. What a change this was for Irish agriculture and especially for the Irish dairy industry! Through all the years creameries had struggled with a shortage in milk supplies. Now Europe was faced with the problem of butter mountains and milk lakes.

Because of the vision of the then Group Managing Director, Reddy Brennan, and his management team, Avonmore was one of the first Irish Co-ops to recognise the need to increase production as quickly as possible and thus maximise the position for its suppliers when the cut finally came. It very successfully achieved its objective in this regard by setting up a team of agricultural graduates throughout the Regions to work with farmers both individually and collectively in increasing milk production. Avonmore farmers, including those from the Donaghmore/Monasterevin Region were, therefore, relatively well prepared when the EU Milk Quota regime was introduced and the and the resultant imposition of the Super Levy in April 1984.

Pat O'Neill, replaced Reddy Brennan as Group Managing Director, Avonmore Foods plc

During the period from amalgamation in 1973, Avonmore had acquired either by purchase or amalgamation a number of businesses including Graiguecullen Corn and Coal Company in 1974, J. Murphy & Sons, Graiguenamanagh, in 1975, Welfed in 1977, a 60% investment in D. Walsh & Sons in 1978, Brophys' grain business in Ballacolla in 1981 and Leix Dairies and Kilkenny Creamery three years later. But Avonmore had problems too, apart from the Super Levy, by the mid-1980s. Having to write off an investment of £58,000 with the appointment of a receiver to Clover Meats Ltd in 1984 was a sore blow, at the time, for Avonmore and the pain was repeated a year later when two other ventures supported by Avonmore, Callanwood Ltd and Appledore Ltd were also put into receivership.

Despite these setbacks Avonmore continued to expand its operations. Drogheda and Dundalk Dairies and Bailieboro Dairies were acquired in 1986, which had the effect of doubling the size of Avonmore's liquid milk operations. Production at Bailieboro was discontinued and was consolidated in the Drogheda and Ballytore facilities. In 1985, the new cold storage facility at Ballyragget was completed in association with Norish Foods. In that same year, Avonmore decided to enter the dairy blend business and secured a licencing agreement with Land O' Lakes, Minneapolis. This enabled Avonmore to bring a top quality product to the market quickly, and Avonmore "Gold'n Soft" was launched in mid-November of that year. The value of sales in 1986 was £241.8 million, up from £22 million in 1974.

The amalgamation of Clonaslee Co-op into the Avonmore Group took place in late 1987. The following year, the regional manager, Sean Hearn, revealed that North Offaly Co-op, based in Tullamore, had amalgamated with Avonmore. The premises of Paul and Vincent in the same town had also been purchased. Since 1981, Avonmore had a 43.6 per cent share in Roscrea Bacon Factory. Clonaslee had 18.2 per cent of the issued equity share capital of RBF and this passed onto to Avonmore when the businesses amalgamated in 1987. With the purchase of other shares, Avonmore Foods now owned over 86 per cent of the shareholding in RBF. In March 1988, Avonmore acquired another long established pig processing business, Edmund Burke and Sons of Clonmel.

Avonmore continued in an expansionist mode and management now set their sights on acquisitions in the UK, continental Europe and the USA as well as in Ireland. Spillers Horse Feed business was added in 1988 to the extensive range of animal feedstuffs already being produced within the Group. But the Co-op could not finance a number of other proposed strategic developments from within its own resources. Outside investment was required and it was decided to become a public limited company which would enable it to raise the capital required by releasing some of its equity. The target set for outside investment was £5 million. In a Private Offer placing to Avonmore Co-op shareholders and Avonmore staff in June 1988, £12.7m. was raised while in a public placing on the stock exchange in September 1988, a further £8.3m. was realised. Three years later a further £31.8 million was raised in an Open Offer. If 36.5% of the equity of Avonmore was now in private hands, much of that was bought by farmers themselves and together with the 63.5% still retained by co-op shareholders, farmers retained a firm control of the business. The principal activities of the Group at the time were the processing and marketing of dairy-based food products and ingredients, the processing and marketing of liquid milk and fresh milk products, the processing and marketing of meat products, the manufacture of animal feedstuffs and fertilisers and trading in agricultural produce, especially grain and agricultural inputs.

Record profits of £9.5 million were achieved in 1988, an increase of 43% over the previous year. The Group acquired an initial 42% shareholding in T.H. Goodwin and Sons Ltd, a liquid milk, cream and cheese business based in Shropshire, England and an agreement to purchase the balance of the shareholding was also agreed.

CHAPTER THREE

The Battle for Westmeath

Milk is the basic raw material for the dairy industry. An adequate milk supply is the fundamental requirement for a successful creamery business. There have been bitter battles between neighbouring creameries for milk supplies ever since the industry evolved from its home-made butter status in the latter half of the 19th century. Indeed Donaghmore was conceived during one such milk war that threatened the survival of the industry in the country during the 1920s and owes its beginnings to a rationalisation plan formulated by Dr. Henry Kennedy of the IAOS, which brought hostilities to an end. During its formative years, Donaghmore had to fight off repeated raids on its territory by other co-ops and this book records some of those unneighbourly confrontations.

But the biggest and most publicised milk supply battle in the industry's history was not fought out between neighbouring creameries, but between a co-op controlled company, fully supported by ICOS, and a publicly quoted company, which was part of the every growing business empire of a cattle baron. This was the battle for Westmeath Co-op. Westmeath was a relatively small player in the national context with an annual supply of 13 million gallons. This was a tiny part of the almost 900 million national total. Yet when the business was put on the market in the spring of 1989, it pitched into competition two giants in the farming industry, Avonmore Foods and Food Industries, and resulted in a bonanza for the Westmeath shareholders.

As much as 71.9% of Avonmore Foods, which had gone the plc route in 1988, was still owned by the farmer shareholders of Avonmore Co-op while Food Industries, represented the non-meat food interest of beef-baron, Larry Goodman, who owned 68% of the shares. Food Industries had got a toe-hold in the dairy business when it acquired Bailieboro Co-op in the previous year. That acquisition was, in its own right, a historical breakthrough because, prior to winning the battle for Bailieboro over Killeshandra Co-op, most people believed that it was not possible for a public company to buy a co-op.

Mr. Goodman won that battle hands down and let it be known that it was only the beginning and that other co-ops were being short-listed for takeovers. His attentions next turned to Westmeath. As part of his campaign strategy, he brought satisfied Bailieboro suppliers on board to preach the Goodman gospel that competition, rather than co-operation, was good for the Westmeath and Offaly farmers. The battle had begun to win the hearts and minds of the 1,950 voting shareholders of Westmeath. It was fought out with the intensity of a closely contested by-election. There were information meetings held in hotels, community centres and on street corners. There were campaigners with placards marching in the towns and around the countryside and tons of pamphlets were in circulation. It was the big farming and business story in the national and regional newspapers and on radio and television. Moreover, each shareholder was targeted on a personal basis by a squad of well motivated and high powered campaigners from either side led by Avonmore Group Managing Director, Pat O'Neill, on the one side and Larry Goodman himself, on the other. Personnel from the Donaghmore region were to the fore among those drafted into the battlegrounds around Mullingar, Tullamore, Clara, Moate, Birr, Kinnegad, Kilbeggan, Rahan and Raharney to help win the battle as it was projected not only for the well-being of Avonmore but for the co-op movement as a whole.

As the competition warmed up, the stakes were upped much to the delight of the Westmeath shareholders, whose shares had been stagnant for years. Avonmore submitted an offer estimated at £8.5 million on 15 February 1989. The offer was recommended to shareholders by the chairman of Westmeath Co-op, Gerry Farrell, and his committee. But the battle was far from over. Food Industries kept raising the stakes, so much so, that a mere week later the Avonmore bid had almost doubled again.

The bidding frenzy continued until voting day, Friday, 7 April, when in the region of 1,600 farmers converged upon the Community Hall in Moate, Co. Westmeath, to deliver their judgement. The ballot went Goodman's way by 786 votes to 626. It now seemed that the Goodman rollercoaster was unstoppable. He now had half the beef industry under his control, he was one of the big two operators in the grain trade, he was rapidly expanding in pigmeat, he held large property holdings and owned slices of two major multinationals, which included a recent personal purchase of £75 million worth of shares in the giant Unigate concern. He had just won a major victory at the expense of Avonmore and the rest of the 1,000 million gallon dairy sector seemed ripe for his picking.

Bitter tears were shed in the Donaghmore/Monasterevin Region, where committee members and shareholders had worked tremendously hard to swing the vote Avonmore's way. Almost to a man they had rallied around the flag at the call to arms. They had left their farms early in the mornings and had spent long hours in the field each day in their attempt to woo the Westmeath Co-op shareholders into the Avonmore family.

ICOS laid the blame for the defeat at the door of the "dry" shareholders, who had no strategic interest in the day-to-day running of the co-op and whose interest lay in cash rather than in the future of milk supplies. IFA President, Tom Clinton, said that the shareholders had expressed a free choice in deciding, which was their absolute right. Macra na Feirme president, Padraig Walsh, a Laois farmer who had actively campaigned for the Avonmore bid, labelled the result "a sad day for Irish farmers". He warned that farmers needed to control what happened their produce outside the farm gate more than ever as they entered the 1990s.

It was a bad result for Avonmore and the co-op movement but, as far as they were concerned, they had lost a battle and not the war. Pat O'Neill said emphatically afterwards that Avonmore remained a powerful and vibrant company and that it would continue to develop its business at home and abroad. Goodman's star was most certainly in the ascendant. It was soon to take a nosedive, however. Avonmore quickly shook off the trauma of a high profile and costly defeat, and continued on its upward spiral just as, indeed, its Group Managing Director had predicted.

Raheen Staff in the early 1980s

Back (l. to r.): Fint Brennan, Seán Fitzpatrick, Dan Carroll, P. J. Nealon, Joe Carroll.

Middle (l. to r.): P. J. Kavanagh, Seamus O'Dea, Joe Delaney, Joe Clooney, John Fitzpatrick, Pat Sinnott, Pauric Fleming, Billy Morgan, Dick Malone.

Front (l. to r.): Gerard Lawler, Tom Carroll, Mary McCabe, Seán Hearn (Manager), Annette Duff, Marie Morgan, John Joe Collier.

At the Donaghmore Shop Open Day in 1988 were (l. to r.) Lucy Hyland, Frank Hyland and David Hyland pictured with rugby star Mick Doyle.

CHAPTER FOUR

Dramatic Expansion

The battle for Westmeath Creamery had been a diversion of energy and resources during the first half of 1989 but once the shareholders there had made their decision, Avonmore sought and found other business opportunities elsewhere. By 1993 the extent of the operations had expanded to six countries and employment had grown from 1,381 to 6,219 during those six years. Avonmore was now heavily involved in niche markets in consumer products and food ingredients in Europe and the USA. The turnover from markets outside Ireland had grown from 40% of the total to 73.4%. The injection of private capital had enabled Avonmore evolve from being a major player in the Irish dairy industry to becoming an international food giant.

Turnover at Avonmore grew from £263 million in 1987 to break the one billion mark for the first time in 1993 at £1,129m. Borrowings rose from £23m. to £91m. but Pre-Tax Profits grew faster from £6.6m. to £29.2m. during the same period. The Dairy Division turnover had expanded over threefold but the most significant development over these years was the takeoff in meat product sales, which had accounted for a mere £4m. in 1987 but by 1993 amounted to £454m. or just over 40% of total turnover.

Irish Country Bacon Ltd. (now Irish Country Meats) was acquired in 1989 and this greatly complemented the Roscrea Fresh Foods operation. The product range was by then well established in Europe, Japan and on the home market. It was decided to establish an International Meat Division with offices in the UK, USA and the Netherlands. Turnover at £54m. had almost doubled from the previous year.

In 1990, Bopa Ireland Ltd., a pork processing plant in Clara, Co. Offaly, was added to the Group as were Ashmount Foods, a sliced meat business in Bradford, Yorkshire, and Skellan (Pig) Farms. Turnover for the year was £93m. In 1991, Avonmore invested heavily in Roscrea and Rooskey, Co. Roscommon. The list of acquisitions grew further in 1992 with the acquisition of UMP plants at Ballyhaunis, Ballaghadereen and Camolin, a fifty per cent interest was taken in the Master Pork Group, while other businesses were purchased in Germany and the UK. The well-positioned Avonmore meat operation was, by 1993, selling product into 25 countries.

The Avonmore business boosted farmers' incomes by £350m in 1994. Farmers had also seen their share prices in the plc jump from 45p to 135p and the Co-op had benefited from dividends from the plc of over £11m. in the previous six years. Of the 3,282 people employed by Avonmore in Ireland, which accounted for a wage and salaries bill of £50m, 175 were employed in County Laois, the homeland of Donaghmore Co-op.

About thirty of these worked in the Provender Mill at Portlaoise, which now produced 200,000 tonnes of animal feed along with 25,000 tonnes at Bagenalstown and 15,000 tonnes at Avonmore's Springmount Provender Mill. Most others worked in Donaghmore and in the other retail outlets. Donaghmore's turnover at just under £1m. for 1994 was 10% of the group's total Home and Farm sales, Mountmellick sales were just over £1m. while sales at Raheen and Spink accounted for a further 10% of the group's total.

External factors were causing fresh concerns to the Irish dairy industry in the mid-1990s. Consumer trends were changing and there was further consolidation of the retail sector internationally. The EU Agenda 2000 entailed proposals to reduce market supports for milk, beef and cereals and further liberalisation of international trade was high on the World Trade Organisation's (WTO) agenda. The Irish dairy industry was facing a period of enormous change and challenge. The main focus was on the consolidation of the industry in Ireland and the UK. The issue of critical mass and strong market positions in processing and marketing was being closely examined by the big players in the industry, including Avonmore Foods plc and Waterford Foods plc. Merger talks began between Avonmore and Waterford but they broke down because of the difficulty on agreeing on the valuation of assets. Discussions between the companies were restarted in April 1997 and resulted in a merger on 4 September 1997. The merger proposal was supported by 99% of members in Avonmore Creameries Ltd and 86% of members in Waterford Co-operative Society Ltd. The new company was known as Avonmore Waterford Group plc and John Duggan became its first chairman. The company name was changed to Glanbia plc in 1999.

Group policy began to focus more on businesses with strong market positions. By 2000, it had consolidated its position as the country's leading pigmeat processor. In 2001, the Group's fresh pork operations held the number two position in the combined British and Irish markets. Meanwhile it had disposed of its Irish beef operations in 1999 and had sold its Camolin lamb plant in 2000. Following a strategic review in 2002, the Group decided to exit the UK consumer meats and food service distribution businesses.

At the end of 2002, Glanbia was an international dairy, consumer foods and nutritional products company with a growing reputation for innovation and advanced manufacturing processes. The Group is one of the world's leading cheese manufacturers and suppliers of dairy-based nutritional ingredients, as well as being a major European dairy processor. Glanbia holds key positions in its chosen markets. These include:

- No.1 pizza cheese producer in Europe (in joint venture with Leprino Foods)
- Top cheese producer in UK/Ireland region
- No. 4 producer of American type cheddar cheese in the USA
- Leading global supplier of advanced technology whey proteins and fractions
- Ireland's leading dairy processor
- Irish market leader in fresh milk and fresh dairy products
- Top Irish and major UK pigmeat processor
- Ireland's leading Agribusiness

CHAPTER FIVE

Future Challenges

Here John Moloney, Group Managing Director of Glanbia, reflects on the past thirty years and assesses the challenges of the future for farming and, in particular, the dairying industry.

"Irish agriculture and the food processing sector has successfully completed over three decades of development since EU membership in 1973. This development was built on the foundations, which were established in the years prior to EU membership, especially in dairy co-operative societies, such as Donaghmore and with the formation of Avonmore federation of co-operatives in 1965. During the first decade after EU membership, Irish agriculture responded to the improved market situation by more than doubling the output of milk in the country and achieving similar expansion levels in the other sectors of livestock and crops in general. Farmers adopted new methods of production and invested heavily in on-farm facilities. Likewise co-operatives in the processing sector expanded their processing capacity to cater for the increased volume of farm output.

"The current level of development and the associated investment base will prove to be an important foundation in the years ahead, which are expected to present significant challenges for the farming and the co-operative processing sector. These challenges will arise from the CAP reform agreement reached in June 200 and also from the Doha WTO Round.

"Looking forward over the next thirty years of development and adaptation, what will be critically important will be the farm plans and co-operative agribusiness strategic plans, which are crafted in the coming years in response to what is likely to be a very challenging era. The policy and related changes should be assessed in a complete sense. While it is important that the sector should be fully aware of the threats that the changes are likely to give rise to, it is even more important that all involved in the sector exploit the opportunities that are also available to the sector. Some of these opportunities may relate to the flexibilities that CAP Reform decoupling may present, especially on multi-enterprise farms, which may be in a position to specialise in one sector such as milk production. Another related opportunity is that the sector needs to decide on appropriate restructuring to unlock potential production opportunities. A focussed strategic approach of this nature will allow producers to leverage up their farming strengths to the optimum and thereby minimise the exposure to the obvious threats of reform.

"Very often at a time of rapid change, such as the present, we can all see the negative sides of the change and run the risk of failing to see the opportunities because of an excessive focus on the threat of change. Now, in particular, we should remind ourselves of the vision and commitment of earlier generations of farmers in this region. In addition, we need to maintain a spirit of persistence and a focus on appropriate development. However, we need to draw up plans for the future, which are based on prudent assumptions relating to potential market prices. This applies equally to the co-operative processing sector, which needs to meet the challenges as well. General wisdom in the sector concludes that, if the collective agribusiness sector pursues this approach, it will optimise its future opportunities in overcoming these challenges."

John Moloney, Group Managing Director of Glanbia.

Epilogue

The Donaghmore story as an independent operator may have ended with its amalgamation with Avonmore in 1973. But its identity within the bigger group has survived and it still provides an important service and good employment in County Laois, the Midlands, and the North-East.

The number of people employed at present at the Branches is just a fraction of the number in them at the time of amalgamation. Many workers were replaced by modern technology and working practices such as the forklift, computerisation and bulk deliveries of feed and fertilisers. The situation is similar in most other Branches.

The Glanbia Agribusiness outlet at Donaghmore[1] and other Branches supply a wide range of goods, and provide advisory services to all farming sectors and related activities in the Region.

The Donaghmore Influence on Glanbia plc

Donaghmore Co-op is now a small cog in a very big wheel that is Glanbia plc. But that, in no way, should minimise the important place it commands in the history of Glanbia. Through its representatives on various committees it will continue to play its part in influencing the future of Glanbia. The Co-op principle of one man, one vote, still applies. In his Introduction to this book, Mr. Walsh, Minister for Agriculture, defines Donaghmore as "the acorn from which the giant oak grew".

John Moloney, Group Managing Director of Glanbia, sees Donaghmore Co-op as an important part of the deep heritage of Glanbia. "Our group is firmly rooted in the small co-operatives that were established at the end of the 19th century and into the 20th and which provided hope, organisation and a future to farmers in times of great economic adversity. These small co-ops have amalgamated over the years to form the modern day Glanbia, which is active across the globe. It is a wonderful story of transition.

---

1. Employees at the Donaghmore Branch in 2002: Joseph Nolan, Michael Whelan, John Murphy, Barry Still, Trevor Walsh, John Gilmartin, James Phelan, William Finane, Noreen Beehan, Patrick Daly, John Kinahane, Diarmuid Everard, Anthony Delaney, Murty McWey, Conor Phelan.

Employees at the Raheen Branch in 2002: Cecil Allen, Sean Walsh,.Laurence Lalor, Seamus Morgan, Helen Cahill, Peter Dunne, James O Dea, John Burke, Hubert O Leary.

Employees at the Spink Branch in 2002: Michael Delaney, Enda Cassin, Brendan McWey, Brendan Keogh, James Ring, Peter Lalor, Ellen McGuire.

Employees at the Mountmellick Branch in 2002: John Lowndes, Donal Bergin, Lucy Deffew, Michael Milner, Leo Dunne, James Conroy, Kevin Martin, Val Horan, Claire Dunne, Brian Reddin, Charlton White, John Carroll, Seamus Flanagan, Paul Hogan, Declan Egan, Vincent Callinan, Alice Conroy, Tina Phelan, Graham Whelan, Herman Joubertj, Peter Ging, Carol Champ, Conor Dowling.

"As we move forward in a new millennium, much has changed but the challenges to dairy farming and dairy processing remain. Happily, Ireland is now a more prosperous place to live. Seventy-five years ago the challenge was to organise dairy processing to serve domestic markets and near neighbours. Today our market is global and we must compete against world scale organisations and increasingly do so at near world prices. For us as producers and processors that means continued and deeper focus on scale and efficiencies and international competitiveness. Once again we must organise ourselves to secure our future. Our history in Donaghmore shows us that we are equal to that task", Mr. Moloney stated confidently.

"Today Glanbia carries forward the legacy of Donaghmore with pride and honour. We know where we came from and we respect the struggle and vision of our founding fathers in Donaghmore and elsewhere. A real triumph of co-operation over adversity."

SECTION TWO

Reflections

Donaghmore has been Good for Spink and Spink has been Good for Donaghmore

JOHN MILLER

John Miller was elected to the first Area Advisory Committee in Spink in 1970 and became its first secretary. Two years later he was elected to the Committee of Management of Donaghmore Co-op Society. He was a member of the Board of Avonmore Farmers Ltd. from 1973 until its amalgamation with Avonmore Creameries Ltd. in 1976. John has been a Council member through the various phases of Avonmore to the present day now under the Glanbia flag and has been a Board member since 1994. He is also a member of a number of subsidiary Boards of Glanbia.

"My first involvement with Donaghmore was in going to collect day old chickens in Spink. I didn't even know where the place was at that stage. I stopped at a house on the way to enquire where it was and I was met by an ex-teacher of mine. She directed me to Spink Creamery. I began doing business with them from the time I was 14 or 15 and was still in Timahoe.

"As regards getting involved, I suppose the deciding factor was one Sunday after Mass in Timahoe and the late John Quigley, a very respected man in the community, approached me to see if I would go and do a training course in Donaghmore. I agreed to go and there were around 12 to 14 people involved in that training under Malachy Prunty of ICOS. A number of people on the course have gone on to do different and perhaps better things in their lives. One such person was Liam Hyland, who actually got involved in politics during that course and didn't finish it. He went on to represent rural communities in the Dail and in Brussels and he as done it very well.

"A committee was formed in Spink; there hadn't been one there previously, and I was elected the first secretary. After a couple of years I was elected to represent Spink on the Regional Committee. At that time, 1972, it was the Committee of Management of the Donaghmore Co-operative Creamery Ltd. Among my fellow travellers from Spink at that time James Cooney R.I.P., Murty McWey, Padraig Culleton R.I.P., and Michael Walsh R.I.P. I was the young gossoon travelling on that load.

"I remember going into the boardroom in Donaghmore for the first meeting and was sitting beside a renowned person who had been very much involved in the Society, the late George Galbraith, a man for whom I had tremendous respect. He gave me some timely advice on how to handle the situation and what way to participate. Some of the advice I got would still be very clear in my head. About three or four years after that I was elected to represent the Donaghmore/Monasterevin Region and the Clonaslee Pig Co-op on the Avonmore Board and I am still there today."

Agricultural Inspector

"John O'Meara was the first qualified agricultural advisor employed by Donaghmore. I benefited from his advice when I purchased the farm in Spink which was very much on the ball, I would have to say. He spent about four or five years in Donaghmore and then he moved to Macra na Feirme. After that he managed a big operation for Cement Ltd.

"There are an awful lot of advantages being involved in a co-op. Dealing with milk is the big business and grain to a certain extent. You sent the milk off and you didn't know what you were getting for it, but it finished up you got what it was worth, half way into the following month. That was one advantage. Another is grain which was mainly put into compounds (feed rations) and went back to farmers. If we go back to 1947, the time of the big snow, rations (feed) would have been unusual. People kept a bit of their own grain and got it ground, and some oats made into oaten meal. That's all the feed that was there, as well as hay, turnips and that sort of thing. Anyone who grew beet got beet pulp. Many people grew beet mainly to have access to the pulp. The co-op has helped the animal feed situation in a big way

"The biggest advantage was that you could predict to a fairly close degree what you were going to get from dairy farming. There wouldn't be any doubt about that and that is still the situation. Although, I suppose, at present with the Fischler proposals and World Trade talks it's a bit more up in the air than at any time in that last forty years.

"Donaghmore had an important input into the Spink area. It gave us a market for what we produced; a guaranteed market anyhow. It gave people encouragement to stay going. There were areas where people couldn't participate in tillage to any great efficiency and it gave them the option to produce milk for cash and cash flow is very important.

"The late Andy Mahon was a Monasterevin representative on the Board and on our regional committee. His aunt lived where I am living presently and he spent holidays there as a child. He told me his aunt milked a fair few cows in that particular time and when the Creamery closed, probably around 1920, they had no market for their milk, so they decided to churn it. The system of disposing of the butter was that the makers brought it in to Abbeyleix and sent it on the bus to Monasterevin. Andy collected it off the bus and brought it by ass and cart to Portarlington to sell it. Maybe that exemplifies the importance of not having a Co-op to sell your milk to and consequently, and it says the same for the importance of having it today.

"There was an important social aspect too over the years. All the news, rather than through the media, was transferred through the creamery in years gone by. It was a sort of semi-social gathering tied in with doing their work and people could get a lot of satisfaction from it. I suppose there was always an eye kept as well on how many churns individuals had and it was a measurement of how well they were doing or otherwise.

"A friend of mine one time described anything starting in the country (rural area) as a 'hole in the ditch'. At the time the people started our creamery at Spink initially, there wasn't even a hole in the ditch. I must compliment them on their foresight in getting someone in to make a gap to build a creamery that is still serving us to the present day, and a few of those people are still with us. At the time half the people would have said 'are they a bit crazy or what to build in a desolate area like that?' I think the attitude would have changed considerably as the years went by, however.

"One might ask why the creamery was built in Spink with the central at Donaghmore, 25 miles distant. The people in Donaghmore had an interest in this area because there was a creamery in Ballyragget and having one here was one way of marking them. Spink was a suitable area for dairying, because there weren't many other options that you could do in the farming line, other than store cattle, perhaps. They were looking at Timogue, near Timahoe, for a while before deciding on Spink.

"There has always been a strong bond between Raheen and Spink. The Raheen people were very involved in setting up the creamery in the Spink area. When I go back to earlier years and see the friendship that was there between the people who travelled to Donaghmore for regional meetings, you could see there was fairly strong loyalty there between Spink and Raheen.

"There would be a little bit of competition between them for store business, but it was always done in a good-natured way, and still is. I suppose when we look at Ballyragget, Castlecomer, Spink and Raheen, we are now all the one.

"There have been people involved in the business who would have regarded Spink as being a nuisance and wanted the place closed, but there was a fairly resilient group around the place who would see that that wasn't going to happen, because it was an important aspect of the area. Apart from the social aspect, it was the only employer that was in the area and there could have been twelve or thirteen people employed there in the better times.

"I can remember one time the big store in Spink was filled with people when there was a threat that business might not be continued as it was; telling people that a place is going to close is a great way of getting out a crowd like that, and they did show up in numbers.

"It was recognised too that, when there was a scarcity of milk in the earlier years, Spink was the one that ensured that Donaghmore continued to function. I'm from Spink myself; about 35 years ago I blew in. I would regard them as a very loyal people around there. They did have options here but all the milk was delivered to Spink and consequently to Donaghmore. I suppose Donaghmore butter had a very good name at that time. It was a market leader in Laois anyhow.

"As regards federation and amalgamation, I suppose that's an aspect of continuous movement that's still with us to the present day. We have recommendations from consultancy firms that we have three main processing plants in the entire twenty-six counties. The fact that amalgamation was a success was a tribute to the people who were heading up the different areas at the time, the likes of Bobby Bennett, John Duggan and George Galbraith, and their ability to convince people that it was the right thing to do. History will say that the work of these men led directly to Ballyragget at present. It put us in a position of having the best milk processing plant in Ireland and comparable to anything in Europe. Only that they were so well equipped with government Ministers in Kilkenny, we might have had that plant in Laois.

"There were people with reservations about amalgamation. I was involved very much at the time. What was a big issue was the fact that they wanted the skim milk for processing. The position on farming at that time was you fed new milk to calves for 5 or 6 weeks and they were then changed over to skim. When you had the separating plant in Spink, the cream was sent on to Donaghmore by lorry every day; Martin Lalor was the lorry driver at the time. The skim was returned to the producers. I'd say that was the biggest negative element at that time – the fact that farmers were not going to have skim milk. There were pigs on nearly every farm at that stage, not very big fattening units, but there would be pigs fattened and there would be a couple of sows nearly everywhere. The skim milk was a very important part of that feed process.

"Donaghmore had moved on to compounding and the fact that there was pig farming going on, added to sales in that area. It was another added dimension, some people got very big into pigs. In my own place I would have benefited from the fact that I had a rather large piggery that would hold 90 to 100 pigs. There was good money in them at that time. If you were, like I was, in the process of trying to build up the farm facilities and build up stock, it gave you the possibility of earning what is regarded now as a second income.

"Farmers got a higher price for their milk that enabled them buy the compounds but it took a little time to get used to the change. We were told that we were getting a balanced compound, but it took a little convincing to change the mind-set, that there was, for instance, a difference between the compound and feeding the pigs with water and skim milk. There was a difference in the product. It took a little bit of time to get that changed, even though we had a totally balanced diet coming out of the bag. I suppose there was a perception that they wouldn't thrive as well if they weren't getting the milk. Skim milk was an important part of Ballyragget's processing at that stage, in any case.

"I think there is a very good system of representation in the Glanbia situation, which was formed by the joining up of Avonmore and Waterford. We are able to convey any information that is needed along a line up and down, which is important that it goes both ways. I would be proud to say that something that arose in Spink could have finished up at the Board level and, the questions raised getting a definitive answer. People wouldn't realise that could happen when you are talking about a multi-billion euro business.

"What we have, if we start off with Spink again which is the one I'm most familiar with, we have an area committee there with about twenty-four farmers on it. We have at least two meetings every month and the local management attend those. Also, being the Board member, I'd bring back information from the Board. We have other areas similar to Spink. We have Donaghmore, Raheen, Mountmellick, Clonaslee, Monasterevin and Tullamore. There is an area committee in each of them and they have their representatives who come to the regional meetings which are held in Portlaoise. At our last meeting, about ten days ago, we were joined by six Premier members who would be feeding into that. They were liquid milk (for shops and house to house deliveries) suppliers and shareholders. That's part of the changing scene. One of the most difficult tasks down through the years was to convince uncertain people, after they had started their co-op and built a new creamery, to come and join in with the regional committee.

"They would have been a bit apprehensive at the time, but we developed into a fairly united group. As we became bigger, area committees and regional committees became more important. Maybe as we were farther and a bit more distant from the power base, they definitely needed us.

"Macra na Feirme has been an important organisation over the years and has had an influence on the way that younger people in particular were thinking. We are having a problem in farming at present in that they are becoming an aged group, there are not enough young people involved in it. Maybe a good bit of it is the pessimism that is being preached, not all of it as it should be. Young people at present have a lot of other options. They are all educated to a fair degree. It was different forty years ago when, if you went to the Christian Brothers and got your leaving, it was a fair step.

"Going plc in 1988 was a big step. Was it good or bad for the farmers? I'd say it's all positive. It gave us the necessary funds to develop and to bring it to the stage it is at today. Also there were a good few shares dispensed through farmer shareholders. People are inclined to forget that there is a dividend paid on them, both plc and co-op. The co-op shareholders haven't got a dividend for the past three years, but they will be coming in the future.

"The money that's invested there is showing a return way above bank rates at present. In relation to loyalty, after the merger with Waterford, our Co-op found itself seriously in debt. There was a campaign started where we went around to shareholders again looking for an advancement of money for five years, and the result of that exceeded all expectations. So it did prove that if there is a need and you approach shareholders in the right way, you will get your results.

"We are a plc but the Co-op has the major part of the shareholding, and the Co-op benefits from the dividend paid by the plc. What people don't realise is that Glanbia at present is a big business and about 55% of it is owned by the farmers through the Co-op, and about another 20% is owned by farmer shareholders in the plc. So anything that the plc creates in the way of profits, probably about 70% of it is going back to farmer shareholders.

"It's difficult to predict what the future holds, but rationalisation is the name of the game. I don't know whether I'll be thanked for making this statement. Since the merger there has been major money spent investing in rationalisation, and particularly in the processing plant in Ballyragget. My belief is that there are other Co-op PLCs further back from that and they will have to make that investment sooner or later. It was difficult at times to explain to farmers that there was a big investment, and you had to pay the interest on that but that we'd eventually see the benefits of it. I think, at this stage, the debts are very much under control and there isn't any reason why we shouldn't, at least, be one of the best co-ops in the country. If there was further redevelopment of the Dairy industry, our investment to date would have to be taken into consideration.

"As regards the future of smaller farmers, the biggest problem is that no-one can tell you, and anyone who does attempt to tell you is just taking a shot at it. In the last forty years it has been the hardest thing to predict. Even to predict what the situation will be in a year's time is difficult - particularly in the context of the Fischler proposals and the talks going on in the World Trade Organisation. They are major and they are going to have an effect on farmers, big and small. What I will say about farming is that it is not always the size of the farm but the ability of the farmer to adjust to the changes and run an efficient operation. Scale will offset some of that but it will never match commitment, and maybe a bit of satisfaction in doing the thing well.

"I am the Glanbia representative on the Laois Leader Board and happen to be chairman of the Agricultural Committee. Initially it was Pat Brophy, then Joe Delaney, God rest him, and John Carroll who, along with myself, have been representing Glanbia on the Leader Board. Agriculture is my main interest and second is tourism. These interests are not altogether divided when we talk about rural communities. There is a budget there allocated to agriculture. We are in the process of developing a project with Slaney Meats and ICM, Camolin, to give people who buy into that operation, quality assured marketing under a Laois Glenbarrow brand. We have formed a partnership with, if I may say so, one of the better groups within the country with markets all over Europe. It is very much a consumer orientated business. Products under that brand are being launched in the county.

"Reporting back from the Board of Glanbia to all the regional and area committees as well as to all the branches in the Donaghmore/Monasterevin region is a big commitment. What keeps me going is that I enjoy doing it. I have a lot of friends in all the areas. I try to get to most of them for at their every second meeting. I cannot get to all of them. Each area had a representative on the council and they convey information back to their area committees. Being at as many meetings as I can, keeps me up to speed to on what is on people's minds and what their needs are. It's a two-way thing. You have to be aware of what farmers' needs are and, you respond to that.

"The Donaghmore/Monasterevin region represents probably the biggest and most important grouping in the amalgamation. It's expanding with the incorporation of the Premier members who are in our region. We are talking about the representation that would enable us to have a second Board member in the region. I wouldn't foresee any immediate changes and if there are changes, it will be after my time.

"I always believed we should have realistic ambitions and work to achieve them. Even from the football point of view, when I was eleven, a man named Mr. Sayers[1] came to teach us and changed the whole outlook in Timahoe. We were in one of the antiquated schools and there was a mirror and a mantelpiece. He always conveyed to us the importance of winning a county final and having a cup on the mantelpiece. We achieved all those ambitions when we won U14, U16, Minor, Intermediate and Senior. After achieving senior success, we probably sat back a little seeing as we had achieved the highest peak. It was as good a team as was seen for a long time. Then to win a junior I had to go back and start again. I eventually won it. I was about thirty-seven, and more or less in an advisory capacity!

"When I moved up to Spink, I saw individuals there as good as we had in Timahoe, and some had won finals with other clubs. But being an isolated area it was only the better ones that got to play somewhere else. That's something I'll take credit for, in helping to start a new club in Spink. We actually succeeded in winning

1. Jim Sayers is a native of Kerry but has spent most of his life in County Laois. He was primary school principal for many years in Timahoe where he became a revered figure for his contribution to the community and lives now in retirement there. He was full-back on the Laois team that won the Leinster senior football title in 1946. That was the last Laois team to win the title until July 2003 when, under Mick O'Dwyer, as manager, the midland county swept to victory in the final against Kildare. Jim's grandson, Padraig Clancy, played at midfield on that team. John Miller, himself, hails from a family steeped in GAA history. His brother, Bobby, was a leading inter-county player in the 1960s and '70s and another brother, Dick, is currently chairman of Laois GAA.

six county titles in four years, three leagues and three championships. There were some very good footballers in Spink. They would have emerged to a large extent from the work done by Enda Condron, who was a teacher in Knock school.

"My second ambition in life is to make a success of the Glenbarrow Farms brand. As part of the LEADER + Programme, Laois Leader has been working with Laois farmers to produce high quality, traceable and certified quality assured beef and lamb. Because of a unique partnership between Laois farmers, Irish Country Meats, Slaney Foods and Teagasc as well as Laois Leader, Laois lamb and beef are now being processed under the Glenbarrow label.

"We have brought on board some expertise in the marketing and PR fields. I suppose it's an extension of the Co-op thing to see if we can deliver some little bit extra to farmers. If you have the right kind of stock it will deliver about eighteen euros of a mark-up. I suppose at a time when everything seems to be going down, that seems a change in direction. Slaney and ICM Camolin get buyers in on a fairly continuous basis from all over Europe. That brand and their standards will be presented to all the buyers for supermarket groups, Albert Hinds, Marks and Spencers and so on. The hope is that if you could get a line to someone like Marks and Spencers, it would be quality rather than quantity that would appeal to them. It's beef and lamb we are talking about at present. The Glenbarrow brand was launched on 22 May 2003 by Dr. Patrick Wall of the Food Safety Authority of Ireland. I hope that it's a winner. I'll pack in taking on ambitions after that.

"Talking in the context of part-time farming and small farmers, a lot of them are moving. But there has been a good deal done with Leader in retraining people for different things. There are probably half or more of the farmers in the county with a wife working or on an income from some other source.

"Glanbia presently, in the pig situation, is dealing with up to 40% of pig production in the country. Roscrea, which is being expanded at present, Edenderry and Rooskey, where the fire was, are the bigger units. It will cost about five million euros to replace that asset at Rooskey. In relation to Avonmore's involvement in the meat business, it could be said that if Donaghmore had not invested £1000 in the Clonaslee Pig Fatting Unit in 1962, Avonmore may never have got involved in the meat business. The business deal was between Donaghmore being a shareholder in Clonaslee and Clonaslee being a shareholder in Roscrea. I suppose Roscrea saw a need to get bigger and that is how Avonmore got involved.

"As regards the Provender Mill being located in Portlaoise, I suppose it was semi-compensation for taking the processing plant to Ballyragget. It is a solid employer. There are only about eight employed on each shift but, when the demand is there, it is doing three shifts. There is also management and sales people to be taken into account and a lot of people outside, such as hauliers, are benefiting as well. One of our own people (from Spink), Martin Gorman, is manager there at present.

"My family have always been involved in farming but I must be quite unusual in the situation today in that I have three lads farming with me at present. I have five sons, the oldest is in the Garda and the fifth lad didn't move far from farming. He is in horticulture and is quite good at that."

Donaghmore Promoted a Lot of Benefits for Farmers

R.P. BENNETT

 **R.P. Bennett, who lives at Lismore, Knockaroo, was chairman of the committee of management at Donaghmore from 1967/'73, was vice-chairman of Avonmore from 1981/'86 and was a member of the Board of Avonmore from 1973/'93.**

"I was always led to believe that I accompanied my father on bringing in the milk on the day Donaghmore Creamery opened for business. I was told this by my father and it was often mentioned in conversation. But I cannot actually recall being there.

"I do remember, however, events before that day in 1927, particularly my father going out canvassing for suppliers, which was a vital factor in getting the Creamery going. My father was on the first committee and also the first management sub-committee of four. We had eight cows at the time and we delivered the milk ourselves. We lived at The Glebe, Donaghmore, in those days, which is opposite the Creamery. We hadn't far to go. Most others had longer distances which sometimes caused transport problems.

"The Glebe was the old rectory for Skeirke, where the first co-operative in Laois was founded in 1898. It had no premises but purchased farm inputs for its customers. Ballybrophy station was used as a collection point. The merchants of the area were opposed to it. They saw it as a threat to their own businesses and put pressure on farmers not to supply their milk. It lasted only two years.

"I remember, as a young boy, bringing batteries to the Creamery to be recharged. One had to go up the big stone stairs, where the offices were located. The manager, William Grogan, and the secretary, J.P. Kelly, worked there. One of them would take the battery and put it on the charger. I would return a couple of days later to collect the battery.

"When I came on the committee in 1946 there was a tension in evidence at the meetings and in the Creamery. Politics was at the heart of it. Donal Grogan, the son of the first manager, William Grogan, had just been appointed and there had been a lot of controversy surrounding it. The Grogans were 'roaring' Fianna Failers and J.P. Kelly was a strong supporter of Fine Gael. Donal was a qualified creamery manager but the committee appointed someone else initially. The Fianna Fail section on the committee wanted him appointed and party supporters gathered outside the creamery when the meetings were taking place to decide on the appointment. Some even climbed up to the windows and were looking in, in order to put pressure on the committee.

"J.P. Kelly was a most capable man, who gave an awful lot of service for very little payment; he put a huge amount of work into it when Donaghmore was tottering. He was the man who encouraged me to go onto the committee and I always got on well with him. He was a man of great integrity and he liked to deal with people who were straight and honest. He was an autocrat. He liked having things his own way. He ran the place and ran it well. He always tried to influence committee members before meetings. He had loads of brains and he was usually right in anything he pushed forward. I could be critical of certain things he did but, I must say, that I have nothing but the height of admiration for him.

"The carters (who transported milk to the Creamery) were a very important part of the operation. When I joined the committee, the milk supply was going down every year; so much so that by 1947 the total intake of milk was only 144,000 gallons, not much more than when the Creamery started. At one meeting it was proposed to close down altogether. The carters built up rounds for themselves. They would bring in the milk and deliver back the skim milk and other products. They had a great relationship with the suppliers. It helped keep up the milk supplies, especially at critical times.

"The first milking machine, run on a small petrol engine, was introduced to the area in the mid to late 1940s by Richard Howard, an uncle of mine. He was a progressive farmer and was also one of the first to introduce a tractor, which he used during the years of compulsory tillage. The average farmer had 10 to 12 cows. But it was very much mixed farming and everyone was largely self-sufficient. Ploughs were worked by horses bred by the farmer. There was no such thing as going out and selling cattle and buying more. You bred and reared your own calves and foals. You grew your own food. The vegetables were mostly cabbage and turnip. There was very little buying from the outside. You had your own milk and pig meat and that was the staple diet as far as meat was concerned. You bought your own flour and you baked your own bread.

"I remember being in a house and baked beans had only been out a short time. The lady of the house said: 'We are having baked beans for dinner today and you must be ready to eat them because the minute I take them out of the tin they are going to go off.'

"At dinner time the spuds would be heeled out in the middle of the table, perhaps on an Irish Press, or something like that. You peeled the spuds on to the paper and you read the news at the same time.

"The compulsory tillage during the war brought about a big emphasis on tillage. This helped the store trade and seed assembly at Donaghmore. Most of it was due to J.P. Kelly, who got the agency for Ranks and they built on that. All the grain came in sacks in those days, all different weights. It had to be put into barrels (weight measure). One barrel of wheat weighed twenty stone and the poor fellows were bent in two from carrying them. A sack of barley weighed 16 stone and oats 14 stone. Packing 20 stone sacks into railway wagons, carrying them in off a lorry was heavy work. The men had to walk up a plank and stoop down to get in through the doorway.

"The co-op benefited farmers basically by providing a market for their produce. Selling things was a bit haphazard. For instance, if you were into grain, you bought your seed and your fertilisers and you knew the co-op would buy what you produced. It gave milk producers a place to sell their milk instead of making their own butter. They got the skim milk for their calves.

"Donaghmore promoted a lot of benefits for the farmers. For instance, the co-op bought a tractor, plough and binder during the war years. These were hired out to the farmers who needed them to do their tillage and cut their corn. The co-op ploughed for a lot of people who wouldn't be in a way of doing it for themselves. The farmers kept some corn for themselves. They could have it dried, stored and ground, if necessary at the co-op.

"The hatchery was set up at Donaghmore (in 1947) after Mr. Dillon, the Minister for Agriculture, announced at the Show Society in Rathdowney, that he was going to drown Britain with eggs. The hatchery gave great scope for the ladies. Those who reared turkeys knew they could sell them in Donaghmore. Before Christmas we used to buy in the turkeys and dispatch them. Day old chicks could be bought from the hatchery and reared into laying pullets. The co-op bought the eggs.

"The co-op started silage making in the area. We took on a number of people who made silage for farmers and we collected the money for those contracted with the work. That great man in the IAOS, Mr. Kennedy, got people interested in making silage and we promoted it here.

"The land was terribly deficient in ground limestone. It was one of the big factors against increasing production. If you didn't have enough lime in your land you weren't getting the maximum out of it when you were applying fertiliser. There was a limeworks in Lisduff, owned by the Byrne family, that we bought and put in more machinery. We ground the limestone and got farmers interested in using it. That was another big plus. The limeworks never made a profit but it provided a good service. It became run down in time and the decision to eventually sell it was a correct one.

"We appointed an agricultural instructor, John O'Meara, in 1964. It took a long time for the County Committee of Agriculture to accept the idea. He stayed with us for a few years and was replaced by a man named O'Malley. We had to agree with the County Committee that we would share his time with them. We eventually agreed with the Department that we would pay the instructor's salary but that he would be employed by the County Committee. That remained the situation up to the time of amalgamation. There were not enough qualified people in the County Committee to service the area properly and by the co-op providing an instructor it did an enormous amount of good to improve farming in the area. The County Committee may have had their reservations because it probably thought we were crossing into their area. When Alex Sweeney came along we worked out great with him as we did later with Michael O'Connor.

"The decision to appoint joint managers did not work out well. J.P. Kelly was secretary but he was also, effectively, the general manager. There was friction in replacing him. Donal Grogan and Billy Wallis both wanted the job. It was decided to make them joint-managers. It was a compromise. J.P. Kelly did not agree with the decision. He said that only one person could run a business. Eventually ICOS got involved. Jim Joyce came down some meetings. I was chairman at the time. He came to me several times to resolve the joint-managers' issue. Billy Wallis was his choice for manager. A special meeting was called and it was agreed that Billy Wallis would become general manager. Donal Grogan was to become manager of the dairy, under Wallis. Donal Grogan was not in the best of health at the time. The vice-chairman, Michael Walsh, and myself had to go to tell him he was no longer joint manager. It was one of the hardest things I ever did in my life. The man collapsed in the chair. He was very upset and eventually left for Macroom."

How Co-operation Benefits Laois Farmers

MICHAEL O'CONNOR
Former Chief Agricultural Officer, Teagasc, Co. Laois

"I first heard of Donaghmore in 1968 when I was trying to promote silage making in the Shanagolden area of Co. Limerick. I was fortunate to hear of Billy Wallis, Co-op manager, who had successfully overcome similar problems in Co. Laois, with the help of its agricultural advisers John O'Meara, and later, Michael O'Malley. Donaghmore organised groups of farmers with planned fertiliser programmes and cutting dates. To get a commitment from suitable silage contractors the co – op paid the contractor when the job was completed with deductions from the farmer's milk cheques; this gave security to both contractor and farmer. It was an innovative and important service to farmers who in the difficult economic circumstances at that time, were struggling to realise the potential of their farms in terms of improved grassland output and herd expansion.

Michael O'Connor

"I took up appointment in Laois in March 1975 as Deputy Chief Agricultural Officer with special responsibility for training and advisory programmes for the county, under the guidance of Alec Sweeney C.A.O. Alec was a committed Donaghmore supporter. Names such as Bobby Bennett, Billy Wallis, Jack Quigley and Bill Delaney are some of those I recall whom Alec admired, for their progressive attitude, support for farmer advancement and their total dedication to the Co – op; Donaghmore was Mecca to them.

"The spring of 1975 was a most distressful period for farmers; cattle prices were very low and calves couldn't be 'given away', leading to overstocking and very little land closed off for winter fodder. In mid–May we held a farm demonstration in Coolrain to cater for one of the worst–hit areas. The field we selected was bare; we advised closing up, fertilising and making a clamp of silage in the corner of the field. Suddenly a voice shouted, "that's a b— —-s of a job". I approached him afterwards to be told that he was only trying to stir up the farmers to think further; he also happened to be a member of Donaghmore Advisory Committee. Twenty-three farmers in that area made silage for the first time and no doubt my so-called friend (L.D.) influenced many of them to put thinking into practice."

Joint Approach

"Up to the end of the seventies the agricultural advisory and training services were under the control of the County Committees of Agriculture, comprised mainly of public representatives and co–opted members. Well known Donaghmore Committee members such as Bobby Bennett, Chris Horan, Finty Phelan and John Joe Dunne were valued members of the Laois County Committee of Agriculture. Bobby Bennett later became vice chairman of Avonmore Foods, Chris and Finty were members of Laois County Council and John Joe Dunne represented Macra Na Feirme. The Laois Committee of Agriculture recognised the important role of Donaghmore in farm development in conjunction with the county advisers. Each year the Co–op. regional committee made an input to planning the county advisory programme as well as providing financial support. This close co-operation and integrated approach was unique at that time and, from the mid 90's onwards, it was used as a model to develop closer links between co-ops and Teagasc advisory services nationwide."

Campaigns

"Entry to the E.E.C. in 1973 offered immense opportunities to develop a thriving agricultural industry with new horizons for dairy products, meat and grain but the quality of the products became an important issue. Milk with the high bacterial counts and chemical contamination could not be converted to quality products demanded in the new high-price markets. With the help of Brendan Graham, Regional Manager {later Avonmore/Glanbia group secretary}, Michael O'Reilly and Jim Clifford a joint campaign was launched and put into action to help farmers to produce milk of the highest quality and store it in refrigerated bulk tanks on the farms. This was a most challenging task and demanded perseverance, patience and understanding on the part of the farmers, Co–op and advisers. Great progress was made in spite of the difficulties farmers were experiencing at that time in relation to upgrading of facilities, water quality and availability of funding. The joint Brucellosis campaign, to identify reactor cows in herds, helped greatly to prepare farmers for the compulsory eradication scheme that followed."

Programme for Developing Farmers

"One of the most successful joint initiatives was the Low Income Farmers Programme in 1977. These farmers were seen as non-progressive and resistant to change. Dr. Neils Roling, University of Wageningen, the Netherlands in his study, "Extension and The Forgotten Farmers", stated clearly that lack of opportunities, relevant

The late Jim O'Keeffe who joined the county advisory service in Laois in 1964 and played a major role in developing dairying in the county.
Jim later became Deputy CAO for Laois.

to their needs, rather than resistance to change was a key factor in influencing progress. He also found that such farmers learn most, not from very successful farmers but from those one step better than themselves. Groups of such farmers were formed around each Co-op branch with time-critical meetings held on farms during the year. The adviser and the Branch Manager supported by the Branch advisory committee worked jointly in getting the farmers to participate; the co-operation of the Branch Manager was crucial due to his intimate local knowledge and the respect with which he was held in the community.

"At the end of four years work (1977-1980) an assessment of the programme was carried out by Oliver Dillon, adviser (now CAO Co. Louth) in conjunction with the faculty of Agriculture, University College Dublin. Progress was spectacular. An extract from Dillon's analysis is worth mentioning: "The progress made by members of the Laois Dairy groups is a tribute to their capacity to share information and ideas. The adviser was an integral part of each group and the exchange of information took place in a location where all were relaxed and unthreatened. There was a mutual trust and respect between the adviser and group members. It was this bond, as members put it, that encouraged them to change so many facets of their farm business.

"Between 1997 – 1980 group members increased dairy cow numbers by 49%, while non-members decreased by 2.4%. Group members also increased milk sales by a staggering 87.3% while others were scarcely able to remain static. Major improvements were also recorded in milking and housing facilities, winter feeding and grassland productivity. All this progress gave rise to more focused financial management and better farm incomes. But the most illuminating comment of all from group members was that their quality of living and that of their families improved a hundred fold".

Quality Silage

"The late Joe Delaney, Branch Manager, Raheen, with the support of Sean Hearn, Regional Manager, was much involved in the success of the Laois Quality Silage Competition. Between 1984-1999, in conjunction with Laois I.F.A. and I.F.I., silage quality improved rapidly from a low base (65-68% DMD) to 73-75% DMD. This paid off handsomely in improving yield of milk and beef from a grass product grown on the farm.

"Joe also spearheaded the 'grassland renovation without ploughing' project; farmers on difficult soils benefited most from this technique with minimum soil disturbance. It could be said that Joe relied on two good computers, with the better one hidden somewhere close to his brain!

"In the late '90's water quality and soil nutrient management became serious issues and a serious challenge for all farmers for the foreseeable future. Here, John Carroll, Branch Manager Mountmellick, in conjunction with I.F.A., I.F.I., and county advisors provided invaluable assistance with the launch of Nutrient Management Awards Programme to make Laois farmers aware of the problems and remedial action required."

A Success Story

"The overall success of Donaghmore is immeasurable. Looking back, 1927 was a period of economic stagnation, poverty and emigration. (Maybe it was appropriate that the founders of the Co-op established their base in "The Workhouse"!). It took courage, foresight, dedication and hard work to establish the Co-op and especially to get the support and trust of the farming community in spite of the political and religious differences that existed at that time; it was a lesson in co-operation without any divide. This aspect of the development deserves more comprehensive study. The challenge in the first thirty years was immense. Donaghmore success was built on sound policy making in the boardroom, with very active regional and branch advisory committees to support the regional and branch management. The communication process from boardroom to farmer, teamwork and trust were some of the more important factors in maintaining the loyalty of the farming community."

The Future

"The number of milk producers in Laois declined by one-third in the past decade. The greatest fall out has been among those producing under 20,000 gallons who did not have the resources to expand and create viable units.

The First Farm School for Young Entrants to Farming was held in Laois in 1967.
Among them were full-time and part-time farmers, successful businessmen, co-op committee members and community activists.
First row (l. to r.): Tom Lalor (Durrow), Ml. McEvoy (Ballacolla), Tim Sherman, Matt McDonald (Timahoe), Tom Doyle (Timahoe), Alan Clegg (Portlaoise), Pat Byron (Ballybrittas).
Middle row (l. to r.): Tom O'Loughlin (Rosenallis), Gerry Russell (Clonaslee), John J. Dunne (Mountmellick), Cyril Pratt (Emo), Wilfred Deverell (Coolbanagher), Lionel Broomfield (Ballyfin), Eamonn Duff (Ballyfin).
Back row (l. to r.): Inset: Gay Lalor (Durrow), Willie Dunne (Durrow), Matt Doyle (Ballacolla), John Ging (Portlaoise), Tom Kelly (Abbeyleix), Tim Gorman (Ballyroan), Peter Bennett (Timahoe), Joe Quigley (Timahoe), Mark Delaney (Timahoe), Pat Phelan (Portlaoise), Denis Feighery (Clonaslee).

"It is likely that one-third of Laois farmers will have farm enterprises capable of generating a viable income by 2010; the remaining two-thirds will have to engage in alternative on-farm or off-farm activity to make-up the income shortfall.

"This new scenario offers a serious challenge to policymakers, food processors, research, development and training agencies to ensure the social and economic fabric of rural areas is maintained.

"The elite group of commercial full-time farmers must be highly trained, even to third level standard. Teagasc has already upgraded its training programmes in conjunction with Institutes of Technology with entry to courses through the C.A.O. system. Successful graduates of these courses can progress to University if they so wish and this should be encouraged.

"Such farmers must also be financial management wizards and capable of achieving efficiency standards comparable with the best in the world. The availability of additional land to farm commercially will be a serious issue with leasing, partnerships and other arrangements taking precedence over land purchase. Skilled hired labour could be a limiting factor due to the industrial wage level but lifestyle must not be allowed to deteriorate at any cost."

Part -Time Farming

"The 'Family Farm' is an important concept in rural Laois and every effort must be made to support and protect it. Part-time farming is not of recent origin; it has been camouflaged where the wife has an off-farm job and the husband on the farm has the status of a full-time farmer. Where the farm is not capable of generating adequate income to support and educate the family, then a decision must be made on how to make up the shortfall.

"Farmers have many skills and with further training they are much in demand for well-paid jobs. Such farmers should make a special effort to upgrade their skills

Laois developing farmers visited the milk processing factory at Ballyragget in January 1980. Included in front are Bobby Bennett, Bill Flynn and Fintan Phelan and others members of the Donaghmore Advisory Committee. Included at back are advisors Fintan Monahan and Tom Everard.

rather than drifting into manual or labouring occupations, which are vulnerable in periods of recession. Training agencies are now aware of the need to adapt courses suitable to the needs of farmers where employment opportunities exist.

"It is important to ensure that the standard of farming is maintained but some adjustment and changes may be necessary; careful farm planning and work organisation are essential to ensure that the family enjoys a better lifestyle and standard of living. It is essential for policy makers to note that part-time farming will be a major contributor to the economy of rural areas."

The Environment

"Much has been said and written about environmental issues, with the negative aspects dominating most of the comments. The quality of the air we breathe, the water that flows through the farms, the landscape and heritage sites all influence the image of the foods produced as well as tourism potential. The development of our basin peatlands, formed over the past five to ten thousand years, has made an enormous contribution to employment and prosperity of our towns and villages. When all the peat is extracted wouldn't it be fitting that these sites would be developed as 'The Great Lakes of Laois'."

Amalgamation

"The close working relationship between Donaghmore and the County Advisory Service was built on trust, loyalty, mutual respect and a firm commitment to promote the welfare and a better standard of living for farm families in Co. Laois. Of course, there were areas where independence of thought, policy and actions were sacrosanct to both organisations and these had to be respected.

"In spite of the amalgamation process, firstly Avonmore and later Glanbia, Donaghmore did not lose its identity but became an important player in the bigger organisation. Great credit is due to Board members under former chairman John Duggan, former chief executives, Reddy Brennan and Pat O'Neill, and the present incumbents, chairman Tom Corcoran and chief executive John Maloney, for their recognition of the Donaghmore culture.

"Donaghmore has reason to be proud of its achievements and we, the citizens of Laois, owe a debt of gratitude to the founding fathers and the dedicated management and staff.

"As Henry Ford once said: 'Coming together is a beginning, staying together is progress and working together is success'."

Memories of Donaghmore
Co-operative Creamery Ltd.

GREGORY C. TIERNEY
Former Secretary ICOS

"My first contact with the Donaghmore Co-op was in 1960. I had joined the staff of I.C.O.S. (or IAOS as it was then known) in late 1957 as Regional Officer covering a very large area of South Leinster and North Munster. "There were ninety co-operatives in that region and all expected service from the ICOS official assigned to that area. Nevertheless my contact with the Society continued on a very regular basis up to the time I left for Brussels in 1973 to establish and manage an office there for I.C.O.S. By the time I returned from Brussels the co-op was already integrated into the Avonmore group.

"Over the period of years, during which I had very frequent and intimate contact with the Society, there were three main issues with which I was involved and which were of great importance to the Co-op. These were:

1. the question of the structure of Management in the Co-op
2. the purchase of the business in Mountmellick (*Editor's note:* See chapter on Mountmellick for Mr. Tierney's comments on this topic)
3. the preparation and adoption of a complete amendment of rules.

"Before dealing with these, however, I would like to relate a small story involving the then secretary of the Society, J.P. Kelly. He and I had been working in great detail on certain legal problems that had risen in regard to the milk carters. As was the practice in other parts of the country, where milk was collected by carters, it was usual that they would bring back to the farmers small quantities of farm requirements, particularly animal feed. A local Garda, who may not have been well disposed to the co-op, took the view that this involved the carriage of non-exempt goods (milk was exempt) for reward. As the carters did not have a licence to carry on such a business, they were deemed by the Gardai to be in breach of the law and were summoned to appear in court. The case eventually ended up on appeal in the Four Courts in Dublin in October 1961 and both J.P. Kelly and I were obliged to attend. He attended as Secretary of the Society and I, as an observer on behalf of all the other dairy co-ops in the country who had a milk cartage system.

"It was expected that the case would end before lunch and that we would go our separate ways at that time. The judge, however, decided to adjourn at 12.30 and to resume at 2.30pm. At that time – the early 1960's – traffic was very light in Dublin and I had, like most others in the city, been in the habit of going home for my main meal of the day at lunchtime. A quick phone call to my wife established that J.P. would be very welcome to join us 'provided he was willing to take pot luck'. This presented no problem to him and we were quickly on our way. I was only married a few months at this time and at home we liked to experiment a little with food. What I did not explain to J.P. was that on that day we were going to have a curry and my wife and I liked our curries very spicy.

"So 'pot luck' took on a whole new meaning but he never flinched and left a clean plate behind him. What I did not know at the time was that J.P. Kelly suffered from severe stomach problems from which he never had much relief but, despite that, he went back to the Four Courts as if nothing had happened. I imagine that he must have suffered later that day.

"I cannot remember what the precise outcome of that stage of the legal process was but I do know that after discussions with the then Minister for Justice, Mr. Erskine Childers, about the problem, an instruction was issued to the Gardai advising them to ignore the carriage of small amounts of farm requirements for farmers by milk carters. The carters continued to bring back farm supplies and there was no further interference."

Management Structure

"In 1961, the committee decided to appoint Donal Grogan and William (Billy) Wallis as Joint General Managers. In the records of ICOS for the time this is described as a temporary arrangement. In fact it lasted until 1970 and led to many problems in the interim. It was not a happy arrangement and led to the start of the holding on a regular basis of 'private meetings' of the committee.

"This meant that no member of the management staff, including the secretary, were present at such meetings. On the other hand I attended on a regular basis. It was common for a normal meeting of the committee to be scheduled to follow these so-called 'private meetings'. At that meeting the practice was to formally propose, second and adopt a resolution encompassing any decision of the 'private' meeting without any discussion at all.

"From a reasonably early stage it was clear that problems about areas of responsibility and jurisdiction were arising. The position of the Society's accountant came into the picture as well because of concerns on his part of a perceived loss of status on the appointment of joint general managers. His position was eventually clarified on his being appointed in 1964 as secretary/accountant even though it required further clarification in June of that year.

"Although the position of secretary/accountant was reasonably well clarified, there continued to be a level of tension between the joint general managers themselves. The private meetings of the committee continued to be held and ICOS was consulted all through this difficult period. Eventually a number of events took place which enabled the committee to overcome the problem. By 1970, Donal Grogan had health problems and decided to retire early on mutually acceptable terms, which had been proposed by ICOS to the chairman of the Society. As a consequence the committee decided to appoint Billy Wallis as sole general manager."

Complete Rule Amendment

"Throughout my long career with ICOS I was involved with dozens of co-operatives in arranging for the adoption of rule changes. Sometimes they were partial changes to the rules but quite often they involved the adoption of a completely new rulebook. Admittedly, even in this latter case, many of the existing rules would be carried forward to the new rulebook.

"Nevertheless in any case where a new rulebook was being prepared every rule in the book was capable of being changed. This invariably led to a long-drawn out process of discussion at committee level.

"In the latter part of 1970 Donaghmore Co-op faced that prospect. At the July meeting of the committee it was decided to appoint a sub-committee to work with myself on the preparation of a draft new set of rules to replace the existing ones. The intention was to hold a Special General Meeting of the members by the end of November to seek their approval for the adoption of those new rules.

"Although the target date was not met, there was a delay of only about ten weeks and the meeting was in fact held on 8th February 1971. Bearing in mind the time needed for printing the proposed new rules and the amount of notice to be given to the members, it is reasonably certain that the sub-committee had in fact concluded work, which in many other co-operatives would take double the time.

"Although I had been involved with Donaghmore Co-op on various smaller amendments over the years the speed which the Complete Amendment was handled in 1970 impressed me and was an indication of the efficiency of the working methods of the committee."

J.P. Kelly - The Inside Story

RICHARD KELLY

Richard Kelly

Richard Kelly, Ballymeelish House, Bally-brophy, former employee of the Donaghmore Co-op Creamery and Avonmore, is son of the late Mr. J.P. Kelly who, as Co-op secretary, was its main driving force for almost 40 years.

Richard has a copy of the original plans for the Donaghmore Workhouse, which were drawn up by his late grandfather in the middle of the nineteenth century. At that time Richard's grandfather lived in the stately house presently occupied by Richard, his wife and family, at Ballymeelish, Ballybrophy. This was the ancestral home of the Kellys and up to the early years of the twentieth century, was an estate of approximately 400 acres. All but 20 acres of the land was purchased by the Land Commission.

Here Richard gives his personal memories of the inimitable J.P., a legendary figure in the success story of Donaghmore Co-op.

"My earliest memories are when we lived in Fruitlawn, Abbeyleix. That was around the mid-1940s. During the war he had a little Ford van that he had a permit to oper-ate and a petrol allowance. He also had a car which he wasn't allowed to operate because of the petrol shortage. We'd go to second mass in Abbeyleix on Sundays and from there we'd go to Spink and collect 20 gallon cans of cream, then on to Raheen and collect one 20-gallon can of cream, and take the cans back to Donaghmore. That way the cream was delivered on Sunday. That would be the summer time Sunday job he had.

"Any work problems about Donaghmore were never discussed in the house. He had agencies for Ranks, Suttons, Powers, and Batchelors Peas as well. He would have worked eight days a week if there were eight days to work.

"In dealing with problems they were sorted out there and then. Wherever the problem arose he put pen to paper and gave his opinion. Everything was recorded and he had no codology about things.

"My father had a great way with words and never used a spare word where one wasn't needed. He often talked about the IAOS. There was a Gregory Tierney there and they got on like a house on fire because Gregory's idea about doing something was to say "this is what you want and I can see what you want". He

J.P. Kelly

would bring Gregory down to Donaghmore and say "this is what we want to do, is this the way we should do it?" Gregory would go back and draft it out and send it down in the post and that was it.

"Before Gregory there was a man called Mr. Ebrill, an engineer from IAOS. In later years, when I had a shop in Rathdowney, a rep. came in to me and we got talking and it turned out that his wife was Ebrill's personal secretary in the IAOS. When he went home and told his wife, she said that Mr. Ebrill and Mr. Kelly got on extremely well, and that they had often been in contact both by letter and by phone.

"You didn't try to mess him about, or pull the wool over his eyes, because he'd go through you for a shortcut. I'd admit that I was literally afraid of him, even when I was working in the Creamery. He was my boss as well. I remember one particular morning when I was working in the shop (that was the old shop that wasn't one eighth of the size of the present shop). He came in and looked around the place and asked who had swept the floor that morning. I replied that it had been me, and he ordered it to be done again because it was not swept properly. So I proceeded to do it again and as it was a concrete floor, I sprinkled water on it and gathered up an extra bit of dirt and put it in the bucket. He saw me putting the brush away and said, 'Are you trying to tell me that floor is swept?' 'Yes', I replied. 'Behind that pile of buckets there is a cigarette box', he said, 'and it was there yesterday'. He then told me that if I had swept the floor properly the cigarette box would not have been there. That's one of many such incidents that I remember. His motto was that you did it right or not at all.

"When I started in 1953 your typical day was, even though my father was leaving home in the morning, you got up on your bicycle and cycled down in hail, rain, or snow. He'd pass you on the road and he'd be standing at the clock when you arrived. If you were supposed to be there at 8.15am and were a minute or two late, he'd ask you why were you late. He treated me the same as anyone else. They had a form there at one time which you had to fill in to explain your misadventures, be it lateness or anything else. You literally had to give reasons why you shouldn't be fired. I got ticked off by Billy Wallis one morning for being late and he asked how he could be expected 'to tick off lads out in the yard when you are late'.

"He'd want to be in good humour and everything going right for him the day he'd say to you, even in the evening if he was clocking out at the same time, 'put your bike up on the back of the car'. If things weren't right or he had something on his mind he'd just get into his car and that was it. When you got home you brought in the cows, milked them, and did anything else that needed to be done.

"Physically, if you had something wrong with you, he was the most kind-hearted man going and he never raised his voice other than to command you to do something. If you didn't do what you were told, you were told a second time. You automatically knew what you had to do. I remember one year we went off with the Macra to the Isle of Man for the August weekend. We left the Isle of Man about midnight, and I felt sick on the boat, not from drinking beer or anything, at that stage

IRISH VOLUNTEERS.

BORRIS-IN-OSSORY.

23rd May, 1915.

SIR,

A Meeting of all Members of the above Company will be held in the Parochial Hall, Borris-in-Ossory, on Wednesday, 26th Inst., at the hour of 7.30 p.m.

Your attendance is earnestly requested.

BUSINESS :

1. To consider Report and Balance Sheet, copy of which I enclose.

2. To appoint a Delegate to act with your Captain on Battalion Committee.

3. Adjourned discussion with reference to Band.

4. To arrange for New Drill Field

5. To appoint Officers and Working Committee for 1915-1916,

6. Any other business that may arise.

Faithfully yours,

MICHAEL CAHILL, Hon. Sec.

To Each Member.

Irish Paper.   M. Fitzpatrick, Printer, 99 O'Connell Street, Limerick.   Irish Ink.

J. P. Kelly was a member of the Irish Volunteers, commanded by John Redmond, and for a time was secretary of the Borris-in-Ossory division. These two items of memorabilia comes from his collection courtesy of his son Richard Kelly.

A DANCE

WILL BE HELD IN

Donoghmore Union Buildings,

On Sunday, 18th Sept., 1921.

Proceeds in aid of Volunteers.

Dancing Commences at 8.30 (Irish Time).

Gent's Ticket   =   =   6/=

you barely had the ten bob for the trip and perhaps a few shillings to spare to get chips or something. In fact, everyone on the boat got sick coming home. We arrived in Dublin, came down on the bus to Rathdowney, cycled from Rathdowney to home, and got into bed about 6.30am. At 7.30am the blankets were pulled off me and, when I looked up sheepishly, my father said, "You have a job to go to". There was no sympathy there. I was glad to come home and go to bed early that night to recover lost ground.

"My grandfather was involved in politics. He was a Nationalist and was the first Vice-Chairman of Laois County Council. My father was Treasurer of the local branch of the Irish Volunteers in 1915 and was also interested in politics. At one time he stood for election to Laois County Council at the request of Fine Gael. He didn't do an Oliver Flanagan on it. He just sent out a few circulars to people. At that time, things within politics were pretty dirty – they still are. He was doing well in the counting of votes, anyway. Votepapers were put into different piles. This particular individual was seen to lean in over the table and say to whoever was counting the votes, "take so many out of that bundle and put them aside". The person who saw this came back to my father and my father questioned it with the Registrar. "The Registrar said he couldn't check it out and my father replied, 'In that case, you can have it'.

"Religion was never a barrier with my father. He got on with every Protestant in the county. The first committee had Bobby Bennett's father, Jim Cooper, Herbert Thompson and Jacob Thompson. That's four Protestants out of a committee of twelve. This increased to five out of sixteen in 1928 when the four members from Raheen were elected, including George Galbraith. There was no one more loyal to the Creamery than the Protestant members.

"My father bought a threshing set and hired two men to operate it and it was hired out to local farmers. He also had a grinding mill which he gave to the Creamery for a year when he was encouraging the committee to provide a grinding service for the farmers. He used to keep his own farm accounts up to Profit and Loss figures, which was unusual in those days

"One time when Mr. Grogan, the creamery manager, was on holidays, there was some messing going on in the dairy. J.P. challenged those involved and two of them gave him a bit of 'guff'. He asked them to wait outside the office, collected their cards from the rack, made up what they were to be paid, put it into envelopes, gave it to them and, pointing to the exit door, said, 'Now boys, that's the way you came in'.

"The same thing happened over in the hatchery. When I was able to drive a car, I was sent down on a Sunday morning to look after whatever surplus chickens were in the loft over what is now the boardroom. The hatchery was where the boardroom is now and overhead, beside the Hammer Mill, the surplus chickens were kept there under lights and sold off as quickly as possible. The hatchery lady was supposed to be there on Sunday mornings and when I went there this Sunday around dinner time, there were about twenty or thirty chicks dead because she never came in to give them feed and water. So she 'got the hatchet' on Monday. Mr. Grogan, who was away when this happened, just as he was when the lads from the dairy were fired, took exception to both sackings as he felt he should have had some say in these matters. But he didn't win.

"When we came over here to Ballymeelish from Fruitlawn in 1950, he had an accident when a wheel came off a grain dryer and he was hospitalised for nearly six months. He never got a penny's compensation for all the time he was out. He had to pay all his own hospital bills and expenses.

"When the ESB came along he wired everything in this house himself; and when the ESB man came to connect it up, he found only one fault in it. That was on a two-way switch in the hall. We were the first house around here to get the power. He wired it all out of a book he bought in Easons for 6d. No matter what problem arose in relation to things mechanical, he just thought about it and came up with an answer. He had an old car after the war and the engine went in it. He bought an engine from Hennessy's of Castledermot and put it into the car himself. He would take out an engine and grind the valves himself. He kept books on everything including the manuals on all his cars and he would refer to them whenever he had a problem.

"He was an excellent father to us in every way he could. You weren't idle when he was around, he always got you to do something. We had great regard for one another at all times, but he didn't take any messing from anybody, that was one thing about him. He was serious at work and had a serious attitude to life. He ruled with an iron fist at home as well as abroad. He believed God created you to work and that was it. Honesty was his middle name."

The Local Creamery was Very Important to Raheen

JOE BUTLER

Raheen Creamery was opened in 1928. Joe Butler began working there on 11 April 1932 and he was there until he retired in 1979, the vast majority of those 47 years as manager of the Branch. It could therefore be said that the history of Raheen Creamery revolves largely around the presence of Joe. This is Joe's story, told in his own words.

"Raheen was started mainly through the efforts of George Galbraith and Fr. Coyne, P.P. A committee was set up and the original members included: George Gabraith, Peter Salter, John Tynan, Billy Bergin and Tom Mitchell. Fr. Coyne was not on the original committee but he encouraged parishioners to get involved. He got them to draw loads of gravel, sand and other goods to the site. A lot of the requirements were supplied with no cost involved and the tradesmen gave their time free. There were no buildings of any kind there at the time so the creamery was the first building erected, on land owned by Pete Salter which he gave for a nominal fee.

"A Corkman, Tim Kelleher, was appointed manager. John Lalor, of Corbally, was in charge of the engine and also dispensed the skim milk, helped to keep the boiler fired to maintain the required steam level, attended to the washing up and anything else associated with the general routine of milk intake. For a while, these were the only two who worked there.

"There were not many suppliers at the start but gradually the numbers began to grow. Among the first people to contribute to that increase was a Pat Lalor of Coole, who, with his horse and dray cart, started to collect cans of milk around the areas of Raheen, Roskelton and Clonkeen.

"That improved the situation for perhaps a year or so, until the economic depression of the early 1930s set in and the financial situation dictated that the manager had to be let go. As he was leaving, Kelleher turned over six or seven pages in the platform book, which was used to record the milk intake, put an 'X' mark on a particular page and said 'If you reach this page, it will be a miracle'. He expected the Co-op would be closed in weeks rather than months.

"There were about fifteen suppliers at the time. Initially, milk intake was only three days per week and I was dispensing the skim milk and helping with washing up and so on. Soon after my first day, John Lalor and myself agreed to swap jobs and I was then in charge of milk intake, a position I held for quite a long time.

"When the first dairy at Spink was taken over by Donaghmore in 1935, myself and John Lalor used to cycle up there on the three non milk days (in the autumn/winter time) to do repair work on the old buildings.

"Times were tough but the Co-op did not close. I must pay tribute to the late George Galbraith and the committee members from here who did everything possible, including cycling over to the monthly committee meetings in Donaghmore, a round trip of forty miles, free of charge in all kinds of weather, to help keep the ship afloat. In later years, when finances improved very slightly, a car would be sent to collect George and others but that was the only assistance given to them.

"Things gradually began to improve with more milk suppliers being recruited in the 1940s. Around 1950/51, John Seale of Clonboyne became the first milk carter with his own lorry to climb the little hill, which was the raised platform at the intake point. From small beginnings, he moved on to larger lorries, and eventually, even on his biggest lorry, he had to erect an upper deck in order to cope adequately with the increased milk supply. He was in turn followed by other carters. Among the names I can remember were Gerard Grace, Bill Delaney, Mick Lalor, Mick Bergin, John Young, Fint Delaney, Felix Bennett, Jack Conroy, Tom Delaney, John Malone, Jim Dunne, Chris Horan, Andy Lambe and Kevin O'Riordan, with varying types and sizes of vehicle.

"In the early 1940s there was no store in Raheen, but some goods would be brought from the old store in Donaghmore and sold to Raheen customers. At the time, Paddy Keyes of Ballycarney, Portlaoise, was contracted with his lorry to deliver the cream from Raheen to Donaghmore, and on the return journey, he would bring back a few bags of meal and millstuff. Joe Conroy of Cashel was the driver of Keyes' lorry at the time, and he was later followed by Ned Bergin for some time. He also collected milk around the Cashel and Ballyroan areas for a short while.

"Soon after that time, the then secretary of Donaghmore Co-op, J.P. Kelly, drew up plans for the first store in Raheen. A man named Gaynor from Donaghmore area, a builder by trade, was sent over to mark out the site and get the job started. It was then given over to local man, Mick Lalor of Corbally, a brother of John, who had left at the time, and myself, to complete the building in our spare time.

"So, in the early part of the days, it was the milk intake and then the hard slog of building with mass concrete in afternoons and evenings. Blocks, of course, were as yet unheard of, and indeed, would be for quite some years to come.

"Eventually the building was finished and the store trade increased rapidly. Soon after that, a small mill was built at the rear of the dairy and a roller/grinder was installed. By this time, there were two more staff in Raheen, and Donaghmore had procured their own lorry.

"Ned Bergin, who was previously on Keyes' lorry, was brought in to drive the Donaghmore one for a while. During the war years, petrol was very scarce, and the lorry was converted to use gas. It was a rather dangerous contraption while it lasted, but thankfully no injuries or damages occurred. Ned eventually quit that job and was replaced by Mick Lalor, with Ernest Keegan taking over from Lalor in the dairy."

Steam power

"The engine in the dairy was driven by steam. That posed its own problems in the war years, when fuel was scarce. At the time, Laois County Council were giving out turf banks on Derrykearn bog, and the Co-op bought four or five plots. They procured a team of workers to cut and save the turf, which was used to run the engine. Joe Ryan, who worked in the Co-op, was put in charge of the bog men.

Initially, there was no turf shed, so they drew it up to George Galbraith's haggard in Corbally and clamped it there. They would then bring down a load at a time to keep the Co-op's flame burning. Eventually, a turf shed was built. Its walls consisted of poles, obtained in a wood in Blandsfort, near Ballyroan. It had a galvanised roof and held most of a year's crop, but still some had to be stored in Corbally.

"Although lucky enough to have the turf, it was a full time job keeping a good fire in the boiler. After a time, we got a diesel engine, which apart from turning the wheels in the dairy, enabled us to install the roller/grinder machine.

"Because of the small staff, it was often a case of returning after normal hours, to do some rolling and grinding. When the dairy was in operation, there would not be enough power to drive the mill at the same time, which meant we had to come back in the evenings to get the other work done.

"Engine and boiler maintenance and repairs were generally done by ourselves. I remember on one particular Saturday night, we had parts of the steam engine all over the floor. With the engine stopped, the lighting system soon failed, and we had to resort to using candles. When I got home at last, it was five o'clock Sunday morning. I got washed and cleaned, had a snack for breakfast, went to first mass at eight o'clock and then down again to the Co-op for milk intake.

"On one occasion, a staff person put in separator oil instead of diesel in the engine. The result was that the engine began to run much faster than usual and we were unable to stop it by the normal way, even after disconnecting the feed pipe. Eventually, I rolled up a large sack into a roll, pushed it against the flywheel and gradually it came to a halt. It was perhaps the most terrifying incident to occur there in all my years.

"I remember another incident with the boiler. It had not been in good condition for a while and was not supposed to have too high a pressure. There was a safety valve which would let excess steam pressure blow off. The valve included a fairly heavy ball, fitted onto a bar. It could be moved along the bar to a point which would allow the excess steam blow off.

"However, in order to operate it properly at lower pressure, we had to cut it in two pieces and therefore have less weight to resist the steam pressure. It seemed that at a previous maintenance job, the now flat part of the ball was put back on the bar, with the flat side turned in and too near the end of the bar. This meant that there was hardly any resistance to the power of the steam, which had by now increased to a very high level and steam was blowing all around. We tried to get the valve ball moved out along the bar a little, and gradually we managed to reduce the pressure. With a number of horses and donkeys prancing around just outside the boiler room, added to the noise from the steam, it was a rather frightening experience.

"Then there was the chimney pipe from the boiler up through the roof, which was made of timber with tarred felt on the outside. Although there was a galvanised area around the pipe, when turf was used instead of the original fuel, which was coal, it tended to send up much more heat to the top, with the result that the roof actually was set on fire a few times. Thankfully, it was seen very quickly and any major damage was avoided.

"The lighting system was home made. At first, my brother-in-law, Frank Graham, encouraged me to try a wind charger, which we did. He helped me with the making of the unit, procured a dynamo and produced a lighting system. I had it in my own house in Raheen for some years, but then, as the wind spinner was fairly high and not so easy to manage, I decided to bring the dynamo down to the creamery and also my old batteries, and got them linked up with the drive shaft and produced our own electric light. In the meantime, we had installed a charger, which helped keep the batteries powered, but, of course, when the engine was not running, the lights would soon fail, as the batteries run down. We later installed a diesel engine, which was easier to operate but it too would require ongoing maintenance and at least one major overhaul each year. Again, we had to undertake any such work that was necessary. Our home-made effort was only a 12 volt set up but it did its job for a few years until we got connected to the ESB in the mid 1950s. I think it was there for about 15 years.

"We provided a much needed service to local people by charging batteries for them. They would bring in their radio batteries which were linked up to the big batteries on the dynamo system. We could charge about six at a time. They were only two volts and our max was twelve volts. We would check them for levels of distilled water and sulphuric acid. People really appreciated this service.

"There was a large increase in the milk supply in the 1960s. The old building was not suitable for the extra work now and it was decided to erect a new dairy. This was completed in 1967. It was a great novelty at that time with a lot of automation involving a conveyor belt system, which went all along the outside platform, bringing in the cans of milk, taking the cans and lids through a washing and steaming process, before carrying them back out again to the platform for reloading on to lorries.

"The chief mechanic involved in setting up the system was from Sweden. His name was Eric Oleffson. Although it was generally a very good system, there were times when there were minor problems, particularly with the cans and lids going through the wash system. If even one can or lid got misplaced, it would upset the remaining lot all through, and would result in a wrong lid being replaced on each can.

"In the early 1970s the issue of returning skim milk to the suppliers began to wane and this would eventually cease altogether. It was also around that time that some of the cream from Raheen was sent to Kilmeaden Co-op because Donaghmore could not handle all its intake. It was prior to the setting up of the factory in Ballyragget.

"When the bulk milk collections started, around the late 1970s, it was the beginning of the end for the new dairy, as far as milk intake was concerned. It was also the end of an era for the milk carters. During those years, the store trade had increased a lot and the carters acted as messenger boys for a great many of the suppliers, bringing out items from a pound of butter to several bags of meal. They did this despite the fact that on nearly all the lorries there was an upper deck to cope with the increased volume of milk available at the time. That store trade had increased quite a lot and we bought a second lorry in order to cope with the extra demand. Deliveries were now being made to many outlying areas, particularly around Clonaslee, Rosenallis, Camross and so on before the premises in Mountmellick was acquired. When the carters eventually ceased to operate, it had a dramatic effect on the store trade."

Grain intake

"The late J.P. Kelly was an agent for Ranks of Limerick. Although there was no storage at the time, we began to buy grain from the farmers and bring it in to the rail station in Abbeyleix. It was then transported to Ranks. The handling of sacks of wheat with perhaps 25 to 30 stone in each one was hard labour and there were many tired limbs and sore backs as a result.

"When we were finished at the milk intake, we would set out to collect the wheat and were often unloading at the station up to 10 o'clock at night. We were fortunate to have a friendly station-master, who was willing enough to allow this.

"Apart from being very hard work, it was also very dangerous, particularly loading into wagons with a roof, which meant the workers had to stoop down in order to get in through the doorway. Sometimes, they had to walk on ramps, in order to access the wagon. Those ramps were moveable, often quite loose, which added to the danger involved.

"Later on, when we had a store available, the grain was brought into the store, where it was barreled into 20 stone sacks for wheat and, at a later stage, 16 stone sacks for barley and 14 stone sacks for oats.

"When no wagons were available or there was no space at the grain depot, the grain would have to be stored at Raheen. When storing was necessary, it meant having to pile up the sacks, two, three or even four high, up to rafters. This was indeed very hard and dangerous work and pay in those years was very low. Around that time also, Donaghmore acquired a grain drier and they also had much more storage space than in Raheen. That helped to relieve the situation in relation to space. Some time later in Raheen, we got a small drier. While it helped a little, it had a rather slow output and it had to operate around the clock.

The war years – the ration years

"I remember the war years when ration books were in operation and the hardships it imposed on so many people. There was no way you could get butter, flour or tea unless you had a coupon. At one particular time, we had a very small quantity of seed wheat left over at springtime – maybe a bag or two – which we ground into wholemeal and provided a welcome meal for a few people.

"In some cases, the farmers were allowed to keep a bag of wheat for their own use. They in turn would bring in a few stone at a time to make wholemeal for their own use. All in all, though it was quite a struggle, people managed as best they could.

"In 1941, when the foot and mouth outbreak occurred in Ballacolla, members of the LDF forces patrolled the area to ensure that all necessary precautions were observed. Customers and suppliers would be sprayed with a mixture of washing soda and water. Around the skim milk outlet area, they had to build an enclosure, put a quantity of the same mixture in it, and through which horses and donkeys had to pass. The donkeys especially did not like the idea but rules were rules and through it they had to go. The skim milk also had to be boiled and cooled. This posed a problem too as the facility to cool the skim was not there.

"Everything would have to be in order when the dairy inspector called. Charlie O'Connor was the first such person we got to know in Raheen. Charlie was a very nice person and although he might appear without any warning, he was always very fair and if he did find something amiss, he would always give a gentle warning to have it rectified before his return.

"The Co-op used to buy eggs from people, which was not quite in order as you had to have a suitable special room for that purpose. I was in my little office with Charlie nearby, when a local person stepped in with a basketful of eggs. I went quickly to the door and somehow got the basket under cover somewhere nearby. I'm sure Charlie knew what was going on but he made no remark.

"As the milk supply increased, more water was needed for cleaning purposes and we had to sink a second well. However, some time later, the owner of the land outside the premises was doing land reclamation and this resulted in a draw off of water from one of the wells. Loughlin Moran of Shanahoe was contacted and he helped restore the supply by lowering the well much deeper. At a later stage, when the new dairy was being built, we had to procure yet another well nearer to the new building. Liam Rohan, also from the Shanahoe area, was responsible for finding a very good source of supply, which was badly needed.

"When we were building a second large store back in the fifties, we procured a block making machine which made one block, 18"x9"x6", at a time. It was quite a slow process. You packed in the mortar mix and added in some small stones, making sure not to let any near the corners. As each one was packed, a lever was pulled, which brought the pallet, on which the block was packed, upwards and it was then carried away and left on level ground to dry out. Next day, they were turned on their edge, a slight tip released the pallet and the block would be carried to a storage place, to dry out further before being ready for use.

"When we started selling manure in those years, it came in two cwt bags, which were not so easy to handle as they were generally wide and low sized. Then, we procured a horse-drawn manure spreader. It was very useful for the farmers, but being rather wide, it caused problems on the roads, and where lanes or narrow gates were involved, it posed a problem for the people concerned.

John Hosey, on behalf of the Raheen local area committee makes a presentation to Joe Butler on his retirement as manager at Raheen in 1979.

"The late Joe Ryan was the operator of the spreader and also a horse-drawn sprayer which was there before the spreader. There was quite a large amount of washing soda and 8 pounds of bluestone and 40 gallons of water to make enough to spray a quarter acre. That procedure was generally repeated two or three times in a season."

Two great men

"J.P. Kelly was gruff in manner, no airs or graces about him, but he was dead straight. You knew where you stood with him. He was a very honest, straightforward man and he didn't hide his feelings. If you were not pulling your weight, he'd let you know it very quick. He could drop in anytime. Most of the time he had a motor car but during the war years, when petrol was very scarce, he had a pony and trap. He was living in Fruitlawn then, which is between Abbeyleix and Shanahoe. In earlier years he had a motor bike. So, it was motor bike, motor car, pony and trap and then back to the motor car again. He had a great brain. He could figure out anything, whatever was needed in the line of building or machinery, what line to take and, at all times, what was best for the Society,

"George Galbraith was another very straight man, a man who was always looking ahead. He was a great friend of Fr. Coyne and was a regular visitor to his house. They got on well together. Although they were from different religions, religion was never an issue at Raheen. Farmers big and small and of different religions all worked well together – there was no friction. With George Galbraith and Fr. Coyne there to set an example, relations could only be cordial.

"George had seen service in the Great War and was wounded in one of his arms, so he did not have full use of it, but otherwise he was a very active man and a man with a good sense of humour.

"George was down in the Co-op one evening and he remarked to me: 'Joe, I can foresee the day when we will have to spray out our effluent somewhere, it will not be allowed in the river. If we could get access to Mrs. Keegan's field across the river, it would be in our interest. We may never want it, but I'm pretty sure we will.'

"I was deputised to try and make a deal with Mrs. Keegan to purchase the land. I managed to persuade her to come with me to the auctioneer and sign the deeds. That gave us some leeway but we would still have to cross John H. Talbot's ground. So again, I was deputised to meet him. The Co-op was willing to swap a portion of good land for his more swampy type land near the river. Talbot seemed a bit suspicious about that idea and some committee members tried in vain to sell the exchange idea to him. Eventually Paddy Shiel convinced him that he was getting a good deal and all the necessary signing was completed. That was a typical example of the type of person George Galbraith was. He was so right about the need for extra ground, as it was only a couple of years later we had to spray the effluent from the Co-op out on that land.

"Raheen Co-op was important to the farmers and when it got going fairly well, it provided a lot of local employment. There were up to twenty five people employed there during the peak years. During these years also, there were two lorries and they were kept going full-time bringing in supplies and delivering out lots of feed stuff, manure, seed and so on. The grinding/rolling mill was also going at full blast in order to maintain supplies of ground and rolled barley. Yes, Raheen was very important to the area."

Memories of Raheen Creamery

SEAMUS HOSEY
Senior Producer in RTE Radio

"One of my earliest memories as a child growing up in the Parish of Raheen in County Laois is of going to the creamery with my father. The trip to Raheen Creamery in the black Ford Prefect car, with the trailer swaying in tow, was never a singular or simple excursion to deliver the silver cans of milk or to bring home a bag of pig meal or a roll of barbed wire for fencing. The business transaction of the day was only one of the reasons or excuses my father, like most other farmers in the area, travelled to the creamery almost every day.

"Raheen Creamery was in reality the social hub of the parish and the wider world where you met the neighbours and where, in the days before local radio or even telephones were common, you heard the vital and important news of the parish and further afield. Not just births, marriages and deaths were discussed but who got a good price for pigs at Abbeyleix Fair or how store bullocks were selling at Portlaoise Mart or whether it was time to spray the potatoes against the blight or warning signs of the dreaded blood murrain in cattle. Someone in Roskelton broke a hip and was in Portlaoise Hospital or someone else was housebound and needed shopping done.

"The talk that drifted across the creamery yard ranged wide and far as my father warmed to the task: Clonad's chances against Abbeyleix in the hurling match on Sunday or a progress report on how rehearsals were going for the play in the parish hall or what new attractions the curate, Father Brennan, had up his sleeve for the Sports Day. Politics came into it too, of course, where seed, breed and generations were known and how every last vote was likely to be cast in local or national elections. Truly, all of human life was there and Raheen Creamery was the hub of a wheel whose spokes radiated to all corners of the rural community.

"Having finished my Leaving Certificate in the summer of 1968, in that no-man's land of waiting for the exam results, I worked in Raheen Creamery. Apart from earning untold riches of £7.7s.6d a week, I had a great opportunity to observe at first hand the importance and vitality of the creamery in the lives of the people I knew and grew up with. Besides the very important employment it gave, Raheen creamery was at the very heart of the economic, social and community life of the parish and the wider Laois hinterland. There was something historically appropriate in the fact that Tenakill House, just over a mile from the creamery, was the birthplace of the great Irish patriot and political thinker, James Fintan Lalor. He was to become the powerful national advocate of the belief in "the land of Ireland for the people of Ireland." Although he died in 1849, the logical progression of the Young Ireland struggle Lalor espoused led to the later Land Act Reforms which indirectly gave birth to the Co-operative Movement. That Irish Co-operative Movement in turn fostered the growth of institutions such as the network of creameries of which Raheen was such a vital and thriving example.

"Working in the General Office in the long summer of 1968 you looked out on the creamery yard with its constant activity and bustle and felt proud to be part of an institution that touched the daily lives of so many people. Manager, Joe Butler, presided in a kindly and patriarchal way over a staff who kept the many and varied services of the creamery functioning smoothly. In the office, Ger Lawler, Annette Dunne, Stella Burke and John Burke initiated me into the mysteries of taking the urgent A. I. calls every morning and filing the all-important coloured dockets which, in an age before computers, kept the system ticking over. Telephone calls came in from farmers, often in remote areas, looking for the A. I. man to call to cows who were unused to seeing a man in a collar and tie where formerly the more romantic encounter was in a field with the gentleman with horns and hooves. Between clocking in and clocking out there was lots of laughter too and a running commentary on the foibles and follies of customers and staff alike where individuality was not only tolerated but difference and eccentricity positively encouraged.

"If the office was the head of the creamery body, then the shop was the heart. Here life was a constant passing parade where customers came to browse or bargain or maybe even buy when the milk cheque was good. The staff had to be expert in everything from advising on shades of paint for a bathroom to the durability of hoes and rakes and the life expectancy of enamel buckets. When life was not too hectic in the shop, Tom Carroll might burst into song with "Doonaree" or Joe Delaney might regale the company in his quiet and humorous way with an account of some ordinary encounter in the creamery yard which he would transform in the magic of the telling.

"All that hat was another time and another place. Raheen Creamery was then part of a national network and has since moved on to become part of an even bigger international corporation. In celebrating Raheen Creamery and the dozens of institutions like them that emerged in the early days of the new Irish State, let us remember the men and women of vision who founded them for the important role they played in giving Irish farmers a sense of self-determination, self-confidence and economic prosperity. Let us celebrate too the vital role they played in not only providing work locally in the dark days of unemployment and emigration but also in giving a sense of community, identity and local pride to so many in rural Ireland."

The People who Pioneered and Kept the Business Going in Hard Times Should Not be Forgotten

JOHN GALBRAITH

John Galbraith served as accountant and secretary of Donaghmore Co-op, where he worked from 1942 until 1976. He is son of the late George Galbraith, one of the leading figures in the history of Donaghmore Co-op and first chairman of Avonmore Creameries.

"I started in Donaghmore during the war years. Donaghmore had become very involved in organising the growing of wheat over a fairly wide area. They were agents for Ranks of Limerick and used the local rail station at Ballybrophy to transport the grain at harvest time. This business secured the future of the Co-op, financially, over the war time.

"My first work included handling of grain, weighing it and doing the necessary book work involved. At the end of that harvest, one of the clerical staff, Gretta Grogan, left to get married and I applied for, and got her job. The word 'clerical' covered a varied range of work. You would take any outgoing post down to the local post office in the village, at five o'clock in the evening. If there was a message for the dairy, you ran down with it. Someone might want a box of butter and you might have to carry that out for them.

"In my early years there, I was staying in 'Digs' in Rathdowney and went home to Corbally on a Saturday night. It could be around 8pm when I'd get home.

"The principal people with whom I was in contact in those years were J.P. Kelly and William Grogan, who was the first manager. They were people who saw a lot of life in the raw, and I learned a lot of things from them, that you would not learn in school or university.

"You realised very quickly that you did not choose what you might do, but you did what you were told and as quickly as possible, or else you got a boot in the tail.

"Milk arrived in all sorts of vehicles in those days from Denis McGaughy with a wheelbarrow, Stephen Campion with a donkey and cart while someone else used a bike to carry their can, which contained, perhaps, only a gallon or two. You could say that anything with a wheel on it was used to bring in the milk. Milk, of course, was weighed by the pound. The abbreviation usually used for the pound weight was lb or lbs and a gallon was 10.8lbs. You had to tot up those figures at the end of each day's intake. At the end of each month, the totals in lbs were converted into gallons and a value was set for each supplier. Farmers would buy back butter made from their own milk, so to speak but, during the ration period, they had to be content with their allocation just like everyone else.

"Most suppliers would want their skim milk for pig feeding and some would take extra in addition to their allowance, which was 80% of what they brought in. Others would not require any at all. There would usually be a good demand for any skim available.

"Sometime within the third week of each month, the management committee would fix the price of milk per gallon, and then, the value of each person's supply was calculated and, after all deductions had been stopped, their nett pay cheque was issued. Some of those cheques were for very low amounts, perhaps two or three pounds, but money was scarce and they were as much looked forward to as if they were for a hundred pounds.

"When the store trade started and farmers bought goods, some could easily have bought more during a month than what their milk would cover and end up owing money to the Co-op.

"During the real peak of the harvest, we would often have to work a twelve hour, seven day week, and some temporary staff would also be brought in. Although the wheat came into Donaghmore there were perhaps ten agents calling on the farmers and procuring the wheat on behalf of Ranks. They got a commission of maybe three pence or sixpence per barrel.

"It is important to note that during the war years, from the late 1930s and well into the 1940s, wheat growing was our lifeline, nationally. Compulsory grain production was the order of the day. During those years, the Department of Agriculture got a dozen Fordson tractors. They were rationed out to certain outlets around the country, where they could be used in the promotion of grain crops, wheat growing especially. Donaghmore got a tractor and plough and this was let out to plough for farmers. They also got a reaper and binder for the harvest time. I had to drive that tractor at times and indeed was out until twelve at night a few times. Talk about the things we did!

"To supplement working, a corn grinder was installed at Donaghmore for animal feeding. This service was a blessing to the community and provided a steady cash income to the Co-op. The Government put in place a lot of restrictions. Commodities that we were used to, such as tea, sugar, bread and so on, were rationed to a bare minimum per week.

"Vital supplies were short, the most serious being petrol. Private cars were off the road and rationed quantities were allowed to industry. Donaghmore equipped a lorry with what was called a gas plant, which ran on gas produced by burning anthracite in a burner on the lorry. It's not difficult to contemplate how unsatisfactory that was and the depths to which we were reduced to carry on. Turf was brought in from the area to heat the boilers in the processing plants and an allowance of petrol was also made for that purpose."

The big snow in 1947

"That bad spell started about mid February and lasted until March 17th. The only way you could travel was to walk, cycle if possible, and use a tractor. That was a pretty tough time, while the snow lasted. There was a little Allis Chalmers tractor on the premises and we had to use it to get around and go to the station, if need be.

"There was a chick hatchery operating there in the early years. I think about 24,000 eggs were set down every week. There were two incubators working: one held 16,000 and one held 8,000. One third of those produced chickens every week, which were 8,000 chickens. This was quite a big operation, while it lasted, and it was the one time that the farmers' wives could do something in their own right, when they came in for a box of chickens. They would of course take a few stone of chick meal, which helped to keep the wheels turning.

"During that cold spell in 1947, those incubators had to be kept going, by whatever means, or the hatch was dead. Indeed, it did happen a few times. We bought an ex-RAF alternator in England to be wired up to the hatchery so as to have alternative power, if the electricity went. But it was not an automatic changeover and I often spent hours watching a set of dials to ensure that the voltage remained at a certain level because if the voltage was too high, it was 'lights out' for the eggs and chicks.

"There was a cable wire linked from the hatchery to Donal Grogan's house. If there was any change in temperature during the night, a bell would ring and Donal would, and often did, run across the yard in his night clothes to rectify the problem.

"Strange as it may seem, you could put a dozen chicks in a cardboard box and they would arrive safely at their destination, which might be as far away as Donegal. But you had to ensure that they were at Ballybrophy station in good time and it was a problem at times, finding somebody available to get them there in good time. I don't think any other co-op in the country had a hatchery business, certainly none as big as Donaghmore.

"The hatchery business called for producing chick meal which, under the brand name of 'Diamond', sold for many years. We also had a van on the road collecting and buying eggs and poultry. In the slow return to normality, sales of Diamond meals increased and a plant was installed to cater for the extra needs.

"The natural result of the pick up after the war was the opening of a store, to make available to the suppliers and customers generally, normal farm and domestic requirements. Milk producers were on the increase and suppliers from the outer regions around Clonaslee, Geashill and Mountmellick area, who sent their milk to Raheen, had no retail outlet near them.

"The Co-op was almost a social centre in that the farmers gathered there regularly and there were so many things that they could get in the store. Of course, many of them were milk suppliers and could go in and order the normal requirements, for both domestic and farm, and have it charged to their milk account. It was a barter system of a type.

"The Co-op was the biggest employer in the district and with mostly permanent staff. They did not take on many part-timers, except during the harvest time and perhaps in spring time.

"One particular service introduced in the 1950s, and at that time was looked upon as the 'silly service', was the A.I. service. Most people had no idea what A.I. meant and the older people in the farming community were very reluctant to discuss it. Then in 1964, an Agricultural advisor was appointed to help promote agriculture to the best possible level.

"As the Co-op expanded, there was a need for someone to look after the accounting system and I was given that job. In trying to keep up with the needs, they procured an accounting machine. It was a N.C.R (National Cash Register) and it was a great asset at that time. It was for doing the customer accounts, it cost around two and a half thousand pounds and would be regarded as the forerunner of the computer. That was in the 1950s and I found it quite hard to convince the management of the need for it.

"After some years, and with continued expansion, there was enough work there for a full time accountant to keep tabs on everything. Again, it was put to management, agreed, and a Mr. R. Cumbers was appointed. He remained for quite some time and eventually he left soon after the Avonmore take over around 1974. He was replaced by a Mr. K. Quigley, who remained just a few years until Avonmore rang the changes.

"When J.P. Kelly retired in the 1960s, I was appointed to his job, as secretary, and that was a very varied occupation. That's where I ended up, when Avonmore decided that they were going to do all their own work.

"Credit must be given to those who took the decision to ensure that Donaghmore, and the branches at Raheen and Spink, stayed in business, in the interest of shareholders and the local community. Costs were cut to the bone. Wages, which were not high, were reduced. Those who took management responsibility worked long hours for a modest income.

"In the late 1960s, Donaghmore acquired the established and well known shop in Mountmellick, known as Pims. The owners were retiring from business and made contact with Donaghmore management indicating that they would like to see the business being continued in the same manner as Pims had run it for generations, serving the general public and farmers.

"That idea was a wonderful gesture on their part and the opportunity was a golden one for Donaghmore. It was not very long afterwards that Donaghmore acquired a similar premises, known as Smiths, which was next door to Pims.

"The Department of Agriculture was keenly aware of the need for standardising the quality of butter production and for improved marketing. This resulted in larger units being formed and Avonmore was one of the biggest of these. This meant that work done individually by these units, including Donaghmore, was now taken on by Avonmore. It also meant that people with particular skills were deemed unsuitable for modern methods and were made redundant. When Avonmore took over, I was deemed as unemployable and so ended 34 years of service.

"The people who pioneered and kept the business going in hard times and gave their talents for poor reward, by comparison with today, should never be forgotten. The result of their labours was handed on to another generation. The person who comes to mind as the brains of the place was the late J.P. Kelly, whose foresight, vitality and endless go, without doubt, created the very successful business which Avonmore had the pleasure of absorbing into their group."

The Co-op has been Great for the County

MRS. MAEVE WALLIS

Billy Wallis, General Manager of Donaghmore Creamery 1969-'73 – Joint Manager 1960-'68.

Maeve was an employee of Donaghmore Co-op for many years and is widow of the late Billy Wallis, former General Manager of Donaghmore

"I joined the creamery around 1947/48. In the office was the boss, J.P. Kelly, and the dairy manager, Donal Grogan, and about a year afterwards Lily Dowling joined. Down at the bottom of the office there were two windows. People knocked on the window and you shot it up to see what they wanted. Sometimes they were looking for a docket for skimmed milk, other times it was for items of hardware. There was no hardware shop and it was all kept in a storeroom down below the office. I knew nothing at all about hardware and I'd say to them, 'Look, I'll go with you and you can pick up what you want and I'll get a price for you'.

"Then they opened the new shop in the yard. At that time you had to weigh things in half-stones, there was none of the modern things. You weighed up _ stones of chicken mash, _ stones of flake meal and _ stones of everything for the shelves on the counter. They would ring up and say, 'Can you come over and weigh up with us'. We would go over. It was a scoop scales with the weights on it and you weighed your ½ stones of everything and you had to shake it down in the bag. You had to fold the bags properly, they were sticklers for the folding of the bags – you had to learn that. You would get told off if they were not folded properly.

"Then the hatchery was opened. You took orders for chickens and you got in the eggs from the people. You knew how many dozens of eggs came in. One door on the incubator had the eggs and the others had the chickens. They were changed after about ten days when they tested the eggs to see how many were infertile and how many were good. You took orders for 75% or thereabouts. The customers would tell you where their nearest station was and we would ring up the train stations to see what time the next trains were running. Donal Grogan would take the chickens to the train in the early morning.

"The cards went out for the delivery of chickens on a Monday. We'd take them to Ballybrophy and they would be dispatched on the mail train even if it was a bank holiday. Then he learned to sex the chickens. Pullets were much more expensive than cocks. Some of the cocks you couldn't give away We had Light Sussex, Rhode Island Reds and Leghorns, and then we had a Rhode Island Red and a Leghorn crossed.

"On a certain day the eggs in the hatchery would have to be tested. You had a little box with a bulb in it and a little hole for an egg. If you could see the little chicken in it, you would put it back on the tray in the compartment. They sold the infertile eggs as liquid eggs in tins. They broke them in to tins and they sold them to bakeries. The chickens had to be dealt with all in the one day. People were waiting for them and, if they didn't arrive, all hell broke loose. . We advertised them in the daily papers and people would order the chickens from that. We sent them to Galway, Wexford, Mayo, and all over the country by bus and train. So the name of Donaghmore Creamery was known all over the country

"We had poultry instructresses who used to come. There was Olive Clinton in Abbeyleix and before that there was Miss Doyle from Borris-in-Ossory. She became Mrs. Dwyer. The head inspector was a Miss Golden, a very precise and grand lady. There was a Miss O'Neill first, Peggy Moriarty and then Betty Brennan. We also had trainees from the Department of Agriculture at different times. Don't ask me what they were doing. But they would be here for six weeks and then they would be gone. Maybe they were blood testing. You didn't get to know them very well in six weeks.

"They also had turkeys, geese and chickens at Christmas time. They had pluckers and an egg grading machine. I used to be fascinated with the grading machine. If an egg was two ounces it dropped off at one place, and if it was two ounces and one eighth it dropped off at the next one.

"It was another forward move when the AI (Artificial Insemination) was introduced. The farmers would ring in but often they didn't know how to explain what they wanted. We had to ring in the calls to Dovea. This day I rang Thurles 110 as usual and a very precise girl answered. She took down all the information and then she said 'this is all double Dutch to me, are you sure you have the right number?' 'I said 'Is that Thurles 110?' 'No!' she said, 'this is Thurles 111 – the Ursuline Convent!' I remember the poor nun and I'm sure she was flabbergasted to get all that kind of information.

"At that time you could overhear on the phone and I overheard my father (a Garda) one day talking to the Superintendent's Office in Abbeyleix. Someone had stolen a watch from a shop locally and he was reporting it to the office. I said to him when he came home 'Did you get anyone for stealing the watch?' Needless to say he was surprised, to say the least.

"We had to do many things. I didn't have much to do with the milk accounts but we had to write the cheques with pen and ink. And you did all that by hand. Then we did all the envelopes by hand; it was easier than putting each one into the typewriter and typing out the name and address. And if we had a slack time, we thought nothing of washing out the office. We would go over and get deck scrubs from the shop and wash out the office, or tidy up the stationery. You kept yourself busy.

"Bill was a very kind man and very honest. He didn't believe in backhanders or anything. He hated the thought of someone wanting to take him to lunch because he felt obliged then to buy from that particular person and he didn't want that commitment. In later years they had a group called AIM (Associated Irish Merchants). Arthur Cope, Norman Gillespie in Carlow, Mervyn Shaw and Bill were on the buying committee. They'd meet the clients in Dublin or sometimes, Carlow, and the business would go long into the evening or night. I used go along with Bill because he wanted someone to talk to on the way home in case he'd fall asleep at the wheel.

"One time in the Creamery, in the latter end of his days, somebody wrote him a very threatening letter and told him he would shoot him on sight, and to make his peace with God. He was very worried about it. The fellow that the Gardai suspected knocked at the hall door and asked to see Bill. Bill went out to him and the man said 'Come out to the car with me, I want to talk to you personally'. Bill said 'no, there is no one here but you and me. Whatever you have to say, say it'. He didn't say very much and off he went. I often wondered if Bill had gone out to the car what would have happened. It was a very difficult time. I don't know what it was all about. Maybe the man applied for a job and didn't get it. There was a lot of that.

"There was another woman who felt obliged to come down to the house and she'd give me two dozen eggs in the hope that her son would get a job, and I would feel terrible. She arrived with a live turkey one time and I said 'Look missus, I don't want it, thanks very much', and she said 'Oh, but I brought it all the way for you'. She thought if she greased my palm, I'd have a word with Bill. But there was nothing I could do, he either wanted them or he didn't. I couldn't influence him one way or the other.

"He was always very busy and he worked very hard coming up to the spring. He had to have the fertiliser in and the seed corn and it was a lot of hard work. Then he had to work on a price-list. My brother was an army officer who served in the Congo. He brought home a bottle of Vodka for Bill, and no one knew anything about Vodka at that stage. Bill was working on this price list on a Sunday evening. He was sipping away nicely at the Vodka and the next thing, when he stood up, the two legs went from under him and he said, 'Oh, there is something terrible wrong with me'. Sure when we looked at the bottle he had half of it sipped. So I said, 'the best place for you is in the bed!'

"Bill liked meeting people, and liked knowing people. The locals, he knew them all when they came in with their asses and carts. They would sit in the shop and discuss the topics of the day. Some of them sat up on the counter and there would be a great conclave.

"But in later years I was in the office and one of the farmers had a particular knock on the window on a Friday morning. I'd go down to him and he'd slip me in two bars of chocolate. On hearing the particular knock, Lily would look at me and say, 'it's your turn to go and get the bars of chocolate'. They were decent people, very decent people.

"There was a lot of corn sowed. I used to do the bushel weights and assess the moisture content before they got this modern machine that you put the ground-up corn into. First of all there was a special little oven and there were tins and each tin weighed a particular amount. You had a list on the side of it as to what the tins weighed. So you weighed the tin to make sure it was the right one you were using. You put five grams of wheat into it and you did five or six of them, and you put them into this little oven for a stated length of time. Then you took them out and put lids on them before putting them into a vacuum – a glass jar. When they got cold you had to weigh them and you knew how much you put in and whatever came out, you subtracted one from the other, and by that way you knew the moisture content of the corn. But you knew anyway for a start because if the bushel weight was low you had a lot of moisture. The higher the bushel weight, the lower the moisture. You would bring in ten or twenty bushel weights and you had to write them into a book. It was a busy job.

"Bill could put a grain of wheat into his mouth and chew it and he could work out the moisture content from that. Often when I would be doing the moisture test he'd say to me, 'do it again, you are wrong'. He was that accurate. You see the farmers were paid on the moisture and you had to be accurate. The moisture content was written on the dockets and there was a variation in the prices. When it came to drying the corn you had to do it slowly. But he had good lads like Mick Finnane. Now he was a great workman. He was in the mill in Donaghmore. There were others too and they knew what they were about.

"I had to keep track of the sacks that were given out. You had a big ledger and you wrote down everybody's sacks and what came back under the grain and what came back loose. And they were jobs that all disappeared when they got all this new-fangled bulk stuff.

"I remember Billy going to England with Bobby Bennett to an agricultural show on one occasion. Both men were tired after a long day at the show. When Bill came home he said to me 'I was so bloody tired at the end of the day that I hopped into bed to go asleep. Bobby put me to shame when he knelt down to say his prayers'.

"I used to do the germinations on the corn. The seed corn came in during the spring. You had little dishes and blotting paper and the blotting paper had to be damp on the bottom. You then counted 100 seeds onto the blotting paper, put another sheet of blotting paper over them, and a sheet of glass over that, and we would have the shelves all full of these. That was always done before we would sell any seeds. If the germination was poor, Billy would be on to the supplier. This was seed that he had bought from some firm and he would have to test the germination before he could stand over it and sell it to whatever farmers wanted it. J.P. Kelly would go to Athy on a Tuesday and make the contacts. There was a Captain Redmond in Popefield, Athy, and there were the Greenes and I don't know who else. But Billy could never write Captain Redmond's address as Popefield, he always wrote it as Poefield. I would always be looking out for him when he was writing a receipt or a bill or anything and always correct it if there was a mistake. That was only a small thing but it used to give us a laugh up and down.

"Billy got on great with J.P. Kelly except when J.P. was in bad humour. J.P. went his way and nobody interfered with him, you know, it was as simple as that. They had a lot in common. For one thing they both recognised good workers.

"J.P. was a very strict man but he was very fair and honest. You mightn't always agree with what he said but he was fair. We had two big tables in the office and Lily, Donal Grogan, J.P. and myself sat there. We had some lovely outings with the committee and the management team. The yard workers would have an outing as well and the committee helped pay for the bus. We went to Ardnacrusha, Wicklow and Wexford among other places. Bill and me got engaged before we went on one outing, a cruise on the Shannon, and they played a special request for us. I was at work on the Monday and I didn't have the ring on. J.P. gave me a poke and he said, 'come on, show me!', and I said 'What'? 'Come on', he said, 'show me the ring'. And I said, 'What ring?' I got my bag, took the ring out and showed it to him. 'What is it doing in your bag?' he said. 'It should be on your finger!'

"J.P. Kelly and the Grogans, William and Donal, didn't get on too well. I'm not sure of the reason why, but I suspect that politics and the fact that peoples' jobs were not clearly defined, may have been, to some extent, responsible for it. But JP would never ask you your political affiliations.

"Billy never fancied the Lisduff quarry end of the business. He was big into expanding the walls, if you like. That was his idea – to expand the business. I don't know much about Lisduff now, I really don't. At that stage he kept a lot of his worries to himself. Maybe he thought I wasn't interested if he started talking, I don't know. At the time I'd say I'd have given a fortune for sensible conversation. All I know about that now, he went around to the farmers and explained that they had bought it. I know one particular man he went to and explained that they had bought it and the man said, 'We know who to complain to if our windows are broken'. And right enough the next time they had explosives his windows were broken and they came right down on the roof of his house too. The explosives mustn't have been properly co-ordinated or whatever.

"Billy was also very forward thinking in the fact that he was responsible for getting John O'Meara (Agricultural Advisor). That was a new thing at the time and he was a great blessing. He was paid by the Creamery and he went out to help the farmers make the best of what they had. Herbert Stanley down the road is always saying he wouldn't be where he is today if Bill hadn't advised him and gave him credit when it was necessary. He knew his customers in a lot of cases, who to give credit to and who not to give it to, who would pay up with their corn or who would be heading off to Athy with it.

"One Christmas Eve there was a hell of a flood in the mill and he had to organise all the staff to lift the corn up out of the wet. He must have had twenty men on Christmas Eve and then he took them into a pub when the day was over and bought them all a drink. They all worked very hard and he said they were entitled to at least a drink for all their hard work, even though they were going to get paid for the day. He felt they had worked over and above the call of duty.

"At one stage I said to Billy, 'You've a lot of hardware, but you have nothing to encourage the women to come into the Creamery. Why don't you buy in tea-sets and things like that?' He said, 'That's a good idea, I'll think about that'. And he did. They began to stock fancy goods that the women might buy for wedding presents. They also had open nights for a week once a year and everyone got a cup of tea. They had demonstrations of washing machines and a deep-freeze. They had a lot of people there. They had the Odlum's Home Adviser and the Bolands' representative giving out recipes. And the women used to come in droves. They organised buses and brought them in from various areas. Then at the end of the week when it was over we would have a party down in the committee room. Everyone would do their party piece. It was a get-together for everyone and it was most enjoyable and everyone felt their work was appreciated with this little hooley.

"The wages were very poor. When I started I got two pounds per week and you went up by five shillings per year. It wasn't an awful lot by today's standards. When I left in 1956 I was earning £6-10-0. I went back for the harvest in 1957 to keep track of the sacks and do the bushel weights, and I got £7-10-0. That was the top end of the wages at that stage. I saved up all my money and at the end of the harvest I bought an Electrolux with a polisher. Admittedly Billy gave it to me at cost price, and I bought an outfit for myself. I bought a dress, a coat, a hat, a bag, and a pair of shoes out of what I earned in that harvest.

"Billy and Donal Ward, who was manager in Roscrea Bacon Factory, were directors in Clonaslee. They were involved because things went bottom up there, and they were sent there to put things right.

"Donal Grogan was a lovely man, but he was a dairy man and he thought the dairy should take precedence over everything, do you know that sort of a way? He was a grand man, he really was, but he was distant. Years after I left the Creamery, he was here one night with Bill, and I was still calling him Mr. Grogan. He said, 'Maeve, I'm Donal, for God's sake!' I said, 'To me you are Mr. Grogan and you'll remain Mr. Grogan.' I couldn't just say it, because my father was very particular. If you didn't go to school with him you weren't allowed to call him Joe or Tom or whatever. They were a different breed of people altogether than today. Billy and Donal were joint managers for a time but they hadn't that much in common really. They had different areas of interest outside the job too. Donal was a golfer and Bill wouldn't give you tuppence for golf. But he loved to see the kids hurling and playing games. He used to say, 'when they are tired they will sleep'.

"It is never a right thing to live on the premises as the Grogans did, and it was awkward for them because there were no flush toilets in those days. There was no running water in the house, and whenever they wanted some they would have to go up to the dairy for it.

"Donal Grogan was a very able man. And the dairy was of primary importance to him. It was his whole life really. He was good at adding and laying out things. We got a new churn, from Finland, I think it was, and it did the wrapping automatically. Donal spent days designing the wrapper for it.

"Donal was a book man. He liked to see the books looking nice and the tots all balanced. Billy liked to see the books right too but he liked to see other things done as well. I'd check the cash sometimes too. If we were up, say, six pence, we threw it into a bowl because we might be down the following day. One evening we were down a lot of money because one sale that I had marked on the docket as paid, wasn't paid. Some people are honest, and some are not, it's as simple as that. Bill's father went bankrupt in Borris-in-Ossory years ago because he was taken advantage of. Bill had a ledger for years and years and he was so frustrated and annoyed that nobody ever offered to pay a penny except one woman. Her mother was a widow with three children and she said, 'my mother owes your father twenty seven pounds and when I get money I'll pay it. She didn't, but that's neither here or there, he wasn't stuck for the £27. One day, before we were married, he took out the ledger and he burned it. He was frustrated and annoyed that nobody ever said they owed him money.

"Billy and Bobby Bennett were involved in Co-op Animal Health and Donaghmore used to stock their products. This was a good thing in one way and in another it wasn't, because the farmers did not know what prolonged use of penicillin could do to animals? But I think they were careful enough, if you came back five times in a row they would be asking you what you were doing with it. Here we are now today and there's penicillin in everything, we don't know what we are eating half the time

"Election time came and there was a polling booth at the Co-op. I got a letter advising me that I was to work there on election day. But I didn't look for the job. I told Mr. Kelly what had happened and he said that he had put my name forward. I should have been there all day and my father would have killed me if he knew I took a little time off. I hadn't voted when I went out to work and the man who was in charge of the polling booth said, 'the next car that comes in, you go and do your voting and no-one will be any the wiser'. I went and cast my vote.

"We also had a buttermaker who was sacked and she wouldn't go. She came in as usual. My father (a Garda) was called upon to 'turf' her out. But he said, 'What can I do? I can't catch her physically and throw her out! I couldn't get a whip and whip her out the gate in front of me.' I don't know why she wouldn't leave but she must have had some grievance with the Co-op.

"I remember the purchase of the Mountmellick premises. They were in a terrible state. I went over a few times with Billy after they bought it. I don't know how they carried on as a shop really. But it was great that they expanded a bit. It's a big place over there now.

"We didn't talk about amalgamation very much because I wasn't very keen on it. He went for it from the point of view that it would be a bigger outfit altogether than they had in Donaghmore. But afterwards he wasn't very keen on it. You were only a number. Nobody had any interest in you as a person. There was no-one to complain to and he wasn't in favour of that. He thought if you had a complaint you should know who to complain to, but there was nobody who would take responsibility for anything. You also had younger people telling him what he should do. Bill objected to young fellows telling him what to do. He didn't like it. He said he had more knowledge than these young fellows telling him how to run the place.

"He didn't like the way things turned out and he was happy to get out. His life changed after he retired. When Billy was working he thought that if he wasn't there, the creamery would fall down. He genuinely did. But suddenly he had time on his hands. In the latter eighteen months he had no interest in anything. His brain dried up and then he had a heart attack and was rushed to hospital.

"Billy and John Galbraith got on the finest. John was very kind and very nice. He would get his big ledger and spend his days going through it and making sure that the bills were sent out. There were some funny responses. One lady to whom we sent a bill, wrote back and said, 'How dare you send me such a letter, there are other people who would be very glad of my business'.

"We had one milk supplier who bought half a stone of chicken mash every morning and a pound of butter every couple of mornings. We tried to convince her that she should buy one cwt at a time. But no, she persisted with a half-stone every morning.

"We used fountain pens mainly but we also had ink wells on our desks, and that was a terrible job, having to dip the pens in the ink all the time. Later on Donal Grogan and Lily had a calculator when they were doing the ledgers. If the butterfat was 3.60 that was one price and you would have to multiply that price by the number of gallons. If the butterfat was different it would be a different price. Before we got the calculator, all that had to be worked out manually on paper. So it was a great day when we got a calculator. Then they got invoicing machines and other things followed.

"We used to do the stocktaking and Ken Deane was an ex-army man, he was in the shop, and I used to do the writing and he'd do the calling. The top shelf was full of kettles and things like that and Ken would say, 'Put D.P. after every one of them'. I didn't know what D.P. (Drill Pattern) meant and he said it meant they were no good. They would have been returned by customers because they didn't work. They were just left up there to fill the top shelf and make it look good.

"The Co-op has been great for the county and the immediate area. The wages weren't big, but they bought a lot. They were no worse than in any other business but there wasn't the plentifulness of money that there is now. Still men were able to bring up families on what they earned. A lot of people worked for the Creamery and if it wasn't there, I don't know what they would have done. Possibly a lot of them would have gone to England."

Personal Recollections – Donaghmore

Mick Fitzpatrick
(Grangemore, Borris-in-Ossory)

"I started working in Donaghmore on 19 May 1969. At first, my job was to attend to orders for goods from the branches. Tim Finlay and Liam O'Dea were there also, and we worked from a small office off the shop. My wages were £9 per week.

"In the early 1970s, a new type of store was erected. It was a large balloon type made from a fairly strong canvas material. There were two porch-like sections, one at each end, for loading and unloading goods. There were two compressors which kept the air supply at peak day and night and the doors had always to be closed. It would seem that a new store was required at a minimum cost and this was the type chosen. John Fitzgerald, who was in the shop, was now transferred to the 'balloon' store along with me. Our work was as before – checking in goods and supplying the branches, pricing all goods and so on. It served its purpose fairly well until 1974 when a severe storm sent bits of it in all directions. After that, we had to retreat back into the shop until a new store was built. We worked away in the new store for a while and then some of us moved to offices, which were located on the upper decks of some of the old stores down the yard.

"At that stage, perhaps in the mid to late 70s, my work pattern changed and I was now involved in the creditors department, passing invoices and such like. In the meantime, the first computer type equipment was being used. They were known as VDUs and information was punched into them and transferred to Ballyragget for further processing. After a time in Portlaoise, I was moved to Ballyragget, where I was involved in setting up a new coding system for the computers, which had been operating for a few years. Shortly after that, I moved to Universal Providers in Kilkenny, which had been acquired by Avonmore. I remained there for six years, before returning to Ballyragget, where I am still doing the same type of work.

"We had many pleasant annual outings over the years. One particularly memorable one consisted of a bus trip to New Ross, then onto a boat to Waterford, on which we had lunch and some drinks and rounded off with a great day in Tramore. Another memorable one for the opposite reason was the intended trip by boat to St. Kevin's Bed in Glendalough. The boatman had a small boat powered by batteries and with room for about ten people. Some twenty two of us got on board and we had only gone a few yards when one of our group, who probably had liquid refreshments, started prancing about the boat. We almost went down. The owner of the boat told me the lake was 110 feet deep. I was never so scared in my life."

Eileen Fitzpatrick

Michael's wife, Eileen (nee McCormack, from Kilcoran, Rathdowney), worked with Donaghmore Co-op for 15 years. She started in 1967 as a phone operator, which included taking the AI (Artificial Insemination) calls. Eileen, who married Michael in 1974, remembers:

"One particular AI person was Michael Smith, who later became a TD and Minister. I was busy taking the AI calls and passing the messages on to the AI people who would phone in. Then a radio system was set up for transmitting calls to the operators. After some years, myself and some other girls worked as punch card operators, inputting all the milk related figures. We would get the milk sheets from the dairy and input them into the machine. There were special cards for the job and I think a card would do for the week. They would then be sent to Dublin for further processing.

"At a later stage, computers were introduced and we did all the processing in Donaghmore. It was called key editing. After one person had entered the figures, another would do a repeat entry, in order to validate the first entry. Other transactions, such as butter sales, were also done in like manner. That type of work continued until well into the 1970s, when local milk intake ceased."

Margaret Mulvihill
(nee Whelan, Tullacommon, Donaghmore)

"I started in 1928 in Donaghmore and continued until 1929. I was the first clerical person there, having been brought in by the late William Grogan, to assist him at the bookwork.

"William Grogan was the first manager and the only other person there then was the late J.P. Kelly. I was seated between the two of them at a table, so we were a compact little group of important people. One of the first people I recall seeing there was Jack Power, from the Green Roads. He was mainly involved in the milk and cream intake. I was shown how to test milk for butterfat by Mr. Grogan. They were also making butter there. Miss Hoey was responsible for that department.

"My working day was from 9am to 5pm. At mid-day, I used to go to a local house for lunch. The lady, who lived at the top of the hill, could see me leaving the creamery and would have the meal ready when I arrived."

Editor's note: Sadly, Margaret Mulvihill (nee Whelan, Donaghmore) died prior to Christmas 2002. May she rest in peace.

Kieran Hogan
(Coolowley)

"I started in Donaghmore in 1954, in the dairy department, where my principle job was giving out the skimmed milk. In preceding years, that work was done by the late Jack Fitzpatrick and I think there was a Jim Holohan there prior to Jack, who may have been there from the early days of the Co-op.

"After a short time, I moved to general store and yard duties, where I remained until about 1957, when I left to go to America. I returned again in 1960 and resumed work in Donaghmore. When one worked in the store and yard, you had to do many many different types of jobs, like loading and unloading to and from lorries. It was pretty hard work and all done manually - there were no fork lifts, pallets and other labour saving devices in those years. Manure was in two cwt jute bags, so you would have very tired and sore arms after handling many loads during the day.

"Then, you might have to go to the C.I.E. station for loads of cement and the bags would be so hot that you could hardly catch or carry them to the lorries. In the earlier years, I was involved in bringing grain to the station and yes, that was very hard work as well. Later, I was involved with the mixing of the various ingredients for the various meals. It was only a 2.5 ton mixer so it would have been rather slow in relation to requirements.

Joe Nolan
(Ballymeelish)

"I started in Donaghmore in August 1957 at £4 per week. One of my earliest memories is of being told by the late Jack Power, who was in the dairy when they started in 1927, that he weighed in the first can of milk. It was brought in by donkey and cart by local farmer, Stephen Campion, who was also a committee member from the start.

"My first job was at the grain dryer, which was then housed where the museum is presently situated. The first combine harvesters were starting to operate locally, so that meant a greater need for a dryer than before. After some years, there was a second dryer installed, which helped a great deal. Eventually, they were replaced by a much larger one, in conjunction with the building of a large new store. There were a number of lads manning the various dryers, among them was the late Bill Shiel, who was known to be quite a comical character.

"Once when he was drying oats which were growing fairly badly out through the sacks, Billy Wallis, who was in charge of the stores department, came in and remarked: 'It'll take you a long time to dry that, Bill'. 'Sure why wouldn't it?' said Bill, 'when I have to snag it first'.

"I remember a time, probably back in the 1960s and early 1970s, when there was quite a large number of people employed in Donaghmore Co-op. There were 22 ladies and 100 men. Many of those were involved in the assembly of seed grain, which was done in the old mill store, located a short distance away in the village.

"Some of the original lads working in that store were Mick Finnane, Martin Williams, Mick Moore and Ber Bergin. Among the original names in the butter making department included Mrs. J.P. Kelly, Sally Delaney, Rita Nolan, Kathleen Gorman, Kathleen Fitzpatrick and Carmel Williams. A few of the earlier people in the dairy department were Mick Loughman, Jack Power, Paddy McCormack, Thomas Creagh, Bob McKelvey, Paddy Loughman and Jim Somers, who was assistant to manager Donal Grogan. Others, including general repairmen, drivers and helpers who come to mind include Jack Hennessy, Joe Morrin, Joe Treacy, Joe Shortt, Mick and Jack Flanagan, Ned and Har Moynan, and Billy and Nicky Percy.

"Although usually there were specific people assigned to their own particular

Back: **Eileen McCormack, Teresa Dunne, Harriet Moynan, Kathleen Aherne.**
Front: **Teresa Breen, Margaret O'Hara, Sandra Horsburgh on an outing in the 1960s.**

jobs, especially in the dairy department, they could also be expected to fall in anywhere else, as required. You had to be a jack of all trades.

"There were a number of changes around the place during my time there. Where the new grain store was built around the back area, I remember seeing nothing there, only the green fields. Then, of course, the original old dairy was replaced by a more modern one, with mechanical intake. It was quite a change from the old outfit, where you would usually need two people to lift the rather heavy old metal cans. It was hard work, the work week was 48 hours, and the pay was very low.

"But there were the lighter moments too. Once, towards the end of harvest time, me and a lorry driver named Paddy, went up to a farmer in the Camross area, for a load of grain. It was a 10 or 12 ton lorry, and it was almost dark at the time. We had to reverse down a fairly steep laneway to the house where the bags of grain were. When we had loaded all the bags, the farmer asked us in for tea. That was very welcome, but Paddy said we'd bring up the lorry to the road first where it was fairly level. The farmer also came up with us and when we stopped, he remarked on the possible horse power of the lorry. 'I'd say there are a lot of horses in that lorry!' he said. 'Well', said Paddy, 'there are 15 horses under the bonnet and two asses in the cab'.

"Back in the 1960s, a group of lads working in the Co-op started a hurling team, which did fairly well over a long number of years. We won a county final and actually went on to a Leinster final, which ended in a draw, but we lost in the replay.

"On the down side of our story, the very last meal mixing plant

Gemma Bergin, Moira Phelan (Ryan), Lily O'Connor (Dowling) at work in Donaghmore in February 1962.

was actually closed around the same time as I retired, after nearly 45 years, in April 2002. All the meal mixing is now done in Portlaoise. It's a bit sad really to see this happen over here as I think back to the days when Donaghmore had its own very distinctive brand name of 'Diamond' meals. They even had the diamond symbol imprinted on all the meal bags.

"In the earlier years, as the bags were filled and weighed, they were sealed up using a packing needle and twine. In later years, that method was replaced by the electronic stitcher.

"There was a time away back, when there were only two places where a young person in these parts might try for work. One was the brewery in Rathdowney and the other one was Donaghmore. After all, it was set up and run by local people.

"The first milk carter who owned a lorry and collected milk around the locality, was a Bob Mitchell.

"A link with the past, before Donaghmore was set up, was that some of the old buildings, especially where the present museum is located, were used and occupied by the 'Black and Tans'. A stark reminder of that era is the marks of bullet holes in the walls and roof. There is also an old graveyard at the back of the Co-op which was used in the days when there was a workhouse here. Actually, Kieran Hogan was the first person to undertake a clean up job on it.

"In the late 1980s, due to some changes and updating of machinery, a store at the front area became vacant. There was a decision made to set up a museum in the old store and it was given over by Avonmore, as it was then known, to a local committee."

Editor's note: Sadly, Joe Nolan died unexpectedly since this interview with Ger Lawler. Sincere sympathy is extended to his wife and family on their great loss.

Joe Morrin
(Aughafan, Castletown)

"I came to Donaghmore from Bord na Móna in Offaly, where I worked as a fitter. I answered an advertisement and was called for interview with Mr. Grogan and Mr. Wallis. I got the job. It entailed looking after the maintenance of all the machinery in Donaghmore, Raheen and Spink. Before I went there, they had to bring mechanics from Limerick when repairs were necessary and this was becoming too expensive for them.

"Gradually, more machinery was acquired and in the 1950s they got a hammer mill, which was mainly for producing fairly fine meal. Before then, they only had the ordinary grinding/rolling mill. I remember some of the lads were wondering what a hammer mill was and the witty Billy Sheil spoke up and said 'Oh, you have to beat it out through a screen with a hammer and it can't come back'. The production of that fine meal was an essential ingredient in the production of their own 'Diamond' brand of meals.

"In the dairy department, a new can washer and a new stainless steel churn, which could hold two tons of butter, were purchased. Prior to then, they only had two old wooden churns. There was approximately six tons of butter produced every day at peak times.

"On one occasion, there was a break in a part of a boiler in Raheen. They had to get a new part in Dublin. It was due to be dispatched from Dublin by rail, but as it was near the Easter weekend, it would not arrive until the Tuesday and would be too late, as the boiler was required before then. Joe Butler asked me to go with him to Dublin to collect the part. I think it was Good Friday, and we were told the part had been sent on to Kingsbridge Station, (in 1966 became Heuston Station). We went to Kingsbridge and inquired, and of course the person in charge there showed all the signs of expecting a tip for his inconvenience, but there was no tip given. However, after some persuasion, we got the part and headed for Raheen.

"We had now left Dublin and I was simply starving. Eventually, when we got to Naas, Joe went into the shop across the road and emerged with two bars of chocolate – priced at a shilling each – and said 'they will keep us going until we get home'. We arrived back at the creamery and when I brought in the new part for the boiler, he said 'I'll tip up home now and get some tea'. After a while, he arrived down again with a flask of tea. That was economy at its best.

"But that was generally how things were back then, even in Donaghmore. When there was something special to be done, people took their job quite seriously, knowing very well that they depended so much on the Co-op for a living.

"I remember going over to Raheen one day and a man there was putting creosote on some stakes and was growling a little at the idea. I asked him as to what was wrong. 'Nothing at all wrong', he said, 'only some people here think they're going to live for … (expletive deleted) ever'. He felt that the stakes as they were, untreated, should do for a lifetime - but others had very different ideas.

"Mick Lalor is a droll character. I recall one time, he and 'Mog' Fitz came over to Donaghmore for a load of meal. They were loading away, when every now and then, Mog would say 'shhh … stop, shhh ….' so at last when the lorry was loaded and they were down again, they noticed a back wheel was flat. That was what Mog had heard, the air leaking out which, of course, was getting louder as the weight on the lorry increased. 'Well, Janey Mac', said Mick, 'isn't 'Mog' a sharp lad the way he heard the hissing noise'. So they had to unload some of the bags, as the jack was unable to lift the full load, and there were no fork lifts at that time. Hardship was the name of the game.

"One harvest time, during which there was a lot of bad weather, Billy Wallis came out to me with a bill for oil usage and wondered why it was so high. It happened that those who were drying the grain had the heating system turned up to maximum. Billy asked me to go with him to check and I could not see anything amiss. He went to Bill Shiel, a very witty character, to inquire what was wrong. Not getting any reason from Bill, he went to check the fire and said 'Oh, you have turned it up to full, turn it down quickly', he said. 'Do you know', said Bill, 'what I'm going to tell you, sure you couldn't dry this grain, even if you threw it on the fire."

"Once while Ned Moynan was loading a lorry, J.P. Kelly came on the scene. That was not unusual as he always had a keen interest in whatever was going on, especially where machinery was concerned. 'Hmm… the front wheel of that lorry is soft', said J.P. to Ned. Ned retorted : 'You don't see the … (expletive deleted) hard ones at all'. So J.P. just moved on, knowing that with Ned, at best, it could only be a draw.

"That's just how things were. You worked hard every day but still there would always be the more light hearted moments when something or someone's witty quip would induce a good laugh.

"The milk carters were great people too. Not only did they collect and return cans every day during peak times, but they also did the shopping for many houses, which could range from millstuff, cement, hardware items, pounds of butter, cigarettes and AI notes.

"In times when the skim milk was returned to the farmers, and you ran out of it while there was still a few cans left to fill, you'd have to make more skim by rinsing the froth around the sides of the tank with water before it went completely empty.

"There was a small shop in Donaghmore but they wanted a much larger one and also one that had no pillars in the middle. Billy Wallis, Jack Dunphy and I went to Thurles, where there was such a building, in order to see the design. We got the plans and built the shop but erecting the roof was a problem. I had made the trusses but there was no crane to lift them up. I got a long piece of steel, welded a hook at the top, put the steel upright and tied ropes from it all around, so as to keep it upright. We had already fitted a pulley block at the top, and we managed to lift each of the heavy and wide trusses to the top. Then, we had to hold a long ladder, while someone, with a good head for heights – I think it was Billy Carthy – went up and fastened the bolts. It was built in the 1960s and was regarded as a great feat at the time.

"Jim Phelan of Roskelton, who was a builder and tradesman, and was very much involved in buildings at Raheen and Spink, also did some building and repair jobs at Donaghmore. His mode of transport was a bicycle and he would usually stop out when he was working there.

"One time, one of the shafts on the hammer mill broke down, which caused a bit of a worry to the management. Billy Wallis knew of a place in Cork where there was a similar one operating and, after making some inquiries about it he sent me down to have a look and, if suitable, to bring it back. So, he gave me a blank cheque and after seeing that it would suit, a three figure price was mentioned. I did not say who it was for and started to haggle down the price until at last he agreed to sell it for £50. I filled up the cheque for £50 and when he saw the heading on it, he said 'Bejay, if I had known it was for that crowd, you wouldn't have got it for that price'. That was a typical example of management trusting staff and staff honouring that trust. Later that day, I had the mill operating again."

Liam 'Chum' Brophy
(Killadooley, Borris-in-Ossory)

"As a very young lad, I was with my dad who was taking our milk to Donaghmore Creamery on the first day it opened in 1927. As far as I can recall, there was a Fr. Dillon there, all the local neighbours were there, including Stephen Campion, George McKelvey, Bob McKelvey, Whelans, Sutcliffes and many more.

"We supplied milk down through the years until the 1970s when the bulk tankers started. Our old type heavy can was getting rusty and we were told to get an aluminium one and later then we were told to get a small bulk tank, which is still out in the yard.

"Then a time came when they wanted us out of milk because we were too small a supplier. They tried to find fault with our milk but they couldn't find any. Some lad came up from Avonmore, a fella with a gimlet eye, who said: 'Don't take down that milk for half an hour or more'. His idea was that the milk would be gone soft and would not pass the test. Then another lad called and told me: 'Your milk is not going to pass'. I said to him: 'There was a hangman who used to come over to this country from England years ago, Pierpoint was his name, and he had a more cheerful face than you have on you'.

Donaghmore employees – Seamus Phelan, Michael Whelan, Paddy Campion, Mick Moore, pictured in the 1970s.

"It was very hard to take as we never had any problems with TB or anything, but there were no apologies. Some time later, I was down in Thurles and I met the lad with the gimlet eye, and he asked me: 'How is the little pony going with you?' Said I: 'I'm sure you care a ... (expletive deleted) lot about me or my pony. All you wanted to do was to hang me'.

"There was a buttermaker in Donaghmore in the early days. Miss Hoey was her name. She used to play golf out at the back of the Creamery in the evening time. Later then, there was a Stephen Morrissey, who replaced her.

"I remember a ploughing match locally, many years ago, and the first prize was a 10 stone bag of flour, which was worth about ten bob (shillings), at the time. It was a very valuable prize and the cotton bag could be used in many varying ways. There was a company called Suttons, whose name was on flour bags which were sold in Borris-in-Ossory. Those bags were also used to make hurling/football knicks and I remember seeing a local team playing, with the name Suttons written across their, shall we say, rear ends.

"There was a certain woman who seemed to think that farmers were very well off and had plenty of money. She decided to conacre some land and sowed corn. Some of the locals helped her as best they could and when the threshing time came, she was persuaded to have a dance. When the dance was over and we all had left the house, herself brought in to that same room where we were dancing, a sow to have bonhams. A kind hearted woman she was, and sure what happened with the sow, would not have been so unusual in times past."

James Whelan in the stores (1960s).

Rita Coss
(nee Nolan, Rathdowney and formerly Kilkenny)

"I started at Donaghmore as buttermaker in January 1959. At winter time, milk would only be coming in on two or three days per week. After separation, the cream would be cooled down to 38 degrees and when cool enough, would be pumped into churns. After a process of revolving for a while, it would turn into butter. Then, you would drain off the butter milk and rinse the remaining butter, during which time, the churn would be turning.

"When thoroughly washed, the butter would be removed. When the butter was ready for packing into boxes, it had to be dug out of the churns.

"The butter was put into boxes, and sometimes into a machine to produce the 1lb blocks, which would then be wrapped by machine. In my earlier years, it was wrapped by hand. Every so often, the 1lb blocks would be check weighed. When packing the bulk butter into the 56lb wooden boxes, they had to be lined with grease proof paper, which would have been steeped in brine. After keeping a sufficient amount in our own cold store for retail sales to customers and shops, the rest was sent to cold storage depots in Dublin.

"Generally, we would have been able to finish our job within the normal working day, but I recall one particular day, when the power was cut off, that we had to work all that night to process the cream."

John Coss
(Kyledellig, Clough)

"I started as a milk carter in 1945, with a pony and dray cart and collected milk from a few local farmers. In 1946 I got a lorry as the supply of milk was gradually increasing, and my little dray cart was made redundant. I managed to get a loan of £100 and bought the small lorry. Although not a Rolls Royce, so to speak, it did the job for a few years, until the supply increased and I got a bigger one.

"There were times when people would be late leaving out their milk and you just had to pass on to the next stand. Then there was the occasional person who did not have a stand and might be slow to comply with a request to erect one. Most people were lucky enough to have a fairly high roadside bank, on which they would place a few blocks or slabs, so as to have a solid base for the cans. I continued until bulk collection started in 1970."

Christy Fitzpatrick
(Grangemore, Borris-in-Ossory)

"I started in Donaghmore in 1956, in the meal mixing plant, with Lar Dunne and Paddy Campion. After a number of years, there was a new provender plant installed, and I was put in charge. There was a capacity of one ton at a time, and you fed in all the ingredients for the various kinds of meals. You might also have a farmer come in and order a specific mix of their own and I fixed them up.

"Our working hours were generally from 8am to 6pm and quite often we worked up to 10pm, so as to have enough meals ready for dispatch early next day. There was one hour for lunch and half an hour in the evening, with no breaks in between. There were eight lads altogether in that department at peak times.

"On the rare occasions, where there might be a slackness of work in the meal mix department, you would go to the other areas where help was needed, maybe bagging coal or, during harvest time, go to the CIE station with grain or, perhaps, collect cement at the station.

"By way of leisure activities for those of us who had our lunch break on the premises, there would be cards, or skittles or football.

"As regards management, I'd have to say that they always brought in locals to work, and also there were quite a lot of families who had two or three family members there, including my own.

"Joe Nolan and Kieran Hogan were in charge of bagging the meals and it would usually take twenty minutes to prepare a ton of mix. When we had all the necessary ingredients ready for a mix, it went into a large hopper, where it was mixed for a while, and then went through a pipe or tunnel to another bin where it was bagged.

"In connection with the mixing of meals, we always ordered the ingredients ourselves. Some would be from Odlums, Ranks and Bolands in Dublin. We also made up mixtures for spraying potatoes as well as grass seed mixtures, which were done at the old mill house, down in Donaghmore village. All the seed grain assembly was also done down there.

"In preparing grain for seed, there was a huge furnace lit, and it was extremely hot when going at full blast. You would be in there turning grain on a floor, heated by the furnace, using a wide shovel and wearing just togs or shorts. That, of course, would only be seasonal work, but wherever we were, we worked hard and were generally happy enough and glad to have a job.

"In the 1960s, when there was a threat of foot and mouth disease, we had to go through a disinfection process, which included our bikes, but thankfully it was only a threat.

"There was generally an annual outing, which we went on, and always eagerly looked forward to the day. The transport for those outings was usually provided by Mick Lalor's two vans. Mick or 'Mikey' as he was also known, was based in the Raheen branch as a lorry driver and, as such, was a regular visitor to Donaghmore."

Billy Finnane
Rathdowney

"I started work in Donaghmore in November 1969. My first duty was at the petrol pump and I also

Christy Fitzpatrick at work in the meal store (1960s).

helped at filling the skim milk into the cans for the milk carters. I would also write invoices for some customers who had goods brought to them by the carters.

"Sometimes, I would be sent to the station to unload cement from wagons on to our lorries. I would have to remain there all day, maybe for three or four days at a time. Cement was always very hot and hard to handle, as the bags could be stuck to each other. I was at that type of work for about five years, and then I was brought into the shop.

"Some of the other shop staff there when I joined were: Larry and Pat Dunne, Richard Kelly, Billy Wallis, Paddy Kavanagh, Tim Finlay, Liam O'Dea, Jackie Maher, Bertie Horsburgh and Noel Mooney."

Editor's note: Billy remained in the shop and is still there 34 years later, though with a reduced staff.

Paddy McCormack
(Kilcoran, Rathdowney)

"I started in Donaghmore in May 1960, in the dairy department. At the time, there were seven in that department: Jim Somers (Dairy Manager), Jack Power, Jack Fitzpatrick, Michael Holohan, Thomas Creagh, Sean Power and myself. Six of us were involved in milk intake and Sean Power dispensed the skim milk. Regretfully, the other six have passed away and I'm the only one left out of that dairy group of lads.

"The first job each morning was to wash down the dairy, to prepare for the milk intake. The separator would be assembled and some of the other lads would have the boiler lit and steam raised, which was a very important part of the cream separation process.

"In my earlier years, Jack Power and myself did the washing up after all the milk was in and the skim tank emptied. I recall Jack telling me that when he started back in 1927, the very first day the creamery opened, he was very surprised to see the *Stations of the Cross* hanging on the walls – the dairy was actually the chapel of the old workhouse.

"When I think back now about those years, I have to say that everyone did their work very well, and we all enjoyed our work and we were like a big happy family.

"In the very early years, Jack Power often told me that they did not have any aprons or protective wear, so they would watch out for some of the lorries coming in, hoping to get a good sack to use for an apron.

"Also in earlier years when there was only the dairy, Jack used to say that it could be quite lonely in the afternoons as there was only a small amount of milk coming in. In my time, it was a different story, especially at peak times, and even in the slack winter time you could always find something to do around the yard or in the stores. There might be times when I would drive a van to collect windows and doors for Paddy Campion, who was in charge of that department. It was a nice change to get out around the country for a while and admire the scenery.

"There used to be an initiation ceremony for all newcomers in the dairy. A door would be left slightly ajar with a basin half full of water on the top. When you opened the door fully, of course, you got a head rinse. Some might not accept it too well, but you'd be better if you did. However, it was never done in winter time.

"When I started, the hours were from 8.30am to 6pm. You generally would not have to work later, unless a breakdown occurred. When the bulk collection started, the milk was taken in and cooled and stored in large tanks for a while before being transported down to the factory in Ballyragget.

"In later years, I used to go to Raheen and Spink to do quality milk tests, and I also did the same job in Donaghmore. You had to be there for the duration of milk intake and samples would be taken from every supplier. A certain temperature of water was a necessary part of the testing process. The test reading after a few hours would determine the quality of the milk and the subsequent price paid. The longer the test lasted, the better the quality it was and would merit a bonus in addition to the price per gallon paid. In my later years there, I drove a van to Ballyragget factory to collect butter.

"There were many characters working in Donaghmore; none better than the late Bill Shiel, well known for his funny stories and quick wit. If there was any little mistake made by anyone, Bill would bring the offender quickly to heel: 'A kitten opens its eyes after nine days, but you never open them'."

Editor's note: Paddy McCormack is a respected name in Laois hurling circles. He was one of the elite band of Laoismen who have had the distinction of winning a Leinster senior hurling medal and playing with their county in an All-Ireland senior hurling final. Paddy lined out at right corner back in the final of 1949, in which Tipperary defeated Laois.

Noreen Whelan
(nee Hyland, Borris-in-Ossory)

"The first job I had in Donaghmore when I started at the harvest time in 1960 was to keep an account of sacks to and from farmers. I also did the grain tests for moisture, which was done in an old type oven. It was a rather complicated type of work which necessitated great care and attention and which would determine the price payable to the farmer. Jack Hennessy was the man in charge and was always a great help to me.

"All dockets were hand written and when we had finished with them, they were passed into the office department for further processing. Most of those grain tests were done in the front office of the hatchery department and would generally run until the end of a year, or very near so.

"Then, some grain was retained for seed in the following year. There was a germination test done on it. That was done by means of placing 100 sample grains on a container and later we would see how many of those grains sprouted. Any grain which did not meet the necessary standard was used for feed.

"After a few years, someone left the hatchery department and I was sent there. It was only seasonal from January to Easter time. Jack Flanagan, who drove a van on deliveries, would bring in most of the eggs. They were put in an incubator, usually on a Tuesday and Wednesday. The waiting period was three weeks, and there were tests done at intervals during that time. Any infertile ones among them were removed and the remaining good ones would usually hatch out on a Thursday morning.

"An inspector from the department would then come to decide the sexes, after which any orders were attended to. Some people might want females only, others males only, and some would take them as hatched. In later years, the sex tests were done by Richard Kelly, who was a shop assistant. I was helped by Mick Holohan and glad of it too, as some boxes were quite heavy. If any chicks remained after fulfilling all orders, they were taken to a place on one of the lofts in the old buildings and would be fed there. People would come then and buy older ones.

"In the office then, all clerical work was done by hand. Addressing envelopes for the monthly accounts was perhaps the hardest and most important job. At one stage, they put an office in the shop and I served in that for a year or so, taking the cash and selling cigarettes. Then, for a while, they introduced a stock control system, and I worked at that for a while also. We had staff outings and later, when there was a much bigger staff, they organised a dinner dance for the whole region, at which there were over 150, and the only hotel able to cater for it was the Croften in Carlow. I left in 1970."

Tommy Whelan
(Feeragh, Clough, husband of Noreen)

"I started in the yard in Donaghmore in March 1964. Up to then, Donaghmore was dealing with Alfa-Laval for milking machines but around that time, Avonmore took over, and they switched to Fullwood. Danny Phelan and myself were transferred to Fullwood (Ireland) where we remained for about five years, up until 1979.

"I moved to the Avonmore Mills in Portlaoise in January 1981. I was in the additives section for a while and then I moved to the control room. At first, it was day time work only, but then they started operating shift work and required more people in the control room. It was quite a challenge from the other type of work which I had been doing but I got used to it and liked it quite well. I remained there until 1999, when soon after the merger with Waterford, there were redundancies on offer and after 18 years of shift work, I decided to take the redundancy.

An afterthought ... "I remember one Saturday, being sent to the Clonmore area as an extra helper with Mick Flanagan and Tom O'Hara. Tom was sent into a little shop to get a loaf, ½ lb butter and some ham. He returned with goods wrapped in brown paper and we moved on to a house, where we knew we could get a kettle of water boiled. When the kettle was boiled, we brought it out and made some tea and opened the paper wrapper, only to find a Barm Brack, the ½ lb butter and the ham. All eyes fell on poor Tom and he said: 'Sure, what could I do, they had no bread and I had to bring something'.

"Some time in the 1970s, we went by train from Ballybrophy on an outing to Bray. It was a very windy and wet morning when we were leaving, and was much worse when we arrived. The waves were quite high and it was a real storm. We just ran from the train over to Bray Head Hotel and closed the doors. The manager of the resident band was there at the time and he went and got a few musicians to play for us. We had music, eating and drinking in the hotel all day until it was time to depart while, outside, the hurricane continued. It was straight back to the train and home. There was no sightseeing. It was one of those days that I will never forget but we all enjoyed it immensely."

Margaret Fennelly
(nee O'Hara, Borris-in-Ossory)

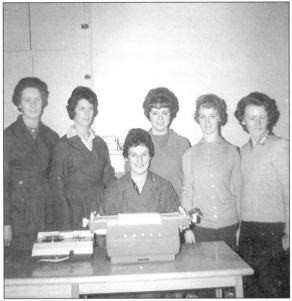

Donaghmore ladies (1960s): Martha Ryan, Mary Maher, Nancy Dann, Margaret O'Hara, Sandra Horsburgh.
Seated: Moira Ryan.

"I worked the switchboard when I first joined in 1965, and then as cashier until I left in 1972. The rapport with other staff and customers was always good. We looked forward to the annual outing each year and there would also be a social get-together every Christmas.

"There was a character working there whose name was Jack. Sometimes he would come to me for a packet of fags and might be short a few pence. I would say: 'Is it the morning after the night before, Jack?' and Bertie Horsburg would say 'Well now you have it, Jack, she has given it to you, right to your face'. So we would have a good laugh over it.

"It was during my years in Donaghmore, that I met Andy Fennelly, who later became my husband. Andy is a Raheen man and worked in the Raheen branch for some years. I left in 1972."

Mick Power
(Green Roads)

"I started in 1951 in the butter department, assembling the wooden butter boxes. There was a Pat Joe Keane also there at the time. It was the late Donal Grogan who showed me how to make the boxes and I was at that type of work for about three or four months before going into the dairy department.

"My hours at that time were 8.15am to 6pm, with only one break at lunch time. I worked in the butter-making department, which involved weighing the 1lb blocks and hand

Back: **Joe Nolan, John Fitzpatrick, Jim Daly, Christy Fitzpatrick, Ml. White, Donie Dowling.**
Front: **Seán Power and Paddy Carey (driver) pictured on an outing in the 1960s.**

wrapping them. The machine dispensing the 1lb blocks was called a rolling machine. Sometime in the late 1950s, they installed a machine wrapper, which was automatic.

"In my earlier years, there would be about four or five tons of butter made per day and this increased later to about eight tons per day. Jack Flanagan was the principal van driver who delivered the butter. Jack Bowe was another and Sean Bergin was the last person to deliver butter for Donaghmore.

"There was a social outing every year but myself and Mick Loughman, who was also in the dairy department, usually had to stay and take care of the milk intake. Milk was at peak supply in summer time and we usually worked about 52 hours per 7 day week. That 52 hour week was as prescribed by the Government, and was posted up on the premises. We got no overtime in those years and you might get some time off in lieu, a few times a year.

"My late father, Jack Power, was one of three lads who were there in the early years. The others were Joe Bergin and Ned Fox. My father was there from the first year in 1927 until 1967. My late brother, Sean, was there from 1953 to 1987. They all worked mostly in the dairy. I actually made the last churn of butter in Donaghmore, although Avonmore had taken over at the time.

"Mick Loughman was a good butter maker, although not qualified. There were a few sealed boxes of butter sent to Dublin each year, which had been chosen by a department inspector on surprise visits. Mick won a cup for being the best in Ireland, which was presented at the Spring Show."

Martin Tynan
(Errill)

"I worked in Lisduff Quarry, under the original owner, Ned Byrne. In those years (in the mid-fifties), as well as the ground lime, they also made concrete blocks. At the quarry, you would load the stones by hand into a tractor trailer and then onto a series of crushers. The stones were made smaller each time and the last crushing produced the fine limestone.

"As the lime became available, it was loaded into lorries for delivery out to farmers. Sometimes, in early morning, there might not be enough time to fill a lorry because of the difficulty of loading the lime. I would get down into a bin and stand on a ladder to try and loosen the lime, which would become stuck to the sides. But you would never go down alone as you could get overcome by the lime dust in a closed area. At a later stage, when better machinery was installed, more lime could be produced, and the surplus to needs was stockpiled.

"My work ranged from loading the trailers at the pit, driving down the tractor loads to the crushers, delivering loads to the farmers, and also, delivering blocks – mostly to people who were building sheds, new houses and extensions. Some of those deliveries were also done with tractor and trailer.

"After a short period in the grain drying plant, I got the job of driver at Donaghmore. I delivered locally to the farmers before being put on the Dublin run. We would collect coal and manure and other goods, sometimes making two runs to Dublin in the same day. Generally, we worked a five and a half day week, but for some time they introduced a rotating system which meant you had to work on some Saturdays all day and perhaps get a day off instead. It was not a popular idea and only lasted a short time. I worked at Donaghmore from 1958 until 2000."

Peter Kilmartin
(Coolowley, Errill)

"Sometime in 1950 Donaghmore advertised for a lorry owner to operate and collect milk on a specific route, on which they had been operating up to then. Only a short time earlier, I had purchased a new tractor and I applied for and got the job. There were about twenty-five suppliers at the time and as the route was already set up, I did not have to canvass.

"At first, I had a little Ferguson tractor and then got one or two bigger ones after a few years. Later again, I got a lorry which lasted until I finished when the bulk tankers replaced the cans.

"My route covered a wide area including Coolowley, Garron, Knock, Garryduff, Errill and Lisduff. There were quite a large number of carters operating at that time but sadly, most have passed away.

"All the skim milk was returned to the farmers, then some would look for extra, while a small few would not want any at all. So the person giving out the skim milk would have to perform a good balancing act to ensure that there would be enough to meet all requirements.

"According to one of the local witty characters, there was a well known 'black cow', which could dispense skim milk when requested, if it was fed well enough. In this case, it was quantity rather than quality."

Peter Bergin
(Kilbreedy, Rathdowney)

"In August 1965 a job as manager of Lisduff Quarry was advertised. I answered it, and was called for an interview which was with Mr. Grogan, Mr. Wallis and Mr. Galbraith. I got the job and was appointed manager. I was the first person to hold that post, as Donaghmore had only acquired the quarry a short time before then.

"There were thirteen people working there at the take over. Ground limestone, mainly used by farmers on land, was the principal product produced, but they also made concrete blocks for a while. However, they discontinued the block-making after a short time, as the machinery was old and rather obsolete.

"A typical day would start at 8am, with only a half-hour lunch during the day, and finish at 5.30pm. In the quarry large chunks of stone were collected and brought to a crusher, and later the smaller bits would go through a mill, and come out as ground limestone. There would be a product called screenings or mill waste, which was sold for yard-filling.

"I was not involved in any of the physical work. I would be directing operations, and looking after accounts, taking orders and seeing that they were dispatched promptly. Springtime was always a very busy time, but we worked all year through and would have a stockpile available when the spring rush would start.

"By way of leisure activities, although we were located a few miles from Donaghmore, we would be included in their annual outings, on their GAA teams and whatever. Most of our orders came through the Co-ops and we also had a sales rep., Edward Keane – who worked for the previous owners. Generally we had two lorries on deliveries, but at peak times we had to hire a few more lorries in order to cope with the demand. Eventually, the Irish Sugar Company became interested (in 1978) and took over the plant, as a going concern – which meant that all the staff remained and I continued as manager until they closed down operations in 1988."

Jack Flanagan
(Tullacommon, Donaghmore)

"It was a harvest time in 1953 when I joined Donaghmore. At first I was in a grain store, handling sacks of grain coming in and going out, and doing jobs such as the store weighing.

"After the harvest I was generally around the yard and stores, as well as painting and cleaning. There was always something to do. If a driver was out sick I would replace him and so on. I eventually replaced Jack Bowe as driver and I remained in the job for the next twenty years until I retired in 1975.

"The van was generally used to deliver out butter to shops and branches. I also used to collect eggs for the hatchery from various supply areas. I would leave empty boxes and collect full ones. I was careful of any boxes falling as I went along some bad roads, but luckily no eggs were ever broken. Every week I delivered out chicks from the hatchery to the rail station, local customers, and the branches.

"I also delivered butter every week to shops in all the surrounding areas, and to many shops in other counties. There was no cooling equipment in the van, so it was not easy to keep the butter from going soft in the warm weather. I would have to keep it changed around in the van as best I could. Once or twice I was asked by a senior shop person to bring back some meat and bone meal in the van. Apart from not having much room it was not nice material to have near butter, so I would not entertain that idea.

"Occasionally when Mick Lalor, who brought the cream from the branches, was on holidays I would take over on the lorry and bring in the cream and deliver millstuff to the branches. My starting time was 8.30am but in the evenings it could be 8pm or later when I finished. My late brother, Mick, also worked for many years with Donaghmore."

Breda Kavanagh
(nee Williams, Grogan, Errill)

"My starting wages in 1972 were £6, after tax deductions. My first job was checking and sorting invoices which were all done manually at the time. There were three lots: cash, credit milk accounts and credit goods or ledger accounts. Noreen Dunne was also in that department with me, and we worked in the main office along with a number of other clerical staff. I would also help when the monthly accounts were being sent out.

"When the invoices were sorted out each morning, the supplier's number and branch identity number were put on milk account invoices, and ledger account numbers and branch numbers on non-milk invoices. Tots would be checked and code numbers and letters would be inserted against items on the invoices. After that, all credit transactions were recorded on customers' accounts. There were accounting machines in later years, but in the earlier years all items on invoices

*Christy Fitzpatrick and Paddy Bannon
on an outing 1960s.*

were written onto statements, using carbon paper and duplicate statements. The top copy was for customers, and the carbon copy was held by the Co-op.

"I also worked in a small office in the dairy department. I would transfer milk intake figures from a platform book to a record book, which accommodated all the figures for a month in one opening, with fifty suppliers' numbers per opening. At mid-month, up to 16 days in the first half of the book would be totted and cross-checked, and at the end of the month the remaining half would be completed. In a similar manner, the credit sales of butter would also be recorded against account numbers.

"When milk tests were done - twice monthly in Summer time - usually by Jim Somers, who was dairy manager, I would write those figures into a test record book, and they were punched onto punch cards by more senior clerks. In 1975 the Co-op procured new computers, which were linked by a special phone line to Avonmore in Ballyragget. At this stage, Mary McEvoy was sorting the daily dockets and would input the non-milk accounts into the computer, while I did the milk accounts.

"Once every week validation sheets were issued in Ballyragget, and someone from there would bring them to us, or I might have to go and collect them. If there were discrepancies they had to be corrected as soon as possible, and punched again. Then after the end of each month, when the accounts came out, all available staff would be involved in getting statements and dockets ready for dispatch.

"In the latter years addressed labels were issued by Avonmore, and this saved a lot of time. So, all milk accounts especially, had to be ready for posting by a certain date each month. When about to leave with the post, we would have to inform the post office, so as they would be ready for the rush.

"We all got on very well together, our work was quite hard and demanding, and everyone had targets to meet and everyone played their part to achieve these targets. In 1986, when computers were installed at the sales counter and other places, the transactions then went direct to Ballyragget, which meant no punching operation in the branches. With less work, redundancies were on offer, and

*Sally Delaney, Michael (Mixie) Kelly, Mick Lalor
pictured at Donaghmore in the 1950s.*

thus came the end of an era for me and a number of staff members in February 1986."

Martin Williams
(Coolowley, Errill)

"In the Autumn of 1954, I started working in the old mill, which is just down the road a short distance, in the village of Donaghmore. My wages were three pounds and twelve shillings per week. That mill was used only to dry and prepare grain for seed. I believe the kiln that was used then is still there, though idle now. There were two other lads there, Mick Finnane and Mick Moore. We worked well together and we became life-long friends, but sadly both men have since died.

"The grain was starting to come in when I joined. It was very important that we took samples from each sack and gave our verdict on their suitability for seed. Whatever was not suitable was dried and would be used for feed.

"The kiln was very interesting and it used coke, a smokeless fuel. We had to make sure that it maintained a consistent level of heat while the drying was in progress. The building was three-storey and there were stone slabs going up from the furnace through a chimney-like space.

"The floor had space for about twenty sacks of grain. It would be spread out over the floor and we used wooden shovels and rakes, to spread and keep the grain turned. It was spread about four inches deep and we had to ensure that it was not over-dried, especially that which was going for seed.

"When a lot of grain was dried we had to move it over near a chute, which would bring it down to the next floor to be put into sacks. There was a slide on the chute that closed off the flow when the sack was full. The whole process would be repeated until all the grain was dried. We knew the names of the various types of grain, and who grew it. We usually worked until around 9pm, having started at 8am, so it was a long day. If we finished a lot which was OK for seed, we would then put on a lot which was only for feed use, and turn the heat down low and leave it there overnight. Then in the morning we would bag that lot, and identify it as for feed only, and leave it away from potential seed. If there was a change in grain (wheat after barley or oats and so on) we had to ensure that no grains remained from a previous kind. So that routine would continue all through harvest from about mid-September to the end of November.

"There were always a few farmers who were sure that their grain was, or should be OK for seed, but we might see it in a different light. Then when all the drying was completed we would have to winnow it to remove any hulls or chaff and identify the various types. For that process, there was a machine with several different screens inside it. The principle of how it worked was similar to a threshing machine. The upper screen had the largest holes, with each of the other three or four screens gradually getting finer down to the last one.

"There would be three outlet points on which sacks were hanging – one for chaff and weed seeds, one for unsuitable seed type, and one for good seed. Then we had to check for moisture. This was done by putting 100 grains in a special tray and, if 90 sprouted it would be passed as OK.

"There were usually a couple of months in winter-time, when drying was stopped, and the whole area was cleaned. Then the seed would be dressed, in readiness for the spring sowing. But you would only dress what you would expect to sell, as the dressed grain could not be used for food.

"At seed dressing time, when using the special powder, we had to use masks as it was very dangerous stuff. We would have a fair idea of what seed was required, and were careful not to have any dressed seed left over. In the off-season, we would return to the creamery area.

"While working in the mill we would cycle up to the creamery, in turns, for a half-hour lunch break, the only one in the day, and get back as quickly as possible to keep the work going.

"The spring season generally lasted three months, from March to May, which meant you worked at grain for six to seven months a year. In the other months, we would go back up to the creamery stores and yard.

"We were mostly in the yard, filling coal into bags and weighing them and leaving them ready for sale. There were only the jute bags at that time, and they held a cwt. each. Coal was in great demand then and a lorry load would not last very long.

"The two Micks and myself were fond of the odd bet on the horses. One Derby day in the late 1950s we had a few bets on the big race. Mick Finnane brought back a little radio after lunch to hear the broadcast. The radio was turned on and the race was about to start when I saw J.P., as he was always referred to, coming towards us. 'Here's the boss, lads,' I said. We had our coats off and Mick Finnane grabbed his and put it down over the radio. But he forgot to turn it off.

"'Hello, men', said JP, 'You're going on well there!' We returned the greeting. He knew we used to do bets at times, and what was going on. Then, winking at me, he said to Mick, 'Your coat is speaking!', and away he went. It's a typical example of how fair and how honest he was. We had great regard for J.P.

"In the earlier years when we were down in the old mill, sometimes if we were working late we'd have a fry of sausages and puddings at the short break, but we never had any eggs. There was a young lad named Donal, who used help out in the mill at times. He must have told his mother about our occasional feed, and she gave him six eggs in a 'brown' paper bag. Now that could be a dangerous word to use in present times, but brown it was. We found out that Donal had left the eggs down in the basement. Unknown to the young lad, Mick Finnane got the eggs and boiled them as hard as rocks, before leaving them back again where he had got them.

"At break time that evening, Mick said, 'Where's the eggs, Donal?' 'Oh, they're in the basement!', and went and fetched them. He tried to crack one on the edge of the pan, intending to fry them. Of course, it didn't break at first, but when eventually it did, he seemed shocked. 'Look!' said Donal in disgust, showing the egg. Mick looked at the egg for a few seconds and then said, 'Janey, Donal, your mother must have great hens, they're able to lay hard-boiled eggs!'

"We all got on very well together, the work was hard, the pay was low, but we had the bit of craic now and again to keep us cheered up. I finished on the 13th of June, 1966."

Billy Percy
(Clonmeen, Errill)

"I worked in all departments of the Co-op for a few years from 1957, before being put in charge of a small lorry on local deliveries. After some time, I was given a bigger lorry. It was then around the 1960s and Donaghmore was a very busy trading centre.

"There would be loads of manure going out to areas outside the county, including many in Co. Tipperary, such as Borrisoleigh, Upperchurch, and Templemore and also around the Birr area and into Co. Galway. Farmers were starting to build silage pits and that meant lots of cement going out to those places.

"Although we were supposed to have a half day on Saturdays, it would be perhaps three or four in the afternoon, before we normally finished. In my earlier years, we often took loads of butter to Dublin and would have to call to several warehouses and wholesale shops to collect goods for the return journey. In those years, it was fairly easy to get around in Dublin. We would usually do around the north side first and then have lunch and continue around the south side.

"In the early 1970s, before Avonmore took over, I used to draw loads of milk to Dungarvan and sometimes to Miloko. When Avonmore did start, I still took milk to Miloko. That could be three times daily and I only had three small tanks on the lorry. Occasionally, I used to deliver loads of skim to Gerry Culliton's pig farm in Clonaslee.

"When Avonmore started to get quite busy, Mick Lalor, from Raheen branch, and myself had to go to Ballyragget, to train as bulk tanker drivers.

"Every day at lunch break in the Co-op, there would be football, cards and skittles, which made up the leisure side of our day. There were quite a lot of young lads around then, in their early 20s, and it could be hard enough to remain on your feet, when they started at football.

"For a while before I finished, Avonmore would close for five or six weeks in winter time, and we would have to take the milk to perhaps Dungarvan, one year, and Tipperary town, another year. That would put a lot of extra pressure on us, especially those drivers covering the areas of north Leinster who, when they had collected from the farms, would have to take on the extra journey with their loads. It could be 6.30pm or later when some drivers would reach Dungarvan.

"No matter what I was at, whether in the yard, store, or on lorries, I always was very happy at my work. I opted for redundancy and finished in January 1993, after almost 36 years."

Sean Percy
(Templequain, Rathdowney)

"In 1965 I was given a job, working at the building of a new shop. That lasted for about three months and then I was put helping on a lorry driven by my cousin, Billy Percy.

"After about four years, I was given a small truck and put on local deliveries. Some years later, in 1974, I started to deliver bulk milk tanks out to farmers, in Laois, and most of the surrounding counties. Those tanks were originally stored in Kells and Freshford, in Co. Kilkenny. But, with the milk supply increasing rapidly, there was a need for a secure store in order to be able to lock up lots of smaller items, such as electric motors and associated fittings. I told them that there were two old stores in Donaghmore, which were idle. So, they took charge of those stores, put new floors and doors in them and that solved a problem of storage space for the Avonmore group.

Mick Lalor unloading cans of cream at Donaghmore, late 1950s.

"During these years, some farmers changed tanks for bigger ones, up to three times a year, and that evolution continued into the mid-1980s. In 1986, as work began to slacken, there was talk of redundancy around the place. A job became vacant in heavy haulage and I was given it. I was drawing loads of assorted animal feeds from Portlaoise mill to all branch locations. I also drew in bulk material from some ports: Foynes, Dublin, Dundalk, Drogheda and Waterford. I continued in that position until 31st of July 1998, when I took early retirement."

Kieran Finnane
(Rathdowney)

"I was just finished in National School at 14 years old when I started in Donaghmore. At first, my principal work was weighing out flour, flake meal, various kinds of animal feed into varying amounts, from a ½ stone up to maybe two stone packs in paper bags, to have a supply ready for customers, as they came in.

"Likewise, nails and staples came in cwt bags at that time, and I would weigh out lots of them, from ½ lb up to 1lb, or perhaps 2lbs, in some cases. Billy Wallis was in charge of the shop department then. I then moved on to serving customers. Items like plough fittings and other machinery parts, would be in a store, off shop, and I would help in that area also, when required.

"After some years, they started dealing in plumbing and bathroom fittings, and I became very much involved with those. Then, as group water schemes were starting in many areas, we stocked all the various piping and fittings required. Among the bigger schemes was one in and around Errill village.

"Around that time also, probably the early 1960s, there were grants available for farmers, who wanted to have water piped around their lands. Pumps for that purpose were also a big selling item in Donaghmore. Then,

Donie Dowling, Larry Ryan and Billy Mansfield at Donaghmore in 1966.

after approximately three years, I progressed to buying, first in the plumbing department and later, in the timber and hardware departments.

"Firms, such as Brooks-Thomas, Unidare, Wavin, Thomas Corry, John C. Parkes, Heatons and Dockrells were leaders in their fields in those years. Some others who worked in Donaghmore during my time were: Bertie Horsburgh, Paddy Kavanagh, Richard Kelly and Paddy Campion. After I left there, other members of my family came in. Seamus and George came and went and Billy, who came in over 30 years ago, is the only one of our family still there in the shop department. Our father, Mick, worked in Donaghmore from 1952 to 1975. So we had a strong family connection with the place.

"Back in the 1960s, I would go to Raheen and Spink, to take their orders for goods – most of which were in my plumbing department and then when Mick Lalor came over with the Raheen lorry, I would organise the load for both branches.

"Donaghmore was a great place to work and I always enjoyed being with work colleagues, both male and female. All in all, I had a great seven years there. I left in 1965 and went to a Dublin firm, Heiton McFerran Ltd, who were well known builders providers and steel stockholders. We used to deal with them for many years and I learned of a job opportunity with much better pay, and so I was fortunate to procure a job with them.

"Some years later, I changed jobs again and finally, I set up my own business venture, namely, Finline Furniture, which was a big challenge and thankfully, I'm doing pretty well so far."

Gemma Bergin
(Donaghmore)

"My first work, in the mid-1950s, was checking and adding milk figures in the dairy, on farmers' milk cards. Later then, I progressed to filing dockets, typing and attending a reception window. I was fortunate enough to have typing and short-hand knowledge when I joined. Also at the reception area, customers and milk carters would come for butter and cream. Those butter and cream sales would be charged to the customers' accounts, while any sales which were paid for would be accounted for by a different method.

"After that, I was wages clerk for a while, and did creditors ledger transactions too. We used pencils, biros and fountain pens. The better quality fountain pens, such as Parker and Watermans, were used especially for entries into the milk record books, milk summary and all the more important books. Blotting paper was a must whenever you had to use a fountain pen.

"Occasionally, I would assist Mr. Galbraith in checking bank accounts. Then, every month when our accounts were being sent out, we would all be involved in that process. Envelopes were addressed, statements and dockets enclosed, and stamps put on. In later years, they got a franking machine, which was a great advantage. They used a slogan with the franking, which read: 'Eat more Donaghmore butter'.

"Sometime in the early 1960s, they procured an accounting machine. It was not fully automatic and we had to do a lot by hand while operating it, but it was still a great step forward. There was always a great working atmosphere in the place, and many happy days on the annual outing.

"When I was wages clerk, the week ended on Wednesdays and wages were paid out on Thursdays. All transactions were manual and the only aid you had was a ready-reckoner. You only had a few hours to prepare the cards for pay-out time."

Paddy Bannon
(Ballymullen, Errill)

"At first in 1952, I was a helper on a lorry, which lasted about four years or so. Work would vary between collecting bags of grain from farmers, bringing it into the store and unloading it. In those years, there was no lifting equipment on lorries or farms, and so lifting sacks with perhaps 25 or more stones of wheat in them was not too easy.

"Other types of grain, such as barley and oats might not be quite as heavy but, still, heavy enough when lifting the sacks off the ground. When wheat was weighed into barrels of 20 stone each, loads were dispatched to Ballybrophy station and put into wagons. Some wagons were open with no roof and were a little easier to load but if you got the covered ones, you would soon realise what hard work was like. With 20 stone of wheat on your back, you walked from lorry to wagon and then you had to stoop and try to ease your way through a narrow door and let down the bag as easy as possible, or otherwise it could burst. At the end of a day, you would have a very sore back and you would repeat that process many times during a grain harvest.

"Apart from handling grain, there would be deliveries of mill stuff around to customers and branches. My driver for the first four years was Andy Bergin from Barney and when he left, I started to drive, although I had almost no experience before then.

"Ah, they were tough times. The auld money was small at that time, a few auld shillings. You would usually start work at 8am but you would never know when you would finish – it could be all hours of the night. If we were back in the yard by lunch time, we would get our bit of grub and some lads would be playing cards, and others at the skittles. As often as not, a row could develop among the players and empty bags or other items could be thrown at each other for a while, but then it would calm down again and everything was fine until the next day.

"Our lorries at that time were just about okay, but on one occasion, I was driving a different one, which was in rather poor shape and the late Bill Shiel was with me. As we trundled along on a bad road, Bill said: 'For F* sake, will ya keep it near the ditch, so we won't have far to shove it, if it breaks down'.

"Before they acquired Lisduff quarry, Donaghmore had a sand pit near Roscrea and I drew many loads of sand out to farmers. They also made blocks there, with a machine which made one block at a time. The two lads operating that were Ned Campion and Joe Hanrahan and although it seemed a rather slow process, they would make a lot of blocks in a day. I drew out loads of them also."

Richard Kelly
(Donaghmore)

"I was employed by the Society for 34 years, from sweeping the floor to being on the Board of Management. Initially I started off in the old shop which was a very small room before being extended to double its size. Then they took the back wall out of it and built an asbestos-roofed extension. Billy Wallis, Ken Deane and Jimmie Fitz were in the shop when I started. Then Jimmie Fitz left and went to England and there were only the three of us there. Bertie Horsburg came out from Williams' in Rathdowney and he brought a lot of custom with him from Rathdowney because Williams' were closing down.

"I worked for a time in the hatchery as a chick sexer for which I had to undergo a course of training. You had to determine the sex of day old chicks. You had this gadget with lights, which you put up into the chick's backside and you could see the ovaries or testicles. Then the Japanese developed a method whereby they could determine the sex by merely looking at the chick's backside. Determining the sex of the chicks was an important job because if the Society, for instance, sold a quantity of chicks as pullets and some of them turned out to be cocks, the Society was responsible.

"The shops developed into selling footwear and then into the electrical end of it when the rural electrification started. We used to buy quite a lot of supplies from wholesalers. Nearly all the stuff for wiring houses from Thurles to Portlaoise was bought in the Creamery. Nobody else was selling electrical appliances.

"We got into white goods, as we called them, such as washing machines and fridges. You had to know everything about a washing machine. The small 'servis' machine took six pounds dry weight while the bigger one took nine pounds. If you sold a washing machine, you had to demonstrate how it worked because no one had a clue. The same thing if you sold a fridge, you had to show them how to turn the dial. We had to know everything about the appliances that came into the Creamery, otherwise you didn't make the sale. You got manuals and you took them home and studied them to see how each appliance worked.

"The shop expanded in time and there were up to twelve working there. From 1971 to 1975 we became big in plumbing. We sold lead and we used ½ inch wastes, this was before Wavin or any of the PVC's came in. There was the white Belfast sink, that was the only one you got, before stainless steel came in. It had a 1½ inch lead trap and a lead waste. You charged so much per foot for the lead waste. You had to roll your own pipe so that it wouldn't kink.

"The biggest boost we got in the shops was when we did the shopping sprees in the early sixties. These were massive sales that went on late into the nights for a week. We called it the Open Week. They were mainly for household goods like washing machines, fridges and cookers. It was in the new shop which was then fully operational. It was a novel idea and very well organised. Bob Cumbers was there at the time and it was his idea. It was advertised for different areas. Roscrea might be on a Monday night. Five or six buses would be organised to bring the ICA and other people from Roscrea and along the road. The first bus load first saw the demonstrations and then moved along to get a cup of tea, sandwiches and buns. After that they came back to make their purchases. Then parties from successive buses went through the same routine.

"We bought in bulk the sort of things that the housewives wanted. We explained that we wanted the Creamery to be there for the housewife just as much as the farmer. We worked hard at it and profits went through the roof that year. It was not so much the profit but the business it generated and making people aware of the facilities we had here. Years later when I was working for Acorn Insurance I called to a couple below Nenagh and when the wife found out where I was from, she

Gemma Bergin, Noreen Whelan (Hyland), Lily O'Connor (Dowling), Mrs. Sophie Kelly on a staff outing in the 1950s.

recalled the great night they had up in Donaghmore at the spree where they bought a washing-machine and a cooker and enjoyed the tea, buns and sandwiches.

"The Creamery has been very important to the prosperity of the area. There were 400 or so jobs there in the late sixties between Donaghmore, Raheen, Spink and Mountmellick. Where would we have been without that level of employment?

"Raheen was always important to Donaghmore but it must be remembered that when Spink was opened in 1935 it was the mainstay. It kept Donaghmore open up to 1939/1940.

"The Creamery was good for the economy of the area generally, even for the shops. The shops were totally against the co-op in the initial stages but they did benefit eventually from the increased economic activity.

"The Creamery took a smaller margin of profit than the shops. The mark-up was only about 25% and you didn't round it off for your own sake. If it worked out at 1/8½ you were expected to get 1/8½ and if Mr. Wallis heard you argue with the lads and say take 1/8, he would ask you what price was on that item you were selling. Of course, because the Co-op was selling at a keen price anyway they couldn't afford to sell below the marked up price. Anyway the Co-op was there to provide a service to its shareholders rather than making big profits. Even when they made a profit, they gave a lot of it back to shareholders by way of dividends, bonuses and shop vouchers. The lowest dividend they paid was 1/- per share (5%).

"I later got involved in transport and was in management, as transport manager, around the time of the amalgamation with Avonmore. A lot of changes took place over a short period of time, particularly when money became more available for people to buy. Donaghmore was sold for the price of a gallon of milk. At the meeting where it was decided to amalgamate, which was held in St. Mary's Hall in Portlaoise, everyone who attended had to produce an admission card. There were a couple of people put there to make sure everyone had

Peter Creagh, Mixie Kelly, Mick Power, Mick Lalor, Sally Delaney, Rody Loughman, all Donaghmore employees in the 1950s.

an admission card. They knew there was going to be a bit of hassle and every-one attending had to be members. Certain members on the committee prevented Paddy Kavanagh and myself getting admission cards from some people coming into the meeting on that night. People were just pushed in, and the barricade that we had put up was removed.

"Others may or may not tell you the same story, but that did happen. We don't know if any non-members got in. But I had been going to AGM's for years where my function was to take admission cards from people coming in, or I knew they were members or whatever. The normal AGM's were held in the Creamery and there could be 150 attending. But this was an exceptional AGM because of all the shareholders in the wider group and the particular interest of the dairy farmers. It was the milk producers that swung it through. There was a meeting held two weeks later in Borris-in-Ossory, a confirmatory meeting, and it was passed by four votes. Had there been four or five more members it would have been stopped. If that had happened it would still have been federated to Avonmore.

"I think it would have been better had Donaghmore stayed out. Look at Centenary. They are totally independent and they have their loyal shareholders and customers and they are doing the business. They have taken over an awful lot of the Donaghmore business.

"Old people that you meet will talk about Donaghmore in the good old days. I'm talking about the whole store trade. Avonmore were only interested in milk, and I don't care what anyone says, they had no interest in anything other than milk. Milk, milk, milk – that's all they wanted."

Paddy Dooley
(Neilstown, Roscrea)

"Billy Scully, who came from a townsland called Summerhill, started canvassing the area around 1957 for milk suppliers. The farmers there had never sent milk anywhere before that. He collected milk from people within five miles of Birr. The area he covered was about 80 square miles, a huge area. He collected it in cans and he was always in trouble with lorries.

"The man who kept him on the road was a man called Joe Thompson, from Borris-in-Ossory, who had a garage. But for him, I don't think there would have been any milk going from our part of the country. He bought a lorry one time from McCormack's Amusements. He went around the country collecting milk with *McCormack's Amusements* written on the side of the lorry.

"At that time in Donaghmore you could get anything, including groceries, and the people would tell Billy what they wanted. He had a remarkable memory, he never wrote down anything and everything he was told to bring, he brought it correctly. He kept it all in his head.

"He was very efficient, the cans would always be brought back in time. But if he wasn't on the lorry and some of the helpers were there, the cans could end up anywhere. They could fall off the lorry along the side of the road.

"What you would have to do, if the cans didn't come back, was to retrace the route that the lorry had taken and call into every farmhouse to see if you could find your can. I remember once having to go off down to Ballybrit and to Leap Castle.

"At that time, as regards the milk collections, the big job was to get the skim milk back before it turned sour, in the summer time in particular. It could be left on the stand for a couple of hours. I'm talking about the 1950's and 1960's. That was always the worry with my mother and father, would the milk come back soon? Because Scully might be late coming, if he had problems with the lorry, I remember that my father devised this method of cooling milk, prior to electricity. He got a length of hydrodare tube, connected the two ends and made it into a circle and bored holes in the tube. The tube was then put around the can and we had gravity flow water at that time and we still have. The source of the water was a well higher up in the Slieve Bloom Mountains and it was very cold and there was great force on it. That was our way of cooling the milk before we got electricity. I know some others saw it and used the same method. That was an ingenious and effective way of cooling the milk. We were very late getting the electricity up there in the Slieve Blooms. It was 1963 when Rural Electrification came to our part of the country.

"My involvement with Donaghmore is relatively recent. I came onto the Donaghmore Committee in 1980 and there are people on it today that were on it when I came in. I still think that Donaghmore has an important function in this particular area. It was the co-operative effort and the foresight of men in places like Donaghmore that made Glanbia what it is today. There was a great spirit of co-operation in the area here in the early days. I don't know if that spirit is still there or not. I think it has diluted to a large extent. But I still feel that Donaghmore as a co-operative has an awful lot to offer the farmers in this area.

"A lot of the co-operative spirit has been subsumed by the bigger Glanbia setup. But there were many factors mitigating against Donaghmore staying independent at the time of the amalgamation. I know that in our particular part of the country there was wholesale agreement. I met very few people in that particular area who felt that it should remain as an independent entity. The advice of Bobby Bennett and others was to amalgamate and their advice was taken.

"I would think that the price of milk would not be as good today had they remained independent. I honestly believe that Donaghmore, had it continued as a separate entity, would have had a hell of a big job to remain functional.

"Centenary Co-op send their milk into Avonmore Creameries. When I was on the Committees it was a great bone of contention that Centenary was doing better than the people who were sending their milk direct to Donaghmore. Had Donaghmore and all the other Creameries not amalgamated, then there would have been no Avonmore with whom Centenary could make the deal they made. Centenary was fortunate that they had someone's coat-tails to hang on to. There is no doubt about the fact, though, that in the bigger entity the individual identity of the shareholder is not what it was.

"I always felt a loyalty to Donaghmore. Not all creamery suppliers had the same loyalty, I'm sorry to say. I would like to see greater development and better facilities in branches like Donaghmore. When I came back to full time farming there was an agricultural advisor in Donaghmore and he'd be available to local suppliers. They were far more accessible than they are now, I'd say. But after a while they did not want to know about the small supplier. One of them more or less said so, and bid me goodbye. I took it up with Avonmore that if they were going to service only the bigger farmers in the area, they could forget about it. Some of the top officials from Avonmore came out to me and they assured me that this wasn't the case. So I got back my advisor again. They sorted it out because the company got to know about it. Had I remained silent, my advisor was gone.

"We live in a severely disadvantaged area. We have about 90 acres of our own and about 40 to 45 acres leased. That would be as productive as about 70 to 80 acres of good land. It couldn't be good land 700 to 800 feet high up in the Slieve Blooms. You get late springs and early winters.

"I regret to say that I think the days of the small farmers are numbered. I know that in my own particular case at home, I took early retirement four or five years ago and my son took over. Now he is working in a job. I was always able to keep a family comfortable without having to go working a shift from 4 to 12. He is all right, he can do that now, but in dairying it's very difficult to be a part-time farmer. With cows calving at all sorts of times, he is lucky I'm there as there is nobody but himself at it. It is a seven day a week job. With all these Fischler proposals and the new World Trade Organisation negotiations coming up, I think that is a tragedy. In areas like ours in the Camross region, where it is an area of disadvantage because the land is not good, what's going to happen to it? Will we be able to get jobs in the local towns? What's going to happen to the landscape? Is it all going to be planted with trees? That's what I foresee and it will be denuded of people. And there are many similar areas all over the country.

"As regards companies like Glanbia, it looks to me that the only thing that matters is what's on the bottom line. Glanbia plc is there to make money and a profit. I'll put it this way, I don't think there is any social aspect to the policy of Glanbia plc at the moment. There were over 40 milk suppliers on our run about 25 years ago and that's down to ten today. There is a need for an agricultural advisor subsidised by Glanbia, to help the smaller farmers today to survive in farming.

"Advisory Committees by the very term of the name, are Advisory Committees, they can only advise. They have no powers, good, bad or indifferent. I have often felt, in the almost twenty years that I was on the Committee (some of that time on the Regional Committee as well) that there was no heed paid to what was being discussed at those meetings by those at the top. You would be very frustrated at times to realise that what you were trying to bring about, wasn't happening or wasn't being given any consideration. There is a conflict there between what Glanbia plc wants and what the farmers want.

"I would say that the committees don't take full advantage of the facilities available to them to make their voice heard. Whether that's a fault of a lack of communication between Glanbia and its suppliers is another question. "Glanbia could improve communications with the ordinary members and would benefit from listening to what the ordinary members have to say. It should encourage more involvement from the grass roots, and think seriously on how they can do that effectively.

"Glanbia plc should take into account the co-operative aspect and the social aspect. They could go the road that they have gone and still have borne in mind the importance of looking after their shareholders and the small farmers."

Billy Mansfield
(Rathdowney)

"Around 1947, J.P. Kelly and Michael Kirwan from Donaghmore, called to people around the Rathdowney area, trying to get people to take shares in Donaghmore Co-op, and asking farmers to consider sending milk to the Co-op.

"They came to my mother, who had been a widow since my father died in 1941,

Jack Hennessy pictured with his son Jim at Donaghmore Creamery in 1950s.

when I was only nine months old. My mother was very interested and agreed to take some shares. As they were leaving, she asked how she could help them in relation to milk collection. They thought it would be a great idea and asked if she could put a vehicle on the road.

"At the time, we were doing hire work for the County Council and we also had a couple of steam engines and threshing machines and two men who helped with driving.

"My mother agreed to put a tractor and trailer on the road with one of the men to drive it. We started on Easter Monday 1947. The tractor was an old type Fordson Major and though I was only about seven years old, I went with the driver and we brought in some few cans of milk to Donaghmore. It was my first time in there and I remember sitting on one of the mudguards as we went along. No roll bars or cabs in those days.

"I thought the whole place looked very dilapidated with long grass, old farm implements and an Allis Chalmers tractor in the yard. There was no shop there then. We went in to the manager to get some more cans, hoping to try and get a few more people to send milk.

"We gradually got a milk round set up, which covered the districts of Ballagh, Clonmeen, Lismoracha, north and south Clonmeen, Kyle, Graigue, Cappalinnan, Cloneve, Harristown, Ballybuggy, Lyroguelane and on in to Donaghmore.

"Some of the people had been suppliers to Templetouhy Creamery and had those big heavy cans with the wide bottom, but as we were passing by their houses, they decided to change over to us. They had been going to Templetouhy by horse and cart.

"Some time in the 1950s, Peter Kilmartin called to my mother to enquire how she started as he was thinking of starting a milk run

Jim Hennessy, Christy Fitzpatrick, Lar Dunne working at Donaghmore Creamery 1950s.

in an adjoining area and would she mind. Kieran Bowe also called around the same time with a similar query. She had no objections to either of them as I was still quite young and could not drive and so she had no plans to expand at that time.

"After some time, things began to improve in Donaghmore. The place was tidied up, a new shop was built, and they were doing grinding and rolling also. Prior to that, a man used to come from Urlingford to Campions of Kyle, with a mobile type of grinder and the farmers around the area would bring grain for grinding and rolling.

"After many years, we decided to replace the tractor and trailer outfit with a lorry. After some time, another carter, Rody Loughman, died and part of his round went to Peter Kilmartin and part of Peter's round was given to me, which meant that we had a much bigger round.

"All of the carters decided to get better organised so we used to have monthly meetings at Mick Lalor's house in Abbeyleix. Our aim was to have a redundancy packet available whenever we would finish. Towards that aim, we made an arrangement with Donaghmore that for every £ we put in, they would do the same.

"There was a good relationship between management and the carters and by that time, there was quite a notable change for the better around the place.

"My time to drive came when I was of age to get a driving licence and I remember bringing out the many and varied items to customers on the return journey. I had to bring out day old chicks on a few occasions. In the earlier years, we even brought the milk cheques out for some time. Also in those earlier years, hygiene was a bit lax. I recall seeing one particular customer putting the milk into a can. She was using a piece of cloth with the strainer which proved to be rather slow so she removed the cloth and I could see that there were straws and other bits of material that one could find around a cow house. So it would seem that sometimes a separator had to extract more than just cream from the milk.

"Some years back, there was a rumour that some of the older buildings might be knocked. At the time, I was a member of Laois County Council and along with another council member, we got a preservation order issued declaring all the old buildings as 'listed buildings'.

"The Co-op movement was so powerful that it was really the greatest thing that ever happened. It gave farmers a new lease of life, having a regular cash flow, being able to get goods through the milk account, and able to organise themselves in a different way. It is such a wonderful organisation.

"The whole management structure at Donaghmore was really wonderful. People like J.P. Kelly and others went out and got money from farmers and others, to help them build their own business. Donaghmore Co-op shows what Irish people can do for themselves."

A group of employees of Donaghmore Creamery on an outing in 1958
Back row: Paddy Campion, Joe Shortt, Jim Crennan, Jack Fitzpatrick, Tom O'Hara, Mick Moore, Ned Moynan, Nicholas Percy, Seán Power.
Front row: John Fitzpatrick, Joe Nolan, Martin Williams, Tom Creagh.

Donaghmore employees on an outing in the 1960s
Eddie Bergin, J. Fitzpatrick, Donie Dowling, Seán Percy, Thomas Whelan, Tom O'Hara, J. Loughlin.

Personal Recollections – Raheen

Sadie Bennett
(nee Galbraith, Corbally, Abbeyleix)

"In the early 1940s during World War II, the country had a severe shock when an outbreak of foot and mouth disease was diagnosed on the farm of Peter Talbot between Ballacolla and Durrow in County Laois. Immediately, all necessary systems were set into action to get this contagious disease under control.

"On account of the amount of work operating in the creamery in Raheen as well as all other creameries in connection with farming, it was necessary to deal with the problem very seriously. The people bringing the milk were issued with rain gear and as each supplier arrived, the man and his outfit were sprayed with disinfectant from a hand operated stirrup pump.

"A channel about 6 inches in depth was dug out and filled with disinfectant. Animals and anything with wheels and the farmers had to pass through it and were thoroughly disinfected. While it lasted, it caused a lot of disruption. Animals or food could not be moved without a permit.

"World War II was at its height and members of the local Defence Force patrolled the roads on a rota basis to watch out for stray animals 24 hours of the day. Eventually everything was under control.

"When Raheen and Spink started, farmers brought the milk to them by whatever way best suited, mainly by horse and cart. That is where the milk was separated and the cream was taken to Donaghmore, where there was a creamery for the manufacture of butter. It was packed in wooden boxes and, from what I remember, each box held 56 x 1 lb rolls. There was great demand for these boxes and women turned them into useful items around a house, mainly seats and hold-all boxes, and covered them very nicely.

"I would say the manufacture of butter was the beginning of the end of making butter in farmers' houses. Some people missed the home-made butter very much, but it did not take long to get used to the change.

"When the creamery went into operation, it had a supply of cans suited to each farmer's need and each supplier purchased whatever size he or she could use. When the cream was taken from the milk, farmers brought home the skimmed milk in their cans to be fed to calves and pigs."

Richard (Dick) Lalor-Fitzpatrick
(Tinnakill)

"My late father supplied milk to Raheen Co-op when it first started in 1928. As far as I can recall, the price per gallon was 3 or 4 old pence, depending on butter

L-r.: Felix Bennett, Leo Mills, Mick Harding, Jimmy Hearns, Pat Lynch. Front: Fintan Graham at Raheen Creamery late 1950s.

fat. If the butter fat was very good, you might get up to 6 pence per gallon. It was pretty hard work at that time, as of course, milking was done by hand and then the milk was transported by pony and cart to the Co-op. As the Co-op was a new venture in the area, activity there was slow enough for some time, but gradually the Co-op idea was growing in confidence and the volume of milk supply began to increase steadily.

"As there was no electricity at the time, you had to use a lantern at milking time in the morning and evening when the days were short in the autumn and winter. I always tried to avoid night time milking by starting early enough to be finished before dark. In most cases, the maximum number of cows would have been around 10 or 12.

"One local man who contributed in no small measure to the advancement of the Co-op was the late George Galbraith, who was a founding committee member and always had a keen interest in the whole Co-op idea. In fact, not only then but as long as he was able, he continued to have a great interest in Raheen and Donaghmore and later in Avonmore. He also had a great interest in livestock and would have been a well-known figure at all the local shows.

"You went down with your milk in those rather heavy cans of the time and got your quota of skimmed milk. Then later, when a store was opened, you brought back any meal requirements. This was very handy as you did all your shopping in the one journey.

"All went fairly well until 1941, when the foot and mouth disease showed in the locality. You could only bring the cans of milk. You could not have any sacks or straw or such like on the cart. Down there, you had to go through disinfectant with the pony and cart and be hosed down yourself also. There were problems also for people who cut turf locally, as they were not allowed bring any of the usual type of material such as straw

L-r.: Gerry Conroy, Jimmy Hearns and Ben Moran, at Raheen Creamery, late 1950s.

and hay, which were used to put over bushes at the top of the previous year's filled up boghole. So they had to manage as best they could with rushes, heather and so on for that one year.

"During the late 1930s and during the war years, the local LDF were active in the area. The late Paul Hurley and myself used to cycle to Abbeyleix, around midnight, and take up duty in the local courthouse until 3 am. We used the old carbide lamps on our bikes and while they were a pretty good light, you could have problems on a wet or windy night. There were usually a few others there also in a room. Our 'B' section was only for the dispatch of messages. There was a radio link with key people outside.

"I remember the late Seamus Dooley being sent out to Derrykearn wood to cut long stakes, which were put up in a large field nearby, owned by the Breen family. The idea was to keep planes from landing. There would also be a certain amount of foot patrol, particularly during that year of foot and mouth to watch out for possible movement of animals from one location to another.

"I recall a particular type of tractor we had, probably in the 1950s. It was an Allis Chalmers, which was bought up in McGees, Ardee, Co. Louth. It was unusual, having its two front wheels – which were called twins – situated in the centre, with only less than a foot between them. It was a TVO model, was fairly 'nifty' on the road, but was not ideal for ploughing or using in drills. Still, we managed okay and used it for 5 or 6 years.

"When Macra na Feirme was set up in Abbeyleix, I served on the committee along with George Galbraith. It was through him that I became a member of the Co-op committee. I was also on the local advisory committee for a few years. In the early 1970s, when Avonmore was set up, it was a great step forward for Donaghmore and Raheen and opened up a whole new era in the Co-op movement, which was of great benefit to suppliers, which by now had increased a great deal."

William McGrath
(Cashel, Portlaoise)

"I joined the local area committee in 1979, having been informed of a vacancy in the Ballyroan district, by the late John Hosey – who was a member at the time.

"It so happened that at the very first meeting, at which I was co-opted, there was also a vacancy for a secretary. I was elected to that post on that same night and remained as secretary for the next 10 years. Later holders of that post were: John Hosey (Jnr), Gerard Phelan and the present holder is Pat Keegan. I have also been on the regional committee since 1987. Jim Clifford was the manager when I joined. He replaced Joe Butler, who retired in 1979, having served in Raheen for 47 years. I enjoyed meeting with other farmers and hearing their opinions and feel that, as a result, we could offer some help and advice to our farming colleagues.

"Going to bulk collection was a very important step forward for the Co-op. That happened back in the early 1970s and it introduced some important changes including a very strict quality control. But it also meant the beginning of the end of the new dairy in Raheen, and lots of cans and many lorries and drivers were made redundant.

"Our milk was collected by Felix Bennett's lorries and later by a local man, William Carter, using a tractor and trailer.

"On one occasion, I had to help a local neighbour to get out their milk for collection. There were three full cans being brought out on the frame of a pram with boards across it – it was a bit weak. So, the man and wife lifted off the first can and on to the waiting trailer. Then I lifted off the second can and of course, the third one just tipped over and the full can of milk spilled onto the roadside. Needless to say, they were not too pleased. One spouse accused the other and said nothing to me, even though it was partly my fault – though not intentionally."

Tony Sinnott
(Ardlea, Mountrath)

"My first job with the Raheen Co-op was in 1941 on Derrykearn bog, cutting and saving turf. Initially, we had to clean and prepare the spreading ground. It was full of trees and briars and had not been used for a long time. There were a number of drains to be cleaned also. Mick Lalor of Corbally, who was working in the Co-op at the time, would come down when finished in the dairy and he helped me to get water flowing through the drains.

"There was no bog hole as such, as the bog around that area had slipped in over past years. So we rolled out huge 'dodges'[1] to one side of the bank and cut branches off the trees, and used them and other suitable material to make a hut between the 'dodges', having left a space between them.

"Jim Phelan of Coole was the principal slane's man[2] and John Lalor of Corbally made the barrows. The spreading bank was two perches wide and quite long. Wheeling out the turf was done in relays. Each person would go about 20 yards and hand over to the next and so on. There were perhaps six lads there generally, and up to ten at times – depending on what was being done.

"The season could be from April to September or October, depending on the weather. When the turf was dry, it was drawn to George Galbraith's yard in Corbally. Some of Galbraiths' trees were cut down to make space for the large amount of turf. A wall was made with these trees, by nailing them to the line of upright trees. They could then pile up the turf quite high and only had to clamp the front rows.

"At that time, there was a kind of laneway, from the main Portlaoise to Abbeyleix road to Galvin's railway house, which continued to the bog. The loads would be brought up to the railway, and the attendant at the level crossing, Johnny Galvin, would open the gates and let them through and up to Galbraiths, which was quite near the railway exit.

"There was one particular day we had a rather slow donkey with a cart full of turf, when the donkey decided to stop for a rest – while crossing the railway line. There was soon a shout from a junior Galvin to get that … (expletive deleted) … ass off the line, as there was a train due any minute. So we had to almost lift the donkey off the line. Sure, it was a bit of a laugh for a while but there was a little hint of worry there also. The harvesting of turf lasted for maybe five or six years.

"I just recall a time when there was a poultry market held at the Co-op for a few years, just before Christmas. There was one year, a goose flew away. Myself and another man were sent to try and catch it. It got into the river stream nearby and escaped. Years later, I met the man and asked him what ever happened. He said 'I caught it that night'. He did not tell me if it was the goose or the 'flu' he caught."

Liam McCabe
(Colt, Ballyroan)

"My first contact with Donaghmore was in 1952, when, as a qualified electrician, I was wiring the house of J.P. Kelly. When finished with him, I was asked to do some jobs in Donaghmore, including the hatchery.

"The dairy and stores were the chief buildings there at that time and there was only one motor required to drive the mill roller. Then they installed a grain drier in the front buildings, where the museum is now. When I was wiring the dairy, there were fitters there from Limerick, putting in tanks, stainless steel pipes and other equipment. I could not start my work until they would leave each evening, which meant that it was often three or four o'clock next morning when I would finish so that the creamery could take in milk later on.

"There was one particular night that I fitted fourteen motors. It was only some time later that I found out that J.P. Kelly had placed a bet with someone that the majority of the motors would go in the right direction. So, by mere luck, 13 of the 14 were right and J.P. was delighted.

"Over the next forty five years, I was engaged to do all the wiring jobs in Donaghmore, and some branches – mainly Raheen and Spink, and a little in Mountmellick.

"I started my training in 1941 with the ESB in Portlaoise and it continued for five years. Then the rural electrification started in 1948 and I left the ESB and started on my own.

"One of the first places where I worked was in Clonaslee in 1948. I only had a bike, and on it, I carried a step ladder, cables, and tools – all of which could weigh a cwt or so. Living in Colt, I would stay out during the week and cycle home at weekends.

"The first car I bought was a baby Ford for £30 in 1949. It had very little more than the engine – no brakes, no lights, and so on - so after a few 'escapes', I decided to get a van. That was a big step forward as, apart from getting me and my ladder and tools around the country, I was able to go to Dublin for my requirements, rather than having them sent by rail to Portlaoise, as there were no wholesale outlets down the country in those years.

"So, after starting to contract with Donaghmore, as time progressed, so did my work. With many new buildings, and the need for bigger and more high-powered motors, I was always kept very busy."

John Seale
(Clonboyne, Portlaoise)

"In 1950 or 1951, myself and my neighbour, Andy Carter, had a chat about milk and decided to go to Mr. Butler, who was manager of Raheen branch, with a view to putting a lorry on the road to collect milk. He informed us that he would not do so because it would not pay the Co-op to do so.

"So I decided to approach people, starting locally and going up to Derrough crossroads in Ballyfin. At first, some people were not very interested in the idea but after a while, they decided to give it a try anyway. Money was scarce at the time and I could not afford to buy a good lorry. I went to England to a wedding and had

Staff at Raheen Creamery late 1950s
Back (L-r.): Tom Scully, Dan Burke, Mick Carroll,
Tom Carroll.
Front: Joe Ryan, Dan Drennan, Mick Lalor.

a chat about the idea with my sisters over there. They gave me £200 coming home, which was regarded as a lot of money at that time. Wondering as to how best to spend it, I went to a man I knew in the business, the late Dick Morgan. He sold me a small 30 cwt. lorry, and I started collecting milk from the grand total of just six suppliers.

"With that lorry, which I bought for £115, I was more often under it than over it. Anyway, I carried on with just the six suppliers and I used to send little notes to farmers, saying I would meet them at a certain crossroads and at a certain time. There I would stand on my little soap box, to try and encourage them to increase my load. None of those people had ever sent milk to a creamery anywhere and perhaps some may not even have been aware that the Co-op was there at all. So, every now and then, I would go and say to those who were sceptical: 'did you ever change your mind?' 'Well, I did, and there's another fellow down the road – you might know him – he's changed his mind too.' At that stage, it was more of a cost on me, than a profit. Gradually, after a lot of trying, my load increased to around 15 collections. I kept going and when summer time came the next year, I had less empty space on the little lorry.

"The old lorry was my livelihood but keeping it going was often a problem. I recall one day coming from Ballyfin, when the housing split and 14 studs fell on the

Pictured at Raheen Creamery late 1950s
Back (L-r.): Jim Harding, John Maybury.
Front: Dan Burke, Ned Moynan, Mick Harding and
John Carter.

road at Derrough cross roads. All the oil leaked out and there were just two studs left at the top of the cracked housing. I had a full load and I was very worried as to how I was going to get the milk to Raheen. I somehow got word to Joe Butler. He sent out a lorry to bring in the milk I had collected.

"Sometime after that I was in Raheen and was called into the office by Joe Butler. The late J.P. Kelly, who was one of the principal people in Donaghmore from the start, was there also and said to me: 'Seale, have you any money?' 'I haven't Mr. Kelly' (which I hadn't). He suggested that I should buy a new lorry, a bigger one. He said that he knew of a two ton lorry being available and that we would get the money somewhere! He asked if I would go with him and we agreed on a day and went to Hennessy's of Castledermot – the Austin dealers.

"There was this lovely shiny lorry, only ten months old, taxed for the year and I nearly got a pain in my eyes looking at it. A price was given for it. 'Would you like it John?' 'Sure why wouldn't I, Mr. Kelly, it's only 10 months old and as good as new!' He put up the surety and I bought the lorry for £300. I went and collected it soon after and I felt I was on top of the world in that cab. I'm not sure what became of the old one but I think it went to the scrap heap.

"In the late autumn and winter time, the supply always fell back a fair amount and you might only have half the amount of milk coming in. Again, Mr. Kelly was aware of the situation and he suggested that perhaps I could do other work in the slack time. I'd buy turnips and take them to Dublin and bring back a load of manure. That would amount to a good day's wage for two days a week. With the milk supply gradually increasing over the next few years, I found I should go for a larger lorry and I bought a five ton Austin. I still retained the two ton lorry and continued the two way transactions.

"The bigger lorry had an added advantage during the harvest time, when I was able to bring in loads of grain. As time passed, I was able to get bigger lorries as the needs arose. In addition to the milk runs, I could draw grain in and out, manure, timber and other goods to and from Dublin, and even up North. During the good years, I had to get a top deck or tier fitted in order to cope with the expansion in milk supply. The tier held approximately half the amount that would fit on the floor.

"Of course, you also had to do a lot of shopping for your customers, according to what space you had. Anything from 1 lb of butter to maybe half a ton of meal and that happened over a span of 25 years or so, up to when the cans gave way to the bulk tanker.

"When bringing back goods to suppliers, you sometimes were expected to do a little above what might be regarded as normal. On a particular day, a farmer wanted a quantity of a particular brand of meal, which he regarded as being the best. I'm not sure if the brand required was in stock or not, but anyway, I brought a different brand out and the person would not accept it. So it was brought back again and changed into a sack with the favoured brand name on it and returned to customer on the next visit. The customer was delighted, saying that the other brand was no use at all. The pigs did not notice any difference, as I never heard of any complaints or any reduction in their numbers.

"During the better years, when my loads were quite large, I had to have a helper, but I held out as long as possible, as I simply could not afford to pay one. There were problems also where suppliers did not have a stand or platform for their cans – which in the earlier years were quite heavy – and you had to plead with them to erect a stand or the milk would not be collected."

Fintan Graham
(Rathbrennan, Portlaoise - Vet. Surgeon based in Mountrath)

"I hail from Rathbrennan, near Portlaoise, and the first milk collected from around our area was brought in by Jack Corcoran, who was actually from around the Clonkeen area. I remember my late father went around with him canvassing for suppliers. Up to that time, people were making their own butter and feeding calves with the milk. I think that would have been around the early 1950s. Jack had a rather small lorry and did not continue for too many years. The collection was then continued by the brothers Jack and Jerry Conroy from Ballyfin area, which lasted for a number of years, and was then taken over by Felix Bennett. I think that was around 1957 and Felix remained on that run, until he died in 1963.

"In the earlier years when Jack Conroy was driving, I would go with him when I had holidays from the N.S. In later years, when I was a student in college, at holiday time I drove for and helped Felix Bennett, on a few occasions. He had other helpers/drivers at various times, such as Patsy Heffernan, Jack Bowe and Pat Lynch.

"After Felix died, Mrs. Bennett continued to operate the lorry and also, because of extra suppliers and extra work, put a tractor and trailer on a different route under the command of Andy Lambe. I think that continued until the bulk collection started.

"Felix covered part of Ballyfin, into Portlaoise via Mountmellick Road and out around Eyne, Rathevan, Ballyclider, Ballyroan, Abbeyleix and out to the old original creamery at Raheen via the main roads."

Seán Reilly
(Rathmoyle House, Abbeyleix)

"I was first elected to the committee of Donaghmore Co-op, Raheen branch, in 1957. The vacancy occurred by the retirement of the late Rody McEvoy. My name was proposed by the late George Galbraith. I remained a member for 25 years, until 1982. My late father, Tom Reilly, was one of the earliest shareholders.

"We were usually picked up for the monthly meetings in Donaghmore by Mick Lalor at 6pm. Other members along the route included Mick Walsh, Murty McWey, George Galbraith and Paddy Shiel. Those meetings would start at 8pm and we would usually be home between 1 and 2am the next morning. It was all voluntary on our part. We were fortunate enough not to have to cycle there, however, as apparently some members had to in the early years of the Co-op.

"I recall that at one particular meeting, when manager Billy Wallis informed us that the bushel weight system for grain, was being replaced by a metric system. I suppose it was a sign of things to come later, when the European bosses would dictate what we might or might not do.

"Joe Butler had his little office in Raheen at the end of a store. I bought a sheep shearing machine from Joe and 2/6 per month was stopped from my account to pay for it. That would have been a common enough occurrence in those times, when money was scarce and a half crown was worth a lot.

"One thing the committee looked forward to each year was the annual outing. They were organised by the late J.P. Kelly, and everything was always set up and timed very exactly. On one occasion, our trip was to Dublin airport. George

L.-r.: P. J. Lalor and Paddy Fitzpatrick packing the shelves at Spink Shop in 1980s.

Liam Brophy, Killadooley, bringing milk to the Creamery in the 1970s.

Famous hurlers D.J. Carey and Declan Ryan pictured with Julie Ann Lupton at Donaghmore Open Day in November 2002.

Hurling star D.J. Carey pictured with Christy Fitzpatrick at Donaghmore Open Day in November 2002.

At Donaghmore Open Day in November 2002 were Kilkenny hurling star D.J. Carey and Gerard Lawler.

Opening of Avonmore Home and Farm Shop at Spink, Circa 1987
(L.-r.): Betty McGuire, Trudy Nealon (Portlaoise Mill), P. J. Lalor, Carmel Fitzpatrick,
Tim Costigan, Jack O'Shea, Fr. Kelly P.P. Ballinakill), Fr. Cummins (Heywood), Pat Alley
(Avonmore), John Miller (Area Committee), Hugh Harkin (Manager Feed Division,
Portlaoise Mill), John Carroll, Jim Ring, Paddy Fitzpatrick.

Presentation of I.S.O. 9002 by the Minister for Agriculture, Joe Walsh, in 1991 at
Portlaoise Mill
Front row (l. to r.): Seamus Coady, Kieran Delaney, John Comerford, Brian Brennan,
James Fitzpatrick, Tom Salmon, Eamon Delaney and Peter McEvoy.
Back row (l. to r.): Seán Hearn, Mary McEvoy, John Scannell, Mary Larkin, Dave Delaney,
Seamus Greene, Padraig Fleming, Mary Donoghue, Nicky Mulhall, Minister for
Agriculture, Joe Walsh, P. A. O'Neill, Geraldine Cullen, Tom Kerr, Trudy Nealon, Shirley
Bennett, Denis Bergin, Donal Williams and Derek Gaffney.

Staff, present and former, with some famous guests at Donaghmore Branch Open Day on 5/11/'02
Front row (l. to r.): John Kinahan, Noreen Behan, Kilkenny hurler D.J. Carey with the McCarthy Cup, Conor Phelan, John Kilmartin, Branch Rep. Diarmuid Everard, Tipperary hurler Declan Ryan, Paddy Daly and John Galvin.
Back row (l. to r.): James Phelan (Area Manager), Murtagh McWey (Branch Manager), Diarmuid Doran, Billy Finnane, Anthony Delaney and Joseph Walsh.

Donaghmore 1974
Back (l.-r.): Mary McEvoy, Geraldine O'Gorman, Teresa Fitzpatrick, Teresa Breen.
Front: Noreen Dunne, Noreen Hyland.
(Three had birthdays on same day – 20, 21, 22).

A selection of old dairy equipment preserved at Donaghmore Museum.

Presentation to Richard Palmer (Shanahoe) – National Milk Supplier of the Year 1982
Front row (l. to r.): Seán Hearn, John Miller, Richard Palmer, Maureen Palmer, Bobby Bennett and Bernard Rochford.
Second row: John Kirwan, Patrick J. Phelan, Hugh Cole, Liam Delaney, Laurence Phelan and Padraig Culliton.
Back row: Bill Delaney, Murtagh McWey, William Maher, Michael Delaney.

Pictured at Donaghmore Open Day on 5th November 2002 were present and former committee members

Front row (l. to r.): Liam Delaney, William Maher, Bobby Bennett, Loughlin Campion, Thomas Phelan, Patrick Duggan, John Dunne, Laurence Phelan, Freddie Bailey, Martin Bergin and Murtagh McWey (Donaghmore Area Manager).

Back row (l. to r.): Niall Bennett, Donal Hynes, Patrick Dooley, Joseph Morrin, William Carroll, Seán Bergin, Sylvester Phelan, Thomas Hogan, Trevor Walsh, Canice Hyland, Joseph Walsh

Near the end of grain season in Raheen – September 1998.

The Donaghmore hurling team that won county honours in 1986

Front row (l. to r.): Donal Williams, Seán O'Dea, Jimmie Fitzpatrick, John Byrne, Jim Ring, Tommy Gorman, P. J. Gorman, John Bergin, Michael Fitzpatrick, Pat Fitzpatrick.

Back row: (l. to r.): Joe Nolan, Jimmie Daly, Seán Hyland, P. J. Lalor, Val McCartney, Liam Phelan, Peter Grey, John Tynan, Michael Dowling, Jimmie Hanlon, John O'Dea, Owen Coss, Billy Moylan and Padraig Fleming.

Presentation to Bobby Bennett to mark his retirement from the Board of Avonmore in 1993

Front row (l. to r.): Pat Brophy, Martin Keane, Lar Phelan, Tom Kelly, Bobby Bennett, Thomas Mather, John Miller, Liam Delaney and James Cooney.

Middle row (l. to r.): Michael Delaney, Michael Igoe, James Shortall, Murtagh McWey, George Byrne, James Mahon, Brian Fox, Bernie Rochford, John McEvoy, John Dunne, Paddy Dooley and John Nolan.

Back row (l. to r.): Patrick D. Brickley, Michael Mahon, Chris Horan, Hugh Cole, Billy Flynn, Paddy McHugh, John Delaney, Richard Whelan and Gerry O'Brien.

Galbraith and myself were up at the top area, watching planes take off, when we heard a shout from J.P.: 'Do you know what time it is, the bus is leaving.' So, while we were perhaps two of the most likely to observe a time schedule, there we were, caught by the ever keen J.P.

"Perhaps on the same outing we were in some hotel or restaurant, when a waitress brought some cups to our table. She held them with her fingers inside the cups. A very annoyed J.P. told her quite firmly to take back those cups and have them washed and, in future, to catch them properly by the handles when serving customers."

J.J. Campion
(Rushin, Mountrath)

"When Tom Delaney started as a carter, near the end of the 1950s, I sent milk with him for a while and later, my son continued until the new regulations about updating cow sheds were introduced. So, we gave up at that stage.

"I was elected to the local area committee in Raheen in the early 1970s. At one of those meetings, one member asked Reddy Brennan of Avonmore, who was present, why farmers should continue to supply milk when there was already a 'milk lake' in the country. Mr. Brennan advised all present to continue sending milk as a time would come when a quota system would be set up and the more milk the farmer sent, the higher their quota would be. That was very good advice as the quota system did indeed come in a year or so later.

"I enjoyed being at the monthly meetings, which were always sure to provide a good lively debate and of course, there was sure to be a few awkward questions raised. Also, the annual social event, whether an outing or otherwise, was always eagerly looked forward to. When you attain a certain age you have to retire, but I was allowed to stay on for some years extra, but with no voting rights.

"One of the memories that people of my age group has, is about certain items which were available through the black market outlets, of which there were a few in every town and village, and some of the rural huckster shops. Tea was perhaps the most common among those items. There was one such place in a local town. One day a woman called to get some tea but the shop was closed. She called to a house nearby and inquired if they knew where the shop owner might be. The man of the house inquired if she was looking for anything in particular. The woman said she wanted to get some tea. Now, there was quite a large family in this house, and they had accumulated a big amount of tea. The man of the house said that he had a couple of pounds of tea that he got from the local shop and that she could have it for £2. The woman was delighted. Later, the woman was back in town again and called in to the shop. She told from whom she had got the tea, and that the man had told her he had bought it from that same shop. 'Well, indeed he did not get it from me', said the shop-owner in disgust. When she had left, he went out to tell off the informant. 'I didn't know that you were in the black market as well', he complained.

"One time many years ago, I was in the Mater Hospital in Dublin and there was a staff sister there, who was from my own area of Rushin. One day she said to me 'Do you know who I have in here as a patient?' I said I didn't and she said 'The president, Mr. De Valera. Would you like to see him?' I said I would love to see him.

Joe Ryan, Jimmy Hearns and Dan Burke at Raheen Creamery, late 1950s.

So she took me to the private area where he was and I had a great chat with him for an hour or so. We talked about the economic war era and he had great praise for the loyalty of the small farmers during that time. 'They stood by me when others were against me,' he said. 'When I went for election in Clare, the small farmers and the workers all stood by me.'

"I remember the hard times well. Pims of Mountmellick used to buy pigs every week at the pub in Ballyfin and I recall a local farmer who had four pigs, which weighed 16 stone each, and all he could get was £2 apiece for them. Another man sold a sow for £1-10-0. I went to a man who had potatoes to sell and I bought a barrel for five shillings. Times were very hard and only that the farmers had their own milk and butter, it would have been so much worse.

"Talking about tough times, 1947 was a very bad year. We had a crop of wheat in a low lying field. At harvest time, it was very wet and I remember walking along the headlands and looking across the field. You could see a green tint all over the crop, where the wheat had sprouted and was growing, with water still lying on the ground. I tried using a mowing machine and horses but had to abandon that idea, as the horses were sinking in the muddy ground. We also tried a binder and likewise that failed. There was only one option left – to cut it with scythes, which we did.

"Because of the emergency that year, people from towns were asked to call to farmers all around to offer help. We got our 5 acres cut and stacked and later in October, the weather improved and we were actually able to use a tractor to draw the wheat from the field. After we threshed and took the grain to a local miller, I told him that a few bags were not too good. 'Forget about it', he said, 'it's wheat and that is what we want'. If that happened now, you would not get rid of it so easily and you'd consider yourself lucky if it were taken for feed use.

Pictured at Raheen Creamery late 1950s
L-r.: Gerry Conroy, Joe Ryan, Jim Harding and Pat Lynch.
Front: Jimmy Hearns.

"Before I finish I'll tell you another story. Myself and a friend were visiting a certain house one night years back, when only a few houses had TV. There was the mother and two of her three sons and the TV was turned on at the time. It had been bought by a third son, who worked in Dublin. We remarked to her, how lucky she was to have a TV. 'Ah,' she said, 'it's grand to watch the news and other programmes but Lord save us, there's some awful things on it, in front of the young lads.' The 'young lads' were nearer to 60 than 50 and we didn't get any idea of how often they were allowed to watch it."

Editor's note: It is with deep regret we note the passing of J.J. Campion since this interview. Sincere sympathy is extended to his wife and family.

Essie Galvin
(nee Lalor, Corbally, Abbeyleix)

"My brother, Johnny, worked with the creamery in Raheen from the day that it opened in 1928. He had to cycle to Donaghmore for a week or two, to learn how to operate the steam engine. Tim Kelleher was the manager at Raheen. He was from Cork but was staying in a house in Colt, which was owned by the Galbraith family. For the first few years there were only the two of them there.

"Johnny left in 1934 and went to England, hoping to get a better-paid job. He was only earning 10 shillings a week while in the Co-op. After Johnny left, my brother Mick went to work there for a short while, driving an old gas lorry. It was very cumbersome and hard to manage and, as far as I know, it had solid rubber wheels. In the meantime, Joe Butler and Ernest Keegan had come to work there. Mick collected a few cans of milk around the area, and took the cream to Donaghmore also. Mick stayed for a few years, then he got a job in Portlaoise. Sometime in the early 1950's, he went to Australia, where he remained until he died some years ago.

"In 1954 my brother, Johnny, was back on home soil again and, with Jim Phelan of Roskelton, also a tradesman and builder, was involved in building the bigger store at Raheen. Towards the end of the job, in November 1954, when they were plastering the walls, the P.P., Fr. Coyne, died. They immediately had to abandon the plastering to go dig the grave for Fr. Coyne, who had been in Raheen for many years.

"In the very early years in Raheen, on a wall in the creamery, there was a small oblong type of plaque, done in concrete with the initials 'J.L.' thereon. One day J.P. Kelly was going through a nearby door, and seeing the letters, he enquired from Johnny as to who did it. Johnny did not do it and told him so. J.P. said, 'Well, whoever did it wasn't doing much for the creamery'.

"Also in the very early years there was a dry toilet down in the wood, which was between the river and the creamery. It seemed that it was used only by the manager, from Cork. On one occasion an inspector called, and after he paid a visit to the loo and found that it was not as good as perhaps it might be, he suggested that it should be cleaned. 'Well,' said Johnny, 'I'll clean out no toilet after any Corkman!'"

John Galvin
(Essie's son, Colt, Ballyroan)

"In the late 1960's when I worked in Kelly's Structural Steel Co. I was involved in making the first steel portions for the factory in Ballyragget. The first job I started

A happy group at Raheen Creamery 1950s.
L.-r: Joe Ryan, Joe Bonham, Mrs. Bonham, Anne Mulhall
and Ben Moran. Front: Jimmy Hearns.

in Raheen in 1979 was making doors for the new dairy. Its original ones were wooden and, with so much water splashing around, wooden doors were not a good idea.

"It's ironic that some of my work involved knocking stores or sheds that my uncle, Johnny, had been involved in building. While I was dismantling the new dairy in 1997, I fell from the roof and was in hospital for a few days but, thankfully, I had no serious injury. I began to think that, perhaps, I was having bad luck for what I was doing.

"Uncle Johnny often mentioned that, at the rear of the creamery, there was a bog hole or two near the river, which flows by and forms the boundary on one side. In relation to the bog holes, local people will know that it's only a few hundred yards to a corner of the local Derrykearn bog, where turf had been cut many years ago.

"One of my uncles often told me that when the store was being built, a type of hammer – property of the company – was lost somewhere in the building. It was a special implement, known as a slater's tool. The management was very annoyed, lots of questions were asked, and they were convinced it was stolen. Many years later, when that same store was being knocked to increase the yard space, I was dismantling the roof and I found the long-lost tool."

T.C. Phelan
(Coole, Abbeyleix)

Tom Phelan, Fox-boro, and formerly of Coole, was in Raheen Creamery, with his father, on the day it

Pictured at Raheen Creamery in late 1950s.
L.-r.: Tom Carroll, Jimmy Phelan, Mick Carroll,
John Maybury, Seán Tyrrell, Joe Ryan and Jim Bonham.

opened. He was only seven years old at the time but clearly remembers bringing in the milk, "just the one can", by donkey and cart.

Fr. Coyne, P.P., was a neighbour and kept some cows. Paddy Holland worked for him and brought down his milk to the Creamery. Tom also remembers a horse and dray passing his door with cans of milk.

In his early days the Phelans, like so many other small farming families, used to separate their own milk and make their own butter with a turn-over churn. Fr. Coyne was a customer for their butter and they sold some in nearby Abbeyleix.

During the war years, classes in agriculture and cookery were held on different nights in the old school at Raheen. The young men would go to the agricultural classes and the young ladies to the cookery ones. But often the lads would have as much, if not more, interest in what was going on in the cookery classes. "Perhaps it was the delicious odour wafting over the hill that drew the lads like a magnet in that direction," Tom surmises. "On one such night the lads knew that it was chicken that was on the menu. A few of them gathered outside the window at the rear and someone shouted: 'If that's a cock, you'll all crow on the way home.'"

Tom recalled selling bonhams in Abbeyleix for as little as fifteen shillings. "Sometimes I might have a few stronger bonhams to sell and a 'jobber' would ask what I wanted for them. I would allow myself for a bit of a drop and would look for twenty three shillings. The jobber would say, 'I'll give you a ploughman' – and the deal was done." The ploughman was the old £1 note.

A surprising windfall came Tom's way one day as he was going to the fair in Abbeyleix with a pig for sale. He met a friend on the road who told him that there was a buyer down from the north, parked on the Raheen side of the town, who was anxious to buy as many pigs as he could before they were snapped up at the fair. Tom was advised to look for a little extra for his pig. He was hoping to get £13, so he looked for £16. "Let it in here," said the buyer, pointing to his trailer. "A chance meeting had put an extra three quid in my pocket that day," Tom reflected with a smile.

The Burke connection –
(Tunduff, Abbeyleix)

The late Dan Burke worked in Raheen from 1949 until the late 1970s. Most of his work was in the dairy but on non-milk days, he was willing to fall in wherever he was required, in the store, at grain or on the lorries. Dan continued to work up to the time the bulk collection of milk started in the late 1970s.

Dan's son, John, started in Raheen in 1959. He did general store work and various jobs including testing milk. He was a helper on the lorry driven by Mick Lalor for some time. After a few years in the office, John was appointed as sales representative around 1970, and he still works in that capacity.

John's sister, Stella McHugh, started in Raheen as a typist in 1965. In her time there an N.C.R. Odhner accounting machine was introduced. It was considered a giant step forward at the time. On it, the monthly milk accounts statements were produced, and those with a cheque value were then sent to Donaghmore to have manual cheques issued. Stella worked in Raheen for about ten years until her marriage.

Jim Phelan
(Coole, Abbeyleix)

Ger Lawler, who carried out many of the interviews mentioned in this book, was told by Essie Lalor, that a local woman, Maggie Kelly, who lived about 200 yards from Raheen Creamery, used to come down her field to the little river, which forms part of the Co-op boundary, cross over the river by means of a wooden plank and collect a bucket of water from the creamery well. It was the only source of water in the immediate vicinity. Jim Phelan was able to confirm this.

Jim also told him that George Galbraith and Martin Farrell of Cromogue, were two people who worked on levelling the site for the new creamery back in the 1920s. "There was a bit of a hill on part of the site, which may have been sandy, as across the road in what was Dowling's land, there was a small area of hill, which contained a sandpit."

An interest of Jim's was the local bog. He has a happy story to tell about it. Martin Keegan, father of Ernest, who is mentioned in Ger Lawler's reminiscences, used to cut turf there. "Martin's wife was on the bog one afternoon rearing turf and, while crossing a plank over a partly filled-in bog hole, she slipped and fell in. I was the last person leaving the bog and, luckily, I heard her cry for help. I got her out and on to the cart and took her to her home."

Mick Lalor
(Ring, Colt, Ballyroan)

Mick Lalor worked in Raheen from 1952 until 1978. He took over from Ned Rothwell as lorry driver covering many areas, including milk collection, delivering cream to Donaghmore and later to Ballyragget. But the greater part of his work was in bringing in and distributing the millstuff and fertilisers.

Mick's truck could carry over twenty tons of fertilisers and he would usually do two runs a day from New Ross or Wicklow. "In the earlier years myself and a helper would load by hand. At a later stage there was a type of a lift fitted on the end of lorries. It was spring loaded and a bit cumbersome. Then later, fork-lifts and pallets were introduced and that surely was a welcome innovation," he says.

Mick recalled that in later years the millers introduced a smaller 4 st bag which was much easier to handle than the bulky ones of old. The smaller bags were ideal for making pillow covers, he related.

During some of his earlier years, he collected milk for Spink Creamery. He started in the Ballyroan area, then on to Timahoe and into Spink. "While returning with the cans, you would usually have some bags of meal to deliver." He also drew milk into the old creamery (McDonnells) in Spink for a while.

In later years, he drew milk to the Avonmore plant in Ballyragget. "In fact, I was the first lorry driver to draw milk in there," he stated. "I was now starting at 4am and you could never say when you expected to finish. Maybe when I got home, there could be a message from people whose tanks were full and I would have to help them as best I could. I also had to take milk down to Kilmanagh and, generally, I would clock up over 300 miles a day, for a year. Then, around 1976, I got brucel-losis. I had the symptoms for a couple of years, but eventually I was unable to continue and had to bow out."

Gerard Lawler
(Colt, Ballyroan)

Gerard Lawler, originally from Colt, and a chief researcher for this book, worked for Donaghmore Co-op, mostly at the Raheen Branch, for over fifty years. He was only thirteen years of age and on holidays from school, "having done the primary cert, which in those years was completed in 6th class. I was still wearing the short pants which were the norm for boys in those days." He was down in Raheen one day and the manager, Joe Butler, told him there was a job going and asked him would he be interested? It was a choice between a job and going back to school. He took the job.

His first work was in the dairy department, mainly dispensing the skim milk and washing up. He would also give a helping hand with lifting the cans of milk and emptying them into a weighing-in tank. Joe Butler, apart from his manager's role, would be involved in milk intake. Joe Ryan was in the store and Ernest Keegan in the dairy.

Each supplier had a milk record card. The manager would note on it the amount of milk received, measured in lbs, and the amount of skim milk to return to the farmer. Ernest showed Ger how to dispense the skim milk.

"From a large galvanised tank, resting on two supports, four feet high, a fairly large outlet pipe fed the skim milk into a round galvanised tank, with a scales hanging from a pulley, which moved along a support unit. At the outlet of the round tank a cloth, usually made from a flour bag, would hang to enable the skim flow into the cans without splashing. That was the ideal situation but there could be some old-style shorter cans or a cart lower than the usual, which could cause some problems."

Ger explained the entire separating process from his vast first-hand experience. "The first job in the dairy was to light a fire in the boiler to raise steam, which was a vital component for every phase of the dairy operation. Turf was the usual fuel in my time, but coal and timber could also be used. The turf was stored in a large shed, adjacent to the old dairy. Steam would be raised to a recommended pressure. There was a glass pipe on the outside of the boiler, within a protective glass case, which indicated the level of water in the boiler. While the boiler was heating up, the engine would be started. From a pulley on the engine, a long belt went up to one of a number of pulleys, fitted on a long shaft, which extended from wall to wall across the dairy. For some operations a second pulley ran idle beside the operating one. One such example was on a water-pump. Each morning you got a bucket of water and a siphon and used it to raise water, which was pumped from a nearby well. There was a lid on top of the pump and when water appeared, you moved a lever which brought the belt on to the spare pulley and closed the lid. Then the belt was pushed back on the other pulley and water was pumped up into a large galvanised tank, located high up near the roof, so as to give a good gravity feed.

"There was a piece of timber inside the tank from which a piece of twine was strung over a spool at the top and down to the bottom of the tank outside, with a large weight attached. When the tank was full, the weight outside would be at the bottom. Then you could put the belt on the idle pulley until required again.

"While all that was happening, parts of the separator would be assembled. A heavy bowl was first fitted on a spindle, followed by a second unit on which the

"Spike" McCormack and John Seale at Raheen Creamery 1950s.

discs were placed. There was one special heavy disc which was last on and there was a clamp which was designed to fit over the discs and then screwed onto the bowl and tightened.

"At that stage you would generally be ready to start taking in milk. If there was a second staff person available, he would empty the milk into a weighing scales. It was weighed by means of two different weights, which you moved by hand along two slide bars, with weight figures printed on them. If the weight was over 100 lbs, you used the bigger one, and for less or in between each 100 lbs, you would use the smaller one, until the bar tilted freely up and down. Then, having taken a sample, the milk was released into a much bigger tank underneath by lifting a lever.

"When there was a certain amount in the bigger tank, you could start the separation process. Firstly, the milk went through a pipe into a heater. The flow was controlled by a lever valve which was partly opened in order to avoid an overflow in the heater. The heater was, in principle, similar to a cylinder in a domestic hot press. The cylinder which contained the milk, had an outer shell inside of which water was heated by steam which in turn heated the milk in the cylinder. This was necessary to separate the cream from the milk. The cream was pumped through a pipe up to and over a cooler, which was on the upper floor of the dairy. The cooler had a hollow section inside through which cold water flowed. The outer part was in circular ridges over which the cream flowed. It would be cooled when it reached the bottom channel and then flowed into the large twenty gallon cans.

"As soon as possible after taking in milk from suppliers, you would go and give them their allocation of skim milk. There were some non-suppliers

Jack Bowe, Joe Ryan, Jim Harding, John Maybury and Pat Lynch at Raheen Creamery late 1950s.

who would buy quantities of skim for animal feeding, and some small amounts would go for home baking. There was always a balancing act needed to meet demand. The skim was also pumped from the separator up to a tank, and because it was hot, it would form a froth, which would adhere to the sides of the tank. If the froth rose very high a quick sprinkle from a water hose around the sides of the tank was needed.

"When all the milk was in and the skim dispensed, the washing up began. For the separator parts and other items of convenient size, a large galvanised tank was used. A steam pipe was linked into the bottom of this tank for heating the water, and washing soda was added. It was great stuff for cleaning but hard on the hands, especially the soft, young ones. For other equipment, such as milk cans, the water was heated in a galvanised bucket by use of a steam hose.

"Alongside the wash-up tank, there was a set of draining boards fitted on a wall, which was part of the upper raised platform. On these boards were placed all the separator parts, including the numerous discs, can lids and so on. In later years when the milk supply increased, one might not be able to do the washing-up before lunch. In these cases you would put all those items in the wash-up tank and cover them with water. Otherwise you would have a much harder job in getting them clean. When washing up, a stiff bristle brush, with a short handle, was used.

"In the early years, a lorry from Donaghmore would come to collect the cream, which was in twenty gallon cans, and quite heavy. The lorry floor would be at least six inches over the platform, which meant it was quite difficult and dangerous to load the cans. The lorry would bring back the empty cans, which would have been rinsed only, at Donaghmore. They had to be washed as soon as convenient.

"During the washing-up you were conscious of two factors. You had to keep a regular check on the boiler, add fuel as required, check the water level, and control the air-draft inflow, so as not to have excess steam blowing off. The second matter was the large volume of noise coming from the engine and the various wheels, belts and pulleys. To be heard you had to shout quite loudly."

Other tasks
When the work in the dairy was done, Ger had to turn his hand to other tasks. In the store, he learned how to weigh and bag flour and animal feeds.

In the harvest time, the wheat was moved to a separate store to be taken by lorry to Abbeyleix station for transfer to Ranks of Limerick. The barley and oats were usually sent by lorry to Donaghmore, where there were better storage facilities.

At the end of the season Ger, using Joe Butler's bicycle, would sometimes deliver the cheques for the grain to the farmers. It was a type of racer bicycle with a very high saddle and drooping handlebars. These posed quite a problem for a little lad like Ger. But he got by.

He had to learn quickly too, the routine of grinding and rolling. This was a loud process and there was a lot of dust. There were no goggles, ear muffs or protective clothing at workers' disposal in those days. Farmers would come with their oats and barley. Each sack was weighed and then emptied into a hopper. This was a wooden structure three feet square at the top and tapering down to a small square opening at the bottom of about six inches width. The grain flowed onto an elevator shaft, one of two through which a belt with small containers attached very close to each other, would rotate upwards next to the hopper, picking up grain in each little bucket as it passed. At the top, after turning over, the grain would empty into a smaller hopper, which was located just above the top of the roller/grinder feed inlet point.

Before starting to roll or grind, the belt running on an idle pulley, was moved by lever to the working pulley and, with an empty sack in place, the process could begin.

For rolling, one inside roller was turning quite fast and the outside one was edged towards it by slowly rotating two adjusting handles, until the rollers met quite firmly. For grinding, one inside round steel section was fitted with little ridges, very near each other, while outside that a second steel plate, with matching ridges, was spinning fast. This would be edged inwards by a control wheel which was locked into place, when the correct texture was reached.

"After my first year or two, I was called into the manager's office to help sort dockets, address envelopes and so on. His first office was small, with only one table. He (Joe Butler) designed a simple small collapsible table, which was fitted on a side wall. He marked a few places on the wall for screw holes, gave me a hammer and rawl tool, showed me how to use them and rotate it after every blow, and away I went – tap, tap, tap … The table was soon ready.

"That was a great idea where space was limited. When set up, it was 2½ ft. X 1½ ft, at standing height, and when hanging by the wall, it would only be about 2½ ins wide.

"After four years, I was brought in full time into the office. A little narrow table was installed which meant a lot of sideways movement for the both of us.

"The only writing equipment was a Parker fountain-pen and two kinds of pencils – black lead and what was called purple or indelible lead. The manager had a biro pen – I think it came on the market shortly before I started in the office. It was a good quality pen, with a unique type of refill. The modern refill is a straight tube, which extends to near the top of the frame, but the original one came up to the same area, and then turned and extended down about half way, quite near to, but not touching, the upper tube.

"The first alternative to be used was the Biro Minor, a long slim pen with just a straight tube. From memory, I think it retailed at 4/-. They were much better than the fountain-pens when using the duplicate statements and carbon paper – although the fountain-pens were still used quite a lot.

"Milk testing was done monthly, and twice monthly in summertime. The purpose was to produce a butterfat test, which would determine the price per gallon. The testing process was complicated and could be dangerous. There were 24 glass vials, in a special wooden container. A measure each of alcohol, milk and acid were added. The milk would be preserved by special tablets. After the three mixtures were added, the vials were sealed by a rubber cork, then put into a round container with 24 copper tubes, and covered with a lid.

"Before going into the round container, the box they were in was covered and shaken for a few minutes until a certain colour appeared. Then after adding each one into a tube in the round spinner, a lid was secured and they were spun for a few minutes at a certain speed. The spinner was turned by hand, with a slot in the handle to release it from the spinner every few minutes. When spun enough, it was allowed to slow down and was helped a little by pressing lightly against the side with a cloth or similar item. The lid was removed and the reading could begin. If there were absentee suppliers, there was an 'X' marked against that number on the record sheet. There was also a marking guide in the spinner, where you put in the first vial, so you started to read from that point. At the last spin, if there were less than the 24, you would leave certain spaces empty so as to have a proper balance. If necessary a dummy was put in to create the balance.

"On the vials there were markings, and by adjusting the rubber cork carefully in or out, the readings of each test were obtained. After the 24 tests were read, the corks were removed and the vials were emptied into a channel, in which a light flow of water was running and flowed on to outside and into a gulley. Then they were rinsed, drained well by shaking and the whole process would begin again, until all the tests were done.

"When the samples were taken each day, the bottles, which contained a small amount of lead shot and a preserving tablet, were shaken before and after a sample was added. The shot would keep the milk from sticking to the bottles, which were glass, similar to milk bottles. There were two sets of bottles, which involved a lot of extra careful washing each month. A Department inspector would also carry out random tests, a few times a year.

"When at the end of the month the manager would determine the value of milk, based on the butterfat test, he used a ready-reckoner for that purpose. When all transactions relating to milk were finished, and the value worked out, the relevant details were sent to Donaghmore, from where the cheques were issued. These were returned to the branches and sent out to suppliers. Non-supplier accounts were sent out directly from each branch.

"In the office, a small solid-fuel stove provided heat during autumn, winter and spring months. A smoke pipe from it extended through a wall and linked into another pipe outside, which extended to just above roof level. It would be usually brushed clean once a year. The first time I had to clean it was on a cold, frosty morning, without gloves or any other protection. Suffice it to say, I had more than just dirty hands without the help of hot water.

"There was only one telephone, which was generally used by the manager. It was an old style type, with a winding handle on one side. Calls were made and received through operators, who were based in Abbeyleix Post Office. If you had to make an outward call – say to Donaghmore 3, which was at HQ – you turned the handle, lifted the receiver and waited for an operator to answer. You identified your own number – we were Abbeyleix 16 – and asked for the required number. If it was local you might be connected immediately, otherwise the operator would phone back. When finished, you gave the handle a short turn.

"The manager owned a rifle, and sometimes he would have it in the office. Once, when there was a few inches of snow on the ground, there was a rabbit in the adjoining field, about two hundred yards away. He (Joe Butler) showed me how to handle the rifle and to take a shot. I aimed for one eye, so as to give it a fair chance, but the barrel of the gun must have been slightly crooked. Sure how else could I have missed?

"One of the first things I learned about store work was the existence of microbes. They were noticeable, especially in the flour and meals. Although unseen, if you checked the top of a bag of flour or meal each morning, it would be quite smooth. If you observed the meal, which would not be so fine, you would actually see it move.

"During my earlier years, when the manager, Joe Butler, was on holidays, Mr. Wallis from Donaghmore would come and do the relief for the two weeks. He had

***Willie Manning, Andy Fennelly, Liam McCabe, John Maybury and Jimmy Phelan
pictured outside new dairy at Raheen, 1967.***

a little Austin which he parked in a garage during the day. When going home in the evenings, he would sometimes show me how to start it and reverse it out into the yard.

"That same garage was used to park the Co-op's own lorry, a two-ton Austin. The driver was Ned Rothwell. He would also explain to me how to start the lorry and how to use the clutch. Occasionally I was sent as a helper to Donaghmore with Ned. The longest journey I went on was when he delivered a load of butter to a warehouse at Sir John Rogerson's Quay in Dublin. The butter was packed in 56 lb wooden boxes. Whenever I went as helper I kept a keen interest in every move and gear change, as done by Ned. However, there was no driving on the roads for me until 1960, when I got my first bone-shaker, a well-worn old style Morris Minor.

"In the late 1950s we started selling petrol at Raheen. The pump was a hand operated one, which had been in use in Donaghmore. It issued a gallon only each time so if you had a tank near full, and if you did not have a spare can, there would be a spillage.

"In early 1972, I was transferred to Donaghmore, which meant a longer distance to travel to work. Initially the clerical work was quite variable but it soon developed into more serious work, such as compiling all the necessary figures for, and completing, the tax returns every two months.

"In mid-1975 a staff person left Raheen and I was recalled there. This again was a challenge, as they had installed a new cash desk in the shop and I was put in charge of it. That meant being responsible for all cash transactions, in and out.

"Avonmore had become the umbrella body in 1973 and that signalled a change in the whole working procedure at Donaghmore and its branches. While in Donaghmore, on the first day under Avonmore, there was a one hour token protest held outside the buildings. All, except a few very senior management people, were involved.

"Although computers had been introduced for the debtor accounts and the milk department in 1973, they were not used in the retail area until 1986. After some teething problems, the new system worked smoothly. For the first five years there was a big heavy mainframe machine in the office, which governed the workings of all computer screens in the shop and offices. Every week I would have to download material onto a floppy disc, identify the dates held on it and store them in locked boxes. If that was not done, the system would clog up and the issuing of dockets and so on would slow down. That system was changed in 1991 for a more updated version, which did not require disc change. With either system, at the end of the evening, I would reel off a sub-total list of transactions for the day, and if all appeared okay, then a final list would be printed off. On the older system, a change of date for the next day was set up, but the new one would change automatically at 24.00.

"And there my story ends. It's true to say that working with the Co-op played a big role in my journey through life. There were ups and downs but for the most part it was an enjoyable and rewarding experience."

Editor's note: Ger Lawler retired on 3 October, 1998, having worked over fifty years with Donaghmore Creamery Co-op. His long and dedicated service was marked by a special presentation made to him by management and staff at a function in Harding's Hotel, Abbeyleix, a short time after his retirement.

Liam Rohan,
(Anngrove)

"My interest in the Co-op follows on from my late father, John Rohan, who lived in Corbally, just a short distance away from Raheen Co-op. He was on the committee in the very early years and often mentioned that he and the late George Galbraith and others would cycle to Donaghmore for the monthly meetings during the worst of those rather lean years of the economic depression.

"In fact, he often told us that on one such night, on their return journey through Abbeyleix, he was fined for not having a light on his bike. I often wonder would any of the present generation, myself included, have done what the people of those times actually did. To set out on a bike from Corbally or somewhere similar and pedal to Donaghmore and sit in a cold hall or room for some hours sorting out the affairs of the Co-op and planning the future. That requires one to have such a dedicated interest.

"I heard him telling that in those early years, they (committee members) went around to all prospective milk suppliers, looking for half a crown subscriptions to become shareholders.

"My father bought this place (Annegrove) in 1934 so most of his activity would have been in the first six years. I also have been involved for many years in committee and council activity but father time has caught up with me, and I have moved on. Jim Delaney of Derrygarron has replaced me on the council and like me, he also has a direct link with the past as his late father, Bill, was a council member and also a milk carter.

"People back at that time really had foresight and determination. People, for the most part, were not so well-educated, especially during the depression and war years and yet what started as a tiny acorn, grew to be a mighty oak.

"As far as I know, my father did not send milk until about the mid 1950s. A local

Liam Rohan won the All-Ireland Senior Ploughing Championship in 1986. Here he is being presented with the Supreme Trophy by Derek Johnston, Managing Director of Esso. Also in picture is Liam's wife, Bridie. Liam represented Ireland in four world contests: 1982 (Tasmania), 1985 (Denmark – 5th place), 1987 (Austria) and 1988 (Iowa, USA).

lady, Moira Conroy, started to bring a few cans from her home in Gortnaclea with a car and trailer and had room for more and collected from ourselves and a few more people in the locality.

"Before that, as with most other farmers, we separated the milk and my mother made butter, and any excess butter we had, was sold to local shopkeeper, the late Larry Malone. I had to do my share with the separation and churning also.

"We had an old small separator and from time to time, the little disks would wear down and need repairs. The late Kieran Dowling from Cappanaclough was handy with a soldering iron and he would do the necessary repairs.

"After some time, we were increasing our cow numbers and decided to get a new, larger separator. That was a very big decision in the early 1950s. The ESB was still some years ahead, so there was plenty of hard work involved. You had to separate at each milking and I would be turning the handle while some other family member brought up the buckets of milk and of course, it had to be separated while warm to get the maximum amount of cream.

"Around that time also, we replaced the old end over end churn, with a stainless steel one. We had twelve cows at the time and decided to get one more. There was only room for twelve in the shed and the newcomer was very quiet and would stand outside chewing the cud until a space was ready. There was a quiet one among the twelve also and when finished, she would be let out and the one waiting would just walk in and go into the empty space and await her turn.

"It was probably a short time later that Moira called to see my father to chat about her idea of carting milk to Raheen. She, of course, would be getting compensated for so doing. That was an introduction to creamery milk supply, and some few years later, a much bigger area was initiated for milk haulage by the late Fint Delaney from Cappanaclough, who started with a lorry.

"For a while after we started sending milk to the creamery, we still separated some and made the butter, especially at weekends in summer time, as the lorry would be going much earlier on a Sunday morning. I think the dual operation only lasted for perhaps a year or so and the separator and churn were sold.

"At one stage, my father was considering getting a milking machine, driven by a petrol engine, but eventually decided not to. In fact, we stopped sending milk for a while and went on to suckling and we fed milk to calves for a while.

"In 1966 after I got married, I took over from my father and decided to increase my stock. I had the grazing area laid out in paddocks for the sucklers and the electric fence was very useful too and we were able to move the cows every few days. We had forty-five cows. About 10 years later, we began to think that if we sent the milk to the creamery, we would have a better income and much less hardship.

"So, after some time, and having got some advice from an agricultural adviser, I decided to revert back to sending the milk to the creamery. We did, of course, do mixed farming all the time.

"Around the mid 1970s, I contacted a man from the North of Ireland, whom I knew, and talked to him about my intended plans. He was also a dairy farmer. He thought it was a good idea and he invited me up to see him. He knew of an impending sale in Belfast and on the sale day, I went with him and we bought two loads.

"He brought down a load of twelve animals to my yard, and his commission charge was a fiver per head, that was £60, for the return journey from Belfast. The average price that I paid for those cows, most of which were pedigree stock, was £220 each for springers and some were calved.

"I had a slight problem at the time, as we were building a milking parlour and it was not yet finished. I had a chat with my neighbour, the late Dick Palmer, telling him about the calved ones, and a few more were due very soon. So, he said to bring them down to him and he would milk them until our parlour was ready. When we got going, we were milking around eighty-five cows and the bulk collection had started by then.

"At first, we were advised by the Avonmore adviser to get a 400 gallon tank. Before very long, they said we should get an 800 gallon one and, though hard to believe, it was not so long before they said we would need a 1300 gallon tank. That was very annoying and added extra costs to us as the allowance for the previous two tanks, though almost new, was very little.

"So, that was our introduction to milk supply in a worthwhile way. It was a decision that was never regretted and we were lucky by the fact that the quota system was introduced in the early 1980s.

"We would have to say that things have changed quite a lot over the years and the Co-op has expanded greatly and is providing a great service and has provided a great service down through the years. For example, a manure spreading service was a great benefit for a lot of farmers, especially those in the lower acreage category.

"Yet, when we created Avonmore, as we knew it for some years, we were told that our buying power would be so great that it would enable the Co-op to be most efficient for the greater benefit of the customers. They would be able to pay more for milk, grain and so on. But that picture did not seem to materialise as we had expected.

"Even under the Glanbia name, things did not appear to run smoothly and they had to dispose of a number of acquisitions to keep the ship afloat. But I suppose times change and part of the problem comes from those large superstores who have tremendous buying power.

"So these are factors that, in fairness, we have to allow for and they are problems that have arisen in the last few years that maybe were not there before. Perhaps, we should also say that if the Co-op had not been there down through the years and the situation was left to private merchants, then we could be paying a lot more for farm inputs. While I may be inclined to grumble from time to time, I still deal with the Co-op for all our requirements."

L. to R: Stella Burke, Willie Manning, Tom O'Regan, Loughlin Moran, Joe Delaney, John Burke, John Carter and Liam McCabe, pictured outside new dairy, Raheen 1967.

Alf Harvey – Contractor and his team at the building of new dairy in Raheen in 1967. In picture are: Jimmy Phelan, Dinny Dunne, Tom Moore, Tommy Hutchinson, Andy Duff, Jimmy Clooney, Alf Harvey and Jim Campion (with hammer).

Personal Recollections – Spink

Ben Moran

These are excerpts summarised from the late Ben Moran's article titled 'My 40 Years in Spink' which was published in the booklet Avonmore Spink – 1935/'85. *Ben worked at Spink for 40 years and retired in 1975. He died in 1997.*

I believe there was a private creamery, known as Mulhalls, in Spink at the turn of the twentieth century. Around 1906, a group of Spink farmers formed a committee, got their neighbours to contribute share capital and built a creamery. The milk was separated and butter was manufactured from the cream. Eighty per cent of suppliers' deliveries was returned as skim milk. Things were going well and they built a shop. The following years a bakery, forge and a pig slaughtering house were added. A travelling shop in the form of a horse and cart was put on the road which serviced the needs of the local community and bought eggs.

War broke out in 1914, which lasted four years. Coupled with this was the Rising in 1916 which was followed by the Civil War. All of these events eventually brought the creamery business to a standstill. In 1920 the Creamery went into liquidation and all the assets were sold. Fortunately for the shareholders, a local well-off bachelor put up money and cleared the debts. Once again it was back to the farmers doing their own churning and selling their own butter.

In 1934, Donaghmore Creamery came to Spink with the idea of opening a branch in the old creamery. 'Once bitten, twice shy' – the locals would not take part in the shareholding. Donaghmore decided to take a 20 year lease. They renovated the old building and installed a separator, boiler, tanks, pumps and an engine.

Spink Branch continues to provide an important service to farmers over a wide area.

Tim Costigan driving at leisure in Spink, late 1950s.

In July 1935, two months after the opening of Spink, I started work in the Creamery. I was the man who gave out the skim and did the washing up. When this was done and also on Saturdays and Sundays, the manager (Paddy O'Leary) and myself would get on our bikes and scour the countryside looking for new suppliers. We got carts to bring in the milk and I remember Mr. Donnelly from Abbeyleix undertaking to do the Luggacurren run on a year's contract for a halfpenny per gallon. After one year we were taking in milk from Clopook, Raheenahone, Luggacurren, Ballyadams, Ballintubbert and Ballaghmore. CIE were recruited to collect the milk and did so for a number of years. I went out with the CIE driver on one of his first runs. We called to a farmer who had promised to supply. When we arrived at the house the driver put down the window and asked the lady if she had the milk for the creamery. "Sure we only keep a couple of cows. 'Tis mostly sheep we keep," was the reply. "I'm sorry, ma'am,' said the driver, "but we don't collect sheep's milk."

Donaghmore, and likewise Spink, paid for milk at a price per lb of butterfat. Ballyragget, who were the opposition, paid a straight price per gallon. You can understand how confusing this was for farmers. At the time the price per lb of butterfat was 8d-10d and Ballyragget's price was 4d for every gallon supplied. During those years, many locals continued to churn and sell their own salted butter in the local shops, even as far away as Athy.

When war broke out in 1939, Billy Wallis was manager at Spink. Because there was no transport, suppliers in outlying districts could not get their milk delivered. Every commodity was in scarce supply and rationing was the order of the day. All private cars, of which there were very few, had to go off the road because there was no petrol. Only doctors, priests and hackney men were allowed a limited number of coupons for

Martin Lalor at hand operated petrol pump at Spink Creamery late 1950s.

emergency journeys. Coupons were needed for tea, bread, butter, flour, sugar, and most other foodstuffs.

The government made an order for compulsory tillage. This, in effect, greatly reduced milk production around the country. Spink was lucky since most of the land in this area was not arable and milk supplies did not suffer greatly.

In 1945 petrol could not be got for the lorry. To try and keep the show on the road, the engine was changed to gas. This operation was unsuccessful and we changed to charcoal, which greatly enhanced the performance of the truck.

Even through those terrible years, Spink had managed to open a new store, which sold seed for wheat, barley and seed potatoes. We stocked flour, pigmeal, pollard, bran, and other household requirements. The only manure available was basic slag, ground rock phosphate and sulphur. Anybody sowing beet collected the manure at Abbeyleix Railway station.

In the spring of 1941, a bombshell struck Spink. Foot and Mouth disease broke out all around the area. There was an immediate clampdown on all herd movements. Ten guards were drafted in to Ballinakill to oversee the restrictions. The creamery was subjected to severe restrictions. It was closed down for milk intake until we got set up to pasteurise the skim milk. Mr. Kelly was sent for, as he was an expert on steam engines. I directed him to Joe Foyle of Knock, who fortunately had an engine. After a lot of modifications and failures we had to call it a day as the engine did not raise enough steam to boil the milk. We sent the milk to Raheen to have it pasteurised and then brought back again. Donaghmore eventually bought a steam boiler and the creamery was operating once more under very strict Donaghmore inspection.

My job every morning was to fill my knapsack sprayer with disinfectant and spray the people as they arrived in the yard, together with the cans and the donkeys, the horses and the carts. The farmers, as you can gather, did not take too well to being sprayed and they were supposed to wear protective clothing but many did not. Regardless, they had to be sprayed and this was hard on their clothes.

My second job was to give out the skim. After pasteurisation the skim was boiling and it was given out this way as there was no way of cooling it. This operation made the donkeys and horses nervous as hot spatters of skim would hit them on the hips and make them jump. The drop lids on the churns of the time were very convenient for holding one or two pound rolls of butter. Some farmers forgot about the hot skim and ended up with a right mess on the lid when they reached home.

The summer of 1946 was one of the worst in history and most of the hay rotted in the fields. This was followed by the worst winter of all time. In late 1947, the effects of the previous year's disasters began to wear off and things began to look up again. Donaghmore bought a new van which travelled all around to farmers' houses buying fowl and eggs and turkeys at Christmas time.

In 1949, the government removed the subsidy from farmers' butter and this effectively signalled the death of home churning. The farmer's wife could no longer compete without the subsidy so this heralded a sudden demand from farmers to supply milk to Spink Creamery. The late Pat Lacey from Luggacurren put a lorry on the road, we fitted him out from Donaghmore with a load of new cans. By the end of 1950 we had 12 carters bringing in milk to Spink. These were: Pat Lacey, J. Keyes, J. Phelan, D. Costigan, P. Bowe, G. Grace, P. Kelly, J. McDonald, D. Dunne, M. Kehoe, and the Raheen lorry with the 'Skipper' Rothwell covering

L.-r.: Patrick Costigan, Jimmy Deighton, Tim Costigan, M. Shelly at Spink Creamery 1950s.

Cullenagh and Timahoe. As milk increased in the following years, tractors, trailers, and some lorries gradually replaced the horses and donkeys.

In 1953, the 20 year lease was up and it was decided to build a new creamery on a site about one mile from the old creamery, bought from Tommy Lennon. The new creamery was opened in April 1954. Everything was new and this included a stainless steel pasteuriser, tanks and a separator. The only transfer from the old creamery was the old oil engine.

We had great trouble getting a water supply. After some failed attempts we resorted to a man with a sally rod and he pinpointed a spring just inside the gate. The well was bored to 300 feet and this gave us a permanent supply at 800 gallons per hour. We got our first electricity in 1955. This was a great novelty to us all. We now had light and power at the pressing of a button.

I was appointed manager for six months in 1954. Spink had a poor record in retaining managers. There were no fewer than twelve appointed between 1935 and 1955. The Department would only allow qualified managers to run the creamery. After a lot of discussion, the Department agreed that if I sat an examination they might agree to my appointment. The secretary of the Department of Agriculture, Mr. Phelan, took charge of the examination in the Club House Hotel, Kilkenny in 1956. Luckily I passed the test and was appointed manager. From then on I attended the monthly committee meetings in Donaghmore to account for Spink and discuss its needs.

L.-r.: John Doyle, Patrick Costigan, Jimmy Deighton, Peter Kelly, Christy Cahill, Tim Costigan and Ben Moran, enjoying a two minute break at Spink Creamery – late 1950s.

Tim Costigan
(Spink)

Tim Costigan was manager at Spink from 1975 until he retired in 1998. His father, Timothy, was the first milk supplier to Spink Creamery.

I started in Spink in 1949. Donaghmore had a hatchery and produced day old chicks. The chicks would be delivered to each branch, and I often had to deliver some boxes out to local people on my bike. My first job was taking in milk at the platform. I can remember my first pay packet was £1-7-6. Subsequently I was transferred to the shop where I remained until I was appointed manager, on Ben Moran's retirement, in 1975.

My initial years were at the first old co-op, which was in premises owned by a McDonnell family. A new creamery was built in 1954 and later another new one was built in 1968 by Jack Quinn and sons of Abbeyleix.

Taking over from Ben Moran (as manager at Spink in 1975) was not easy. Having worked with him until he retired in 1975 was a great experience and pre-pared me well for the task ahead.

With amalgamation (with Avonmore in 1973) there were major changes. Farmers could now have their milk collected by road tankers from bulk tanks on their farms or on the roadside. Milk was no longer taken in by weighing scales but instead a tanker was parked in the creamery yard which took the milk direct from the suppliers and on to Avonmore. The hauliers became redundant. We were sad to lose these men because they had been responsible for the expansion of our store and milk business.

The results of these changes and our entry into the EEC led to a huge expansion in milk production. Milk intake in 1975 was 1.5 million gallons and this increased threefold to 4.2 million gallons by 1985. This brought with it an enormous rise in our store business activities. To cope, we had to make major alterations at Spink. The old creamery and store were demolished; the whole yard was resurfaced and a new shop and store were built. Pallets and forklifts became the modern way of handling bulk goods.

Billy Wallis

General Manager of Donaghmore Co-op from 1969-'73 and Joint General Manager from 1960-'68, worked at the Spink Branch from 1941-'43. Billy Willis died on 25 October 1990. These are excerpts summarised from an interview published in Avonmore Spink – 1935/'85.

I commenced work in Spink in July 1941, having previously worked in a general hardware store. In 1941 the number of milk suppliers was 43. Both Ben Moran and myself canvassed the area on our bicycles after work. We found it difficult to convince farmers and their wives to send their milk to the creamery, as new milk had always been fed to calves and, as well as that, they had been making their own butter for sale locally. We managed to increase the number to 81 suppliers by 1943. In 1941, at its peak, the daily intake was 550 gallons. By 1943 this had increased to 900 gallons daily.

Murtagh McWey.

In 1943, the late J.P. Kelly asked me to look after the grain intake and to establish a store business in Donaghmore. While in Spink my weekly wages were £2-10-0. There was a government freeze on wages, so by altering my position I was able to avail of a 10/- per week increase in pay – and in those days 10/- was a sizeable sum of money.

Murtagh McWey
(Spink)

Summarised excerpts from an interview published in Avonmore Spink – 1935/1985.

When Donaghmore opened a branch in Spink, all the dairy farmers in the area changed (from Ballyragget) to the local creamery. Some of it was carted by the late J. Dooley from Ballypickas. Most of the farmers brought in their own milk by horse and donkey. In fact, the animals were so used to going to the creamery that when the farmers wanted to go to Abbeyleix, the donkeys would not pass the creamery yard. In many cases they had to enter the yard premises before they could proceed any further on their journey.

During the war years, compulsory tillage greatly reduced milk production in many areas. But for the milk supply to Spink during those years, Donaghmore would have had to close down as a creamery.

In 1944, Spink got its first member onto the Donaghmore committee. The late Michael Walsh represented Spink from then until 1979. In the early 1950s I was elected on the management committee. The meetings were held at night at Donaghmore Creamery. I used to cycle to Abbeyleix to meet the Raheen members. From there we were all taken to Donaghmore in McCoy's hackney car. The main task was to fix the milk price for the previous month's milk. There were no guaranteed prices then, milk prices were poor and it was always difficult to strike the right balance.

Stock-taking took place on every 31 December. I have vivid memories of plodding through the snow to

James Cooney, Luggacurren was a member of Committee of Management for Spink at Donaghmore for many years. He was also for a time chairman of Laois County Council.

be at Spink by 6pm after the shop had closed. When the job was done we would go up to the late Mrs. O'Connor, who would have a fine big meal ready for us. This was a special night!

Sheila Walshe
(nee O'Connor, Loughteague, Stradbally and Spink Public House)

"Our family moved to Spink in 1939, to run a grocery shop and pub until 1949. The creamery building was still there, but the creamery itself had ceased to function long before that. The only local link we became aware of was that a Ned Burke, who lived in Aughnacross, worked there. We rigged up a grinder and our own electric supply from the old engine there and some batteries, which were charged from the engine.

"When we came to Spink, the only creamery in the area was the one down in McDonnells. Francie McDonnell had a grocery shop there also. There had also been a creamery in Timogue, near Timahoe, and it was only about a mile from where we lived in Loughteague. It was privately owned, I don't know by whom, and we supplied milk there. But I think it had a rather short life also. There are some or all of the old walls still there, near an old church.

"When we started living in Spink, it was around the start of the war years, and they were tough times. The ration books were in use and we had to ration out the tea and other scarce items. Trying to get supplies was a big problem. The foot and mouth disease came around that time also, but as far as I know, it didn't affect anyone in our area.

"There was a mill in Stradbally, owned by Frazers, and we would get some wheat rolled there. We would try to sieve it through a silk stocking to get some wholemeal flour.

"I remember one time, in the 1940s, when there was snow on the ground, a funeral was trying to negotiate its way up the hills around our house at Spink. It was a motor hearse and it was unable to pass, so whatever few people were with it had to stay in our house overnight. We had to bake bread to help them out as best we could. They were going from Abbeyleix to near Carlow."

Christy Cahill
(Timahoe and Portlaoise)

"I worked with Patrick Lacey, who lived in Clopook, near Luggacurren, for about four years, in the early 1950s carting milk to the old Spink depot in McDonnells. I then transferred to John Keyes as helper and driver.

"By this time the new creamery was in operation and there was plenty of space to move around. There was always a great social atmosphere in the place. Some of the staff, and some of the carters also, would have their lunch there. There would usually be a game of cards and the banter and 'craic' was always enjoyable.

"Among the areas covered by Patrick Lacey were Luggacurren, Moyadd, Wolfhill, The Swan and Spink. John Keyes' area included Timahoe, Garryglass and Boleybeg. I also did a few Sunday morning runs into Raheen for John Seale.

"One day, a travelling journeyman called into Spink. I think he wanted some milk.

There was a bit of banter with him and when leaving he said, 'Back *Mr. What* in the big race tomorrow, and you won't be sorry'. It was the Grand National and all the gang backed 'Mr. What' and, of course, they won. They would have given a few bob to the stranger in appreciation, but he had left the area and was never seen again.

"I moved on to a new employer but I certainly enjoyed the work, and the company of those that I encountered during my time in the milk business in the 1950s."

Tommy McDonald
(Kyle, Timahoe)

"In August 1961, when John Keyes was drawing milk to Spink Co-op, his helper had just left him and he took me on in his place. He lived in Knockbawn, which was just a short distance away from Spink on the Carlow side. His route was through Blandsfort, Moneenard, Timahoe, Orchard, Guileen, Aughamaddock, Stradbally, Timogue, Loughteague, Coolnabacca, Garryglass, and Graigue.

"At that time he only had one lorry and from Graigue he would take in the load to Spink, get the skim milk, and return direct to Timahoe, where he had a trailer parked, and unload all the cans of skim on to the trailer.

"Then he would set off for a second load out the Portlaoise road, on to Cremorgan, Raheenduff, Cullenagh, Cashel, Ballyknocken, Easter Hill, Lamberton, Ratheniska, Cork Road (Stradbally), Portlaoise Road, into Timahoe and on to Spink. That second load of skim was delivered to the suppliers as normal, en route back to Timahoe, where the first load was reloaded on the lorry and delivered to suppliers.

"The volume of milk gradually increased over a few years, and in 1962 John bought a new lorry but it had not as yet been used. Now, within a week or so after buying the lorry, John died, and the transaction was cancelled on the night of his wake and the lorry remained in the garage.

"But soon afterwards the amount of milk was so great that Mrs. Keyes had to buy the lorry again, and she got her cousin, Mick Kehoe, to drive it. The Reg. no of the lorry was BCI 794.

"The usual story for all milk carters applies here also and you would always have to bring out messages of various sizes, from pounds of butter to bags of meal. You could have a little space on the lorry in winter time, but at peak times it was not so easy. Sometimes we might return to Spink for meal and other goods after delivering all the skim.

"It continued like that up to the mid-1970s, when bulk collection started and the cans became redundant. After that I got a lorry of my own and was hired by Spink to draw loads in and out. I remained at that until 1991.

"It was hard work but we had some laughs too. There was one lady who would not have the milk out in time. She was a jolly sort of lady and one morning I said to her, 'I'll bring you back a new one today'. She said, 'What?', and I said, 'A clock, it will get you up earlier and you will be able to have the milk out in time!' 'Feck you and your clock', she said, and went back into her house laughing.

"The late Ben Costigan, who worked in Spink, came with me one day as a helper. He was on holidays at the time. We were going along somewhere around Cullenagh, when a cat crossed the road ahead of us. I applied the brakes and Ben, who was on the body of the lorry, slid along the floor with some of the cans. He put out his hand over the side of the lorry, knowing I could see him in the mirror, and said, 'Don't mind them, they have nine lives, but I have only one!'

"In later years when I had my own lorry I got a lifter, or type of fork lift, which was carried on a trolley behind the lorry. I worked that for two years before Spink got one. I tried Ben Moran in Spink and Joe Butler in Raheen, but neither of them could give me permission to use it. But Joe suggested I try Mick Mackey, who was transport manager in Ballyragget. I did some drawings for him and explained how it worked and it appealed very much to him. It seemed the pallets were the main problem and he suggested they charge for outgoing pallets and credit them on their return. Soon the problem was solved. Pallets were acquired and the lifter was introduced at both branches."

Bob Moran
(Ballinakill)

Bob Moran, who resides in Ballyroan, started carting milk to Spink Creamery in the late 1930s. He was only 15 years old and was helping his father, who had been collecting the milk in his horse and dray from the day the branch opened there in 1935. His older brother, John, followed on from his father, who was a brother of the father of Ben Moran, who became a legendary figure at Spink Creamery.

Bob remembered many of the milk suppliers on his route. "We were living in Ballinakill when I started. We had a pub there. We had a small drop (of milk) ourselves, and then proceeded to Kennedys of Bride Street, Rices, Drurys, Kennedys of Ironmills, Tom and Jack Egan of Kilcronin, then on to Hylands of Moate, Kavanaghs of Boleybawn, Muldowneys (a heavy full 20 gallon can) and Dorans of Dysart. I would have to unload the cans there, near a wart-stone, because there was a very steep hill. Then on to Tod Walsh of Moate, Pete Jackman, Dan Cranny of Ballypickas, John Boylan, Tom Lalor, Delaneys, Babs Foyle, and Cass, from the Knock area, and so on to Spink. Before that I would have gone back down the steep hill and reloaded the few cans which I had left there earlier.

"Then I delivered the skim milk back to the farmers. My starting time was 9am and I finished around 7pm. I got into Spink around 1pm. The few locals would usually be gone back home by then. I think there was another auld lad, who had a long dray and two horses also drawing there at the time. He drew milk from the Wolfhill area."

During the time of the depression Bob and a friend, Pake McMahon, cut timber with a crosscut saw and sold it to the nuns in the convent at Ballyroan. Bob also took potatoes to a market in Castlecomer and got five shillings for a twenty stone sack.

Bob then offered an interesting little snippet from times past. He believes that, in the 1920s, there were three cottages built in Ballyroan for £30. "That's a tenner each", he explained.

It was tough work back then but there were the lighter moments too. Bob, a man with a delightful sense of humour, recalled a man named Ned Dea, who had a stripper cow at a fair in Ballinakill in the 1930s. She was fairly skinny and two Dublin lads were trying to make a deal for her with Ned. The going rate for a cow would have been from half a crown to 50 shillings. They offered him five shillings, at which Ned

Ben Moran (left) borrows Paddy Sheil's hat on an outing in the 1950s.

turned to the cow and said: "I'll take you home again, Kathleen."

He also remembered a witty character by the name of Boylan who came from around Blandsfort. He went with a mare to a fair in Kilkenny. A buyer was interested and asked: "Is there a foal in her?" "I don't know", said Boylan, "I was never in there".

Bob then told the little story of the farmer who kept a sow and her "clutch" of bonhams in the kitchen of his house, beside the fire. "People used to feed skim milk to sows at the time. The skim milk had the effect of making the sow pass wind quite often, with more than a little noise and a fairly strong whiff also!"

Bob thought of another story. "There was a man named Tom, who lived in the Durrow area. He used to collect dead animals. A favourite saying of his was 'Ah, worse could happen'. It so happened that his wife died in Abbeyleix Hospital and a messenger brought him the bad news. He was unable to read so he got the messenger to read the letter for him informing of his wife's death and other details. His reaction was, 'Ah, worse could happen'."

Tod Walshe
(Moate, Ballinakill)

Tod Walshe, from Moate Ballinakill, recalled Bob Moran collecting the milk and bringing it to the Spink Creamery. "We sent most of our milk to Dublin. His family also supplied surplus milk on Sundays to the old creamery, "where the public house is now. There were no trains on Sundays", he explained.

Martin Lalor
(Moate, Ballinakill)

"In the early years, I was in the dairy department for milk intake, and in the store for the remainder of the day. My wages were around £3 per week.

"In the early mornings, before milk came in, I would weigh small quantities of flour and mill stuff and at spraying time, I would weigh out various quantities of washing soda and bluestone, which were the ingredients for potato spraying.

"In those times, people did not have to contend with buying those pre packs of nails and other items like they do now. If a person required only a few ounces of fine nails, or netting wire staples or a quarter pound of ordinary nails, you would weigh out whatever they required.

"Sometime in the mid 1960s, they procured a grinding and rolling mill, and I worked in that also. In spring time especially, there would be a big demand for manure. All manure was in two cwt bags, and there were no fork lifts then. If store space was scarce, you had to pile them up as high as you were able, and that was pretty tough.

"Some years later, they got a type of portable elevator, which was called a creeper. It had a small petrol motor and was not too easy to start – so you would always make sure not to let it run dry of petrol.

"In 1966, I started to drive a small two ton lorry, which was originally in the Raheen branch. It was used mainly for bringing meals from Donaghmore and deliveries out to farmers. I would also collect cement from Portlaoise and Ballybrophy stations. In the late 1960s, they got a bigger lorry and I had to draw cream from Spink and Raheen to Donaghmore.

"Generally, after unloading the cream, you would have to bring back a load of mill stuff and put the empty cream cans on top of the load of meal. They were 20 gallon size, pretty heavy, and not so easy to manage

"Getting the cement from the railway wagons was one of the hardest jobs that any driver or helper did. It would be extremely hot and very hard to handle. The building of silage pits was starting in a big way around that time – the late 1960s and into the 1970s – and demand for cement was quite brisk."

Lighter moments

… "One day, a department inspector called to check if proper diesel was being used in lorries. While one particular lorry was being checked, the driver remarked to the Inspector: 'I suppose you do catch an odd one?' 'Oh yes, I do, indeed', said the Inspector, 'but you're okay anyway'. But he failed to notice that the driver had a can of coloured diesel on the lorry, inside a milk can, and was feeding the engine from it, while the lorry tank had the proper diesel in it.

"Somehow, I don't think that he was the only driver using a similar system. Another staff member, the late Johnny Butler, was a jovial and witty character and one day, a priest came in for a bag of layers mash for hens. He told Johnny to put it in his car, a Volkswagen, while he went in to pay and get a docket. When Johnny looked for the layers mash, there was none left, so he put in a bag of barley meal, instead. When the priest came out and saw the barley meal, he would not take it and said: 'Johnny! I wouldn't give my hens barley meal'. 'Well Father', said Johnny, 'sure you can't leave them hungry either'."

List of Spink Branch Managers

Paddy O'Leary, William Wallis, John Everard, John Keane, J.F. O'Sullivan, P.J. O'Driscoll, Paddy McAdams, William Keane, Dick Stapleton, Brian Connellan, Ben Moran, Timothy Costigan.

List of Spink Employees 1935-1985

Tony McDonald, Larry Doone, Paddy Walsh, Gerry Walsh, Patrick Costigan, Martin Lalor, P.J. Lalor, Michael McEvoy, Jim Ring, Paddy Fitzpatrick, Ben Costigan, Dan Costigan, James Deighton, John Dea, Paddy Lalor, Murty McDonald, Dan Phelan, Mrs. Philomena Mealy, Mrs. Mairead Bergin, Mrs. Carmel Hennessy, Miss Betty McGuire, Paddy Delaney, John Butler, Tommy Doyle, Gertie Foley, John Fitzgerald, John Kennedy, Edward Kennedy.

Courtesy of Avonmore Spink – 1935/'85.

Personal Recollections – Mountmellick

In this interview recorded by Michael Igoe, Mountmellick area committee members, Billy Flynn, John Joe Dunne, Sean Young and Bernard Rochford, reflect on aspects of how Donaghmore spread its wings to Mountmellick and its influence on developments there and in Clonaslee[1] over the years.

John Joe Dunne: I met Colm Costello and Malachy Prunty of the IAOS in Brussels one night in the late 1970s. They related a story of the acquisition in Mountmellick and its amalgamation into the Donaghmore structure. Colm met the late Mr. Bailey from Summergrove one day in the offices of the IAOS in Plunkett House in Dublin. This stately gentleman from outside Mountmellick informed Colm that he was a farmer and his wife and himself had a large business in Mountmellick. They were trading under a number of headings but they were particularly dealing with a lot of local farmers, doing their business and giving them credit and the farmers in turn coming in at the end of year and paying their accounts. The Baileys were very appreciative of the amount of business they got from farmers and, as they were retiring from business and had no successors or family, they wanted, as a thank you, to offer their business to the farming community.

They were retiring, they wanted to sell and move on, and they had no idea how to put this into effect. So they went to the IAOS for guidance and after discussing the matter with Colm, they came up with the idea that there were two options. One was to form a co-operative in the Mountmellick area. The other was to deal with the existing co-operative in Donaghmore, which had a lot of experience and expertise in running a business.

The whole principle that Mr. and Mrs. Bailey worked under was to return the business to the farmers with some cash upfront. But also confidentiality was paramount to any discussions. Mr. Bailey warned them that any breakdown in confidentiality was going to scuttle the whole project, that he would withdraw immediately and there would be no re-opening of negotiation. So it was decided to place enormous trust in two members of the board of Donaghmore. From my recollection these were the late George Galbraith and Bobby Bennett who, thankfully, is still with us.

A number of meetings were held and negotiations proceeded rapidly. Mr. Galbraith and Mr. Bennett were invited to visit the premises in Mountmellick and were smuggled in almost in the dead of the night, to keep the confidentiality and secrecy on board. Eventually agreement was reached in principle, subject to the board's approval. When they discussed the sort of strategy to take, they realised they couldn't release the vendor's name to the board. On that basis, they put their proposition to the board and as Colm Costelloe said to me, it was unheard of that

1. Further information on Clonaslee Co-op appears in the chapter on Clonaslee.

332

a board would accept a business proposition from two of their members without knowing the details and the facts. It showed great confidence in the two people involved.

Billy Flynn: The rules were changed to allow the Mountmellick area to develop as a branch of Donaghmore, similar to Raheen and Spink. As a result of that there was an area advisory committee set up and a change of rules gave Mountmellick area two members on the board. The two members were, as I recall, Gerry Culliton and Chris Horan. Within the next couple of years, there was a third member of the board elected from the Mountmellick area – Bernie Rochford.

Bernard Rochford: Yes, there were three of us then from Mountmellick on the committee of management at Donaghmore. I have nothing but praise for the other members of the committee. There was great harmony and appreciation of what everyone was doing.

Billy Flynn: The buying of Smiths, in my recollection, was the most interesting piece of the whole scenario. When Smiths came on the market, the local committee felt that it had to be put together with the Pims part of the business or it would prove disastrous. But the Board in Donaghmore felt it was going to be a very severe financial pressure for them to buy it at that particular time. Mountmellick had only become a recent part of Donaghmore and it was going to put a lot of pressure on finances to buy another premises in the region. There was a number of area committee meetings, held outside the town to maintain confidentiality, so that there wouldn't be any movements noticed. We met about five times, and eventually the board gave us the message that they couldn't see themselves being able to buy at that particular time. A number of people on the committee said that it was now time to put our money where our mouths were and they suggested that we put together a fund to give a loan to the board over a year or two period, to help them to buy the premises. We felt that strongly about the necessity to buy it. At the end of one night's meeting, where there was only one committee member missing, there were slips of paper passed around and the members marked what they could afford to give. My recollection tells me that there was about £22,000 to be collected from that particular meeting. Immediately after that, the Board of Donaghmore went along and, seeing that there was such a strength of will in Mountmellick to have the premises bought, they decided to buy it, when it came up for auction.

It certainly was one of my greatest ambitions to see it happening and it was tremendous that there were so many people on the committee who had the strength to lend money to buy it. Since then, it has gone from strength to strength in Mountmellick and we are all delighted that it is still a strong branch.

John Joe Dunne: I would feel strongly that across the areas from Rosenallis, Clonaslee, Ballyfin, Mountmellick, the fact that there were a lot of farmers updating their farms and starting to work to serious farm plans and improve their farmyards, stock and breeding, they seemed to all come together. There seemed to be a great nucleus and energy there. That went hand in hand with the purpose of Mountmellick and the integration of Donaghmore. I think also that during that period of the late 1960s and early 1970s, the whole EEC issue was to the forefront. We were associate members and then full members. There were discussions about Mancholt and the excitement of getting away from the domination of the British market and having an open market with all these other countries. This injected into people a great enthusiasm and expectation. Again I think it was fortunate for the whole project on that basis to have these two things coming together and the opportunity to extend our business as farmers as well farmers' ownership and direction of their business.

Sean Young: Obviously there was a necessity for additional funding to progress the Co-op. The overall Co-op at this stage was Donaghmore, Raheen and Spink, as well as Mountmellick. We were working as a team at this stage and, I suppose, in fairness to other areas that had already put up their capital and share funding, there was a big drive to spread the shareholders right throughout the whole area that the Co-op was serving. That wasn't going to happen by sending out a circular and people were not going to come in with their cash and cheques. There had to be a selling and marketing job done on that. The area committee took on a big responsibility, supported by some of the staff, of calling around to their neighbours in little groups, chatting to them about it and selling the idea. It was a tremendous success. I suppose we were focusing at that stage on milk producers and people who were committing themselves to a future in milk. One could argue that they were captive customers in one sense but they were ones who were going to have a direct income and bearing on the Society. It was a big move forward but it wasn't just the money, it was buying into a share of the business. But you were also doing other business with the Co-op and promoting it to the non shareholders in the area, and trying to extend the business.

Billy Flynn: One of the things that I regretted was that for two or three years after the introduction of the Capital Contribution Scheme,[2] there was a lot of opposition to it. There was a feeling that this was a levy on us that we need not be paying. The opposition went on for a number of years. However, after we went plc, there was no need for such schemes.

Clonaslee adopted a system whereby 50 pence per pig was paid in capital contributions in the same way that the quarter pence on the gallon of milk. When the amalgamation of Avonmore and Clonaslee took place, some of the shareholders in the most recent Glanbia set up from Clonaslee were the biggest shareholders in Glanbia – because of the capital contributions deducted from their pig payments. Two of the shareholders from Clonaslee were, indeed, the largest shareholders in Glanbia.

One of the aspects of the positive nature of what was happening in Mountmellick, was that it spread back into the formation of Avonmore itself. When the discussion first started on amalgamation it was very evident that the farmers themselves were a bit more positive than the management people, whom you would naturally expect would be a bit worried about their own positions. Consequently, the first few meetings were a little bit slow to develop before the farmers drove it and before the final decision was made.

John Joe Dunne: I would agree. I think the very fact that agriculture in Laois and Avonmore expanded so rapidly was because there was a great Macra base in Laois at that time and a great lot of young people coming into agriculture. People were up for it; they were up to looking at new ideas, and the new ideas and the excitement propelled us all on. These new ideas were about purchasing, selling

---

2. A scheme started in 1973 whereby a quarter penny per gallon of milk supplied was stopped for the purposes of building up the capital of the society. The scheme lasted from 1973 to 1984 and for every £1 contributed, the supplier received a £1 "C" share in the Society. The contribution was a half pence per gallon for part of the time.

and marketing at a higher level; getting more people involved; cutting the costs of the gallon of milk or tonne of grain; sharing our capital contributions; having this mighty plant in Ballyragget. This was very exciting and we were young and up for it. Looking back it's very hard to know if all that hadn't to happen, where we would be. Certainly, I don't think any of the decisions at that stage were wrong. I think they were very good and positive decisions and they did increase the income of farmers in this area. I think we all responded back at farm level too to that excitement and we all started to build our milking parlours and improve our stocks. It was happening at different levels; at an individual level, at an area level, and also at a collective Avonmore level.

Obviously, you know in hindsight there were a few mistakes made along the line. But you never do anything without making a few mistakes, whether individual or collective mistakes. But the project overall has been a success.

Billy Flynn: The acceleration of milk production was phenomenal during Reddy Brennan's early time in Avonmore. He increased milk supply for quite a number of years by 16 or 17%. The great pity was that he didn't get a few more years before quota came because we'd have been very strong quota-wise if they had followed the way he had driven the increased supply situation.

John Joe Dunne: It may be asked to what extent the decision to amalgamate with Avonmore was influenced by the fact that the Donaghmore milk plants could no longer cope with the greatly increased milk supply without spending a lot of money which they didn't have and were already sending their surplus milk to Ballyragget. To turn that argument around, if we didn't go into Avonmore none of us would have increased our milk as fast as we did so we'd have a lesser quota today. There was a very active committee here who were always involved and very progressive about trying to create better services and facilities and be attentive to what was on the menu. The purchase of Smiths was obviously a very key decision but that didn't mean that the committee had all their work done. It started to look at things like the gateway, the bad state of the two shops where we had a business and at a staff who were working in very poor conditions. The services were being delivered out of very pokey holes and long counters and stuff having to be packed away that couldn't be seen.

The building of the new shop was a huge investment but it was also a vote of confidence in the people who were dealing with the business. I think the committee too had a big role in it, not alone with planning it, but in getting a decision from Avonmore to provide the capital investment. Maybe we have moved a bit away from that; I personally believe that we have. We don't seem in the last seven to ten years to have the same influence on decision-making or input into it. It's not because there are different people at all, and I wouldn't dream of suggesting that, maybe it's because the business is at a level where you can't do that – I don't know why. But I think it's a great pity not to have participation down at the ground level, other than on paper.

Billy Flynn: I suppose though the strength of the Co-op thinking and progression in Laois particularly and in Kildare and other small co-operative organisations that came into being such as IFAC, the Irish Farmers Accounts Co-op, Laois held the strongest groupings in the country at the time it was formed. Consequently, the county had one seat at the Board, which wouldn't have been the norm from the national point of view. I must say that IFAC has certainly played a big role in the financial advisory business and in farming in general.

Frank White
– reflects on a long association with Mountmellick Branch

"Me and my late brother used to go clean out a place here in Mountmellick. Comer Conroy owned the store and it had flag floors on it. That's where the butterman[3] used to buy the butter. I never met him because he'd be gone by the time we got home from school. The butter would come in from the farmers. All we got to wash out the place was a kettle of hot water. There was no such thing as Fairy liquid in those days. It was a fright to clean out – you would break your neck on the floor. The butterman had an utensil that he used to stick into the butter. You would see them doing it now with cheese when they are testing it. The reason he had it was that someone one time brought in a big turnip and covered it over with butter and got paid for it.

"He'd buy any kind of butter so long as it was butter. Some of it had hairs in it and some would have a blue streak through it. But it all went to Cork and there was a factory there that used to purify it and, as a matter of fact, it came back to Pims in Mountmellick. I sold it myself and it came back under the name of Black Swan – there was a black swan on the front of the packet and it was marked 'factory butter'. I also used to get butter from Drinagh in County Cork, and it was pure creamery butter. But a lot of the people coming into Pims would look for Black Swan. They always used to look for the Black Swan. Although it was only marked factory butter, there was more the taste of country butter off it than there was off the creamery variety.

"I went in to work in Pims in 1942, during the War, in the bottle store. It was at the rear of the grocery shop in the square. We had a ladies' drapery shop downstairs, we had a gents' shop upstairs and we also had an office there. Moving on again we had a butcher's stall – Peter Graham was the chargehand when I was there. Next came the provisions' shop and Sam Holmes, Pat Finlay and myself worked there. Then there was the hardware and Robert Patterson from the North of Ireland (there is an estate now called after him in Mountmellick) and Charlie Sands, were the two head men in it. We had the yard man, Mick Seale, and his son, Michael. Down at the end, we had a carpenter's shop. We used to call it 'the hut' but there was machinery in it and Jimmie Hayes, Jim Carroll, Jim Dunne and the old man Bill Wall worked in it, making the wheels for the horse carts. They also made coffins there as well and bog barrows. Then we had the forge and old Paddy Hayes, Jimmie's father, worked in it. He was a great blacksmith. We had the bacon factory as well and there were a good lot of men working there. The head man in it was Ned Whitford and next in line to him was Joe Molloy.

"When I went there, there were no Catholics employed in the office, in the drapery or in the hardware. There was one Catholic man employed in the grocery. He worked in the wholesale end upstairs and he only came down at dinner time. So I was the first Catholic man to go into the office. I understood the ration books well and that's why I was brought in there. When I finished there, I went on to the provisions' shop and I worked under Sam Holmes. The Bacon factory was taken over by Dennys and they started an abattoir for killing cattle and sheep as well.

3. The 'butterman' referred to was the late Cornelius Dennehy, from Millstreet, Co. Cork, aged 30, who was murdered on 17 August 1938. Dermot Smith, from the Rushes, Wolfhill, Co. Laois, was convicted and hanged for the murder.

"The wages when I started was 15/- in the old money, it would be 75 cent today. The boss man at that time told me not to tell any of the others as they only had 12/- per week. The boss would give you anything bar money; that was the type of man he was. He didn't like to see senior men smoking behind the counter as it was a bad example for younger men.

"In 1969, Mrs. Bailey came into the grocery where I was working at the time and told me that Donaghmore had bought the business. She said she would approach Mr. Wallis and see if he would take me on the staff. I was taken on in the hardware and was in control of stocks in the yard and millstuffs

"I was delighted to get the job. My wages doubled straight away. Pims never paid a wage. I met the old man about a month later. I was carrying a part of a plough across to a car in the square. He said to me 'you are working now anyhow' and I said 'if I am, I'm getting paid for it'. We were delighted with the Donaghmore takeover.

"Someone would come down for layers mash and we wouldn't have it and they would take something else. Then the stocks would be out, only a little out, but you wouldn't be happy when you couldn't balance them out completely. I went into the shop after the three months and I worked at general hardware, selling nails and timber and different things. Then after some time, a fellow left and the boss man, Larry O'Rourke, said that they were going to put me in the glass store. I said I knew nothing about cutting glass – I never cut glass in my life. But Larry said 'you will not be long learning'. So I got in on it anyhow.

"After some time, the man that was in charge of the plumbing left and the manager came to me again and said that he was going to put me in charge of that department. I said I didn't know anything about plumbing. It all went by numbers – a tee was 318, a straight joiner was 310, a male/female was 312. I got to be an expert in all the numbers. When people came in some of them wouldn't know exactly what they wanted, and I'd say to them 'Explain to me what you are doing' and when they would explain it to me, I'd know exactly what they wanted. So I did very well in the plumbing.

"A daughter of mine, Olive, worked in the office for a couple of years and she got on very well. My son, Charlie, was anxious to come in during the holidays and Mr. Wallis took him in for a couple of months. He was put in charge of the tools. We had a great lot of tools at that time and he was great at them. When the holidays were over, Billy Wallis pleaded with Charlie to stay on but Charlie said no, as he wanted to go back and do his Leaving Cert. So he went back, got his Leaving and then came back. He was delighted with the job and was in charge of all the tools. He did the ordering and knew what contractors and other people wanted. He is in the job 30 years now and I believe he is very popular with the customers. He took after his father!

"It was good for business to have a good mixture of Catholics and Protestants on the management committee. I always found that about Donaghmore – there were no exceptions, anyone could go in to work in it whatever religion you were.

"The advisory committee were a good crowd; they were a great help to us at the counter. We might have some complaint to make. We might be short a man in one area and we would need and we'd mention it to one of the committee men and he would bring it up at a meeting with Mr. Wallis. They could also come in and tell us if there was a bit of slackness in some area.

"The customers were very happy with the change over from Pims to

Donaghmore because we were carrying a lot of extra goods. If we wanted something in a hurry we were able to get it from the head branch in Donaghmore. We had a van coming every week from Donaghmore. Sean Bergin was the driver and he used to bring over a lot of stuff. A lot of the millstuffs were brought in by Mountmellick man, Mick Reddin. The Co-op was great for the farmers.

"On Saturdays we worked from nine to nine. The town at that time was working from nine to eight and we were used to working until eight. The extra hour made a difference. It seemed to be a very long day. We were there looking at each other and that made the hour longer altogether. If anyone did come in, they only came in for a chat at that time. Donaghmore wouldn't agree to change back and we threatened that we would go at eight anyway. Mr. Wallis brought a few people from Donaghmore with him to cover the extra hour. You wouldn't be doing much business from eight to nine when the other shops were closed. People who came in on a Saturday night, left in their order and their eggs and butter and they'd go down to confession. They'd call back later before eight to collect their stuff. It was straightened out very soon after. We were very happy after that.

"There were some characters too. I remember in Pims' time there was a man in the hardware and this lady came in. She was getting married and buying a bed. Some time earlier he had sold her mother a fork and had overcharged her for it. He told her the price of the bed. 'Well, now', she said, 'if you done my mother in the fork, you are not going to do me in the bed'. That was true; that happened. I remember one fellow coming in to me, a long time ago, he was about seventy at the time and we were talking about friends and relations. He said 'My mother used to say it would take a church to hold your relations but a pulpit would hold your friends'. It was a true saying.

"When Donaghmore took over, Larry O'Rourke became manager, Johnny Martin was second in command and, I suppose, I could have been third in command to a point. There were only three keys to the safe and I had one of them."

John Martin
(Tyrrellspass and Mountmellick)

"I started in Pims on 01/07/1963, under the manager, Tom Dooley, who was from Durrow, Co. Laois. I hailed from Tyrellspass in Co. Westmeath. After about three years, Dooley left and Mrs. Bailey, who was proprietor of Pims, appointed myself and Larry O'Rourke, who was already working there, as joint managers. We continued in that role until February 1969, when Mrs. Bailey sold the premises to Donaghmore. Under the new title, Larry was made manager and I was appointed assistant to him.

"After the changeover, Mr. Wallis, who was manager in Donaghmore, brought me over there for three months, to learn their way of trading. After about four years, we came under the Avonmore umbrella, but our work continued much the same as before. Donaghmore later acquired another premises, Smiths. Avonmore did some alterations to those premises and built a new shop, which is still trading, now under the name of Glanbia.

"At Pims, I was dealing in just general hardware, but under Donaghmore and Avonmore, there were also meals, fuels and other goods in the retail side and I did a lot of the buying as well.

"In later years, as business increased, we were responsible for various departments. Mine was mainly veterinary, mill stuffs and fuels in the yard, at which I continued until I retired in September 1997."

" In Smiths, before Avonmore took over, there was a staff man named J.L. Martin. A local man, Bill Redmond, used to say to me that there is a J.L. Martin, a John Martin and there will be a third Martin working here. Many years later, my son, Kevin, came to work there, was there before I left and is still working there with Glanbia."

George Kerr
(Ross, Ballyfin – farmer, supplier, shareholder and customer in Raheen and Mountmellick. Also, a near neighbour to Victor Sands)

"My family's first association with Donaghmore/Raheen was in 1952. John Seale had been collecting milk in some areas, and was eager to enlarge and extend his route. He called a meeting at Irey Lane in the spring of that year. He had canvassed around the locality, and quite a good crowd turned up. John explained his idea and what the advantages for us might be, in becoming creamery members.

"Someone asked: 'What will we rear our calves with, John? What about this blue water that you would bring back to us?

"Oh", said John, "Don't mind the look of it, that is wonderful stuff for the calves."

"We took him at his word. Most of us had small cow numbers at the time. We got some of those rather large heavy twelve gallon cans, and we were advised to erect a stand at the roadside.

"We were about 150 yards from the roadside, and the only way of carrying the cans was with a bog barrow, and that job fell to me. We continued that way until 1954, when we acquired our first tractor. So we struggled and progressed, and are still supplying to what is now Glanbia. When we started we had about twelve cows, which produced two cans of milk.

"Johnnie was a great timekeeper. 8.30am was his time at our stand, and you knew to have it out before then. Of course, like all the others around, ours was milked by hand, so you had to start quite early.

"Our hand milking continued from 1952 to 1965, at which time our cow numbers were about 20. My parents were the principal milkers, but my brother and I did our fair share also. In the earlier years, we had no ideal way of cooling the milk. Only in the late 1950's, we got our own well and were able to route a supply of water to the milking area. We continued at that until 1976, when the bulk collection started. John Joe Collier came around then, to advise us about this new idea. We got a 400 gallon dairy cool tank.

"As time went by, prices improved and we saw the advantages. Gradually our cow numbers increased and then the plank on the back of the tractor was not big enough, so we started to use a trap cart. One time I was doing so, and on the road I would have to reverse back to get near the stand. I saw Johnnie Seale coming some distance away and just as I started to reverse, the lever which kept the trap closed down must not have been fully in place, and up goes the cart and the lids flew off the cans. Johnnie had little or no milk that day. The heavy cans were later replaced by much lighter aluminium cans.

"As was the case with other suppliers, because of the early start on Sundays we would keep that milk, separate it, and make butter for our own use. In earlier years, we also churned and made butter – some of which we would sell. That, of course, was part of the running of farmers' households – big and small.

"In later years, when the system changed, and skim milk was not sent back, one advantage was that the cans came back scalded and clean, and would only need a quick rinse. When they had skim in them for a few hours, it was not so nice trying to clean them.

"In 1976 the bulk collection started. We got a 300 gallon tank, and we altered our entrance to let the tanker lorry come in. I did not regret the passing of the can era. No way. We decided to put in the milking parlour, starting with a four unit, and adding two more units, about two years later. That same six unit plant is still there and last year, in 2002, our son David and I reckoned that over half a million gallons of milk have gone through it in that time. I'm retired now and David has taken over since 1994.

"We used some of the aluminium cans to hold milk for the calves but we let the Hydrosen wash into the cans and that was a bad idea – it caused holes to come in them. We did most of our dealings in Raheen and later in Mountmellick, mainly after I was proposed for, and elected, on the area committee. But in both places, we got a good service, and got on well with management and staff."

Victor Sands
(Irey, Ballyfin – farmer, milk supplier, shareholder, and customer in Raheen and Mountmellick).

"When John Seale canvassed around this area in or around 1950 my late father, Robert, along with other farmers in the locality decided to send milk to Raheen Creamery. We started with two cans – the old heavy 12 gallon ones – and we had to erect a stand on the roadside. We were fortunate enough to have a stream running at the back of the cow-house, and we made part of it deeper, so as to be able to put the cans into it up to the shoulder near the top. It was ideal for keeping the milk cool, and I don't think we ever had any sour milk returned. I remember my mother would sometimes remark on seeing a number of pink labels on some cans, when John Seale was on his return journey – especially during the warmer months.

"The skim milk was of great value to farmers for feeding to pigs and calves. My father always fed it to our pigs, and you would know the pigs which were given the skim – their skin would be snow white. They would thrive very well on it and of course they would also get barley, potatoes and so on. My mother used to churn the cream and make butter. When people started getting butter from the creamery, they found it very different and hard to get used to.

"In our own case, because the lorry was going much earlier on Sunday mornings, we used separate the Saturday night and Sunday morning milk, and mother would make butter, which she continued to do for many years.

"The milking was done by hand for many years also. I remember putting twelve of those heavy type cans of milk on the stand. The hand milking continued until 1960s.

"My mother and father did most of the milking of around twenty five cows, my brother did some also and would get the cans out to the stand before going to school. It was very hard work but that's how things were, you just had to do it, as with many other things. There were never many complaints about creamery milk. It was the first big income from cows and was a big improvement to the farming scene.

"We had a very good milk carter in John Seale, who was always very dedicated and timely. He would always arrive around 8.50am and would return quite early, which meant that the skim would be nice and fresh. The pigs would stand quiet and listen for the sound of his lorry, knowing that something appetising was on the way.

"My father usually went over to Raheen with a car and a trailer, whenever we required mill stuff or other goods. He always had a great regard for Joe Butler, who was the manager then. Nowadays all milk is collected in bulk, and while we still call to Raheen at times, most of our trading is with the Mountmellick branch, which is much nearer to us. When the bulk collection started, a lot of people were somewhat reluctant at first. It meant quite some change to the schedule to what they had known and lived with for so many years. In many cases, the usual entrance to people's yards were not suitable for those bigger lorries, and reluctantly farmers had to provide suitable entry points to their farmyards, at fairly high cost. People who perhaps lived a distance away from public roads, and also, the smaller supplier could find themselves in real trouble and have to cease supplying altogether.

"Neither religion nor politics ever came into the running of the creamery, none that we ever noticed anyway."

The Donkey Serenade

"Somewhere along his route John Seale had a customer whose clock must have had a liking to slowing down a little, as he was usually a bit late getting down to the roadside with his milk.

"One day he left a note for John, saying: 'Come up for the milk, the jennet is gone.' And John wrote a reply on the note, saying: 'Leave the milk where it is, the lorry is gone'."

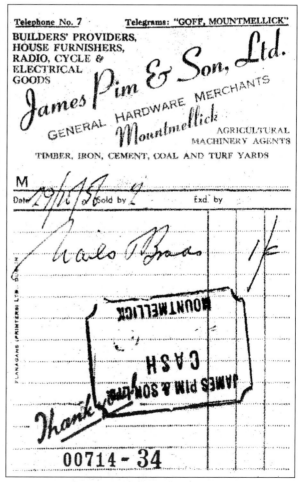

Cash sales docket issued by James Pim & Son from 1956.

Personal Recollections – Macra na Feirme
– good for farming, rural Ireland and the co-operatives

Michael Igoe chaired a round table discussion on the important role of Macra na Feirme in every aspect of rural life with some prominent members of the organisation – Liam Holohan, Liam Rohan, Tom Phelan, Willie Clegg, Billy Flynn, Hugh Ryan and James Costello.

M acra na Feirme has had a very positive influence on rural development and country life since its foundation in 1944. While it has grown into a strong national organisation, Laois and surrounding areas has played a central role in its formation and development. The county, for instance, has provided three national presidents and has been the launching pad for a number of important initiatives helpful to farming folk countrywide.

Macra has provided a great training ground for young farmers in organising and managing their affairs. Most of the leaders of farming related bodies in recent decades have honed their debating and management skills in Macra. The organisation has also worked closely with the co-operative movement and has been supportive of the work of individual co-ops and also of the amalgamations of smaller co-ops in forming larger more economic and competitive super co-ops such as Glanbia.

Billy Flynn of Clonaslee recalled a training course for young farmers jointly organised by Donaghmore Co-op and Macra in the late 1960s. John Miller, now a director with Glanbia, as well as Bobby and Freddie Bailey, were also involved as was Liam Hyland, MEP, before he became involved in politics.

Tom Phelan, Chairman of Donaghmore Area Advisory Committee, remembered a similar course being run jointly by Avonmore and Macra in the 1980s, one of many organised throughout the country. About fifteen young farmers from the whole Avonmore area took part. It was an excellent course, he recalled, and most of those taking part later became actively involved in the Avonmore/Glanbia structure.

One interesting development that emanated from Laois was the Farms Accounts School. Macra, together with the IFA and the Laois Committee of Agriculture, headed by Alec Sweeney, CAO, came up with the idea and helped get it off the ground. It grew into a national event in which Billy Flynn became involved along with Peadar Murphy and Donal Cashman, who was its chairman.

Macra members were always in the vanguard of change and in the ever constant pursuit to improve farming methods and the rural way of life. The organisation was very active in promoting rural electrification and in encouraging rural dwellers to seek a connection to the national grid. James Costello remembered how active Laois members were in the campaign for rural electrification. Clonaslee was, he believed, the first area in County Laois, to be switched on to the scheme.

As regards amalgamation, Billy Flynn, was of the opinion that without the influence of Macra, Donaghmore members may not have voted for amalgamation. He had just become involved in the Donaghmore Committee along with John Miller while Chris Horan, Clonaslee, had been on the committee for some years at that time. "This debate on amalgamation was happening at a time when IFA members were on the ground canvassing for Ireland's entry into the EEC," Billy related. "There was a meeting in Mountrath held in connection with amalgamation and the proposal looked dead at one stage, although some members of the Board were very keen on it. There were a few speakers that night from the younger generation and they probably swung the meeting in favour of their proposal. One of the main angles addressed was that Ireland was out looking for full membership of the EEC, not associate membership, so the young people's advice was to go for amalgamation now and not have to go cap in hand later. One man who was very influential for the proposal was George Galbraith."

Liam Rohan, Shanahoe, also remembered just how committed George Galbraith was to amalgamation. "He was talking about it even when there was no meeting taking place. He was spreading the message wherever he could. He was the most dedicated Macra member that I ever knew. Most of us came into the meeting in Abbeyleix on bicycles at the time but George would walk all the way in from Corbally. Eventually when cars became more plentiful someone might drive him home. He rarely missed a meeting and would get involved in all the topics that we, young lads, were discussing. He was very influential and very helpful. He was as enthusiastic as if he were a young chap himself."

Liam Holohan nodded agreement. "I remember getting involved in Abbeyleix Macra and working with George Galbraith on the Abbeyleix Show Committee. There was a lot of inter-action between the Show committee and Donaghmore and George and Sean Reilly were very influential, especially when we were looking for sponsorship. That inter-action was passed down to my time and Tom Phelan's. Regarding Co-op sponsorship in my time the most influential people were Sean Hearn and Joe Delaney. In our time Laois ran at least two national competitions that were sponsored by Avonmore."

Tom Phelan was also full of praise for Joe Delaney. "Joe was, in a sense, a Macra man even when he was at home. You were going through an open door when you went to see Joe. Because he always had the best interests of Macra and Avonmore at heart, he would never see your organisation stuck, even when sponsorship money was tight."

Billy Flynn added his praise of Joe. "It was generally taken throughout the Donaghmore region that Joe was a man of commonsense. He was probably the one man who had no letters behind his name but was absolutely Mr. Commonsense."

Willie Clegg believed that Mountrath Mart would not have started up but for the involvement of Macra members. "Macra gave young rural people the confidence to stand up and express themselves. That was why a lot of enterprises, like Mountrath Mart, got going," he stated.

The presence of Macra members on Area Advisory Committees as observers was a useful exercise, according to Tom Phelan. They were invited on board by

Avonmore and the tradition has continued, although those co-opted now are not necessarily Macra members. That is because Macra numbers have fallen.

Liam Holohan mentioned that getting members to take up positions of chairman, secretary or treasurer or to get them involved in organising competitions is very difficult now. "It is a situation that has been developing for the past ten years or so", he stated. "They don't want to take up positions of responsibility or to commit themselves or their time. The whole social aspect has changed too", he informed. "Back in the late 1970s or early 1980s there were four Macra halls in Laois; Portlaoise, Abbeyleix, Mountmellick and Mountrath and they were busy places. I remember a Thursday night in Abbeyleix when there were over 1,300 people packed into the hall in Abbeyleix for Big Tom or some other singer. Now younger members want to go elsewhere, to pubs and places where there are more comfortable surroundings."

James Costello wondered are co-ops like Glanbia more dependent now on chief executives and if less heed is taken of the committee system. He feels certain that if the system was worked to its full potential, the committees would wield more power. He agreed with former Avonmore chairman, John Duggan's, assessment of the committee system that any member who had a problem or needed information was never too far from his local committee member and could have his queries dealt with by him. The means of communication were there from the top to the bottom and from the bottom to the top.

The influence that John Duggan had on Macra and the influence that Macra had on him, in the Avonmore context, were highlighted by Billy Flynn. He said that, as chairman, Duggan drove every part of Avonmore on the same basis as he had operated within Macra. He had learned well from his days in Macra.

Although it is becoming increasingly difficult to attract new members into Macra, Hugh Ryan felt that there is still plenty of scope for the organisation. "I think that it is doing good work still but for a more limited number. I think it is extremely important, particularly in the interest of other organisations such as the IFA, ICMSA, ICA, GAA or the co-operatives, that you train young people. We could be a little despondent about leadership and the future. If you take a young farmer, or the not-so-young, he is living, and is going to live in a more competitive world. If he is to survive he has to be good. If the vast majority are good for themselves, they will be good for their organisation too. I wouldn't be too despondent. There are a number of good young people out there and I think that they will make their contribution, whether it's on their own farm, at co-op level or whatever."

SECTION THREE

Extending the Frontiers

Mountmellick Branch after the acquisition by Donaghmore Co-Op.

Mountmellick in more recent times.

MOUNTMELLICK –
a success story that began when a rare opportunity presented itself

Mountmellick Home and Farm Store is now a well established and very important part of the Donaghmore/Monasterevin regional operations of Glanbia. The story of how the Mountmellick business was brought under the co-operative wing of Donaghmore is an unusual one. Greg Tierney, now in his retirement, was involved in the acquisition as an official of the ICOS. He takes up the story.

"In June of 1968 I received a visit in the ICOS offices in Merrion Square in Dublin from a Mr. and Mrs. Bailey from Mountmellick. I had no idea at the time of the purpose of their visit. It quickly emerged that they owned a business in Mountmellick, which was involved in the supply of farm requirements. Mrs. Bailey explained that they wished to retire but as they had no family members willing to take on the business, they wished to dispose of it at a fair price to the farmers in the area. I was asked if I could arrange to have a co-operative established to represent those farmers but in such a way that there would not be much publicity about what was happening because of the risk that competitors would use the knowledge to damage the business.

"I indicated that there would not be major problems in starting a co-op but that I did not see the point as there was already a co-op (Donaghmore) serving farmers in the area. Furthermore, I pointed out that it would not be possible to avoid publicity when forming the co-op, as it would be publicity that would be necessary to ensure a successful campaign to raise sufficient capital to buy the business. Discussion took place on the possibility of having discussions with Donaghmore without the risk of publicity and I promised to see what could be done.

"Subsequently I chaired a meeting in the home of Baileys on July 12th. This meeting was attended by the Baileys and a Mr. Kelly from Portlaoise (presumably an adviser) as well as Messrs. Grogan and Wallis. A valuation of the business had been carried out by H. Lisney & Co. and this formed the basis of the discussion that day. Following that meeting the Chairman of the co-op was advised of the proposal but the absolute necessity for strict confidentiality was impressed very strongly on him. Eventually he agreed that management could progress the matter to the final stages without advising the committee, provided it was clear that no agreement was final until approved by the committee. Furthermore ICOS was to be involved at all stages and in fact the engineering staff of ICOS surveyed the premises on behalf of management without raising any suspicions amongst staff in Mountmellick or in the town.

"A letter dated 13th September 1968 was sent to Mrs. Bailey advising her that the Chairman had authorised management 'to investigate the proposal to a considerable degree without referring the matter back to the committee' and she was

In the Retailing Excellence Awards for 1995/96, Mountmellick were the winners in their category in both years.
Front row (left to right): Alice Conroy, Michael McCann, Billy Murphy, Paul Hogan, John Martin, Charlie White, James Fitzharris.
Back row (left to right): Seán Hyland, Joan McRedmond, Leo Dunne, Michael Fitzpatrick, Michael Fox, Vincent Callanan, John Brennan, Paddy Weston, Thomas Callanan, David Hyland.

advised that contact should be made directly with the secretary, Mr. John Galbraith. I am also aware from my own attendances at meetings of the committee that the chairman sought the approval of the committee for the management together with ICOS to be authorised to negotiate the purchase of an unnamed business for an unspecified sum provided that the final agreement would come before the committee for approval. That approval was given and indicates the level of confidence that the committee had in the chairman. What is equally remarkable about this whole transaction is the speed with which it was concluded bearing in mind the requirement for absolute confidentiality.

"The first date on which management was involved directly at all was July 12th and exactly two months later, Mrs. Bailey could be advised that management had been given authority to negotiate to a near final stage. In the meantime the chairman had sought and received outline approval for the management to negotiate. Although the letter to Mrs. Bailey conveying that information was sent by ICOS on 13th September, it is remarkable that a letter could be sent by the Society to ICOS on 23rd October thanking us for our help, clearly implying that the deal had been concluded."

Pims were a Quaker family who had come to Mountmellick in 1740. Over many years they had catered for a wide variety of trading requirements, especially grocery, hardware, clothing and bacon curing. They were wholesale merchants also.[1] Now, due to the goodwill of Mr. and Mrs. Bailey, the expertise and discretion of ICOS and the foresight and management skills of Donaghmore, the hardware and agri-related part of Pims[1] business, one of the oldest trading establishments in the midlands, was safely under the wing of Donaghmore Co-op.

1. Historical information supplied by James Dooley, 32 Patrick St., Mountmellick, and formerly from Clonduff, Rosenallis.

Larry O'Rourke, who came to work in Pims in 1960 and became manager there in 1963, remembers Mrs. Bailey as "a real lady". She was a Pim before marriage. Mr. Bailey, he said, had not much to do with the business. "They made everything. They bound wheels, made horse and asses' carts. There were eight carpenters there. Jimmy Hayes was a carpenter and his father was the blacksmith. It was lovely to see the two of them working there."

There was one major problem at Pims, which was the lack of accessibility for large trucks because of the arched entrance. Larry went to a Mr. White, in the Planning Office of Laois County Council, who told him simply that "if you have to get lorries in, you'll have to get them in". "That was all he said to me and we went ahead and took down some of the adjacent building, which Pims owned. There was no planning application needed", Larry recalled.

A meeting of shareholders was held on 26 February 1970 for the purpose of electing an advisory committee for the Mountmellick area to the committee of management. The general idea was to improve communications and relations between the Society and its shareholders and customers.

It was agreed to divide the area into four sub-areas, Rosenallis, Clonaslee, Ballyfin and Mountmellick. The following were put forward for the committee from these sub-areas: Rosenallis – William McEvoy, Clonaheen; William Shaw, Rosenallis; Sean Young, Drummond and Dan Hourigan, Cloncannon. Clonaslee – Patrick F. Corbett, Ballykaneen; James Costello, Graigueafulla; William Flynn, Rearyvalley and Michael Lalor, Barkmills. Ballyfin – Ralph Thompson, Camplone; Padraig Ryan, O'Moore's Forest; Patrick Scully, Rossleighan and Sean Fitzpatrick, Barkmills. Mountmellick – Michael Burke, Derryguile; Denis O'Rourke, Acragar; John Ryan, Clonsoughy and Bernard Rochford, Mountmellick. Two local members of the committee of management, Gerry Culliton and Chris Horan, were co-opted onto the area committee as ex-officio members. William Flynn was elected chairman, William Shaw, vice-chairman and Bernard Rochford, secretary. At the AGM in early 1971, Mr. Flynn was re-elected chairman and John Joe Dunne became secretary.

The question of purchasing Smiths general and hardware store in Mountmellick was raised in July 1971. The committee of management (effectively the board of directors) was consulted but it was found that providing the finance was a problem. Mountmellick area advisory committee members agreed to go security for £5,000, which was one-third of the asking price. Gerry Culliton told a meeting on 6 August 1971 that the bank had agreed to an overdraft of £15,000 but on the understanding that if more was required, it would have to come from the farmers themselves.

The purchase was finalised a little time later. The committee of management and some senior staff paid a visit to the Mountmellick branch on 8 October 1971 to inspect the premises for themselves. The shop was re-opened and, after some initial teething problems with staff and service, it was soon doing a thriving business.

The first talks of a possible joining of forces with Avonmore took place in June 1972 and discussions continued for the next year before the fateful decision was eventually taken to amalgamate. With bulk collection now on the cards, the milk carters saw that the writing was on the wall for them and they sought compensation in lieu of loss of earnings.

Plans for the new layout of the yard and the new warehouse measuring 135' x 75' were put before a meeting in May 1974.

At the July meeting of 1974, there were claims made that the area committee had no real power but Gerry Culliton pointed out that it was important to use the area advisory system as a means of communications with 'the top brass'.

In March 1975 there were murmurs of discontent relating to the milk price. It was said that it had fallen below all expectations and instead of increasing production, it would drive farmers from dairying. In June 1975, the Donaghmore chairman, Bobby Bennett, told area members that meetings were being held to see if the workers would forego the second round wage increase in view of the fact that farmers had to take a reduction in the milk price. In February 1976, it was decided to write to John Galbraith, of the Donaghmore region, informing him of the "complete dissatisfaction with the milk testing process".

The shop was operating at a loss and there were much deliberation over the changes that were needed to be made. One suggested improvement was to allow the Mountmellick manager, Larry O'Rourke, the same powers to sell as had the Donaghmore stores manager, Billy Wallis. In 1979, the regional manager, Brendan Graham, reported a big increase in business in the Mountmellick Branch for the previous year and then outlined plans for the re-building of the shop.

There was still unease, however, among Mountmellick suppliers about milk prices. The area committee passed a resolution at their meeting in December 1979 that "in view of the heavy commitments and the rising costs in milk production, a rise in milk prices is most essential ..."

At the AGM on 24 November 1980, John Joe Dunne was elected chairman of the area committee and Ralph Thompson, secretary. It was reported that the Mountmellick Branch was doing very good business and it was decided to send a letter to the manager and staff thanking them for their co-operation during the previous year and "especially during the very bad harvest". It was felt that the amount of money stopped from milk suppliers by way of capital contributions was "a heavy burden during a crisis year". In March 1981, a turnover of £0.5 million was reported for the previous three months at Mountmellick.

The estimated cost of building a new shop at Mountmellick was given as £200,000 at a meeting in October 1981. Larry O'Rourke recalls: "Pat O'Neill and Brendan Graham came over one day and walked around the yard. After a little while Pat had his mind made up. 'Go ahead and build it', he said and that was that. Fair dues to Pat and Brendan. When we built it I thought it was the nicest shop in the midlands."

The new shop was operational in early 1983 and at the March meeting, Larry O'Rourke, in his manager's report, revealed that "business seemed to be a lot better and the opening sale was a big success". The official opening took place on 10 May. It was performed by the Avonmore chairman, John Duggan, and Macra na Feirme members provided variety entertainment later. "We got great custom from a wide area, and one of the reasons was that we had plenty of parking space. Women in those days weren't good drivers, as a rule. But they had little bother getting in and out at Mountmellick. In those days husbands would ask their wives to get whatever they needed. That really made the business for us," stated Larry.

There was a suggestion made at a meeting on 7 November 1984 that "the value of one gallon of milk be stopped in 1984 from all milk suppliers who didn't opt out of the scheme" for the relief of the famine-stricken people of Ethiopia.

Chris Horan reported to the December 1984 meeting of worker unrest in Ballyragget. He said that management was endeavouring to bring about an

Mountmellick team who came 7th in the Avonmore Wheatrace results in early 1980s.
Front from left: Vincent Callanan, Seán Doyle, Michael McCann.
Back row from left: Derek Meredith, Brendan Graham (Avonmore Regional Manager),
Gerard Rochford (Chairman), Larry O'Rourke (Branch Manager).

agreement. This entailed flexibility of working hours, which was something, he said, that should apply to all workers.

In March 1985 there was outright condemnation of suppliers who had only gone into milk production the previous year or two with large herds of up to 200 cows. These were the culprits who created the over supply which led to the imposition of the super-levy, it was said. "We, the long standing suppliers, are being penalised and infuriated by these speculators by having to cut back on our own milk supply", one disgruntled supplier told the meeting.

A proposed revised method of milk collection was put forward at the October meeting of 1985, affecting milk suppliers with less than 50 gallons per collection. They would have to bring their milk to selected collection points in an effort to reduce transport costs. A once-off payment of £350 would be paid as compensation.

Best wishes were expressed by the chairman, John Joe Dunne, to Brendan Graham on being appointed Company Secretary of Avonmore. He said he looked forward to working with his successor as manager of the Donaghmore Region, Sean Hearn.

The Milk War continued unabated through the mid-1980s, with price-cutting by different dairies the order of the day. It was very reminiscent of the Milk War of the 1920s which, in that instance, was based on getting extra supplies at all costs, and which led to a major rationalisation of the industry. In December 1986, it was reported that "the latest Brussels package" would reduce quotas by up to 9% over the following couple of years. In addition there was a new milk cessation scheme

Staff members and some spouses at Pim's of Mountmellick in 1969, before PIM's was acquired by AVONMORE

Front row (l. to r.): Mary Dunne, Peg White, Mavis Dollard, Gertie Cox, Sheila Lalor, Joy Odlum, Mary Conroy, Olive Moody, Mary Culliton, Vicky Harris, Hilda Moody.

Second row (l. to r.): Maggie Coss, Maura Murphy, Mollie Hayes, Claire Lalor, Mary O'Rourke, Annie Mundy, Eithne White, Edith Dempsey, Maria Byrne, Frances Bruce, Carmel Dooley.

Third row (l. to r.): Mrs. Tommy Kelly, Terry Dunne, —, Paddy Dunne, Jimmy Hayes, Oliver Hackett, Trevor Burns, John Coss, Luke McRedmond, Paddy Whelan, Frank Gorman, Miss Earl, John Martin, Nora Bailey, G. P. Bailey, Crissy Reddin.

Back row (l. to r.): Victor Cox, Willie Fitzpatrick, Tommy Kelly, Jim Dollard, Herbert Parsons, Larry O'Rourke, Ian Thompson, Albert Mundy, Frank White, Jim Murphy, Martin Dunne, Tony Reddin, Ernest Gill.

introduced for those who wanted to get out of milk. It was assumed that this would lead to a big financial loss and a loss of milk would mean a loss of jobs.

There were strong feelings expressed at the December 1986 meeting, about the continued production of low quality milk by 5% of suppliers. This was down-grading the quality of milk of other suppliers. It was felt that the Board of Avonmore should remove such suppliers from the system with the aid of the milk cessation scheme.

The then regional manager, Pat Brophy, revealed in September 1991 that Mountmellick was lying second in the region as regards sales and he hoped that new improvements would bring the branch to first place in the near future. In 1994 the sales at Mountmellick amounted to £1,050m., which left it in fourth place in the regional sales table behind Universal Providers, Fethard and Mullingar.

Larry O'Rourke served almost forty years in the Mountmellick business, the vast bulk of that as manager. "Looking back on my time there, I enjoyed every day of it, while I was there; and I'm enjoying life twice as much since I left," he was happy to relate. He had the height of praise for the local area committee. "Anything you wanted done or any decision that had to be made for the good of the business, they would help you out. All the committee would come in and air their views. It was a good way of holding the farming community together. Macra members were always very helpful. But Larry, who is now retired, has a word of caution for the current and future operations there. He believes that it was a mistake to "close the front door" because it sent out the wrong messages to townspeople. "You cannot run a business with farmers only. You need the general public too. With eight hundred houses now being built in Mountmellick there is a great opportunity to get some of that extra business."

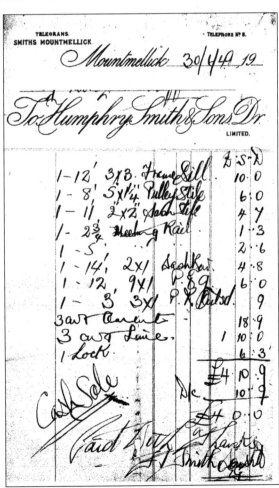

A cash sale docket issued by Humphrey Smith & Sons in 1949.

CLONASLEE CO-OP

Although Clonaslee Co-operative Society was formed in the spring of 1962, its origins date back much further. In 1943, with WW2 at its height, a discussion group was organised in the local Vocational School. Its purpose was to organise lectures, discussions, demonstrations, debates and other activities to improve the educational opportunities, raise standards in farming and rural life and to foster a community spirit which would help promote projects for the common good.

These were lofty aims indeed. The group met weekly during the winter months and monthly during the longer evenings. A lot of interest was generated and it soon had a healthy membership. In 1947 the group joined the Young Farmers Club which was later to become Macra na Feirme. Many events were organised in the 1940s and 1950s and eminent speakers came to talk on all aspects of agriculture and rural endeavour. There were visits to agricultural colleges, progressive farms, co-op societies and Agricultural Institute stations.

By 1960, a new generation of members had emerged, young energetic people full of enthusiasm and fresh ideas. Pig fattening on a large scale was one area identified as having potential for the Clonaslee area. Following a talk given by Agricultural Advisor, Matt Hyland, in Clonaslee in February 1961, on the issue of farming opportunities, Mr. M. O'Connor, manager of the National Bank in Mountmellick wrote to Mr. P.D. Brickley, Clonaslee: "Do you think there is any possibility of starting a co-operative pig fattening society in the Clonaslee area? It looks a likely enough venture to me."[1]

This was just the word of encouragement needed for the resourceful young farmers of   Clonaslee to flesh out the idea. Members looked for a suitable property and gave due deliberation as to how they intended to run the business. On 27 February 1962, the Davis farm at Corbally, Clonaslee, consisting of 130 acres, was purchased for the sum of £10,000 and on 13 April 1962, Clonaslee Co-op was registered under the Industrial and Provident Societies Acts (1893 to 1936). Financial accommodation for the purchase sum was duly given by the National Bank in Mountmellick.[2]

The first forty shareholders, including members of the organising committee, consisted of two clergymen, twenty four farmers, eight business firms and six professional people, all living with a ten mile radius of Clonaslee.

The primary aim of the Society was large scale pig fattening "not for the purpose of accumulating profits for the Society, but to secure a guaranteed market for pigs on a large scale at a fixed and remunerative price". It aimed to raise the standards of pig production in relation to breeding, feeding, housing and management.

In April 1962, the Donaghmore committee discussed a letter from Clonaslee Pig Fattening Co-op looking for support. Members were aware that Mullingar and

1. In a letter dated 24 February 1961.
2. In a letter dated 22 February 1962 from M. O'Connor, Manager of the National Bank in Mountmellick to P.D. Brickley, Clonaslee.

Monasterevin creameries were canvassing Raheen suppliers in the Mountmellick/ Clonaslee area. By joining forces with Clonaslee Co-op a buffer could be created to protect the Raheen supply in the area.

The manager of the National Bank, Mountmellick, had written to Mr. Brickley, chairman of the Clonaslee Society, in March advising him that if Donaghmore decided to make an investment, this fact should be conveyed to the committee of Roscrea Bacon Factory, as it could influence their decision to invest.[3]

Following a proposal by Bobby Bennett, the Donaghmore committee decided, in April 1962, to buy £1000 of shares in Clonaslee provided that they be given representation on the committee there. George Galbraith, from Raheen, and Michael Walsh, from Spink, were duly elected on the Clonaslee committee in October. There was a proposal to raise a loan of £30,000 to erect accommodation for 2,000 pigs but this was considered a little adventurous by some shareholders and in November a decision was taken to proceed with a more modest building, costed at £17,000, which would accommodate up to 700 pigs.

The Clonaslee committee were invited to Donaghmore for an information visit in January 1963 and were entertained to High Tea in Rathdowney later that evening.

In February 1963, the Clonaslee committee asked if they could take shares in Donaghmore, either as individuals or as a Society. Donaghmore responded that it would be desirable that every milk supplier in the Clonaslee area should be a member and that if Clonaslee Co-op were a member, it would enable any trade done by them to be treated as "trade with members". The first four milk suppliers from the Clonaslee area were voted in as members of Donaghmore Co-op at a meeting on 6 March 1963, and the Clonaslee Society was admitted to membership on 10 April 1963.

Local man, Fred Mathews, of "Bellair", Clonaslee, was appointed manager in the spring of 1963. He had been associated with the project from the start and his farm was adjacent to the Co-op owned land.

Following Donaghmore's decision to invest, Roscrea Bacon Factory[4] also became large shareholders in the enterprise. Other co-ops to invest were Rath, North Offaly, Mountrath Livestock Sales and Westmeath Dairy Society.

On 30 July 1963, Roscrea re-affirmed their commitment to the project by agreeing that funds to the sum of £3,600 would be provided for a period of one year, during which time they would hold a lien on the pigs held by the Clonaslee Board to the value of the amount advanced.

The manager's report for 1964 stated that 1962 was a year for planning, 1963 was a year for building and stocking and 1964 was a year of business. But, he revealed that only 80% of the budgeted throughput was achieved. During the year, Clonaslee bought 1,000 tons of meal from Donaghmore. He also reported that a compounding plant had been erected giving an output of 40 tons per week with one operator. This could be doubled by "putting in an extra man", he stated.

Mr. Mathews went on to say that "Clonaslee Co-op could easily have gone out of business during June-December 1964 except for the loyalty of a handful of

3. In a letter dated 23 March 1962 from Manager, National bank in Mountmellick to Mr. Brickley.
4. Roscrea was the first Co-operative Bacon Factory founded in Ireland. It began operations in 1907. The project was spearheaded by Very Rev. John Canon Cunningham. He was dissatisfied with the price that farmers were getting from the sale of their pigs as well as the high level of unemployment that existed in the town of Roscrea and decided to address both problems by building a bacon factory.

members who brought in bonhams at financial loss to themselves, knowing that unless the pig industry has drastically changed, the wheel would turn the other way every bit as far".

Within a few years of opening, Clonaslee found itself strapped for working capital. Donaghmore insisted that the management of the business had to be tightened up at Clonaslee and Billy Wallis was appointed a joint general manager there along with Donal Ward, manager of the Roscrea Bacon Factory.

Bobby Bennett recalls that Wallis did not spend too much time in Clonaslee. He was there to focus the committee's attention on the business end of things more than on the pig rearing end, because that is where they were falling down.

In that same year, 1965, there was a move afoot to establish a pig fattening unit in the Donaghmore area. A committee had been formed, capital was being negotiated and the project was being enthusiastically pursued. But nothing came of it.

At a meeting of the committee of management on 7 March 1966, the chairman, Mr. Brickley, expressed his disappointment as to the manner in which the pig fattening unit was being managed. Thirteen recommendations were made regarding the recording, reporting and accounting procedures at the unit. The manager was also cautioned about his timekeeping. He was expected to be at the Society's premises or farm for 5½ days each week and to be at the pig fattening unit not later than 9am each morning, the memo noted.

In 1968, Roscrea Bacon Factory complained that the loan they had given Clonaslee in 1963 was still unpaid and a new contract was drawn up confirming that the loan was still due and allowing a further twelve months for full repayment.

Thomas Hennessy, who replaced Mr. Mathews as manager at Clonaslee in mid-1968, reported that that when he took over, the Society had not been a viable enterprise. He outlined details of the re-organisation that had taken place to the AGM on 22 August 1969. The revival plan was the brainchild of Roscrea Managing Director, Donal Ward. Hennessy told members that in 1968, the Co-op had purchased 3,031 pigs at a cost of £24,784 from shareholders, that sales from the milling unit amounted to £16,539 and that the farm showed "a successful return for the year".

The balance sheet for 1969 showed a nett profit of £5,226 from a turnover of £101,089. This was increased to £7,149 for 1970. Mr. Hennessy reported that despite the delay in building caused by the 16 week cement strike, by the end of 1970 a Jordan unit was completed to accommodate 2,000 extra pigs. A pipeline feeding system was installed throughout. The nett profit for 1971 was £16,076. Overall business with shareholders had increased by 120% and "provided a guaranteed market and price structure for 11,900 bonhams in a year when market prices varied widely".

Efforts were being made to establish a similar type co-op in the Offaly-Westmeath area. About £9,000 was raised. The IAOS advised, however, that it would be more advantageous that Clonaslee Co-op be developed to service the weaner-producers of Laois, Offaly and Westmeath. In 1970, the majority of those who had subscribed share-capital for the Offaly-Westmeath venture were admitted as shareholders in Clonaslee Co-op. They invested £6,000 into the project and Denis Plunkett was appointed to the committee.

The profit for 1972 was double that of the previous year as Clonaslee's fortunes continued to flourish. The issue of the fee due to Mr. Ward for his part in the Clonaslee profit surge, became a source of embarrassment for the Roscrea general manager, however. He was aware that he was being accused of pressurising the Co-op for payment, which was not the case, he stressed. His company felt that there was an obligation on the bank, rather than on Clonaslee Co-op, to pay him whatever he was due.

In 1978, Roscrea got into financial difficulties. In October of that year, Clonaslee joined with Avonmore and East Galway Co-ops in becoming major shareholders in Roscrea. Avonmore took over Roscrea in 1987 and bought up most of the shares. Purchase of the share capital, rather than amalgamation, was the take-over route recommended by ICOS and preferred by Avonmore, in this instance.[5] P.D. Brickley and William Flynn represented Clonaslee on the Roscrea Board while Reddy Brennan and John Duggan represented Avonmore.

Gerry Culliton was one of the principals in the Rearymore Pig Farm operation.

Bobby Bennett remembers: "Avonmore spent big money on it. We built a new factory. We jointly owned the farm store with Centenary Co-op. Then we built the new mart. The factory, store and mart were all situated on land we bought at Parkmore, Roscrea."

Avonmore had purchased Rearymore Pig Farm, not very distant from Clonaslee Co-op, from Doyles of Newbridge in 1978. Rearymore had been started by Gerry Culliton[6] and his brother, Louis, in 1960, with the help of Gerry's Irish international rugby colleague, accountant, Ronnie Kavanagh. It had accommodation for over 5,000 pigs. They had sold out to Doyles in the mid-1970s. Clonaslee merged with Avonmore in 1988, which effectively doubled Avonmore's interest in the pigmeat industry in North Laois area.

Avonmore were now heavily invested in the bacon industry. Had Donaghmore not become involved with Clonaslee then, perhaps, Avonmore would not have got so heavily involved in the meat business, not only in pigs but in cattle and sheep as well. "There were quite a number of Board meetings at which it was discussed before we got involved. The Board came under intense political pressure to expand the meat business and eventually set up factories in Ballyhaunis and other places," Bobby Bennett revealed.[7]

5. Letter from Gregory Tierney, secretary of ICOS (formerly IAOS) to John Hannon, secretary, Roscrea Bacon Factory Ltd dated 20 August 1987.
6. Gerry Culliton won 19 caps for Ireland between 1959 and '64. He played with the Barbarians when they defeated the mighty Springbok side of 1961. He missed his twentieth cap by misfortune. He played a star game in the final trial for the All-Blacks fixture in 1967 but the big international game was called off, due to an outbreak of foot and mouth disease, a week before the fixture. His conversion to rugby came by chance also. He played county minor hurling for two years and was selected on the senior side when it was found out he had played club rugby and was suspended by Laois GAA Board. That finished his GAA involvement and opened up a more spectacular rugby career.
7. Further details of the surge in Avonmore's involvement in the meat business appear in Chapter 3, Part Seven, Section One titled "Dramatic Expansion".

In 2002, Clonaslee Co-op supplied 30,500 pigs to the Roscrea Bacon Factory and Rearymore supplied a further 18,500. All the pigs supplied from these two units were the progeny of 2,200 sows on the pig farms. Clonaslee Co-op also supplied 100,000 gallons of milk from its dairy farm.

Apart from their importance as sources for Roscrea Bacon Factory, these two fattening units are also important customers of the Portlaoise Provender Mill from which they purchase in the region of 14,000 tonnes of pigfeed per annum, representing 16% of the Mill's annual production of the product. Demand for pigfeed remains constant throughout the year, whereas the demand for other animal feedstuffs tends to be seasonal and weather related. The demand for pigfeed is, therefore, of particular importance to the Provender Mills during the summer months when the demand for other feedstuffs drops off to a considerable extent.

Employees at Clonaslee at December 2002 were: Michael O'Neill (manager), Tom Goroud, Matt Barrett, Simon Hogan, Christy Kelly, P.V. Dunne, Eugene Dunne, Larry Costello, John Casey and Mary Delaney. Employees at Rearymore were: Martin Havill (manager), Pat McRedmond, Michael McRedmond, Tom McRedmond, Michael McEvoy, James McEvoy, Seamus Fitzpatrick, Barney Connolly, Liam Conroy, Tom McLoughlin and Denis Guckivan.

Carrying the milk to the Creamery before motorised transport.

MONASTEREVIN CO-OP

On 20 June 1961, Rev. J. McDonald wrote to the Department of Agriculture seeking information about setting up a creamery in Monasterevin. Two months later, P.T. Donnelly, the Chief Agricultural Officer for Kildare, contacted the Department seeking the services of an organiser to help get the project off the ground.

At a meeting of the NFA County Executive for Kildare on 23 October, at which Greg Tierney of the IAOS attended, it was decided to canvass for milk for possibly two separating stations, one at Monasterevin and the other at Ballytore. The group representing south-east Kildare reported that £1,500 had been promised in a preliminary canvass. A group representing the Monasterevin area intimated that £1,200 had been collected in cash and another £500 signed for. A committee had been formed for Monasterevin and they were determined to erect a creamery in the area. Among those involved on the organising committee were Harold Carter, Andrew Mahon, Christy Mooney, Eddie O'Loughlin, Dr. Kirby, Denis Walsh, M.P. Kelly, Frank Flynn (agricultural inspector), Larry Morrin, P. McDonald, Pat Lawlor, Andy Wilson, Ger Lawlor, Joe Behan, Sean Costello, Dick Slevin, Simon Luttrell, John Boland, Mr. Hutchinson, Mr. Miller and two men from the Emo area.[1]

At another NFA meeting on 6 November 1961, the canvassers reported that £2,280 had been signed for in the Ballytore area and there more farmers to be contacted. A temporary working committee was set up consisting of representatives from Ballyshannon, Ballytore, Moone, Kilcullen, Bigstone, Dunlavin, Baltinglass and Ballymore Eustace. Five delegates were elected to the county committee. It was agreed that both the Monasterevin and Ballytore committees should work together to form a single co-op.

The procedure for canvassing for milk and collecting share capital was that a committee man would bring someone along with him to meet the farmers. Sean Costello recalled doing a canvass. He was driving his VW beetle, a small car for a very big man. He had Pat Lawler with him on the rounds. One day he called to a certain farm. The farmer was not at home but his son was there, talking to a tall stranger at the farmhouse door. Sean let down the window and without getting out of the car, introduced himself. He then told the lad the reason for his visit. "Tell your father I want to collect £10 from him and any more he can afford. We are trying to start up a creamery in Monasterevin." The tall stranger glanced around at the little car, and then said to the lad, "I know what I would do to fellows collecting for a creamery; the same as what we did to them down in Tipperary." In seconds, Sean had emerged from the car, all 6'4" of him and one of the strongest and fittest specimens of humankind. He confronted the tall stranger who was covered by his towering shadow and growled, "What **would** you do?" The poor man turned deathly pale before hastily beating a retreat. Sean revealed, with a broad smile, that he never found out what they "did to them" down in Tipperary.

1. Information supplied in an interview with Michael Mahon.

Monasterevin Creamery in the 1960s.

At a meeting of the joint organising committee on 16 November, Harold Carter was elected chairman and Mr. Doyle as secretary. On 30 November, Andrew Mahon, secretary of the Monasterevin committee, wrote to the Department seeking a licence to set up a creamery.

Greg Tierney advised the IAOS secretary in December 1961 that Monasterevin Creamery was going ahead and that £3,000 had been collected.[2] He also revealed that Ballytore were not, after all, going ahead with their project and he believed that £1,000 of their money might be invested in the Monasterevin venture.

In a letter of 9 March 1962 the Department asked the IAOS to investigate the possibility of the Monasterevin separating station being established by Westmeath Co-op with the help of the share capital already subscribed at Monasterevin. It also expressed fears that the proposed creamery for Tullamore might be adversely affected and suggested that since Monasterevin and Tullamore areas came under the Westmeath Co-op banner, these areas should be served by a single separating station.

In July 1962, there were complaints from Donaghmore and Barrowvale that some of their customers were being encouraged to sign over to Monasterevin. Meetings were held with both co-ops to smooth out the difficulties with boundaries.[3]

At a statutory general meeting (effectively the Society's first AGM) on 6 November 1962, it was noted that the share capital was £5,381. Harold Carter was confirmed as chairman, and the manager, Bobby Cotter, was elected secretary. The relationship with Westmeath Co-op had cooled and agreement was reached with Castlecomer to do the churning.[4] Some of the Monasterevin milk had gone to Mullingar for a short time. Christy Mooney remembered the then manager in Mullingar as being very helpful and how he had altered his creamery's own collections of milk to facilitate the Monasterevin suppliers. But there was disappointment in Mullingar as to the response from south-west Kildare and attitudes there changed very quickly. A Monasterevin supplier, George Byrne, recalled getting poor value from Mullingar for his milk. "I used to fill my churn to the top. The documentation always came back for 80 pounds or in volume eight gallons. It was only when Monasterevin came on stream that I got credit for 100 pounds or ten gallons for my churn of milk. Mullingar knew that we (the Monasterevin suppliers) were only there in a temporary capacity," said George.

2. In an internal IAOS memo dated 18 December 1960.
3. Donaghmore Co-op minutes for April 1962.
4. Donaghmore Co-op minutes for January 1963.

Monasterevin Creamery began operating on 15 January 1963. By the end of the year it had taken in 700,000 gallons. Castlecomer were experiencing difficulties dealing with such a volume of cream. A solution was presented by dividing the Monasterevin cream between Castlecomer and Muckalee Co-ops. In July, the manager, Bobby Cotter, applied to the Department for a central creamery licence. A recommendation from the IAOS was requested in January 1964.

There was a milk intake increase of 43%, up to one million gallons, for 1964. The IAOS had supported the Monasterevin application for a creamery licence on two previous occasions but, in February 1965, they advised the Society that, due to new circumstances, they were not in a position to make any further recommendation. They suggested that Monasterevin should consider coming to an arrangement with Westmeath Co-op, where there had been a change in management.

In March 1965, however, the Department finally confirmed that Monasterevin was a recognised co-op under the Agricultural Co-operative Societies (Debentures) Act and issued a certificate to that effect. By the AGM time on 27 August 1965, the building of the new creamery was already underway. The building costs were estimated at £15,000 and the machinery costs at £25,000. The costs of churning were then estimated at £1,000 per month. The intake for 1965 was over 1.4 million gallons. The new creamery at Cowpasture, Monasterevin, was officially opened by the then Minister for Agriculture, Charles J. Haughey, on 4 July 1966. The milk intake continued to grow spectacularly. In 1966 it was over 1.75 million gallons and in 1967 it had grown again to in excess of 2.3 million gallons. While there had been 230 suppliers on the books when the co-op started, by 1967 the number had grown to 600.

In the spring of 1968, a new boundaries row broke out on two fronts, with Barrowvale and Donaghmore, similar to the situation in 1962. Mr. P. Kelly of the IAOS outlined the boundary lines in detail in a letter to Monasterevin Co-op dated 16 April. The row with Donaghmore centred on nine suppliers who had previously supplied to the Dublin District Milk Board. The Dairy Produce section of the Department of Agriculture and the IAOS got involved, but it was the intervention of the chairman of the Dublin District Milk Board, Martin J. Mullally, that proved most helpful. He advised Donal Grogan that he had not been aware that the suppliers in question were in the Donaghmore area and he wrote personally to the nine farmers involved explaining the situation.[5] Friction sparked again between Monasterevin and the same two neighbouring co-ops in October 1969 over remarks reported at the Monasterevin AGM and published in the Carlow Nationalist. The chairman, Mr. Carter, was reported as saying that "the creamery's aim was to serve the farmers of all the county (of Kildare), as well as those from Laois and Offaly". The Donaghmore secretary, John C. Galbraith, brought the matter to the attention of the IAOS. The Monasterevin manager, Bobby Cotter, made a fulsome apology to the IAOS for the contents of the report. "I very much regret the error in reporting of a statement at our AGM and would ask you to convey our sincere apologies to Donaghmore and Barrowvale Societies for any embarrassment the report may have caused to them. I assure you that the statement as published was an error and was not meant in any way to be unfriendly."

5. Letters from Greg Tierney, IAOS, dated 6 April 1968 to D. Grogan, Donaghmore, from Grogan to Martin J. Mullally, Dublin District Milk Board, dated 8 April 1968 and letter from Mullally to the nine milk suppliers in dispute dated 10 April 1968. (ICOS papers in National Archives).

Monasterevin Branch in the 1970s.

Having to apologise for reports of unfriendly behaviour to neighbouring co-ops may have caused some concern at Monasterevin, but there were far bigger concerns harboured about the results for the year, which were hugely disappointing. The first indication in the IAOS files that there was something amiss was in a letter on 9 September 1970 from the manager, Bobby Cotter, to Patrick Kelly of the IAOS. He wrote that "due to a very heavy financial strain on the Societies' accounts" Monasterevin was in a position to only pay half the due contribution to the IAOS. The full extent of the "strain" on finances was revealed a few weeks later at the AGM on 24 September at which 400 shareholders were present. The losses recorded for 1969 amounted to £18,000 which was in contrast to a profit of £21,000 for the previous year. The reasons for the huge downturn were explained as follows: Gross loss £7004; levy £11,389; production expenses £8,503; overheads £6,535; depreciation £5,556 and subsidies £2,529. Total £41,516. Receipts were up by over £2,000, which left the £39,000 of a difference.

The discussion of the accounts lasted for over two hours and the debate was heated. No statistical back-up was provided and management came in for severe criticism. The main reason given for the decline in fortunes was an 11% drop in milk intake. John Boland led the charge on behalf of shareholders. He continued to ask pertinent questions and demanded appropriate answers. But neither he, nor many of the shareholders present, were happy with the responses.

Colm Costello of the IAOS felt that a more critical analysis of the Society's activities should be undertaken and that his organisation promised to give whatever assistance it could to the Society. Mr. Costello was particularly worried about the trade end of the business which, though small,

Monasterevin Branch in more recent times.

had suffered heavy losses. This was difficult to understand, Mr. Costello felt, but pointed the finger at poor stock control.

The manager came in for criticism at the meeting for the late collection of milk. Suppliers felt that their chances of passing the quality test were consequently reduced. Claims by suppliers that they were receiving poor weights could not be substantiated. Members expressed dissatisfaction with the holding of the AGM so late in the year and there was a proposal to hold the 1970 meeting in March 1971.

Despite these misgivings, the AGM for 1970 was not held until 4 August 1971, at which 100 members attended. The chairman was asked if the committee ever considered sending milk to Avonmore and he replied that they were satisfied that the present outlets were more remunerative and, "in any case", he said, "the cost of transporting milk to Avonmore would be prohibitive". The low prices paid for milk was also criticised. Maurice Colbert of the IAOS explained that Monasterevin's low price, despite a relatively big intake of milk, was due to the fact that the Society didn't have the opportunity of building up funds as other societies had done, and because of the losses being sustained on the store business. A number of members expressed views in favour of amalgamation and, more particularly, a greater involvement with Avonmore.

The outturn for 1971 was also disappointing and "due to the difficult year" the Society again reneged on paying the second instalment of their contribution to the IAOS for 1972.[6]

Shareholders were slow to make up their minds when the amalgamation proposal was put on the table in 1972. Many felt that if they amalgamated they would have no control over their own creamery. George Byrne recalls: "the package was that you would get more money for your milk and, as part of a bigger concern, costs at Monasterevin would be reduced." There were several meetings held on the issue and Reddy Brennan and Bobby Bennett attended one of these. Eventually shareholders were convinced that amalgamation was in the best interests of the Society.

After the amalgamation the committees of Donaghmore and Monasterevin came together to form the Donaghmore/Monasterevin Regional Committee. There were some initial problems but it is generally agreed that the joint arrangement has worked very well. The credit for the smooth transition is attributed to Bobby Bennett's ability as a chairman and his skill in sorting out problems.[7] The butter manufacturing functions were transferred to Ballyragget on amalgamation. A shop was opened at Monasterevin in 1974.

Located in an extensive grain growing area, Avonmore invested heavily in the development of the grain intake, drying and storage facilities in Monasterevin. It became one of the major grain handling branches in the region and was used for the storage of intervention grain. In 2000 it was awarded the ISO Quality Mark for grain handling. Monasterevin provides all the inputs and services needed for grain growing, dairy and dry stock farming as well as agricultural hardware. It celebrated the 40th anniversary of its founding in 2003.

The following personnel worked at the Branch in December 2002:

Lar Havens, Liam Geoghan, Arthur O Connor, Patrick Pollard, Kevin Miller, Aisling Delaney, James Clifford, Redmond Bergin, Jarlet Fahy, Brian Hutchinson, John Fitzgerald.

6. From a letter to Patrick Kelly of the IAOS from Bobby Cotter, manager at Monasterevin.
7. In an interview with Michael Mahon, George Byrne, Jim Garry and Paddy McHugh.

Rev. Dean Jackson turns the first sod for Monasterevin Co-operative milk separating station in August 1962.
Standing immediately behind him is Mr. John Heffernan, Kildare, the contractor.

CONDITION-SCORING AND WINTER FEEDING

A Demonstration on **Condition-Scoring** followed by a discussion on **Winter Feeding** and **Management of DAIRY COWS** will be held on the farm of
Mr. George Byrne, Ballykelly, Monasterevin
on
Thursday, 26 October, 1978, at 2.15 p.m.
under the auspices of Avonmore Creameries Ltd., Kildare Committe of Agriculture, Offaly Committee of Agriculture.

Newspaper cutting re demonstration on the farm of George Byrne, a member of the Monasterevin Area Committee and the Donaghmore/Monasterevin Regional Advisory Committee.

BALLACOLLA

In 1981, the Avonmore grain handling facilities in the Donaghmore/Monasterevin region were enhanced through the purchase of the grain premises of Brophys at Ballacolla. A programme of development followed including the opening of a new shop.

The branch became actively involved in the seeds, fertilisers and agro-chemical inputs to grain growers in the area, as well as purchasing drying and storing the finished product. It also helped to relieve the pressure in the grain handling facilities in the Raheen and Donaghmore branches.

Grain intake in Ballacolla was discontinued in the early 1990s when grain handling facilities in Raheen and Donaghmore were upgraded to handle all the grain purchased in the area. The branch also purchased, packed and stored wool but this activity was discontinued after 1999.

Ballacolla continues to provide a good service to the farming community in its hinterland through the sale of feed, seeds, fertilisers and other agricultural needs and services.

Employees at the Ballacolla Branch in 2002: Val McCartney, Michael Kavanagh, Michael Dowling.

Aerial view of Ballacolla Branch.

Michael Dowling (Manager), and Val McCartney in Ballacolla Branch.

Michael Kavanagh driving forklift at Ballacolla Branch.

NORTH OFFALY CO-OP

North Offaly Co-operative Agricultural Society Ltd. was founded in 1919.[1] It was a general co-op and had no involvement with milk.

A meeting of 29 March 1988[2] discussed a letter from ICOS which advised the committee that it now had a mandate to proceed with discussions with Avonmore regarding amalgamation. It was decided to ask ICOS to help out with updating the share register. Mr. O'Brien felt that the Co-op should seek representation on the Board of Avonmore.

A delegation comprising of Joe Kelly, who took the chair, B. Fox, V. Abbott and J. Mollin represented the Co-op and Avonmore was represented by Billy Murphy and Bobby Bennett. On the question of representation Mr. Murphy explained that North Offaly would have three members on the regional committee (Donaghmore/Monasterevin) and one member on the Council which is next to the main Board. He further explained that the main Board was elected by the regional committees and ratified by the Council. He said that following amalgamation shareholders would enjoy the same privileges as original shareholders, malting barley contracts would be allowed, the shop would be expanded and the site at Arden developed.

John Tyrrell of ICOS attended a further meeting of the sub-committees on 19 April. John Duggan, chairman of Avonmore, chaired the meeting at which the North Offaly delegation also included J. Strong. Mr. Tyrrell revealed that there was a valuation issue relating to North Offaly assets and that there was more clarity required regarding the number of paid-up shares. Mr. Duggan explained that each of the 14,672 paid-up shareholders would receive one 'A' share and 13.18 'B' shares. A dividend would only be paid on the 'A' shares. He also warned that staff might not be maintained at the levels then pertaining.

The resolution in favour of amalgamation was passed at a meeting of shareholders on 30 May 1988.

At the time of amalgamation North Offaly operated from four sites in Tullamore and they owned as fifth site at Arden which was purchased with the intentions of building a new store there, which never materialised. Their high street shop was in William Street where they sold, among other goods, hardware, seeds, drugs, timber, electrical goods, paint and potatoes. At Bridget's Place they dealt in corn and feedstuffs and at their store in Offaly Street the concentration was on seed potatoes, which were sold to customers over a wide area. At a leased premises at the Tanyard, Brussels sprouts were taken in from farmers who were contracted to grow them. The sprouts were prepared for sale to East Cork Foods by approximately 140 seasonal workers over a period of between five and seven weeks each year,

1. Information provided by Brian Fox.
2. The attendance included Mrs. Hynes, J. Mahon, T. Garry, V. Abbott, P. Bracken, G. O'Brien, B. Fox and J. Mollin. Joe Kelly was in the chair.

for about six years.

After amalgamation North Offaly trading activities at Tullamore were developed, increasing further the area being serviced by the Donaghmore/Monasterevin region. Avonmore purchased the provender milling business of Paul and Vincents at Spollenstown, Tullamore. This was developed into a major trading branch and over the next few years the premises and land at William Street, Offaly Street, Bridget's Place and Arden were sold. This phase of development at Spollenstown included the upgrading of the stores there to "Home and Farm Shop" status.

Employees at the Spollenstown Branch in 2002: Ann Dunican, Michael Dunne, Phil Barron, Frank Delaney, Catherine Reilly, Justin Kinsella, P.J.Barron, Patrick Butler, Jim McCarthy, Maurice Grogan.

MOATE

Moate Farm Store is a joint venture formed on the merger of Lakeland Dairies and Avonmore Foods plc. It serves the counties of Offaly, Westmeath and Longford. It is located in the old Roseland Ballroom which was built by former Taoiseach, Albert Reynolds. It offers a wide range on goods and services including feed, fertiliser, soil testing and a full range of agri-inputs. The Branch manager, Tommy Gorman, hails from Spink, County Laois. Other employees at Moate at December 2002 were Stephen Madden and Brendan Heavin.

MULLINGAR

In 1991, Avonmore purchased the Wallace business at The Green, Mullingar, from the Buckley family. This extended the Donaghmore/Monasterevin region to cover parts of Westmeath and Longford. The business was developed by Avonmore to "Home and Farm Shop" status.

In the year 2000, the premises at The Green were sold and the agricultural inputs side of the business was located at a new site in Mullingar purchased from O'Keeffe Foods, at Ballymahon Road, where a new store and shop were built. The concentration in the new location is mainly on sales of feedstuffs, fertilisers and agricultural hardware. The manager is Joe Lalor, who hails from Camross, County Laois. Other employees at December 2002 were John Kearney and Noel McManus.

SECTION FOUR

Appendices

DONAGHMORE WORKHOUSE

T he buildings leased from the Laois Board of Health by Donaghmore Co-op in 1927 were built originally for use as a workhouse in the years following the Great Famine (1845-'49). Poverty and disease were at their height and the existing workhouses at Abbeyleix, Mountmellick and Roscrea were overcrowded. Roscrea, for instance, had basic sleeping accommodation for 900, but housed over 2,000 inmates in March 1851. Mountmellick and Abbeyleix faced similar impossible situations.

The Donaghmore Workhouse was designed to relieve the pressure on these neighbouring institutions. It was built to house 400 inmates but by the time it opened its doors to the public on 23 September 1853, the worst of the famine disaster had passed. Many of the impoverished people for whose benefit it was built had either died or emigrated. Three months after its opening there were 229 poor souls on the master's roll call.

It is difficult for people in 21st century Ireland to contemplate the poverty, hardship and misery that prevailed it this country in the mid nineteenth century. The workhouse was a refuge of last resort for the teeming thousands of starving people living in dire squalor and struggling to survive. It offered the most basic of diets and stable-like accommodation. For this prospect of mere survival the inmates had to conform to the rigours of a humiliating set of ground rules and under a strict incompassionate regime. Families were torn apart on entry and were not allowed to communicate with each other while there. Harsh punishments were dealt out for breaches of the rules.

The grim conditions experienced by inmates in Donaghmore were no better nor worse than other workhouses all over the country. Perhaps its only saving grace was that it survived as a working model for a much shorter span than most. On 30 September 1886 the remaining inmates were transferred to other institutions and the workhouse was closed.

Only ghosts from its stark past were left to roam around the corridors of these stone-clad forbidding buildings. If walls or floors could speak, what tales of horror they could tell! The buildings did survive and were considered for various usages. At the time of closure it was suggested that they would be suitable for a Catholic Industrial School. But the Bishop of Ossory, Rev. Dr. Brownrigg, refused to purchase them as he felt that the government should donate them free of charge to the diocese.

At a meeting of Queen's County Council in June 1912, it was proposed that the disused workhouse be utilised as a home for advanced cases of tuberculosis. In October 1913 the Tuberculosis Committee reported to the County Council their assessment that Donaghmore was a most suitable location for a sanatorium, and that it was capable of accommodating advanced cases from neighbouring counties as well as Laois. The motion was adopted but, for some reason, it was never put into effect. It remained an issue for many years into the future. However, in

Opening of Donaghmore Museum 1993
L. to r: Bobby Bennett, William Mansfield and Robert Mansfield.

November 1930, it was agreed that Donaghmore would not be the most suitable location for a tuberculosis hospital.[1]

In the meanwhile the workhouse was used as a military barracks during WW1. It was occupied by the infamous Black and Tans. Bullet marks in the gable end of the main front buildings, and bars on the window of a cell in the same building, are still to be seen.

It is interesting to note that Donaghmore Co-op committee was given the green light to commence its operations in the old workhouse in 1927. The committee, however, found it difficult to secure a lease for some years from Laois County Council. Although the Society was never informed of the reasons for the delay in the issuing of the lease, it is now apparent that the County Council's deliberations over the location of the proposed sanatorium may have been the reason.

Donaghmore Agricultural Museum

Friday, 28 May 1993, was another historic day for the Donaghmore Workhouse – the opening of the Donaghmore Agricultural Museum. A local voluntary committee was set up in 1989 and they went about the task of restoring the front building

1. *Laois County Council – The First 100 Years* published in 1999 by Laois County Council edited by Teddy Fennelly.

of the workhouse complex for use as a repository of times past in Donaghmore. The Board of Avonmore offered them the building and enthusiastically backed the project.

Today the museum is a unique attraction. It recreates the story of life as it was for the families who lived, and many of whom died, inside these walls during its days as a workhouse. The role of agriculture in the lives of the people of rural Ireland is also highlighted in its exhibits. The machinery, equipment and tools of a bygone era are to be seen here and very appropriately, the dairy section is central to the exhibits.

The official opening was fittingly performed by local man Liam Hyland, then TD and Minister for Forestry and Rural Development and later MEP for the Leinster Constituency. "This very building is a living reminder of the hardships and difficulties that past generations lived through. It was because of the resilience and determination of our ancestors that we can stand here today - free and prosperous – to pay tribute to their work and to put in place a lasting reminder, particularly for our youth, of the way of life of rural people of past generations", said Mr. Hyland.

He added: "It is appropriate that this building should eventually revert to a museum because the building itself is a monument to our local history - from a dreaded workhouse to a creamery, representing the flagship of rural development over the past fifty years." He said that the museum project was a catalogue of community participation and co-operation.

Donaghmore Agricultural Museum Committee:

Michael Delaney, Chairman; Pat Brophy, Regional Manager; John Bergen, Brand Manager; Laurence Phelan, Martin Keane, Joe Nolan (R.I.P.), John Dunne, Bobby Bennett, William Maher, Liam Delaney, Murtagh McWey, Diarmuid Doran, Trevor Stanley.

Opening of the Donaghmore Museum 28 May 1993
L. to r: Timothy Costigan, Branch Manager, Spink; Joseph Morrin, P. J. Butler and
Joseph Nolan.

Donaghmore Agricultural Museum Committee, pictured with guests at the official opening of the Museum on Friday, 28th May, 1993. From left: Pat O'Shea (Chairman, Barrow Nore Suir Leader Group), Pat Brophy (Regional Manager), Lar Phelan, Michael Delaney (Chairman, Museum Committee), Martin Keane, John Duggan (Chairman, Avonmore Foods P.L.C.), Minister for State Liam Hyland, T.D., Joe Nolan, John Dunne, Charles Flanagan T.D., John Bergin (Manager, Donaghmore), Bobby Bennett, Bill Maher and Liam Delaney.

GRAIGUECULLEN AND CRETTYARD

Graiguecullen and Crettyard are two Glanbia Agribusinesses in County Laois that are not part of the Donaghmore/Monasterevin region. Graiguecullen is in the Barrowvale region while Crettyard is attached to the Kilkenny region.

Graiguecullen is a diversified branch offering a wide range of products such as feed bulk and bags, fertilisers, grass seed and veterinary products and services including grain storage, soil testing and silage analysis. The branch produces most of the seed grain for the Glanbia Group and has one of the biggest grain intakes in the Group. Crettyard branch services farmers with goods and services over a wide surrounding area.

Employees at Graiguecullen in December 2002 were: Eamon Quirke (branch manager/area manager, Carlow area), Kevin Hosey, John Fennelly, Pat Culleton, Kathleen Hogan, Sean O'Faolain, Paddy Maher, Oliver Kelly, Gerry Daly, Marie Clancy and Patrick Murray.

Employees at Crettyard in December 2002 were: John Brennan (branch manager), Anne Byrne and Patsy Wilson.

Donaghmore Co-operative Creamery Ltd.

Committee of Management 1927-1973

The Branch represented by the committee member appears in brackets:
D: Donaghmore; C: Coolrain; M: Mountmellick; R: Raheen; S: Spink.

1927-'29	Rev. T. Henebry, C.C. Killesmeestia (D)
1927-'67	Michael Kirwan, Donaghmore (D)
1927-'42	R.F. Bennett, Glebe House, Donaghmore (D)
1927-'47	John Treacy snr., Ballyquaide (D)
1927-'36	Hubert Thompson, Beckfield (D)
1927-'28	Michael Phelan, Donaghmore (D)
1927-'40	P.J. Murphy, Borris-in-Ossory (D)
1927-'37	Joseph Cooper, Coolrain Glebe (C)
1927-'42	Edward Sheeran, Coolrain (C)
1927-'29	James Carroll, Mannin, Rushall (C)
1927-'40	Jacob Thompson, Clonoughill, Coolrain (C)
1927	James Dwyer, Moneymore (D)
1928-'31	John Loughman, Knockiel (D)
1928-'73	George Galbraith, Corbally, Abbeyleix (R)
1928-'32	John Tynan, Ballinree, Abbeyleix (R)
1928-'47	William Bergin, Colt, Ballyroan (R)
1928	Peter Salter, Corbally, Abbeyleix (R)
1929-'37	Richard Wallace, Middlemount (D)
1929-'45	Thomas Mitchell, Tunduff, Abbeyleix (R)
1930	John Thompson, Park, Rathsaran (D)
1930	J.C. Carroll, Mannin, Pike of Rushall (C)
1931-'34	Jerh. Davin, Rathsaran (D)
1931-'40	Richard C. Howard, Kylebeg Borris-in-Ossory (C)
1932	Richard Houlihan, Shragh, Rathdowney (D)
1933	William Moynan, Donaghmore (D)
1933-'35	John Rohan, Corbally, Abbeyleix (R)
1934-'73	John Hennessy, Coolowley, Errill (D)
1935-'66	Patrick J. Kavanagh, Coolowley, Errill (D)
1936-'58	Rody McEvoy, Clonbrin, Ballyroan (R)
1937	Owen McMahon, Mounteagle, Ballyroan (D)
1938-'40	Thomas McDonald, Colt, Ballyroan (R)
1938-'71	Joseph Bergin, Newtown (D)
1941	Martin Brennan, Graigueahown, Spink (S)
1941-'49	Patrick McDonald, Colt, Ballyroan (R)
1941-'42	Robert Mitchell, Castlefleming (D)
1941-'46	John Doherty, Knock (D)
1941-'71	Stephen Campion, Donaghmore (D)
1946-'73	Michael Walsh, Ballyking, Ballyroan (S)
1947-'73	Robert P. Bennett, Lismore (D)
1948-'73	Murtagh McWey, Clontico, Ballyroan (S)
1950-'67	Patrick Shiel, Roskelton, Mountrath (R)
1948-'69	John Treacy jnr., Ballyquaide (D)
1959-'73	Sean O'Reilly, Rathmoyle, Abbeyleix (R)
1967-'73	James Cooney, Monamanry, Luggacurren (S)
1967-'73	M. Gerard Culliton, Highfield, Rearymore, Rosenallis (M)

1967-'71	Padraig Culliton, Raheenduff, Timahoe (S)
1967-'73	Christopher Horan, Wranglestown, Clonaslee (M)
1968-'73	Richard Lalor-Fitzpatrick, Tinnakill, Mountrath (R)
1969-'73	John Kirwan, Donaghmore (D)
1969-'73	Frank Hyland, Bordwell, Clough, Ballacolla (D)
1970-'73	Hugh Cole, Green Road, Ballyroan (R)
1970-'73	Bernard Rochford, Emmett St., Mountmellick (M)
1970-'73	Patrick J. Phelan, Glebe House, Donaghmore (D)
1972-'73	John Miller, Boleybeg, Abbeyleix (S)
1972-'73	Joseph Dwyer, Moneymore (D)
1972-'73	Laurence Phelan, The Glebe, Donaghmore (D)
1973	Billy Flynn, Rearyvalley, Rosenallis (M)

First Shareholders at Donaghmore Co-op (5th May 1927)

No. of shares	Name	Address
12	R.F. Bennett	Glebe House, Ballybrophy
1	Richard Leahy	Rathdowney
3	Miss M. Holland	Rathdowney
2	Patrick Flynn	Rathdowney
1	James Dunne	Rathdowney
6	Peter Thorpe	Rathdowney
2	Jer. Meehan	Rathdowney
8	Ellen Campion	Rathdowney
3	Mrs. K. Tuohy	Rathdowney
6	Delaney Bros.	Rathdowney
5	P.J. Nugent	Rathdowney
1	P.J. White	Rathdowney
5	Mrs. Fitzgerald	Rathdowney
3	Kieran Kelly	Rathdowney
8	Timothy Davin	Eglish, Grogan
5	Maurice Dowling	Castleflemming, Errill
1	Thomas King	Garryduff, Errill
5	Jer. Connor	Garryduff, Errill
2	Mrs. B. Ryan	Garryduff, Errill
2	Mrs. M Nolan	Garryduff, Errill
3	Miss E. Cashin	Garryduff, Errill
2	Matthew Tierney	Garryduff, Errill
3	Richard Moynan	Castleflemming, Errill
6	John Maher	Newtown, Errill
1	George Patterson	Clonmore, Errill
1	Kingsley Roe	Clonmore, Errill
1	Edward Evans	Ballinakill, Errill
6	Henry Pearson	Clonmore, Grogan
6	Andy Bergin	Coolowley, Grogan
4	Mrs. Julia Creary	Castleflemming, Errill
3	John Hynes	Castleflemming, Grogan
6	Michael Kavanagh	Barney, Grogan
4	John Bowe	Mt. Oliver, Grogan
4	Mary Bergin	Coolowley, Grogan
6	John Pearson	Graigueard, Rathdowney
9	Patrick Walsh	Garryduff, Errill
4	Pat Mulhall	Whiteswall, Rathdowney
6	Denis Bowe	Kilcotton, Ballacolla
2	Mrs. B. Bergin	Clonlahy, Borris in Ossory
4	Martin Daly	Castlequarter, Borris in Ossory
3	Mrs. Mary Delaney	Ballymeelish, Borris in Ossory

No. of shares	Name	Address
2	Miss L. Kelly	Ballymeelish, Borris in Ossory
8	Mrs. M Kelly	Ballymeelish, Borris in Ossory
1	Thomas Delaney	Ballymeelish, Borris in Ossory
4	James Costigan	Rapla, Rathdowney
7	Robert J. Stanley	Bawnogue, Rathdowney
4	James MacDowell	Court, Ballacolla
3	Daniel Sweeney	Rathmore, Ballybrophy
3	Patrick Kissane	Rathmore, Ballybrophy
7	Denis J. Breen	Kilcoke, Ballybrophy
3	William Kennedy	Kilcoke, Ballybrophy
10	W.H. Roe	Castleflemming, Grogan
9	William Brophy	Glebe, Ballybrophy
4	Laurence Shelley	Glebe, Ballybrophy
2	Pat Loughman	Raheen, Donaghmore
6	William Murphy	Kilcoke, Ballybrophy
6	Laurence Delaney	Kilcoke, Ballybrophy
9	John Campion	Rathmore, Ballybrophy
3	Edward Purcell	Barney, Grogan
5	Mrs. Campion	Donaghmore
3	John Sutcliffe	The Glebe, Donaghmore
6	Robert Barton	122, Royce Road, Dublin
3	Pierce Bergin	Clonagooden, Borris in Ossory
1	Daniel Phelan	Clonagooden, Borris in Ossory
3	Joseph Bergin	Clonagooden, Borris in Ossory
3	Patrick Delaney	Castlequarter, Borris in Ossory
3	Miss Brennan	Shanboe, Borris in Ossory
2	Daniel Bergin	Shanboe, Borris in Ossory
7	Fintan Wallis	Shanboe, Borris in Ossory
5	Patrick Cavanagh	Shanboe, Borris in Ossory
5	William White	Shanboe, Borris in Ossory
7	P.J. Murphy	Shanboe, Borris in Ossory
2	Pat Kirwan	Shanboe, Borris in Ossory
4	John Brophy	Doon, Borris in Ossory
6	Thos Richardson	Moonfad, Ballybrophy
6	John Grady	Kyle, Ballaghmore
3	R.T. Jones	Rathdowney
3	Patrick Malone	Rathdowney
1	William Quinn	Rathdowney
8	William Jas. Rowell	Rathdowney
8	Michael Gorman	Rathdowney
6	Daniel Quigley	Rathdowney
9	John Loughman	Knockiel, Rathdowney
5	E.J. Hayes	Rathdowney
3	Mrs. Conroy	Rathdowney
3	Michael Moloney	Rathdowney
2	Denis Keys	Ardvarney, Ballybrophy
2	Thos. Rafter	Knockaroe, Ballybrophy
5	Arthur Marshall	Grange, Ballybrophy
8	Mrs. M.A. Bergin	Kilcotton, Ballacolla
3	Robert Proctor	Castleflemming, Errill
2	Miss Lanley	Castleflemming, Errill
6	Robert Mitchell	Castleflemming, Errill
3	W.B. Mitchell	Castleflemming, Errill
3	W.W. Pratt	Castleflemming, Errill
9	William Mitchell	Ballymullen, Grogan, Ballybrophy
1	Daniel Cahill	Rossmore, Grogan, Ballybrophy
4	George Southern	Grogan, Ballybrophy
2	William Delaney	Whiteswall, Rathdowney

No. of shares	Name	Address
2	William Smeaton Jnr.	New Cottages, Rathdowney
2	John Bergin	Levalley, Rathdowney
3	Philip Campion	Coolkerry, Rathdowney
6	Thos. Creagh	Ballybuggy, Rathdowney
6	James Lalor	Ballyedmond
5	James Spooner	Boardwell, Clough Ballacolla
5	Richard Bailey	Grantstown
3	William McEvoy	Ballycoolid, Donaghmore
4	Timothy Fitzpatrick	Kilbreedy, Rathdowney
2	Timothy Fitzpatrick	Ballycoolid, Rathdowney
4	Pat Fitzpatrick	Ballycoolid, Rathdowney
3	John Maher	Donaghmore
15	Michael Kirwan	Donaghmore
6	Jos. Moylan	Ballybrophy
3	John Lambe	Ballybrophy
3	John Moylan	Kilpurcell, Ballybrophy
2	John A. O'Malley	Rathdowney
2	R.R. Mitchell	Rathdowney
6	H.G. Perry & Son	Rathdowney
1	Patrick Quigley	Church St., Rathdowney
6	George Clarke	Ballaghmore Castle, Roscrea
2	Tim Egan	Rosdoraugha, Ballaghmore
2	Richard England	Ballaghmore
3	Timothy Phelan	Ballaghmore
2	Henry Flynn	Ballaghmore
6	Rev. J. Dillon P.P.	Borris in Ossory
2	Dr. R.B. Hennessy	Thorndene, Borris in Ossory.
9	John Kennedy	Jamestown, Borris in Ossory
4	Michael J. Phelan	Donaghmore
12	Denis Loughman	Killadooley, Ballybrophy
8	Michael Maher	Johnstown, Glebe, Rathdowney
3	Patrick Holohan	Knock, Roscrea
2	Thos. Quinlan	Knock, Roscrea
2	Joseph Standish	Knock, Roscrea
3	Charles Doherty	Springfield, Knock, Roscrea
1	Timothy Guidera	Springfield, Knock, Roscrea
1	Timothy Guidera	Rockforest, Knock, Roscrea
3	William Guidera	Knock, Roscrea
2	Timothy Scully	Knock, Roscrea
1	Joseph Delaney	Knock, Roscrea
2	Fintan Bergin	Spafield, Knock, Roscrea
5	Thos. Cunningham	Ballacolla
15	Herbert Thompson	Beckfield, Rathdowney
1	Michael Ryan	Ballytarsna, Borris in Ossory
1	Martin Phelan	Ballytarsna, Borris in Ossory
2	Mrs. Whelan	Sentry Hill, Borris in Ossory
3	Patrick Butler	Bawngorra, Borris in Ossory
5	Peter Guaney	Bawngorra, Borris in Ossory
5	Edward Butler	Bawngorra, Borris in Ossory
3	William Campion	Barnasallagh, Borris in Ossory
3	Loughlin Campion	Barnasallagh, Borris in Ossory
2	John Brophy	Cappagh, Borris in Ossory
9	Thos. Jeston	Sentry Hill, Borris in Ossory
2	Jas. Monahan	Sentry Hill, Borris in Ossory
2	Patrick Brien	Sentry Hill, Borris in Ossory
8	Martin Costigan	Ballytarsna, Borris in Ossory
6	Gerald Thompson	Borris in Ossory
8	Fintan Kiely	Sentry Hill, Borris in Ossory

No. of shares	Name	Address
2	Richard Brien	Derrin, Borris in Ossory
3	John Whelan	Ballycoolid, Rathdowney
6	R.K. Carter	Coolacurragh
4	Mrs. Mary Delaney	Feeneigh, Donaghmore
3	John Byrne	Ballacolla
4	Denis Coss	Currawn, Ballacolla
4	William Byrne	Aghavoe, Ballacolla
2	John King	Akip, Donaghmore
1	Timothy Maher	Palmers Hill, Ballacolla
1	Geo. W. Abbott	Currawn, Aghavoe, Ballacolla
12	R.A.Dagg	Aghavoe, Ballacolla
1	Michael Comerford	Kilcotton, Ballacolla
2	Thos. Cooney	Kildellig, Ballacolla
7	John Walpole	Ashbrook, Ballacolla
3	John Cahill	Rathdowney
10	John Bergin	Ballycoolid, Donaghmore
2	John Walsh	Killesmeestia, Ballybrophy
3	Thos. Kennedy	Killesmeestia, Ballybrophy
3	Mrs. Loughman	Killesmeestia, Ballybrophy
3	James Loughman	Killadooley, Ballybrophy
3	Joseph Young	Tullacommon, Ballybrophy
3	William Whelan	Tullacommon, Ballybrophy
3	Patrick Maher	Tullacommon, Ballybrophy
3	Richard Wall	Killesmeestia, Ballybrophy
5	Rev. T. Henebry C.C.	Killesmeestia, Ballybrophy
2	Edward Fox	Killesmeestia, Ballybrophy
3	William Treacy	Ballyquaide, Ballybrophy
2	Thomas Walsh	Ballyquaide, Ballybrophy
2	Thomas Campion	Killadooley, Ballybrophy
9	Joseph Loughman	Raheenshira
3	Peter Bennett	Garron, Ballybrophy
3	Mrs. Maggie Hennessy	Garron, Ballybrophy
3	Daniel Bourke	Garron, Ballybrophy
3	Daniel Sweeney	Garron, Ballybrophy
2	Anne Davin	Garron, Ballybrophy
3	James Carroll	Garron, Ballybrophy
2	Patrick Maher	Raheenphelan
2	James Delaney	Kyledellig, Ballybrophy
4	Stephen Phillips	Kyledellig, Ballybrophy
6	Charles Thompson	Skeirke, Ballybrophy
6	Michael Holohan	Skeirke, Ballybrophy
6	John Treacy	Ballyquaide, Ballybrophy
2	Michael Delaney	Grangemore, Ballybrophy
4	Richard Holohan	Tullacommon, Ballybrophy
1	George McKelvey	Glebe, Donaghmore
2	Patrick Sweeney	Killadooley, Donaghmore
3	William Roe	Ballykelly, Roscrea
6	Michael Breen	Garron, Ballybrophy
5	Fintan Murphy	Greenroads, Ballybrophy
20	Arthur Dugdale	Donaghmore
5	James Kelly	Ballycoolid, Donaghmore
1	Martin Phelan	Lowran, Rushall
2	Michael Tynan	Peafield, Rushall
2	John Sweeney	Ballytarsna, Borris in Ossory
2	Richard Howard	Kylebeg House, Borris in Ossory
3	John Tighe	Kylemelawn, Errill
4	Michael Peters	Harristown, Rathdowney
2	Michael Kirwan	Johnstown, Glebe, Rathdowney

No. of shares	Name	Address
3	Con Cahill	Rathdowney
8	M.J. Fitzpatrick	Tunduff Park, Abbeyleix
2	Patrick Bergin	Barney, Grogan
9	Mrs. Johanna Breen	Kyledotha, Garron, Ballybrophy
10	Peter Roe	Hollymount, Roscrea
10	Mrs. Carroll	Coolkerry, Rathdowney
3	Michael Tynan	Coolowley, Grogan
6	William Bergin	Newtown, Skierke
4	William Fitzpatrick	Tullacommon, Ballybrophy
1	John Carroll	Grangebeg, Ballybrophy
3	Michael Brophy	Killadooley, Ballybrophy
2	Michael Fitzpatrick	Garron, Ballybrophy
6	Edward Leahy	Ballyreilly, Ballybrophy
1	Richard Percy	Clononin, Borris in Ossory
3	William McEvoy	Creelagh, Rathdowney
4	John Dunphy	Whitepark, Rathdowney
2	Martin Fitzpatrick	Elmfield, Borris in Ossory
1	Michael Nolan	Ballytarsna, Borris in Ossory
6	Michael Nolan	Ballytarsna, Borris in Ossory
5	Richard Thompson	Beechmount, Rathdowney
6	Denis Coss	Kyledellig, Ballybrophy
1	James Phelan	Kilcoke, Ballybrophy
1	Martin Phelan	Kyledellig, Ballybrophy
5	James Dwyer	Moneymore, Borris in Ossory
1	Michael Breen	Coolowley, Grogan
2	Richard McKelvey	Kilpurcell, Ballybrophy
2	William Moynihan	Donaghmore
1	James Moynan	Kilcoke, Ballybrophy
2	Jerome Shortall	Killadooley, Ballybrophy
5	Peter G. Alley	Donaghmore
2	John Rudd	Ballyhegadon
4	Thomas O'Riordan	Donaghmore
2	Michael Drennan	Donaghmore
1	Thomas Byrne	Kilcoke
1	Mrs. Brophy	Bealady, Rathdowney
3	Matt Bergin	Rathdowney
2	Peter White	Coolkerry, Rathdowney
3	Matt Connor	Oldcourt, Clough, Ballacolla
3	Patrick Keys	Bordwell, Ballacolla
2	James Whelan	Ashbrook, Ballacolla
12	James Austin	Glebe, Coolrain
6	Joseph Cooper	Glebe, Coolrain
24	Robert McDonald	Monagh, Coolrain
9	Thomas Thompson	Rosnaclonagh, Coolrain
15	Edward Sheeran	Coolrain
9	Mrs. Anne Delaney	Glebe, Coolrain
3	James O'Loughlin	Glebe, Coolrain
18	James Byrne	Windsor, Coolrain
12	Bernard Higgins	Windsor, Coolrain
30	Cornelius Stretton	Damesfort, Coolrain
9	Thomas Finn	Cahir, Coolrain
9	Margaret Henzy	Cahir, Coolrain
12	Matt Larkin	Coolrain
30	Gerald Delaney	Brooklawn, Borris in Ossory
9	John Hyland	Glebe, Coolrain
30	James Bennett	Cardtown, Mountrath
30	Thomas Troy	Coole, Mountrath
12	Patrick Bennett	Cuddagh, Mountrath

No. of shares	Name	Address
9	William Bennett	Cuddagh, Mountrath
18	Mrs. Ellen Mercier	Cuddagh, Mountrath
30	John Carroll	Camphill, Mountrath
12	Miss Geraldine Roe	Rushall, Mountrath
15	Joseph Keeshan	Derryarrow, Coolrain
12	Arthur McMahon	Cuddagh, Mountrath
24	Timothy Campion	Clonin, Mountrath
6	Michael Conroy	Derryduff, Coolrain
9	Joseph Fitzpatrick	Derryduff, Coolrain
12	Michael Phelan	Derryduff, Coolrain
12	Mrs. Margaret Kelly	Derryduff, Coolrain
18	Martin Gorman	Crannagh, Mountrath
30	Michael Corcoran	Derrynaseera, Coolrain
15	Patrick Doherty	Camross, Coolrain
8	John Gorman	Camross, Coolrain
6	John Dowling	Glenkit, Camross, Coolrain
6	John Dooley	Derry, Camross, Coolrain
6	Denis Delaney	Shrahane, Camross, Coolrain
6	Richard Thompson	Laurel Hill, Coolrain
15	Mrs. Kate Coss	Derryduff, Coolrain
24	Sylvester Phelan	Cranagh, Mountrath
27	Patrick Delaney	Clash, Clonin, Mountrath
15	John Cook	Cranagh, Mouthrath
6	Thomas Phelan	Mannin, Rushall, Mountrath
18	James Casey	Mount Salem, Coolrain
15	Martin O'Rourke	Rushin House, Mountrath
12	Rev. H.S. Anderson	Offerlane, Coolrain
25	William Delaney	Hazelpit, Mountrath

Signed: 5th May 1927 – T. Henebry, C.C. (Chairman)

Donaghmore Branch Area Advisory Committee (1970 to 2002)

Name	Address	Area Represented
R P Bennett	Lismore, Borris in Ossory	Pike of Rushall
Lar Phelan	The Glebe, Donaghmore	Donaghmore
Joseph Bergin	Skeirke, Borris-in-Ossory	Donaghmore
Jerome Campion	Coolkerry, Rathdowney	Rathdowney
Charles Doherty	Ballykelly, Borris-in-Ossory	Ballaghmore
Denis Dooley	Glebe, Coolrain	Pike of Rushall
Michael Loughman	Killesmeestia, Ballybrophy	Donaghmore
John Maher	Newtown, Ballybritt, Roscrea	Ballaghmore
George Murphy	Kilcoke, Ballybrophy	Donaghmore
Michael O Connell	Westfield, Castletown	Pike of Rushall
Michael Parlon	The Leap, Roscrea	Ballaghmore
Albert Roe	Killavilla, Roscrea	Ballaghmore
Michael Maher	Keelough, Pike of Rushall	Pike of Rushall
Paddy Dooley	Neilstown, Roscrea	Ballaghmore
Liam Delaney	Knockbrack, Pike of Rushall	Pike of Rushall
P J Butler	Aughafan, Castletown	Pike of Rushall
John Dunne	Tentore, Ballacolla	Rathdowney/Ballacolla
James Stanley	Coolfin, Rathdowney	Donaghmore
Frank Hyland	Bordwell, Clough, Ballacolla	Rathdowney/Ballacolla
William Maher	Keelough, Pike of Rushall	Pike of Rushall

Name	Address	Area Represented
Charles Campion	Lisduff, Errill	Rathdowney
John Kirwan	Donaghmore	Donaghmore
Peter Loughman	Newtown, Durrrow	Rathdowney/Ballacolla
Joseph Kennedy	Grogan, Errill	Donaghmore
Loughlin Campion	Graigue, Rathdowney	Rathdowney
Tony Bergin	Cooleshall, Roscrea	Ballaghmore
John Hennessy	Coolowley, Errill	Donaghmore
Pat Phelan	Glebe, Donaghmore	Donaghmore
Herbert Stanley	Bawnogue, Rathdowney	Rathdowney
Joe Dwyer	Moneymore, Borris-in-Ossory	Ballaghmore
Stephan Campion	Rathmore, Ballybrophy	Donaghmore
Paddy Phelan	Pike of Rushall	Pike of Rushall
John Roe	Ballykelly, Borris-in-Ossory	Ballaghmore
Sean Bergin	Gurteen, Ballybritt, Roscrea	Ballaghmore
Timothy Doherty	Tinderry House, Knock	Ballaghmore
Tom Phelan	Pike of Rushall, Portlaoise	Pike of Rushall
Thomas Campion	Lisduff, Errill	Rathdowney
Patrick Campion	Kyle, Rathdowney	Rathdowney
William Carroll	Rathmore, Ballybrophy	Donaghmore
Martin Keane	Brockery, Errill	Donaghmore
Trevor Stanley	Coolfin, Rathdowney	Donaghmore
Michael Delaney	Skeirke, Borris-in-Ossory	Ballaghmore
William Delaney Jnr	Knockbrack, Pike of Rushall	Pike of Rushall
Donal Hynes	Larch Hill, Mountrath	Pike of Rushall
Fred Bailey	Grantstown, Ballacolla	Rathdowney/Ballacolla
Canice Hyland	Clough, Ballacolla	Rathdowney/Ballacolla
Gerry Moylan	Derrinsallagh, Borris-in-Ossory	Donaghmore
Victor Butler	Bawngorra, Borris-in-Ossory	Pike of Rushall
Joseph Morrin	Aughafan, Castletown	Pike of Rushall
Neil Bennett	Lismore, Borris-in-Ossory	Pike of Rushall
Thomas Hogan Jnr	Coolowley, Errill	Donaghmore
Paul Hyland	Bordwell, Clough, Ballacolla	Rathdowney/Ballacolla
Pat Duggan	Grantstown, Ballacolla	Rathdowney/Ballacolla
Joe Fletcher	Ballyquaide, Ballybrophy	Donaghmore
Michael Dooley	Neilstown, Roscrea	Donaghmore
James Dwyer	Moneymore, Borris-in-Ossory	Ballaghmore
Sylvester Phelan	Crannagh, Mountrath	Pike of Rushall
Martin Bergin	Grantstown, Ballacolla	Donaghmore
Joseph Walsh	Boherard, Ballacolla	Donaghmore

L.-r.: Gerard Lawler and John Galvin in front of original Raheen Branch Nameplate, with milk testing equipment and aluminium can in front.

Raheen Branch Area Advisory Committee Members (1970 to 2002)

Name	*Address*	*Area Represented*
John Talbot Snr	Corbally	Raheen
Leo Bennett	Tunduff	Abbeyleix
Patrick Sinnott	Ardlea	Raheen
Thomas Phelan	Tunduff	Abbeyleix
John Cole	Tunduff	Abbeyleix
Hugh Cole	Green Road	Abbeyleix
William Sheil	Boley	Shanahoe
Richard Cruite	Ballytarsna	Shanahoe
Richard Palmer	Boley	Shanahoe
Liam Rohan	Kilbricken	Shanahoe
Daniel Conway	Larchfield	Ballyroan
Joseph Corcoran	Crubbin	Ballyroan
Bernie Farrell	Clonad	Clonad
Andrew Doogue	Clonad	Clonad
Patrick Lalor	Lalors Mills	Clonad
J.J. Campion	Rushin	Mountrath
John Lowry	Deerpark	Mountrath
Michael Collier	Camross	Mountrath
George Galbraith	Corbally	Raheen
Sean Reilly	Rathmoyle	Abbeyleix
Richard Lalor-FitzPatrick	Tinakill	Raheen
William Delaney	Rathevan	Clonad
Patrick Keegan, Snr	Rathleague	Clonad
John Hosey, Snr	Corbally	Abbeyleix
Edward Breen	Derrykearn	Raheen
James Fitzgerald	Green Road	Abbeyleix
Fintan Phelan	Forrest	Mountrath
William McGrath	Cashel	Ballyroan
Sean FitzPatrick	Ballyruin	Ballyroan
Walter McDonnell	Shanahoe	Shanahoe
Daniel Cass	Abbeyleix	Abbeyleix
Michael Bergin	Cromogue	Raheen
Rody McEvoy	Ballyroan	Ballyroan
Frank Haslam	Clonenagh	Mountrath
Michael Holland	Trumera	Mountrath
Christy Cullen	Clonard	Mountrath
Patrick McEvoy	Meelick	Clonad
Frank Fogarty	Colt	Ballyroan
Martin Sinnott	Raheen	Raheen
Gerry Phelan	Forrest	Mountrath
John Delaney	Borris	Clonad
Michael Lalor	Raheen	Raheen
Liam Delaney	Paddock	Mountrath
Patrick Keegan, Jnr	Rathleague	Clonad
Tim FitzGerald	Green Roads	Abbeyleix
Sean Tynan	Ardlea	Raheen
John Hosey, Jnr	Corbally	Ballyroan
James Delaney	Derrygarron	Clonad
Michael Bergin	Boley	Shanahoe
Noreen Dooley	Abbeyleix	Abbeyleix
John Talbot, Jnr	Corbally	Raheen
James Phelan	Kilbricken	Shanahoe
Liam Delaney	Rathevan	Clonad
Denis Dowling	Clonard	Mountrath
William Kirwan	Abbeyleix	Abbeyleix
Patrick Parkinson	Trumera	Raheen

Name	Address	Area Represented
Thomas Meade	Redcastle	Mountrath
Patrick Dunne	Coolnacarte	Raheen
Joseph Delaney	Ridge Road, Portlaoise	Clonad

List of milk suppliers to Raheen, circa 1950

No.	Name	Address
1	George Galbraith	Corbally
2	Joseph Moffitt	Raheen
3	Brigidine Convent	Abbeyleix
4	Mrs. Mary Dalton	Colt
5	Mrs. A.S. Bennett	Tunduff
6	Gerard Grace	Colt
7	Thomas Reilly	Oatlands
8	Martin Rohan	Mounteagle
9	Edward Parkinson	Roskelton
10	Mrs. M. Bergin	Roskelton
11	Mrs. K. Hipwell	Oldtown
12	Mrs. B. Dowling	Colt
13	Denis Connor	Raheen
14	Jerh. Shiel	Roskelton
15	Patrick Fogarty	Colt
16	Mrs. M. Lalor-Fitzpatrick	Tinnakill
17	Mrs. Julia Butler	Raheen
18	John Fennelly	Coole
19	Tom Cunningham	Clonadacasey
20	James Phelan	Coole
21	James Ryan	Raheen
22	John McEvoy	Coolnacarte
23	William Rohan	Colt
24	Mrs. C. Mulhall	Coolnacarte
25	James Fitzpatrick	Clonadacasey
26	Mrs. B. McDonald	Corbally
27	Anthony Kavanagh	Colt
28	John Lalor	Clonbar
29	Peter Lalor	Corbally
30	Rody McEvoy	Clonbrin
31	Tom Mitchell	Tunduff
32	John H. Talbot	Corbally
33	William Holland	Ardlea
34	Mrs. Johanna Phelan	Derrykearn
35		
36	Matt Stone	Clonadacasey
37	Mrs. Julia Phelan	Coole
38	Mrs. Nora Tynan	Ardlea
39	Mrs. E. Lalor	Mounteagle
40	Edward Breen	Derrykearn
41	John Rohan	Anngrove
42	Rev. C. Coyne P.P.	Coole
43	Patrick McDonald	Colt
44	Mrs. M.Dooley	Colt
45	Patrick Holland	Coole
46	Mrs. M. Conroy	Gortnaclea
47	Michael Whelan	Clonkeen
48	Mrs. Julia Tynan	
49	John Lalor	Ring

Mountmellick Branch Area Advisory Committee (1970-2002)

Name	Home Address	Area Represented
William McEvoy	Clonaheen	Rosenallis
William Shaw	Clonkelly	Rosenallis
Sean Young	Drummond	Rosenallis
Daniel Hourigan	Cloncannon	Rosenallis
Patrick F Corbett	Ballykaneen	Clonaslee
James Costello	Graigueafulla	Clonaslee
William Flynn	Rearyvalley	Clonaslee
Michael Lalor	Cloonagh	Clonaslee
Ralph Thompson	Campclone	Ballyfin
Padraig Ryan	O Moores Forest	Ballyfin
Patrick Scully	Rossleighan	Ballyfin
Sean Fitzpatrick	Barkmills	Ballyfin
Michael Burke	Derryguile	Mountmellick
Denis O Rourke	Acragar	Mountmellick
John Ryan	Clonsoughy	Mountmellick
Bernard Rochford	Mountmellick	Mountmellick
John Joe Dunne	Graigue	Mountmellick
M.J. Dunne	Ballymacrory	Clonaslee
John McEvoy	Clonaheen	Rosenallis
James Delaney	Cloneygowen	Ballyfin
Sean Baker	O Moore St., Mountmellick	Mountmellick
J. Bowe	Cloneygowen	Ballyfin
Vincent Gorman	Borness	Mountmellick
P.J. Delaney	Graigue	Mountmellick
Thomas Foyle	Clonterry	Mountmellick
H. Dunne	Cloonaghmore	Clonaslee
Andrew Cashin	Clonurk	Ballyfin
W. Sinnott	Clonduff	Rosenallis
P.J. McHugh	Clondarrig	Ballyfin
Fergal Rochford	Graigue	Mountmellick
George Kerr	Ross	Ballyfin
John Dromey	Rearymore House	Clonaslee
Martin Delaney	Graigue	Mountmellick
Denis Whelan	Clonsaughey	Ballyfin
Patrick Corbett Jnr	Ballykaneen	Clonaslee
T. Behan	Cloneygowen	Ballyfin
Derek Meredith	O Moores Forest	Ballyfin
Rory Culleton	Rearymore	Clonaslee
Jeremiah McEvoy	Clonaheen	Rosenallis
P. Duff	Campclone	Ballyfin
Norman Graham	Ballyhupahaun	Rosenallis
Ian Thompson	Campclone	Ballyfin
Kevin Flynn	Rearyvalley	Rosenallis
Thomas Horan	Wranglestown	Clonaslee
J.J. Dunne	Cloonaghbeg	Clonaslee
P. Hyland	Bellair	Clonaslee
Gerry Culliton	Rearymore	The Board
Chris Horan	Wranglestown	Clonaslee
Tom O'Rourke	Kennell's Cross, Emo	Mountmellick
Francis Young	Drummond	Rosenallis
Walter Murphy	Clonduff	Rosenallis
Michael Delaney	Kyletelisha	Mountmellick
David Kerr	Ross	Ballyfin
Ray Lynam	Meelick	Rosenallis
Jerh. Dunne	Pallas	Ballyfin

Name	Home Address	Area Represented
John James McEvoy	Clonaheen	Rosenallis
Tom Fennelly	Tinnakill	Mountmellick
Raymond McEvoy	Garrymore	Mountmellick
Melvyn Bagnall	Kilcavan	Mountmellick

Monasterevin Branch Area Advisory Committee (1986-2002)

Name	Home Address	Area Represented
John Walsh	Grangebeg	Monasterevin/Emo
Chris Booth	Morette	Monasterevin/Emo
George Byrne	Ballykelly	Monasterevin/Emo
Michael Byrne	Ballykelly	Monasterevin/Emo
Tom Kelly	Brownstown	East Kildare
George Pearson	Thomastown	East Kildare
Tom Mather, Snr	Kilnantogue	Derrinturn/Rathangan
Michael Dempsey	Jamestown	Monasterevin/Emo
Michael Flynn	Fisherstown	Monasterevin/Emo
John O'Dea	Clane	East Kildare
Vincent Murphy	Roseberry	East Kildare
Jim Bergin	Rathmore	Cloneygowan
Jim Garry	Cloneyquin	Cloneygowan
Michael Mahon	Grange	Monasterevin/Emo
Pat McHugh	Backwood	Cloneygowan
Tom O'Rourke	Kennells Cross	Monasterevin/Emo
Shay O'Loughlin	Fann	Derrinturn/Rathangan
Larry Morrin	Ladytown	East Kildare
Rd Whelan	Clonard	Cloneygowan
Jim Shortall	Inch	Monasterevin/Emo
Pal Ennis	Guidenstown	Derrinturn/Rathangan
John Daly	Blackhall	East Kildare
Billy Cole	Halverstown	East Kildare
Martin Byrne	Kilberry	Monasterevin/Emo
Gerry Dunleavy	Caragh	East Kildare
John Pearson	Thomastown	East Kildare
Brendan McGlynn	Brownstown	East Kildare
Tom Mather, Jnr	Killinantic	Derrinturn/Rathangan
Tim Garry	Cloneyquin	Cloneygowan
Christy Stapleton	Moyanna	Monasterevin/Emo
Paddy Flynn	Fisherstown	Monasterevin/Emo
Pat McEvoy	Kilberry	Monasterevin/Emo
Robin Frizzell	Kilkeeran Lodge	Cloneygowan
Oliver Dempsey	Jamestown	Monasterevin/Emo
John Joe O'Rourke	Kennells Cross	Monasterevin/Emo
Sean Cawley	Mucklon	East Kildare
Sean Harris	Tipperstown	East Kildare
John Murphy	High Down Hill	East Kildare
Derek Tierney	Cooligmartin	Derrinturn/Rathangan
Joe Moore	Tully Lodge	Monasterevin/Emo
Matt Merrick	Shane	Derrinturn/Rathangan
Pat Jennings	Gallow	East Kildare
Joe Luttrell	Fisherstown	Monasterevin/Emo
Peter McHugh	Backwood	Cloneygowan
Harold Carter	Beech Lodge, Monasterevin	Monasterevin/Emo
Andrew C. Mahon	Grange, Monasterevin	Monasterevin/Emo

Name	Home Address	Area Represented
Denis C. Walsh	Dublin St., Monasterevin	Monasterevin/Emo
Michael Carroll	Clonanny, Portarlington	Monasterevin/Emo
David O'Loughlin	Tullylost, Rathangan	Derrinturn/Rathangan
John Garry	Ballykeane, Geashill	Cloneygowan
Laurence Hart	Newlands, Naas	East Kildare

North Offaly Co-op Advisory Committee Members (1988 to 2002)

Name	Address	Area Represented
Joseph Kelly	Cloncoher	Geashill
Vincent Abbott	Rathue	Kilbeggan
John Mollin	Rahan	Tullamore
James Stronge	Cappincur	Tullamore
Brian Fox	Aharney	Tullamore
Martin O'Grady	Derrybeg	Killeagh
Oliver Claffey	Kilbeggan	
Gerry O'Brien	Barrys Brook	Rhode
Thomas Garry	Ballykane	Geashill
Paddy Bracken	Colhill	
Teresa Hynes	Coolville	Rhode
Thomas Williams	Ballycommon	Tullamore
James Mahon	Ballycommon	Tullamore
Ronnie Bryant	Rathrobin	Blueball
Paul O'Brien	Barrysbrook	Rhode
Robert Cox	Annaharney	Tullamore
Sean Claffey	Kilnalahan	Ballinagore
David O'Connor	Lahinch	Clara
Joe Kelly	Killeshall	Tullamore
Michael A. Guinan	Rahan	Tullamore
Declan Bracken	Wood-of-O	Tullamore
Pat Scully	Attyconnor	Kilbeggan
James Kelly	Cloncoher	Geashill
Vincent Neville	Cloonagh West	Tullamore
Hugh Murphy	Knock	Daingean
James Daly	Kilbeggan	

Spink Area Advisory Committee (1970-2002)

Name	Address	Area Represented
Michael Walsh	Ballyking	Spink
James Cooney	Monamanry	Luggacurren
Padraig Culleton	Raheenduff	Timahoe
Murtagh McWey	Clontico	Spink
William Ramsbottom	Garryglass	Timahoe
Thomas Duff	Ballykockan	Timahoe
John Brennan	Loughteague	Timahoe
Daniel Lalor	Orchard	Timahoe
Patrick Drennan	Ratheniska	Timahoe
John Miller	Boleybeg	Spink
Thomas Gorman	Boleybeg	Spink
William Phelan	Coolnaleen	Spink

Name	Address	Area Represented
Peter Dunne	Kyle, Wolfhill	Spink
Peter Ryan	Lisnagammon	Spink
Richard Foyle	Aughnacross	Ballinakill
Declan Kennedy	Ballinakill	Ballinakill
Martin Rohan	Ballinakill	Ballinakill
John Kennedy	Barnderry	Ballinakill
Michael Walsh	Aughnacross	Ballinakill
Laurence Byrne	Tullamoy	Luggacurren
Andrew Cooney	Coolrusk	Luggacurren
Patrick Stapleton	Clopook	Luggacurren
Joseph Meredith	Southfield	Luggacurren
Andrew Byrne	Luggacurren	Luggacurren
Eamonn Osbourne	Tullamoy	Luggacurren
J.J. Bennett	Lamberton	Timahoe
Eamonn McGrath	Augha dreen	Spink
Vincent Kehoe	Clenagh	Spink
Patrick Lacey	Clopook	Luggacurren
William Murphy	Knockbawn	Spink
John Quigley	Ballygormill	Timahoe
Peter Wall	Ballygormill	Timahoe
Gerald Stone	Scotland	Luggacurren
Larry Kealy	Coolrusk	Luggacurren
Michael Conroy	Raheenahone	Luggacurren
Michael McEvoy	Graiguenahoun	Spink
Jim Walsh	Ballyking	Spink
James Kavanagh	Coolrusk	Luggacurren
Mark Kirwan	Raggettstown	Ballinakill
Paddy Egan	Kilcronan	Ballinakill
James Hennessy	Knockbawn	Spink
John Scully	The Pike	Timahoe
Gay Murphy	Kellyville	Luggacurren
Michael Brennan	The Buildings	Ballinakill
Paddy McWey	Clontico	Spink
Thomas Ryan	Clarbarracum	Ballinakill
John Brophy	Graiguenahoun	Spink
Harry Kelly	Loughteague	Timahoe
John Dalton	Cremorgan	Timahoe
Michael Bennett	Lamberton	Timahoe
Thomas Hennesy	Coolnaleen	Luggacurren
Sean Kennedy	Barnderry	Ballinakill
Richard Duff	Ballykockan	Timahoe
Denis Daly	Garryglass	Timahoe
P.J. Dowling	Fossey	Timahoe
Martin Dowling	Fossey	Timahoe
Seamus Stapleton	Clopook	Luggacurren
Liam Mulhall	Graigue	Spink
Joe Quigley	Ballygormill	Timahoe
Gerard Dooley	Ballinakill	Ballinakill

At the Opening and Blessing of new dairy at Raheen in 1967
**John Treacy, Geo. Galbraith, Rev. Finney, Rev. Fr. Mahon P.P., Raheen, Bobby Bennett
(at back), Rev. Fr. T. Ryan, P.P., Abbeyleix.**

*Presentation in Abbeyleix in 1976 to mark the retirement of Ben Moran and Patrick
Costigan from Spink Creamery. Ben had worked at Spink for 40 years, and half of the
time as manager. Patrick had twenty years service at Spink. (L. to r.): Martin Rohan,
Chairman Spink Advisory Committee, Ben Moran, Patrick Costigan and Tim Costigan,
Shop Manager at Spink.*

On the Avonmore Creameries stand during the walk on the farm of Dick Palmer, Boley, Abbeyleix – creamery milk supplier of the year 1982 – were (from left) Seán Hearn, Avonmore, pictured here with Bill Delaney, Portlaoise and John Hosey, Raheen, both members of Raheen Advisory Committee.

Occasion the announcement of a three year sponsorship agreement between Avonmore and the Charollais Sheep Society of Ireland at Mount Juliet in 1993. Included in photo are:
Front row (l. to r.): Rory Brown, Chairman Charollais Society of Ireland; Joseph Hyland, Avonmore, and Dick O'Hara, Charollais Society and owner of sheep.
Back row (l. to r.): Henry Drea (5th from left), Bobby Bennett (Board of Avonmore, 8th from left), Joe Murphy (Avonmore, 9th from left), and Seán Hearn (Avonmore, extreme right).

Acknowledgements

Sincere thanks to all the people interviewed and to all who contributed photographs, memorabilia or information for this publication.

A special thanks to the following:

Management and staff at Avonmore Provender Mill, Portlaoise

Management and staff at Donaghmore, Monasterevin, Raheen, Spink, Mountmellick and all Glanbia Branches contacted in the research process

Area/Regional Managers: Redmond Bergin, Colm Eustace, Murtagh McWey, John Rice

Branch Managers: Pat Butler, John Carroll, Jim Clifford, Diarmuid Doran, Michael Dowling, Tommy Gorman, Joseph Lawlor, Seamus O'Dea, Michael O'Neill, Jim Ring

Secretaries of the Area Committees: Thomas Garry, Norman Graham, Patrick Keegan, Michael McEvoy, Trevor Stanley

Donaghmore Workhouse Museum Committee

The Co. Librarian and staff at Laois County Library

The Arts Office, Laois County Council

National Archives, Bishop Street, Dublin

National Library of Ireland

Seamus O'Donoghue and staff of ICOS

Centre for Co-op Studies, U.C.C.

Brigid Carroll, Centre for Co-op Studies, U.C.C.

Anne Marie Heskin and staff at FAS – Leinster Express Indexing Scheme

Laois Heritage Society

Patricia Barry, Paddy Bates, Noreen Behan, John Brophy (Video), Joan Byrne, Vincent Callanan, Hugh Cole, Alice Conroy, Bobby Cotter, Rosemary Day, Anthony Delaney, Aisling Delaney, John Delaney, Jim Enright, David, Siobhan, Louise and Eamon Fennelly, Brian Fox, Brendan Graham, Joe Guerin, Hugh Harkin, Alf Harvey (Photographer), Nuala Hayes, Yasmin Henderson, Eileen Henebry (widow of Fr. Henebry's nephew), Chris Horan, Frank Hyland, John Hyland, Martin Keane, Mary Keegan, Bridie Keenan, John Kirwan, Mary Larkin, John Lawler, Lisa Lawler, Betty Maguire, Tony Mahon, Murtagh McWey Snr., John Moloney, John Mulhare, Mary Murphy (niece of Fr. Henebry), Muireann Ni Chonaill, Poilin ni Leathlobhair, Kieran O'Connor, Liam O'Neill, Margaret O'Neill (Grand-niece of Fr. Henebry), Michael Patten, John Phelan, Lawrence Phelan, Sylvester Phelan, Denis Plunkett, Nicholas Purcell, John Roche, Martin Ryan, Michael Scully (Photographer), Ralph Thompson, Charlie White.

Bibliography

The Irish Co-operative Movement: Its History and Development by P. Bolger. (The Institute of Public Administration, Dublin, 1977).

The Centenary Co-operative Creamery Society 1898-1998 by Raymond Smith. (Mount Cross Publishers, Dublin, 1998).

Plunkett and Co-operatives, Past, Present and Future, edited by Carla Keating. (U.C.C. Bank of Ireland Centre for Co-operative Studies, 1983).

Seventy Years Young – Memories of Elizabeth, Countess of Fingall (The Lilliput Press).

Farm Organisations in Ireland – A Century of Progress by Louis P.F. Smith and Sean Healy (Four Courts Press, Dublin, 1996).

Horace Plunkett, Co-operation and Politics by Trevor West (Colin Smythe Limited, Buckinghamshire, 1986).

Towards a History of Agricultural Science in Ireland edited by P.L. Curran (Agricultural Science Association, 1992).

Irish Co-operatives by Carla King and Liam Kennedy (History Ireland, Winter 1994).

At the Sign of the Cow – The Cork Butter Market: 1770-1924 by Colin Rynne (The Collins Press, Cork, 1998).

The Quiet Revolution - The Electrification of Rural Ireland by Michael Shiel (The O'Brien Press, Dublin, 1984).

With Horace Plunkett in Ireland by R.A. Anderson (Macmillan & Co., London, 1935).

Ireland in the New Century by Horace Plunkett (John Murray, London, 1904).

The Workhouses of Ireland – The Fate of Ireland's Poor by John O'Connor (Anvil Books, Dublin, 1995).

The Kerry Way – The History of Kerry Group, 1972-2000 by James J. Kennelly (Oak Tree Press, Dublin, 2001).

Tipp Co-op: Origin and Development of Tipperary Co-operative Creamery Ltd. by William Jenkins (Geography Publications)

Co-op Ireland – Journal of the Co-operative and Food Industries.

The Evolution of the Co-operative Movement in Ireland – degree study prepared for Dublin City University by Yvonne Kerr, 1999).

The Co-operative Movement in Ireland – The Story of a Struggle (ICOS).

A History of the Irish Dairy Industry (NDC, Dublin, 1982).

The Co-operatives of Ireland edited by Robert Briscoe and Michael Ward (Centre for Co-op Studies, U.C.C.).

Ireland's Co-operative Heartland – Ardagh CDS – A History 1891-1974 by John Hough.

Borris-in-Ossory (An Irish Parish and its People) by Hilary D. Walsh F.S.C. (Kilkenny Journal Ltd., 1969).

Laois County Council – The First Hundred Years edited by Teddy Fennelly (Laois County Council, 1999).

The Laois Millennium Year Book edited by Patrick F. Meehan (Portlaoise, 2000).

History of the Queen's County by Revs. J. Canon O'Hanlon and E. O'Leary (Sealy, Bryers & Walker, Dublin, 1907).

Laois – History and Society edited by Padraig G. Lane and William Nolan (Geography Publications, Dublin, 1999).

The Oxford Companion to Irish History edited by S.J. Connolly (Oxford University Press, 1998).

A Proud Harvest – A Centenary of South-Eastern Farmers Co-op (1896-1996) compiled and edited by Michael Sheehan and Larry Sheedy for Avonmore/Waterford Group plc.

A Voice for the Country – 50 Years of Macra na Feirme by Jim Miley (Macra na Feirme, 1994).

By-gone days in Donaghmore

Last night I dreamt of by-gone days, and a spot in County Laois,
'Tis the place where I was born and reared, it's home sweet home to me.
And tonight I know I'll dream again, to leave this foreign shore,
So come with me, in fantasy, on a trip to Donaghmore.

We'll stand upon the river bridge, and look up towards the mill,
And shed a tear for by-gone days, where all the world is still,
And then to meet one's old friends, and talk of times of yore,
And the days of fun, when we were young, in the village of Donaghmore.

The hurling games that we played, with an old and battered ball,
With the old folk there a-watching, as they leaned against the wall.
And sometimes there'd be fisticuffs, when heated tempers soared,
On evenings fine, we passed the time, on the green in Donaghmore.

Stories told by Seanachai, with laughter and with song,
Helped us through the darkest times, when winter nights were long.
To fiddle, flute and bodhran, we gently took the floor,
'til the light of day, we danced away, in our homes in Donaghmore.

I remember well my Father, as he walked behind the plough,
Special words to horses spoke, this work he taught me how;
I followed on and did my bit, 'til my feet were blistered sore,
And I ploughed the hills, and crossed the rills, in the fields 'round Donaghmore.

My Mother too God rest her, a meek and gentle soul,
But strong in heart and faith and love, for us she gave her all.
On summer days when making hay, and the scorching sun would soar.
She would make her way, with the sweetest tay, to the meadows near Donaghmore.

The threshing mill, the sheaves of corn, the sacks of golden grain,
All lost and gone to memory, ne'r to see again.
The thinning and the weeding, and picking spuds galore,
Oh to sweat and toil, in the rich brown soil, of the fields of Donaghmore.

Up the hill and around the bend, there stands the creamery,
It's gates and doors have stood ajar, for three quarters of a century.
As we look back throughout the years, to the days long, long of yore,
When deals were done, and business won, here in Donaghmore.

So let us stand in tribute then, to the men of twenty seven;
Men whose hearts were stout and brave, men of thought and vision.
And today we think of many names, who passed through here before,
With burning pride, they worked and died, for this in Donaghmore.

Composed by Gerard Moylan, Derrinsallagh, Borris-in-Ossory, Co. Laois. Gerard, a farmer, is a milk supplier to Glanbia plc and is a member of the Donaghmore Area Advisory Committee. His brother, William Moylan, the well-known Portlaoise based SIPTU Branch Secretary and member of the Laois County Development Board, worked with Donaghmore Co-op prior to taking up his current appointment.

Index of Interviewees

Co-operation is Cool

In connection with the publication of this book, Laois Education Centre and Glanbia plc have joined forces to launch a joint schools' initiative entitled "Co-operation is Cool". The initiative is aimed at both Primary and Post-Primary Schools in the Laois/Offaly/North Tipperary area.

The aim of the initiative is to promote awareness of co-operation and how it works around us in the 21st century aided by modern technology. 5th and 6th Classes in Primary Schools and Transition year and L.C.V.P. Students in Post-Primary Schools are participating.

The Project Team for "Co-operation is Cool" consists of: Tony Mahon, Director, Laois Education Centre; Paddy Bates, Board of Management, Laois Education Centre; Rosemary Day, Administrator, Laois Education Centre; Jim Enright, I.T. Advisor, Laois Education Centre; Liam O'Neill, Board of Management, Laois Education Centre; Sean Hearn, Glanbia plc and Marie Langton, Group Communications Development Manager, Glanbia plc.

Training for schools

Laois Education Centre will assist all participating schools in preparing Internet guidelines.

Authoring training plus assistance with ICT, digital cameras and the use of scanners will be provided.

Laois Education Centre will also put a competition section on their website so that any relevant material can be archived for access by schools.

Ní neart go cur le chéile

Laois Education Centre
Ionad Oideachais Mhúinteóirí Laois

glanbia

Co-operation is Cool

"TEAM WORK" – An example of working together.

Members of the Donaghmore/Monasterevin Regional Advisory Committee 2002

Front: John Delaney (Secretary), Joe Walsh, Donal Hynes, Martin Keane (Chairman), Liam Rohan (Vice-Chairman), Michael McEvoy, Sylvester Phelan, John Joe O'Rourke.
Middle: Derek Tierney, Norman Graham, Joe Quigley, Peter McHugh, Sean Fitzpatrick, Jim Walsh, Paddy Delaney, Jim Delaney, Kevin Flynn, Paul Ennis, George Byrne, Seán Harris, Paul Hyland, John Murphy, James Mahon, Tom Phelan.
Back: Joe Moore, Michael Mahon, Frank Fogarty, Martin Bergin, Ernest Gill, John McEvoy, Ronnie Bryant, Robin Frizzell, Tom Garry, Pat Jennings.
Inset: Michael Burke.
Missing from photo: Tim Garry, Matt Merrick, Tom Mather.